Alliance Capitalism

Alliance Capitalism

The Social Organization
of Japanese Business

Michael L. Gerlach

UNIVERSITY OF CALIFORNIA PRESS
Berkeley · Los Angeles · Oxford

This volume is sponsored by
The Center for Japanese Studies,
University of California, Berkeley

University of California Press
Berkeley and Los Angeles, California

University of California Press, Ltd.
Oxford, England

© 1992 by
The Regents of the University of California

Library of Congress Cataloging-in-Publication Data

Gerlach, Michael L.
  Alliance capitalism : the social organization of Japanese business /
Michael L. Gerlach.
     p.   cm.
  Sponsored by the Center for Japanese Studies, University of California, Berkeley.
  Includes bibliographical references and index.
  ISBN 0-520-07688-5 (alk. paper)
  1. Strategic alliances (Business)—Japan.   2. Industrial organization—Japan.
I. University of California, Berkeley. Center for Japanese Studies.   II. Title.
HD69.S8G47   1992
338.8'0952—dc20   92-16619

Printed in the United States of America

9   8   7   6   5   4   3   2   1

The paper used in this publication meets the minimum requirements of
American National Standard for Information Sciences—Permanence of Paper
for Printed Library Materials, ANSI Z39.48-1984. ♾

To my parents

Contents

Figures and Tables

FIGURES

TABLES

Introduction

Despite their far-reaching consequences—economic and political, domestic and international—surprisingly little is understood about the patterns of interaction that link Japanese companies. Situated between the internal managerial practices of the Japanese firm and the national and international forces that define Japan's macroeconomy and industrial policies, intercorporate relations in the contemporary Japanese economy are marked by an elaborate structure of institutional arrangements that enmesh its primary decision-making units in complex networks of cooperation and competition. Included here are trade associations among firms in the same industries, large-scale business associations that cut across industries, special public corporations jointly invested in and staffed by private companies and state agencies, and overlapping sets of industrial, commercial, and financial alliances. These mediating institutions have in turn shaped and defined the basic characteristics of Japanese market structure and corporate enterprise.

This is a study of perhaps the most distinctive of these institutions, the intercorporate alliance. There is a strong predilection for firms in Japan to cluster themselves into coherent groupings of affiliated companies extending across a broad spectrum of markets: with banks and insurance firms in the capital market, with *sōgō shōsha* (general trading companies) in primary goods markets, with subcontractors in component parts markets, and with competitors in new technology development. This pattern is clearest when the clusters have been institutionalized into identifiable *keiretsu*, or enterprise groups, which include both the modern descendants of the prewar *zaibatsu* (family-centered holding companies, such as Mitsubishi and Sumitomo) and elaborate chains of suppliers and distributors dependent on large manufacturing concerns (such as the Toyota and Hitachi groups). As is demonstrated at various points throughout this study, however, intercorporate alliances extend far beyond the most formalized groupings and, in fact, pervade much of the Japanese economy.

Understanding how these networks of cooperation operate and the functions they serve has become increasingly important as discussions have moved beyond the realm of academic debates to those of public policy. The keiretsu and other patterns of intercorporate relationships are now at the center of both criticism and admiration by foreign observers. On the one hand, they are attacked as a significant structural barrier for newcomers in the Japanese market. With the continuation of bilateral trade imbalances even after the dramatic rise in the value of the yen beginning in 1985, preferential trading among Japanese firms is seen by U.S. negotiators as a source of market exclusion that continues to operate even after formal barriers imposed by the Japanese government have been torn down. This perception has been heightened by dramatic but unsuccessful attempts by overseas investors, such as T. Boone Pickens, to gain a significant voice in the internal affairs of several Japanese corporations through the same mechanisms of stock acquisition and takeovers that they have used in the United States. A related concern is that as Japanese firms in the automobile and other industries invest increasingly in the United States, they are bringing over their own affiliated firms as suppliers of parts and capital and thereby excluding American competitors.

On the other hand, and with quite different implications, close relationships among banks, shareholders, and business partners are also seen as a potential source of Japanese competitive advantage, particularly in channeling the activities of corporate managers in the direction of long-term growth, profitability, and innovation. A number of observers ask whether the traditional public corporation, with large numbers of dispersed shareholders, has not outlived its usefulness. Taking Japan's banking groups as his model, Michael Jensen (1989) writes of "the eclipse of the public corporation" in the West and advocates the increasing privatization of corporate ownership and the replacement of open stock markets with large-block investments by financial institutions that serve as both equity and debt holders in highly leveraged firms. Similarly, in a special supplement on contemporary market capitalism, *The Economist* (May 5, 1990) suggests that Japan's intercorporate shareholding structure may have done a better job than most Western economies of filling the "vacuum at the heart of capitalism" that resulted from the fragmentation of ownership accompanying the rise of the modern corporation. Approaching the issue from a different direction, Charles Ferguson (1990) advocates the creation of "U.S. keiretsu" in the American computer industry as a means of bringing together financial and technological resources now fragmented among venture capitalists, start-up specialist firms, and integrated computer manufacturers in order to compete more effectively with the intercorporate "complexes" that dominate this industry in Japan. Perhaps, then, Japan has created a set of institutional arrangements that improve on the functioning of such basic institutions as corporations and the stock market, and on the ways they work together to promote economic growth?

These issues strike at the basic structure and character of Japanese market capitalism. Indeed, they raise important questions regarding the optimal organization of exchange in any economy. Is discipline through independent capital markets, notably through hostile takeovers and other forms of shareholder control, the most appropriate means of channeling corporate activities to ensure overall economic efficiency? Or are other, less disruptive, mechanisms for disciplining corporate managements more effective? And are impersonal, atomized markets among competitive traders inevitably the best way of coordinating business relationships, especially in a world of increasing scale, complexity, and technological change? Or is cooperation among companies equally important?

There is, of course, no reason why economic systems need to converge to a single form. Even within advanced industrialized societies, significant differences exist in the nature of the corporation and its role in the economy. Addressing these differences requires a detailed analysis of the specifics of market capitalism—notably in the patterns of trade, banking, ownership, and informal communications among firms themselves.

One of the advantages to studying Japan is the precise data, both academic and popular, available for the study of intercorporate relationships. Despite the abundance of materials, however, research is complicated by the variety of alliances that exist and the terminologies employed, by difficulties in defining membership, and by misconceptions concerning their nature and purposes. The assumption is often made that keiretsu and other alliance forms are uniquely endowed institutions with clearly defined boundaries, when the reality more often is blurred boundaries and overlapping affiliations. For this reason, analysis of specific enterprise groupings must be supplemented by an understanding of the overall intercorporate networks in which they are embedded.

Taking this approach, this study relies on a large-scale new database on important business relationships among large Japanese and large American corporations, described in Appendix A. This database includes information on firms' top-ten shareholders, the amounts of these holdings, and the identity and company affiliations of all outside directors. Data have been systematically coded for a series of key years for the two hundred largest industrial firms and fifty largest financial institutions in both the United States and Japan (see Appendix B for a complete listing). For Japan, information on these companies' top-ten creditors, the amounts of their borrowings, and the identity of their leading trading partners is also coded; this information is not available from published sources for U.S. firms. In the following chapters, these data are used to map the underlying structural characteristics of industrial organization and intercorporate relationships in Japan and compare them with their American counterparts.

The database has several distinctive features worth noting. First, by cutting across major business groupings and including all large, publicly traded Japanese corporations, the database gets away from a problem common in earlier research on enterprise groupings—that of prespecifying membership in groups. Relying instead on overall network data, it becomes possible to derive group patterns empirically, as well as to show patterns that are common among all large Japanese firms. Second, the database is explicitly comparative. Since identical measures are taken from Japan and the United States, it allows for direct comparisons of network structures between the two countries along several variables. Third, the database is longitudinal, facilitating the mapping of the evolution of intercorporate relationships over time and showing patterns of continuity and change. A fourth feature of the database is the broad range of relationships studied, highlighting similarities and differences in structures by market type.

Later chapters utilize this network database to derive a wide variety of original findings and conclusions, among them:

1.   Demonstrating that patterns of corporate ownership in Japan differ substantially from those in the United States. Evidence in Chapter 3 shows that corporate shareholding for large Japanese firms is about (a) twice as concentrated as in the United States; (b) four times more

stable; (c) five times more likely to involve simultaneous board positions among the same companies; and (d) seven times more likely to be reciprocated. The significance of these differences in the basic ownership of the firm is covered in detail at many points in this study.

2.   Measuring in detail the importance of alliance structures in Japan across a range of relationships and market types. Japanese business networks are shown to be strongly organized by keiretsu across three types of ties (dispatched directors, equity shareholding, and bank borrowing) and more weakly organized in a fourth (intermediate product trade). In all cases but product trade, as Chapter 4 indicates, the proportion of transactions taking place with firms in the same group is over ten times higher than the average with firms in other groups, indicating an extremely strong pattern of preferential trading that clearly has important implications for how we understand the nature of Japanese markets.

3.   Showing how these patterns of preferential trading have persisted over time. Because the database used here extends from the late 1960s into the 1980s, analyses are able to map the evolution of relationships. Contrary to prevailing wisdom, results in Chapter 4 suggest that alliance structures in debt and equity markets have remained largely enduring even with ongoing financial liberalization and other changes in the political and economic environment of Japanese industry.

4.   Demonstrating that certain important features of Japanese industrial organization are common to intercorporate relationships among all large Japanese firms. These include stable and reciprocal shareholdings, as well as the linking of transactions across different market types, as indicated in Chapter 5. Alliance forms, therefore, are far more pervasive in the Japanese economy than is commonly recognized.

Overall, these results confirm the existence of alliance structures as a distinctive feature of the Japanese economy and one that continues to thrive into the present day. They also indicate the need for a subtle understanding of these structures, as their importance varies considerably by the type of relationship in question.

Although a variety of alliance forms are discussed in the study, it is the diversified groupings linking major banks and industrial enterprises that receive special attention. The large corporation occupies a central position in industrialized economies, especially in strategic sectors such as finance, basic manufacturing, and international trade. Even in Japan, where the medium-and-small-firm sector constitutes a substantial percentage of total employment, it is the large-firm sector that has been the primary source of Japan's finance capital, its imports and exports, and its major technological and organizational innovations (Okimoto and Saxonhouse, 1987; Patrick and Rohlen, 1987). While representing only 10 percent of the industrial firms listed on the Tokyo Stock Exchange, firms formally affiliated with one of the six largest groups constitute over 40 percent of total banking capital and over half of total sales in certain manufacturing sectors (e.g., steel and nonferrous metals). In addition, the fact that the general trading companies affiliated with these groups handle over two-thirds of Japan's imports places these groups in a special role vis-à-vis foreign traders interested in penetrating the Japanese market.

The significance of these firms extends far beyond even these percentages, however. Many large companies that are nominally "independent" maintain looser affiliations with one or more major groups that do not show up in these figures. Moreover, most large companies maintain vast networks of satellite and subsidiary companies that greatly increase their overall influence in the economy. Over half of Japan's medium-and-small-firm manufacturing businesses serve as subcontractors to larger companies, a fraction that has been increasing over time (Aoki, 1987). Toshiba alone has about two hundred related companies (*kankei gaisha*) in Japan and below those another six hundred "grandchild companies" (*mago gaisha*). Success of the parent firm brings with it increased business for other firms in the parent's network of affiliates, while the failure of a Toshiba, Toyota, or Hitachi would bring down an entire network of dependent enterprises.

Japan's large-scale, diversified groupings also introduce important conceptual issues that prove instructive in understanding distinctive features of Japanese capitalism. Whereas the vertical groups that comprise upstream supplier firms and downstream distributors introduce at the interfirm level some of the characteristics one associates with standard hierarchical organization (notably a degree of centralization of product-related decision making, which is managed by the parent firm), the intermarket groups are less easy to classify. They represent informally and loosely structured "network organizations" among relatively equally sized firms located across diverse economic sectors. Although the financial role of these groupings is most often emphasized, this function coexists with the commercial and industrial activities of member companies in an elaborate structure of relationships across multiple markets. When reinforced through cross ownership, these patterns define strategic control of the overall "core" of the Japanese economy.

Somewhat confusingly, Japanese terminology is vague on the distinctions among different types of groupings. The direct Japanese translation for "enterprise group" (*kigyō gurūpu* or *kigyō shūdan*), is oftentimes used to refer to the major intermarket groupings centered on large commercial banks, but it is also sometimes used by companies in discussing their own family of satellite operations. Toyota Motor Corp., for example, defines the Toyota Group as fourteen key companies, most of which were spun off of the parent company at some point in the past (e.g., Nippondenso and Toyota Autobody). Perhaps as a result of this terminological variation, some academic writers in Japan have taken to coining their own words to describe these forms, among them "intermediate organizations" (*chūkan soshiki*), following a markets and hierarchies formulation, and "networks" (*nettowaaku*) (see, for example, Imai, 1989a).

In recognition of the increasing familiarity of the term, I shall refer to both the vertical and diversified groups as "keiretsu." Although not all observers agree with this usage, the fact is that the term is broadly used in Japan (e.g., in the standard datasource, *Keiretsu no kenkyū*). I have added the modifier "intermarket" where necessary in order to differentiate the diversified groupings that are the main focus of the discussion from their vertical counterpart. Others have referred to these groups as "horizontal" keiretsu because of the similar size and status of their members. This terminology follows directly from the Japanese (*yoko keiretsu*), but it introduces a degree of confusion in English, where "horizontal" typically refers to relationships among competitors in the same industry. These groups have also been termed "financial" keiretsu because of the important role played by commercial banks. However, as suggested above, and again in later chapters, this term defines affiliations rather narrowly and ignores the role played by trading companies and direct business transactions among industrial participants.

These particular groupings fall under the larger category of intercorporate alliances. The variety that alliance forms exhibit and their interaction are introduced in Chapter 1 and discussed at various points in later chapters. Whatever terminology is chosen, it is important to recognize that individual keiretsu groupings represent stylized portrayals of what are actually intricate and overlapping patterns of ties among Japanese companies.

Quantitative analyses of large-firm networks are reinforced at many points by historical and archival works, interviews, and other ethnographic materials. In order to protect the identity of the executives interviewed, individual names have generally been omitted. Where possible, company names have been kept. These interviews were carried out primarily in the mid- and late-1980s. While the executives were often quite frank about what they perceived as the advantages and disadvantages to their companies of different kinds of external alliances, it was sometimes in the interstices surrounding the formal interviews that the most interesting discoveries were made. Perhaps the following example best illustrates this.

I observed in my company rounds an ongoing competition that I took to calling "the beer wars." When I was invited to the company lounge for an after-hours beer at one of the companies where I was interviewing, the brand was invariably that of the group brewery—Asahi at Sumitomo, Kirin at Mitsubishi, or Sapporo at Fuji. Several managers commented that they always ordered their group brand when they were out in public and drank their personal favorite only at home. Thus did intergroup rivalries filter down to the day-to-day level of Japan's corporate managers, making evident the intensely localized way in which these rivalries are sometimes manifest.

This competition has a history going back decades. The first group affiliate was Kirin Brewery, which had been a prewar member of the Mitsubishi zaibatsu. (Even today, one can only find Kirin beer at one's local Meiji-ya, a supermarket chain with a long history of relationships with Kirin and the Mitsubishi group.) In the 1960s, Sapporo began cultivating closer relationships with the Fuji group, so when Sapporo held its ninetieth anniversary in 1966 it used the Fuji Bank headquarters. All core Fuji group companies at the time were invited and the Fuji Bank president opened the ceremonies with a toast, saying, "From now on let's celebrate the end of the year with Sapporo Beer" (quoted in Kameoka, 1969, p. 97). Sapporo the following year became a charter member of the Fuji group's newly formed presidents' council, the Fuyo-kai. Similarly, Asahi Breweries began moving toward the Sumitomo group in the 1960s, and these relationships became considerably closer in the 1970s as a result of Sumitomo's rescue of Asahi from various financial troubles. In response to these shifts, Japan's fourth and last-place brewery, Suntory, has been over the past decade in the process of developing closer ties with the Sanwa group. The comments by the president of Sanwa Bank a number of years ago are worth quoting, as they make evident the importance of business reciprocity in alliance relationships:

> As part of our good partnership policy, our bank has initiated a highly successful campaign to promote sales of Suntory beer and whiskeys among Sanwa group member companies. Suntory's shares of the market have increased significantly in the areas where our bank's offices are located. My

favorite restaurants also have come to always stock Suntory beer and whiskeys. Many of Sanwa group companies, moreover, have switched to Suntory beer and whiskeys as a result of our "Drink Suntory" campaigns. The rise in Suntory's share of the domestic beer market in spite of the exceptionally unfavorable weather conditions this summer can largely be accounted for by our campaigns. Suntory, on its part, urged its employees to deposit their summer allowances with Sanwa Bank and the campaign also proved to be a big success. This type of mutually beneficial accommodation and exchange of territories, managerial know-how and clients is what we call good partnership, a true way of attaining maximum co-prosperity. [Quoted in the *Oriental Economist,* September 1982.]

ACKNOWLEDGMENTS

Over the years in which this project evolved, I have benefited from perhaps even more than the usually broad set of supports—financial, logistical, intellectual, and moral—that any author requires. It is impossible to acknowledge everyone who had some kind of impact on the final outcome, but I would like to mention at least a few of these people and institutions.

Financial support for field research was made possible through the Henry Luce Foundation, the Japan Foundation, and the Japan Society for the Promotion of Sciences. Data collection and analyses used in the quantitative portions of the study were provided through funding from the University of California Pacific Rim Program and the National Science Foundation. Creation of the basic database was greatly facilitated by the skillful research assistance of Christina Ahmadjian, Joan Boothe, Frank Freitas, Peggy Takahashi, and a team of data coders at Berkeley. Joseph Chytry and Patricia Murphy were instrumental in completing figures and tables. In addition, congenial environments for writing and additional forms of support were provided by the Center for Japanese Studies in Berkeley and the Institute of Business Research at Hitotsubashi University in Tokyo. Finally, the Haas School of Business at the University of California has been unusually generous in allowing me time away from campus to complete the project.

Tangible and intangible intellectual stimulation has come from many colleagues and friends. While some must remain anonymous, others do not. Special thanks in Japan are owed to Arai Yoshitami, Goto Akira, Imai Ken-ichi, Kojima Hiroshi, Matsui Kazuo, Nonaka Jiro, Nakamoto Satoru, Nakano Mutsuji, Okumura Akihiro, Okumura Hiroshi, and Ueda Yoshiaki. Among the many people who provided critical comments on earlier drafts of the book and various papers related to it were Paul DiMaggio, Mark Fruin, Mark Granovetter, Robert Harris, Takeo

Hoshi, David Mowery, Charles Perrow, Woody Powell, Vladimir Pucik, Mark Ramseyer, Tom Roehl, Michael Schwartz, David Teece, David Vogel, and Oliver Williamson. Two other individuals merit special mention for carefully reading the entire manuscript in earlier forms—Hugh Patrick and Kozo Yamamura. In addition, my colleague Jim Lincoln has been a great source of intellectual stimulation at Berkeley over the past several years as we have collaborated in developing these ideas and expanding the database in new directions.

No study would be completed without the support of friends and family. Among the many who deserve credit, Mary Dean Lee, Rumi Kanesaka, and especially Laurie Freeman were instrumental in instilling and maintaining my interest in Japan and in the project. Finally, my family, and most specially my parents, have been a continual source of support, even during those long stretches when I was in hibernation with my word processor and a nonexistent correspondent.

NOTE ON JAPANESE USAGE

An attempt has been made to conform as closely as possible to usage in the original source. Japanese personal names are given in the customary Japanese order, family name first, where the work is published in Japanese and in the Western name order where it is written in English. Macrons are used only for Japanese-language works. Company and place names are written without macrons.

Words that appear frequently in the text (keiretsu, zaibatsu, sōgō shōsha) are only italicized the first time they appear. Some of these, of course, have already entered the Western lexicon.

CHAPTER I

Overview

We make our destinies by our choice of gods.
Virgil

The postwar global economy has witnessed what by any standard is an extraordinary reordering. That this has involved competition not only among companies and countries, but also among economic systems, was long apparent when considering the centrally planned economies of Eastern Europe. Ironically, with the dramatic decline of these economies has come an increasing recognition more recently that "market capitalism" is itself no monolithic system. Important institutional characteristics of its contemporary American variant—for example, hostile takeovers, leveraged-buyouts, and other aggressive mechanisms for transferring corporate control—are largely unknown in most European or Asian economies. The patterns of relationships among corporations and other key external actors (financial institutions, government organizations, industrial associations, labor groups) need not be and often are not identical across these economies.

Nowhere are the distinctive characteristics of market capitalism more directly challenged than in the economies of East Asia. With the emergence of Japan and its more recent successors has come the realization that economic development is not the prerogative of countries with a European ancestry. More controversial has been the viewpoint that these economies reflect underlying institutional arrangements to deal with the problems of economic growth that are both different in focus and, in certain respects, more effective in results than their counterparts in other industrial societies. The dynamism now observable in this region was not always so obvious, of course: when President Lincoln's secretary of

1

state, William Henry Seward—perhaps the U.S.'s first great partisan of
the Pacific Rim—tried to build a bridge between the United States and
Asia by purchasing Alaska from Russia, there was widespread doubt
about Asia's capabilities; an article in the *San Francisco Chronicle* at the
time said that Alaska would be the place where "Young America brisk
and spry, shakes hands with Asia withered and dry."[1] But this earlier
backwardness only makes the transformation since then much more
striking.

Among this select group of aggressively expanding economies, Japan's
economic success has been the most extensive and sustained. Japan now
serves as a major trading partner in the global economy, as a model of
economic development (especially for the NICs, or Newly Industrializing
Countries), as a competitive challenger in frontier industries, and, more
recently, as the world's largest net creditor nation and active investor in
overseas markets. Moreover, it has accomplished this while successfully
overcoming three major hurdles during the postwar period: first, the
devastation of the war; second, the oil shocks of the 1970s; and third, the
doubling of the value of the yen against the dollar since 1985.

This remarkable growth and resiliency raises fundamental questions
concerning the nature of Japan's own form of market capitalist economy. Put starkly: is Japan's performance primarily the result of the
effective harnessing of fundamental economic forces within the same
market capitalist institutions as exist in other advanced economies, as
some writers have suggested (e.g., Patrick and Rosovsky, 1976; Abegglen and Stalk, 1985)? Or has Japan crafted new institutions or transformed preexisting institutions in ways so basic that they bring into
question the belief in the inevitable convergence toward a single, universally rational form of economic organization, as others have suggested
(e.g., Dore, 1986; Johnson, 1987)?

These questions are extraordinarily important not only to our understanding of Japan but to more general models of successful economic
organization, development, and growth. The answers have proved elusive partly because Japan continues even now to be a country that is only
vaguely familiar to most Westerners. Perhaps more important, however,
has been the theory gap between our conceptual understanding of economic organization and the application of this understanding to real-
world economies. As Murakami and Patrick (1987, p. xxii) point out in
their introduction to the first volume of the *Political Economy of Japan*
trilogy:

In the short run it may be possible to isolate and analyze certain phenomena on the assumption that nothing else changes, but in the longer run one must take into account an intricate web of complex interactions between economic, political, social, and cultural forces and structures. However, social science has yet to develop generally accepted, comprehensive analytical frameworks that are operational.

How best, then, to understand this "intricate web of complex interactions"?

JAPANESE BUSINESS NETWORKS AND THE KEIRETSU

This study tackles this issue by focusing on the network of alliances among the major corporations that make up the Japanese economy. Intercorporate alliances, as defined here, are *institutionalized relationships among firms based on localized networks of dense transactions, a stable framework for exchange, and patterns of periodic collective action*. As a form of economic organization, they are distinct from both ideal-type bureaucratic organizations, on the one hand, and ideal-type market organizations, on the other. The organizational model is neither that of Alfred Chandler's "visible hand" nor that of Adam Smith's "invisible hand"—neither the solid structures of formal administration nor the autonomously self-regulating processes of impersonal markets— but of hands interlocked in complex networks of formal and informal interfirm relationships.

In the traditional model of formal organization, actors are linked under a common, unified hierarchy. This command structure is designed to ensure high degrees of control over a limited set of exchanges among a prespecified set of actors. Actors within this structure subject themselves to the restrictions imposed by an authority relation (Simon, 1957) and the organization's internal decision-making machinery (Williamson, 1975, 1985). No such unity of command exists in alliance forms. Whether operating through specific institutional arrangements, such as joint ventures, or through more loosely coupled structures, such as informal business groupings, alliances preserve a relatively large degree of formal decision-making independence for their initiating organizations. At the same time, relationships among alliance partners differ from the impersonal, arm's-length markets of textbook theory in that the identity of actors and the history of their relationships are important considerations in actual patterns of trade. Whereas perfect competition implies "social atomization" (Granovetter, 1985) among economic actors—temporary exchanges of convenience among faceless traders—alliances represent coherent clusters of preferential exchange among traders often linked together over the course of decades. In summarizing the distinctive features of Japanese industrial organization, we may point to five general tendencies. Although none of these is unique to Japan, what distinguishes Japan from the United States (which perhaps lies at the other extreme of the transactional continuum) is their pervasiveness and continuing visibility. These defining tendencies are:

1. *Affiliational ties.* Transactions often take place through alliances among affiliated enterprises, creating a vast sphere of economic life intermediate between anonymous markets and vertically integrated firms.

2. *Long-term relationships.* Intercorporate relationships in their ideal form are stable and long-term, relying on diffuse sets of obligations extending over time.

3. *Multiplexity.* Transactions tend to be overlapping, with equity investment and personnel interlocks used to consolidate financial, commercial, and other business ties.

4. *Extended networks.* Bilateral relationships are set in the context of a broader family of related companies.

5. *Symbolic signification.* Active efforts are made to infuse intercorporate relationships with symbolic importance, even in the absence of formal, legal arrangements or contracts.

Networks of business relationships in Japan are most evident when they become institutionalized into identifiable keiretsu. The keiretsu are of two distinct, though overlapping, types. The *vertical keiretsu* organize suppliers and distribution outlets hierarchically beneath a large, industry-specific manufacturing concern. Toyota Motor Corp.'s chain of upstream component suppliers is a well-known example of this form of vertical interfirm organization. These large manufacturers are themselves often clustered within groupings involving trading companies and large banks and insurance companies. The six major groups in Japan comprise three historical alliances directly linked to the former zaibatsu of Mitsui, Mitsubishi, and Sumitomo, and three banking groups centered on Fuji, Sanwa, and Dai-Ichi Kangyo. These large clusterings, the *intermarket keiretsu,* provide for their members reliable sources of loan

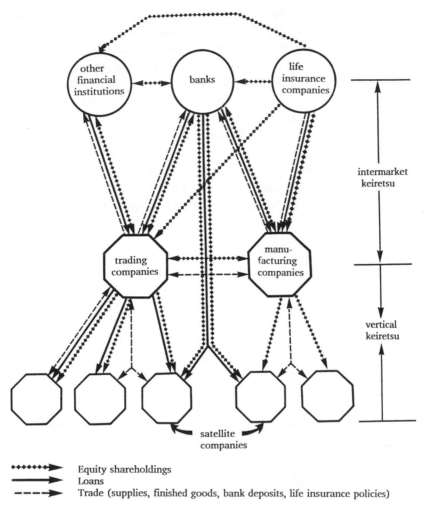

Fig. 1.1.   Debt, Equity, and Trade Linkages in the Keiretsu.

capital and a stable core of long-term shareholders. Moreover, like the vertical keiretsu, they establish a partially internalized market in intermediate products. A basic schematic of linkages within and between the vertical and the intermarket keiretsu is shown in Figure 1.1.

However, it is important to recognize that these are only the most formalized of a wide variety of different cooperative groupings that dominate the Japanese industrial landscape. The keiretsu should be seen as a metaphor for general patterns of interfirm organization in Japan—

as an ideal type in interfirm networks marked by the five characteristics outlined above. As we see in the core empirical chapters, these characteristics are pervasive throughout Japanese industrial organizations (although often varying in precise form). Intercorporate relationships within the most formalized keiretsu therefore share many characteristics with those among ostensibly more independent firms. The alliance terminology captures more flexibly the overlapping richness of these relationships than terminologies based in bounded notions of enterprise groups. For the sake of convenience and consistency with other studies, "keiretsu," "enterprise group," and related terminologies will continue to be used at various points in the chapters that follow; but the loosely coupled sense in which they are interpreted here should be kept in mind.

ARE ALLIANCE FORMS A GLOBAL TREND?

The proliferation of complex new forms of strategic alliances in the United States, the European Community, and elsewhere raises the issue of just how different Japanese patterns of intercorporate relations really are, and whether we are not seeing an international movement toward convergence in organizational practice. The popular and business media have been noting this trend since at least the early 1980s, as suggested in the following reports:

1. In the United States, according to *Business Week*, Silicon Valley has taken the lead in crafting the new rules of competition: "Putting the customer in charge of product design is forging new, tighter relationships between chip suppliers and users. No longer will a sale be just a pact between peddler and purchasing agent; instead, it will require the involvement of engineering staffs and, often, of managements" (May 23, 1983). As part of this "new spirit of cooperation" (January 10, 1983), "Even if they do not acquire each other outright, the various computer, communications, and semiconductor companies may end up aligning themselves through joint ventures, investments, and cooperative deals" (July 11, 1983).

2. In response to international competition, new forms of cooperation have emerged in Europe as well. The *New York Times* (August 21, 1989) reports, "Governments and companies across Europe are teaming up on a large and fast-growing number of projects aimed at making Europe a more formidable competitor for the United States and Japan."

The scale of these projects is increasingly grand: "France, West Germany, Britain and 10 other nations are building a space shuttle at a cost of $4.8 billion. Airbus Industrie, a four-nation consortium, has become the world's No. 2 passenger aircraft manufacturer, behind Boeing. And Europe's three leading semiconductor companies, Philips of the Netherlands, Siemens of West Germany and SGS-Thomson, a French-Italian joint venture—have teamed up on a $5 billion program that aims to build the world's most advanced computer chips."

3.   Similarly, as the Japanese economy moves toward global operations, complex new international alliances are being formed, reshaping the nature of competition in entire industries. A *Japan Times* article on automobile alliances stated a number of years ago (April 4, 1983): "Trends toward the development of a truly global auto industry demonstrate that Japanese car firms and their U.S. and European counterparts are beginning to recognize that the very survival of the world auto industry depends on cooperative integration of limited resources and technical skills. Faced with meeting energy conservation standards and shifting consumer demands, the auto industry is expected to become streamlined and increasingly interdependent, characterized by shifting alliances and intensified cooperation."

Is Japan, then, at the forefront of a global movement toward complex new forms of cooperation and alliance? A variety of researchers have argued that such a movement is indeed under way, as companies search for solutions to the problems of economic organization that simultaneously avoid the shortcomings of the traditional corporate hierarchy, which introduces a host of different costs related to bureaucratic distortions and inertia, and of arm's-length markets, which fail to adequately protect parties in the kind of complex, information-based exchanges that characterize many contemporary business activities. (See, for example, Piore and Sabel, 1984; Miles and Snow, 1987; Powell, 1987; Johanson and Mattsson, 1987; Eccles and Crane, 1987; Jorde and Teece, 1990.) If so, this represents a significant trend in the evolution of the industrial structure of advanced societies.

Nevertheless, important differences remain among forms of intercorporate alliance, especially when comparing the strategic alliances characteristic of emergent industries in Silicon Valley and elsewhere with keiretsu relationships among large Japanese enterprises. Strategic alliances create a framework within which companies are able to cooperate in a set of specific business activities, such as the developing of new technologies. With rare exceptions, however, they do not alter greatly the relationships those companies have directly with each other, their own shareholding structure, or the basic strategic constraints under which they operate.

Japan's major business groups, in contrast, comprise direct and indirect linkages among banks, industrial firms, and commercial enterprises that shape a complex web of interests affecting the company as a whole. They engage a wide variety of activities by opening up sources of capital flows between banks and corporate borrowers, setting a framework for the exchange of raw materials and intermediate product trade, and providing a forum for the informal exchange of information. Most important, they define, through patterns of share crossholding and business-linked equity investment, the underlying ownership structures of their participants—those actors who are assigned ultimate control over the basic decision-making apparatus of the company through the formal mechanisms of corporate control.

This distinction is depicted schematically in Figure 1.2. The strategic alliances that companies craft with competitors and other firms represent a set of focused activities that, while possibly important in the aggregate, do not affect the core integrity of the companies themselves because they are primarily outward-directed and limited in scope. They may be used to help develop new products, exchange technologies, or open up promising markets, but other ongoing business activities among the companies are generally circumscribed and overall corporate strategies are unlikely to be significantly altered.

Not so when a Japanese company's network of ties with its own intermarket keiretsu affiliates is disrupted. Ties to other large manufacturing, trading, and financial firms define basic constraints on the entire corporation: the access it has to capital, the kind of industries it is likely to move into, and the locus of ultimate control over their formal and informal decision-making processes. Should these affiliated enterprises choose, they are able to exercise substantial clout in constraining the management of their members, for they represent a complex nexus of reciprocal interests.

This distinction, of course, is not absolute. Large Japanese companies frequently engage in strategic alliances for technological or market development with the same companies that are their core intermarket affiliates. In this case, their core affiliations help to predetermine the extent of interaction likely to take place among these firms, and this in turn shapes the patterns of cooperation that emerge in the areas of

Strategic Alliances

Examples:

    joint ventures

    R&D consortia

Intermarket keiretsu

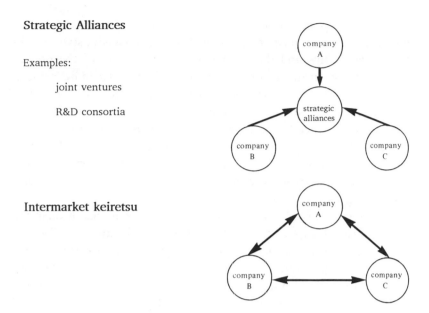

Fig. 1.2.   A Schematic Representation of Strategic Alliances and Intermarket Keiretsu.

business-specific technological and market development. In addition, these firms often take partial equity positions in vertically linked suppliers and distributors that serve business-specific interests for the parent company but represent, in conjunction with high levels of trading dependency, the corporate-wide interests of the supplier or distributor firm.

For this reason, even relatively straightforward distinctions, such as those between vertical and intermarket keiretsu, are rarely this clearly differentiated in practice. Many of the firms constituting the major postwar groupings were themselves at one time vertically linked spin-offs from the zaibatsu. In addition, vertically related firms are often brought into the banking and other relationships that their parent companies maintain with the intermarket groups, indicating that bilateral relationships must be viewed in the context of broader families of relationships.

EARLIER STUDIES OF
JAPAN'S ALLIANCE STRUCTURES

The study of enterprise groupings and intercorporate relationships in Japan has evolved in a number of important ways since the 1970s.

Eleanor Hadley's milestone *Antitrust in Japan* (1970) provides what remains among the most complete analyses of Japan's postwar bank-centered groupings and the impact of the dissolution of the prewar zaibatsu. Hadley writes as someone with long knowledge of her subject, having been involved in early postwar Occupation economic reforms. This background also shapes her perspective, for the main question addressed is whether Japan has recreated in modified form the institutions that the Occupation forces had set out to abolish. Hadley concludes that Japan's postwar groupings are clearly of a different type than the zaibatsu, though loose affiliations remain as a result of Japan's historical legacy.

Also viewing Japan's contemporary business groupings through the lens of industrial organization and its antitrust implications are Richard Caves and Masu Uekusa in their study *Industrial Organization in Japan* (1976). Although addressing a broader range of topics than Hadley, Caves and Uekusa reach similar conclusions regarding the lack of apparent cohesion in the postwar groupings and the difficulty of unified coordination of the kind evident in the prewar period. Their careful empirical analyses do not provide much support for their preferred interpretation of business groups, which is based on market power: the groups do not appear to produce increased concentration, to suppress competition, or to create monopoly profits for group members. Like Hadley before them, Caves and Uekusa are somewhat baffled by just why these groupings exist, although they point to the possibility that the groups might be serving the interests of their constituent banks at the expense of other group firms.

A number of the most finely detailed empirical studies of enterprise groups have been carried out by researchers in Japan. Futatsugi (1976) and Miyazaki (1976) both include systematic quantitative treatments of groups using extensive databases on patterns of share crossholding and other relationships among several hundred major Japanese corporations. A more institutionally oriented perspective is provided in Okumura's (1983) analysis of Japan's six largest bank-centered groups. Okumura presents a wide range of interesting examples of how group processes work in practice and compiles evidence from a variety of sources on the impact of these groupings on the Japanese economy. Both Okumura and Futatsugi emphasize in these and other works (e.g., Okumura, 1975; Futatsugi, 1982) that business reciprocity and intercorporate shareholding are common features throughout Japanese industrial organization and not simply limited to the most visible groupings. This important observation captures a fundamental feature of Japanese capitalism, discussed at greater length in the following chapter and reinforced empirically in various portions of this study—the difficulty of separating capital markets from other business interests that firms have in one another.

As the Japanese economy continued to outperform those of its industrial competitors, the 1980s saw an increasing shift in emphasis toward economic efficiency as an explanation for a wide range of business practices. Just as Japanese personnel practices, such as permanent employment and seniority-based pay and promotion systems, came to be viewed less as legacies of Japan's cultural past and more in terms of conscious rationality in an economy where labor stability and human capital investments are highly valued (e.g., Koike, 1983; Aoki, 1988), so too has economic efficiency, in a variety of guises, emerged as a leading explanation for Japan's enterprise groupings. This shift in thinking has been facilitated by the simultaneous emergence of new approaches to the economic study of organization, discussed in the following chapter.

Among the first writers to take a transactions costs approach to economic exchange and apply it to enterprise groups was Akira Goto (1982). Goto argues that, by organizing collectively, companies are able to avoid the scale diseconomies and the control losses likely in full-scale vertical integration, and at the same time to provide benefits not available in unprotected market exchange. The market mechanism, he notes, "might not be an effective device to trade information because of the characteristics of information as a good, such as strong externalities and the difficulty of appropriation, and because of the ineffectiveness of such institutions as the patent system and the resale prohibition of information" (pp. 61–62). As an alternative to market exchange, business groups serve as a kind of "information club" designed to improve information-sharing among member firms. Close cooperation can in this way be "secured by a set of tacit, informal rules that emerge through a long history of exchange of information and recognition of interdependence, substantiated by financial linkages and interlocking directorates" (p. 61).

Further developing the perspective that enterprise groups represent an efficient hybrid between impersonal markets and internal organization are Ken-ichi Imai and his colleagues (see, e.g., Imai, 1982, 1989; Imai et al., 1982; Imai and Itami, 1984). Viewing markets and organizations as alternative modes of exchange, Imai argues that these modes can coexist within a single organizational form, with enterprise groupings a representative example. In the process of "interpenetration," these groupings simultaneously introduce organizationlike properties in markets (creating a degree of coordination of otherwise-independent companies) and marketlike properties in organization (through a higher level of competition than is common within firms). In explaining the origins of these groupings, Imai adds the useful insight that transactions costs need not be fixed or common; instead, they reflect the relative costs of markets and organizations in any economy. Among the constellation of distinctive factors that exist in Japan is the prevalence of internalized labor markets, which puts pressures on firms to minimize their own size and rely instead on external sourcing through reliable intercorporate relationships in order to ensure stable employment for their core workers (Imai and Itami, 1984).

Efficiency-oriented explanations of Japan's distinctive industrial organization have been applied as well to the study of specific sets of exchanges common within enterprise groups, including those between general trading companies and industrial firms (Roehl, 1983) and those between financial and nonfinancial firms. Special attention has been paid recently to the distinctive role of commercial banks in Japan's capital markets. Using theoretical developments in the economics of financial intermediation, Horiuchi, Packer, and Fukuda (1988) suggest that banks' primary function comes from the creation and integration of costly information on borrowers that is not available to the stock market. Long-term transactions between banks and corporate borrowers improve this information, they argue, resulting in the emergence of "main bank" relationships in Japan in which a lead bank uses its inside information both to provide loans directly to companies and to send signals to other banks on a company's soundness.

Additional evidence for the view that bank-oriented financing creates effective channels of capital allocation in Japan has been provided in a series of empirical studies by Takeo Hoshi and his colleagues (Hoshi, Kashyap, and Scharfstein, 1990a, 1990b, 1990c). Observing that banking relationships are central to the intermarket groups, these researchers explore the possibility that companies with well-defined keiretsu relationships have better access to capital because of the quality of the information obtained by banks. They find that firms with close group affiliations do indeed improve their access to capital.[2] They also find that these banking ties are a better explanation of whether cash flow predicts investment than several standard stock-market indicators.[3] They conclude from this that the intertwined nexus of information and capital flows marking enterprise groupings has created an institutional structure in which Japanese firms can take on higher levels of debt financing with lower levels of attendant risk than their counterparts in America, where debt is relatively diffusely held and bond financing is more prominent (Hoshi, Kashyap, and Scharfstein, 1990c).

A different perspective on the efficiency properties of enterprise groups has also received considerable recent attention. Studies by Nakatani (1984), Aoki (1988) and Sheard (1991) argue that the primary function of bank-centered enterprise groups is to spread risk among their members. This hypothesis points to the distinctive features of Japanese labor markets, notably the high levels of firm-specific capital that are associated with internal labor markets and the resulting absence of markets for managers and skilled workers. These conditions expose Japanese workers to severe risks and encourages managers to stabilize their external business relationships and to create implicit insurance arrangements with other companies should their companies face financial difficulties.

An influential source of empirical support for the risk-sharing hypothesis is Nakatani's study of several hundred large firms listed on the Tokyo Stock Exchange. In a series of regression analyses, Nakatani finds that rates of profitability and sales growth tend to be somewhat lower for firms classified as keiretsu companies, but so too is the variability in these rates. Nakatani interprets these findings as a confirmation of the view that enterprise groupings represent "an implicit mutual insurance scheme, in which member firms are insurers and insured at the same time" (p. 243). More recent studies have extended risk-sharing models theoretically and empirically from the study of enterprise groups as a whole to their various component linkages, including those between creditors and clients (Osano and Tsutsui, 1986; Sheard, 1986), manufacturing firms and subcontractors (Kawasaki and McMillan, 1987), and trading companies and industrial firms (Sheard, 1989).

Unlike the transactions costs explanation, the risk-sharing hypothesis makes no prediction of enhanced performance for Japanese firms that are clearly identified with one of the major keiretsu, since the main rationale is seen to be the buffering of companies' internal labor markets. This is not necessarily inefficient, however. To the extent that workers and managers have large stakes in the firms for which they work, it may be desirable to offer them protection for forms of human capital (e.g., knowledge of how to get things done in a particular factory) that are not transferable elsewhere. In addition, as Nakatani suggests, there may be benefits from the increased stability in company performance that are captured in the form of increased macroeconomic stability, even if not measurable in improved firm-level profitability.

Although most of the research on alliance structures in the Japanese

economy has been carried out by economists, one notable exception has
been the work of sociologist Ronald Dore. In his well-known article
"Goodwill and the Spirit of Market Capitalism" (1983) and in several
books that followed (1986, 1987), Dore points out that transactions
costs in market exchange can vary with the patterns of social and
economic relationships characterizing different countries. For Dore, it is
the durability of Japanese intercorporate relations and their quasi-moral
character that is most striking. The basic principles of relational contracting in Japan, as he sees them, are the sharing of losses in bad times
and gains in good times, the recognition of each partner's role in the
relationship, and the avoidance of using one's positional superiority to
gain advantage.

Unlike the writers discussed above, Dore emphasizes that distinctive
cultural features may be important in explaining Japanese industrial
organization, seeing these patterns as modern-day manifestations of
traditional Japanese notions of social obligation manifested through the
ritual reenactment of well-established relationships. Thus, whereas specific patterns of who may trade with whom may be recent, "what are
entirely traditional . . . are, first, the basic pattern of treating trading
relations as particularistic personal relations; second, the values and
sentiments which sustain the obligations involved; and third, such things
as the pattern of mid-summer and year-end gift exchange which symbol-
izes recognition of those obligations" (1983, pp. 464–65).

Dore acknowledges the possibility that short-term allocative efficiency
is sometimes lost in the course of maintaining these relationships. Nevertheless, like other proponents of risk-sharing models, he believes that
these costs have been offset overall by long-term advantages flowing
from the Japanese economy's adaptability to the ongoing processes of
restructuring inevitable in industrial evolution: "[r]elational contracts, in
this interpretation, are just a way of trading off the short-term loss
involved in sacrificing a price advantage, against the insurance that one
day you can 'call off' the same type of help from your trading partner if
you are in trouble yourself" (1983, p. 470).

STRUCTURES, STRATEGIES, AND INSTITUTIONS: AN INTERDISCIPLINARY APPROACH

This study builds on this prior research, as well as taking it in a variety of
new directions, both empirically and theoretically. In the chapters that
follow, an approach to the understanding of Japan's business networks
and enterprise groupings is developed that is broadly interdisciplinary.

This is the product of a belief that the institutions of modern market capitalism—the intercorporate alliance no less than the corporation or the stock exchange—are the result of a continuing unfolding of overlapping economic, political, and social forces. No single explanation is sufficient, therefore, to cover the wide range of forms or specific patterns of alliance now found in the Japanese economy. The structure of intercorporate relations as it actually exists in Japan is far too intricate, precisely conceived, enduring, and pervasive to be understood solely in terms of single-factor explanations (be they market power, economic efficiency, or cultural determinism). To ignore the interaction among diverse forces, therefore, is to lose important elements in our understanding of the nature and consequences of Japanese industrial organization.

Although interdisciplinary, several strong preferences in the explanation of economic organization will nevertheless become apparent. The first is an orientation toward structural (or network) analysis. This reflects a shift in attention toward complex relationships among actors not wholly derivable either from the aggregation of individual actors (as often assumed in microanalytic economic models) or fully internalized attitudes, norms, and values (common in many culturalist explanations of Japanese economic organization). Methodologically, special attention is placed on the study of concrete structures of relationships that actors forge to facilitate exchange relationships, and especially on intercorporate (as opposed to corporate-level) data. The second, related to the first, is that economic actors view their relationships in essentially strategic terms. This implies that rational action is an intended goal of Japanese corporations. But rationality for any given company—hence, the ultimate criterion by which its actions must be evaluated—is defined not by optimization within a single market or industrial sector (e.g., maximization of profit, sales growth, or employment stability) but across a nexus of interests in the different markets (capital, industrial, and labor) on which it is dependent. Third, intercorporate relationships are set in an institutional context that, on the one hand, shapes the range of options that Japanese firms face when making strategic decisions and, on the other, leads to path-dependent business activities that transcend immediate rationality to include the distinctive histories that the partners bring to their relationships.

The Structural Analysis of Intercorporate Relationships

In a structural approach, concrete networks of exchange become the main unit of analysis, and the focus shifts toward the way specific patterns of interaction emerge and the implication of those patterns for social and economic behavior and performance.[4] Insofar as corporations are the key decision-making bodies in contemporary industrial economies, understanding the patterns of their relationships to other companies becomes an important source of information about their behavior. A "fully structural view," as Mizruchi and Schwartz (1987, p. 3) point out, is one in which "an organization is viewed as interacting with its environment—molding as well as being molded by it—and in which the structure of relations—rather than individual organizations—is the unit of analysis."

This is based in two assumptions. The first is that, in contrast to earlier managerialist theories, in which the modern corporation is seen as largely self-contained and immune from external influence, corporations are instead understood to be strongly affected by other actors in their environment. Managers are constrained, in varying degrees, from acting solely on their own or their organization's interests by their banks and shareholders, trading partners, regulatory agencies, and other external constituencies. Second, and more recently, the organizational environment itself becomes an important phenomenon for study through the analysis of concrete structures of relationships making up the intercorporate network. Associated with this perspective is the belief that economic transactions are not simply decomposable into bilateral transactions, but are organized into complex relationships in which the characteristics of actors' strategies cannot be fully derived from their actions vis-à-vis each dyadic (transactional) linkage.[5]

The recognition that the corporation is subject to external constraint is consistent with the emerging view of the Japanese firm as a constellation of multiple internal and external interests, developed most completely in the theoretical work of Aoki (1984c, 1988). But a structural perspective shifts attention to the level of intercorporate relationships themselves as a major focus of interest in explaining the behavior of firms and their economic performance.

This difference at times becomes important, as when considering issues such as the changing relationships among financial and nonfinancial corporations in Japan, a subject taken up in Chapter 4. A number of writers have suggested that there has been a decline in the role of bank-centered groups during the period from the 1970s to the late 1980s, based on firm-level data showing a shift among large firms from debt- to equity-based financing (e.g., Aoki, 1988; Hoshi, Kashyap, and Scharfstein, 1990a). If we focus instead on the intercorporate flow of capital and the structure of relationships between capital investors and capital users, the impact of this shift becomes far less clear. Equity-based financing continues to be provided largely by the same financial institutions as the debt capital that it is replacing. In contrast to the assumption, based on traditional definitions, that this represents a movement from "indirect" to "direct" financing, an analysis of the actual flow of funds suggests instead that this is essentially a shift from one form of mediated financing to another. The financial institutions that had earlier channeled capital between household savers and corporations through the loan market continue to serve the same function, only now by buying those companies' new securities issues.[6]

This gradual change in financing methods might have great significance if the financial institutions behaved quite differently as purchasers of securities than they do as financial lenders—for example, by becoming unstable stock market investors rather than stable lead banks. However, the analyses in later chapters indicate that equity ties among financial and nonfinancial companies, much like debt ties, continue to be structured in long-term relationships that reflect a complex set of strategic interests among the parties involved—not a movement from administered to impersonal market transactions. As a result, the effects of this shift in the form of financing on the nature of keiretsu-based relationships remains unclear without further substantiation based on the analysis of the concrete patterns of relationships among the firms involved.

This suggests the limitations of studying intercorporate structures from the point of view of data at another (e.g., firm or macroeconomic) level, and reflects the need to improve the empirical record on which the discussion of alliance forms is based. Important comparisons have been left implicit in most previous studies—among them, the differences between patterns of relationships in Japan and those in other countries; between types of relationships (e.g., equity ownership vs. intermediate product trade); between patterns in contemporary Japan relative to those several decades earlier; and between firms with strong group affiliations and those without.

The database used in this study shows that preferential product market trading among affiliated companies in Japan remains very high between general trading firms and some intermediate producers, but is generally much lower when consumer-oriented manufacturers are involved—a fact of importance in assessing the significance of the keiretsu for market access in Japan. The consequence of alliance structures for interlocking directorate positions is mixed, with the density of linkages among companies quite low, as a result of the small number of outside directors on the boards of large Japanese firms, but the likelihood extremely high that the linkages that do exist are with other companies in the same intermarket group.

The pattern of interlocking shareholding, on the other hand, proves to be, if anything, far more important than is generally recognized, a fact that takes on added significance given the increased role for equity-based financing in recent years. Although it is true that the total equity held by affiliated group companies in a typical firm averages "only" 15–30 percent, this ignores two important facts. The first is that many of the shareholders not included in these figures are linked structurally through reciprocal and strategic shareholding positions with the firm, although not formally identified in the same keiretsu. Most large Japanese firms have well over half of their total equity controlled by stable shareholders with a variety of business interests in the company, and in the case of some firms, such as commercial banks and other financial institutions, this figure is over 90 percent. The second is that both affiliated and unaffiliated intercorporate investors are disproportionately represented among firms' leading shareholders. When we look only at the top-ten shareholders, the share of total stocks controlled by companies in the same group rises to over 25 percent in all major intermarket keiretsu and over 50 percent in the older, zaibatsu-based groups. Since these strategic shareholders are the ones best able to create voting coalitions if needed to influence management policy, their influence extends substantially beyond what the raw percentages would indicate.[7]

This factor relates to another of the conclusions of this study: that alliance patterns based on strategic and stable equity crossholdings, as well as reciprocity in trade and financial relationships, are prevalent throughout Japanese industrial organizations and are not limited to the most formal intermarket groupings. The high degree of institutionalization of these network structures points to the need for understanding the contextual and historical forces that have promoted their development in Japan, and also argues against the viewpoint that Japanese industrial organization is rapidly converging toward a "Western" model, as some have suggested.

The similarity in certain important network patterns also helps to explain why empirical studies of the impact of these relationships based on their classification into discretely dichotomized groups (e.g., as keiretsu or non-keiretsu firms) have generally provided mixed results.[8] To the extent that large Japanese firms and the networks of intercorporate relationships they maintain share many characteristics—the product of long histories going back to the prewar period for the great majority of these companies—it is not surprising that performance outcomes flowing from these structures also tend to converge on common patterns.

Chapter 5 reviews these studies and provides new analyses of the sources of Japanese company profitability. In keeping with the findings in several other studies, these results demonstrate small but statistically significant differences in profitability, with firms in clearly defined keiretsu relationships showing lower returns than firms with more loosely defined affiliations. However, these differences are also shown to relate to a number of other characteristics of the companies, most notably to a firm's overall pattern of ownership and banking relationships. These results indicate that corporate performance results from a complex set of considerations beyond keiretsu affiliation itself, and indicate the need to refine analyses of the relationship between network structure and economic outcomes.

The Strategic Linking of Complex and Overlapping Interests

A second characteristic of the approach taken here reflects the belief that economic actors view their relationships from what is fundamentally a strategic vantage point. The alliance terminology conveys the seemingly paradoxical combination of intensive, instrumental maneuvering among corporations for economic advantage and the reality that long-term cooperation is often the best way to pursue those interests. It has a well-established position in the vernacular of political science and anthropology in a way that closely approximates its characteristics in contemporary Japanese industrial organization: an important function of alliances (whether among countries, kinship units, or business corporations) is to serve as a means of creating reliable sources of critical resources and long-term external linkages through which their members are able to carry out their day-to-day activities.[9]

A strategic orientation recognizes that actors consciously seek to improve their own economic and social positions. The emergence of cooperative groupings of firms in Japan is not simply a reflection of culturally determined patterns, for this misses the importance of conscious institutional design in the process and the belief by actors themselves, however well justified, that their interests are being served. Culturally preexisting forms may provide useful "tools" from which to craft new arrangements (Swiddler, 1986), but these tools are utilized by actors to further their own interests and are not simply digested in whole. As Granovetter (1985, p. 486) points out, culture "not only shapes its members but also is shaped by them, in part for their own strategic reasons."

A strategic orientation also implies a second consideration, underappreciated in single-factor explanations of Japan's enterprise groupings. The complexity of the contemporary corporation, the diverse resources on which it is dependent for its survival, and the varied markets it serves have resulted in an equally elaborate structure of networks in which it must maneuver in order to operate successfully. Rational action in this context is defined by optimization not within individual markets but in the company's overall position across a set of interrelated markets.

Theories of intercorporate risk sharing and managerial protection rightly point to the vulnerability of Japanese managers and workers resulting from the prevalence of permanent employment systems in large firms and the lack of an effective midcareer market for managers and skilled workers should their companies fail. In this context, close ties among banks and other companies with implicit agreements for mutual assistance provide important risk-sharing advantages for employees. Share crossholdings offer further protections by creating a stable coalition of shareholders that will vote with management in the event of a dissident shareholder movement or hostile takeover attempt and by providing a reservoir of buffer capital that can be disposed of if necessary in emergencies.

Capital-monitoring models capture a different part of this reality by emphasizing imperfections in the market for investment capital and their resolution through the use of financial intermediaries. Japanese household savers face special problems, including generally poor public-domain accounting information and weak protection by boards of directors that are dominated by inside management. This has led them to rely on banks as investment specialists. Bank-company alliances help to overcome these problems by improving both the quality of information available to investors and the ability of those investors to discipline company managements effectively.

However, it is important not only that alliance structures provide a form of implicit insurance against company failure, protect Japanese managers from hostile outsiders, or facilitate access to capital through improved information flows and governance capabilities, but also that each of these benefits is offered by business partners and financial institutions with which the company is linked in long-term, strategic relationships. Consider the diverse interests involved in two key components of the intermarket groups:

1.   Japanese commercial banks' relationships with their corporate clients include not only receiving substantial loans from the bank, reinforced by equity positions as well as special assistance during times of financial distress, but also (a) managing loan consortia involving other banks; (b) handling a variety of fee businesses from the client, such as foreign exchange transactions; (c) negotiating and financing mergers and acquisitions involving the client; (d) helping the client to find business partners; (e) providing loans to the client's affiliated suppliers and distributors; and (f) managing the savings accounts of the client's employees, whose wages are automatically transferred to the bank.

2.   Trading companies provide a broad range of services for their clients in addition to directly handling domestic and international transactions, including (a) negotiating and writing trade contracts; (b) extending trade credit; (c) hedging exchange rate risks; (d) transporting and storing materials; (e) integrating complex projects; and (f) providing a variety of consulting services related to political, economic, and social conditions in host-country markets.

Firms consciously craft these strategic alignments through intricate and precisely conceived structural and symbolic arrangements. The amount of equity that a commercial bank holds in its corporate clients tends to be directly proportional to the loan, fee, and other business it carries out with the client firm. Similarly, steel companies buy raw materials from general trading companies in direct proportion to the amount of finished steel those trading companies sell.[10] The large corporate clients of these firms also maintain equity crossholding positions, place their own deposits in the bank, and participate in a variety of personnel transfers and joint projects, creating a complex and reciprocal pattern of resource, influence, and information flows.

In this way, banking, trading company, and other intercorporate ties represent multifaceted relationships oriented toward a wide variety of interests companies have in one another and in an extended network of other affiliated companies. The purpose of these relationships is not limited to any single set of considerations (e.g., risk-sharing or improved capital monitoring), for companies do not segment their business activities this easily. Indeed, it is precisely the *intermarket* character of these groupings—in which a broad range of banking, industrial, and

commercial interests are brought together in a community of interest—
that is important to understanding their origins and functions in the
Japanese economy.

This points to the need for an affirmative theory of alliance structures,
recognizing that they serve not simply defensive purposes (important as
those interests may be) but also as a proactive source of strategically
crafted "credible commitments" across a range of complementary business activities.[11] It is the largest firms that are most closely involved in the
intermarket keiretsu, not because of an unusually high need for implicit
insurance arrangements—indeed, these companies are better able to
diffuse risks across a diverse range of business lines than are smaller and
more focused firms. Rather, large companies have the broadest scale and
scope of activities, and the resulting benefits of complementary coordination among these firms, their banks, trading companies, and other
large industrial companies are greatest.

The Institutional Origins of Economic Organization

A strategic orientation to economic organization recognizes that actors
are self-interested. Equally important, however, are the ways that those
interests are shaped by the institutional context within which they take
place. As Simon (1961, p. xxiv) points out, behavior is "*intendedly*
rational, but only *limitedly* so." In part, the limits to rational action are
due to the structural complexity and interdependency of contemporary
economies, resulting in the need for a broad (i.e., strategic) interpretation of how rationality and efficiency are defined, as discussed above. But
economic organization is also constrained by legal and normative restrictions on acceptable behavior, by a priori models of how the world
works, and by patterns of relationships that develop a taken-for-granted
character independent of the interests of the parties involved.[12]

Alliance structures are prevalent in Japan not only because they serve
the immediate interests of their participants but because Japan's distinctive Meiji- and postwar-period history set in motion a series of policies in
banking and securities regulation, antitrust, and corporate law that
proved amenable to their long-term formation. Over time, structures of
cooperation have become institutionalized among firms—that is, seen as
the normal way to do business, both by their participants and by other
members of the business community. Contemporary patterns of intercorporate relationships in Japan reflect distinctive path-dependent trajectories that represent a considerable carryover from the prewar period.

In this way, Japan's alliance structures exist in a context not wholly derivable from the aggregation of individual actions of the participants within them, nor are they easily reproduced in the same form in other institutional contexts.

Microanalytic rational-actor models build from the ground up, starting with the unit of individual transactions and using increasingly elaborated structures to create complex patterns that ultimately define market organizations. Institutional approaches, in contrast, begin with the overall "blueprints" that define and shape exchange relationships and are concerned with the ways macrostructures constrain possible microstructures. Transactions are conceived not in vacuo but in terms of other relationships in the society and the rules that determine which organizational forms emerge. Where a purely microanalytic approach presents the possibility of an infinite universe of organizational arrangements, each most efficient in its own idiosyncratic context, an institutional orientation emphasizes the ways in which historical and structural factors limit the range of forms that actually emerge in any economy.[13]

Ultimately, both approaches provide important information, but it is worth considering where an institutional orientation's distinctive contributions lie. One of the basic conclusions of this study is that Japanese firms—even such progressive and internationalized companies as Sony and Honda—demonstrate patterns of relationships with shareholders, banks, and trading partners that are far more similar to each other than they are to comparable American firms in the same industry. The reasons for this reside in at least two sets of institutional considerations, the first related to the sources of differentiation between Japan and the United States, and the second to the sources of homogeneity of practices within Japan itself.

First, certain pathways of intercorporate action that developed in Japan were restricted legally in the United States. Among the most important, the Glass-Steagall Act in the United States and related prohibitions have restricted forms of intercorporate shareholding between banks and industrial firms that were not proscribed in Japan. These policies were intended to break up the closely linked cliques of financial and nonfinancial firms such as the Morgan trust that existed during the early part of the twentieth century. But their impact has continued into the present, precluding the reemergence of close corporate banking ties during the postwar period (Roe, 1990, 1991). Similarly, a strong legacy of antitrust enforcement in the United States throughout most of the twentieth century has limited a variety of forms of business reciprocity among industrial firms not equally restricted in Japan. Since American law has taken a far more relaxed attitude toward transactions within vertically integrated firms, firms in the United States have sought to use full-scale acquisition to internalize many strategic business operations that their Japanese counterparts manage through interfirm transactions.

Yet while legal and other contextual considerations help to explain why Japanese and American industrial organizations have each followed distinctive trajectories, we need to explain as well the similarity of patterns among firms within Japan and their remarkable durability. This similarity and durability, I argue, is far too great to be understood solely by reference to the interests of individually animated rational actors. This leads to a second set of institutional considerations. In order to understand how patterns converge in common and persistent forms, we need to recognize as well the importance of tacit models of the organizing process that emerge in any economy and become part of the institutionalized way of doing things, independent of the interests of actors involved or its ultimate economic efficiency.

As DiMaggio and Powell (1983) point out, the professionalization of the management function has given rise to widely recognized, standard models of how organizations "should look." For their models of how to organize the personnel function, younger Japanese companies turned to older, established firms, leading to the general adoption of permanent employment and related managerial systems (Gordon, 1985). Similarly, these companies looked to the established firms for their models of intercorporate organizational practices.[14] Just as large American firms adopted the multidivisional corporate form in great numbers after its introduction in the 1920s (Fligstein, 1985), so too did zaibatsu-like holding companies become an increasingly widely accepted form during the prewar period, as the more loosely organized keiretsu did during the postwar period.[15]

As a result of this process of imitation, contemporary enterprise groups have tended to follow similar patterns of membership: each includes a major commercial bank at its center, a large life insurance company, one or more general trading companies, and one or more manufacturing firms in virtually all important industrial sectors. The same general format for executive interaction among affiliated companies has been followed through the use of monthly presidents' councils. And energies have been devoted to signifying these relationships symbolically through group-wide projects that follow one another into new fields.

Institutionalized patterns of keiretsu-based trading have proven extremely durable, surviving intact through capital market liberalization, the emergence of Japan as a technological leader, the internationalization of the Japanese economy, and ongoing shifts in the sectoral composition of the overall economy. In the case of keiretsu-based capital, for example, the proportion of companies' total borrowings and total equity accounted for by banks and other companies in the same group has remained virtually constant since the 1970s, while the proportion of total shareholders that are stable has actually increased throughout this period. In addition, new enterprises spun off from existing keiretsu firms take on patterns of capital investment and trade similar to their parent companies', recreating alliance structures in expanded form and resulting in the gradual increase of overall membership. Today, according to one widely used source, over two-thirds of the companies listed on the first section of the Tokyo Stock Exchange have clearly identifiable banking affiliations (*Keiretsu no kenkyū,* 1990 volume). And among those firms that have formally affiliated through presidents' council membership, none has ever switched groups (see Chapter 5).

This is not to deny that Japanese companies can and do in fact differ in the precise patterns of their external relationships, much as they do in the ways they have implemented their own distinctive variations of internal managerial practices. Nor does it imply that the composition and character of the keiretsu is permanently fixed. Indeed, both differences among groupings and their evolution over time receive wide attention in the Japanese business media, for much as company employees are concerned with how their own firm compares in the intercorporate ranking process and follow this closely, so too do company executives spend considerable time monitoring the strategic linkages that their competitors have forged with other firms. But this discussion also needs to be placed in the perspective of international comparisons, recognizing that tacit models of management, organization, and strategy flow far more easily within than across national boundaries (Westney, 1987) and in so doing come to take on a life of their own. As a result, industrial structures in different countries follow path trajectories that are both distinctive and historically dependent.

Acknowledging the limits to a purely microanalytic approach does not require that we fall back on assumptions that Japan's alliance structures reflect the inevitable consequences of distinctive, unchanging, and widely accepted Japanese cultural values. Intercorporate groupings have emerged in a variety of countries with very different cultural traditions in both Asia and Europe (even if the precise forms that they take vary owing to the emergence of distinctive organizing models and other institutional considerations, as outlined above). Moreover, within Japan we find a degree of precision in the construction of these relationships that is difficult to explain in terms of conformance to an abstract normative order. Where change has been necessary, these relationships have proved themselves adaptable, as when Japanese companies faced extensive proxy fights and market stock acquisition in the 1950s, leading to the rapid increase in share crossholdings during that period (Okumura, 1975). Nor is it true that Japanese cultural values lead in a single, internally consistent direction. As Mark Ramseyer (1987, p. 40) points out,

> Cultural orders seldom constitute coherent logical systems and the Japanese order is no exception. True, the Japanese intellectual tradition has long emphasized harmony, loyalty, and consensus. That same tradition, however, has also long celebrated the misanthropic swordsman who slashes for art, the wily merchant who cheats his way to riches, and the amorous prince who hops from bed to bed. Like any other cultural order, the Japanese tradition is an unstable set of conflicting and manipulable norms.

It is oftentimes argued that there is an unusually strong group orientation in Japan. But in many ways the patterns of cooperation studied here have developed in reaction *against* tendencies of this sort, to counteract the parochializing predilections of closely knit groups. Culturalist explanations for Japanese social organization have generally focused on tightly coupled, vertical arrangements marking traditional Japanese social groups (e.g., Nakane, 1972; Murakami, 1987). Alliance forms, in contrast, must be understood in terms of more loosely organized, extended structures that link widely divergent industries and economic functions. These are not the clearly bounded, insular units implied by the notion of the *ie* (household unit), *uchi* (in-group), or *kaisha* (company), but extended networks of actors in looser configuration with each other. They serve to build ties between cohesive social units, as defined at the company level, but do not themselves approach anywhere near the same levels of internal cohesion.

Social predispositions factor in, of course. There is in Japan—certainly more than in the mobility-conscious social patterns marking urban America—a tendency to differentiate social relationships by the length of time the parties have known each other and the extent to which these relationships are intertwined with other connections (e.g., their university or hometown). Status among leaders in the Japanese business community is conferred less by the conspicuous display of wealth than by one's institutional affiliations and personal *jinmyaku* (vein of people).[16] Appropriate behavior in different settings, such as in the relationship between *senpai* and *kōhai* (the senior and junior parties in a social exchange) is strongly established in the normative order of Japanese society and even in the linguistic structures of the Japanese language, most notably in the language of politeness.

These patterns provide basic organizing models that economic actors are able to use to build and animate their network structures. Among these patterns, as Dore (1983) notes, are well-defined social expectations concerning loyalty and a general preference for dealing with long-term associates rather than unreliable newcomers. Over time, relationships become infused with a social significance that goes beyond the immediate economic concerns of the partners. Self-interest is not abandoned as an explanatory tool, in this sense, but it takes place in the context of the slow building up of business relationships rather than in immediate, conspicuously instrumental behavior.

To understand institutionally the network structures that emerge requires following the precise contours of these relationships by studying the concrete policies and distinctive histories of organizational actors as they interact with this social context, recognizing that network structures are not simply reduceable to a small set of underlying principles or socialized norms. The image of economic organization that results is less one of homogeneous, consensus-driven groups than one of diverse and strategically constructed patterns of alliance-based interaction.

IMPLICATIONS OF JAPAN'S ALLIANCE STRUCTURES FOR ITS FIRM AND MARKET ORGANIZATION

The prevalence of alliance forms of economic organization in Japan has in turn shaped both the nature of its firms and the nature of the markets in which they operate, a topic taken up in the final three chapters. As a preview to this discussion, the main arguments are summarized here.

The Nature of the Japanese Firm

Studies of the Japanese firm have consistently shown much lower levels of diversification than their American counterparts (Clark, 1979; Goto, 1981; Fruin, 1992). In the most systematic of these studies, Yoshihara et al. (1981) recreated Rumelt's (1974) classic analysis with a sample of 118 large Japanese companies. In contrast to Rumelt's findings that 65 percent of major American companies had undergone substantial diversification out of a single strategic business category by the late 1960s, the comparable figure for Japanese firms was only 43 percent. In addition, whereas nearly 20 percent of the American firms had diversified heavily into unrelated areas, less than 7 percent of the Japanese firms had done the same. In summarizing their findings, Yoshihara et al. furthermore found that the diversification levels of Japanese firms was lower than for large firms in Britain, West Germany, France, and Italy as well (although none of these countries had reached the levels found in the United States at the time).

Together these results suggest that the Japanese firm is best viewed as a focused center of closely connected activities dedicated to specific business functions. This is not to say that diversification does not take place. But what is distinctive is the extent to which it occurs through the spinning off of new ventures and the building of external networks of relationships among firms that span a range of industrial sectors. Thus, although Japan does not have an active venture capital market in the American sense,[17] it has crafted a functional alternative that creates a substantial degree of Schumpeterian dynamism in the economy. While the opportunities within spun-off enterprises for high rates of financial returns are generally fewer, other benefits of entrepreneurial firms (social prestige, relative autonomy, long-term career incentives) are re-created in this form. Moreover, the availability of capital, personnel, and technical support from the parent company, as well as access to a partially captive customer base, helps to overcome some of the early disadvantages facing American venture businesses.

Chapter 6 sets this discussion in historical context, focusing on Japan's efforts to cope with the problems of rapid industrialization. Although it has only recently emerged as a technological leader, in many ways the strategic methods of dealing with innovation and technical change have been surprisingly similar since the late 1800s. The organizational model for development has been one of creating new operations as separate companies while linking these ventures into a broader family of enterprises. The present-day intermarket groups are largely composed of enterprises that were spun off from the zaibatsu during the decades before the second world war and were successful in the new markets they were developing. Contemporary Japanese firms have continued this diversification strategy, either by developing their own new enterprises or by bringing in companies from outside, forming overall alliances (e.g., the Matsushita or Hitachi groups) that are every bit as broad in scope collectively as their corporate-level counterparts elsewhere.

In conjunction with the shrinking of the firm's core size and lines of business has come a second transformation in the Japanese firm: a reconfiguration of the roles and relationships among the company's various constituencies. Although it has been argued that the contemporary Japanese corporation is management-controlled, this image is too simple, for it ignores the substantial external constraints under which these firms operate.[18] More important, it ignores who those external constituencies are and what their relationships are to the companies, and the ways in which the answers to these questions determine the strategies and policies of those firms' managements.

The implications of this reconfiguration are clearest when considering the characteristics of company ownership and resulting managerial motivations. It is frequently argued in popular accounts of the Japanese firm and in the business media that Japanese executives rely on a different set of payback criteria and time horizons than American executives when making major strategic decisions or investments. Although it is difficult to get at this issue directly, some supporting evidence comes from comparative data provided in a large-scale questionnaire survey of Japanese and American business managers (Kagono et al., 1985). When asked to rank the relative importance they placed on nine preselected corporate goals, the two sets of managers showed several striking differences. Ranking far most important in senior executives' corporate goals in the United States was return on investment, followed by capital gains for stockholders. In Japan, in contrast, the leading goal cited was increasing market share, followed by return on investment and the company's new product ratio (which was only seventh on the American list). Capital gains for shareholders ranked at the bottom of the list and were cited by almost none of the Japanese managers as an important goal for their company.[19]

To the extent that these represent real differences in the orientation of corporate managements, how are they to be explained? Aoki (1984b, 1988) points in a promising direction by observing that company shareholders may actually be a plural group that have different expectations for the returns on their investments. In his model of the Japanese firm, banks are seen as utilizing their positions as shareholders to push companies to borrow beyond a share price maximizing value. Shareholding for these financial institutions, therefore, is not only for direct income generation but as an influence strategy to increase the amount of loan business they enjoy with the company. Although Aoki's model is highly circumscribed, in the sense that it focuses only on differences between banks and individual shareholders and considers only banks' loan positions in the company, it nevertheless opens the door to a very different way of looking at the Japanese firm and its relationships with shareholders. For if not all shareholders have identical interests, it can no longer be stated with certainty that the goal of the firm is profit maximization (or, more precisely, maximizing the net present value of the firm's earnings), *even if that firm is acting in its shareholders' interests.*

This insight can be developed in a more general direction by exploring the broadly strategic character of intercorporate interests in Japan. The core empirical chapters of this study demonstrate a range of structural differences between Japan and the United States in the nature of shareholding relationships. These include much higher degrees in Japan of shareholding concentration, mutual or reciprocated shareholding positions, and overall shareholder stability. Perhaps most important is the very large percentage of leading equity holders that serve simultaneously as companies' banks and trading partners.[20] Given the multiplex interests corporate shareholders have, their interests will be served in a variety of ways apart from direct returns on their investments.

Many of these interests will lead them to encourage company growth or other goals at the expense of profits. In the case of banks, these interests include not only higher debt-equity ratios but also new fee businesses from the client, increased loans to related companies, an expanded employee base for bank deposits, increased compensating balances, and an improvement in their own equity capital positions through reciprocal shareholding positions (which help to improve their own equity bases in order to meet Bank for International Settlements [BIS] minimum capital asset requirements). This argument can easily be expanded to include trading company and industrial shareholders which, although less prominent as investors in Japan's largest firms, are major shareholders of many medium-sized businesses and have substantial interests in access to steady supplies, improved technical capabilities, and other strategic concerns.

Chapter 7 summarizes these findings and extends the discussion to the institutional character of the Japanese firm that results. Transactions in corporate assets through mergers and acquisitions are shown to be reduced in total number when compared with the highly active American market for corporate control. More important, the transactional process is altered, with certain key constituencies (company employees, banks, and trading partners) having a much more prominent voice than in the United States, and hostile takeovers all but nonexistent. In addition, the internal mechanisms of shareholder representation—the board of directors and general shareholders' meetings—lose much of their importance except as they satisfy the legal and normative requirements in the business community. But at the same time, these mechanisms are replaced by intercorporate substitutes, including presidents' councils, main bank relationships, and personnel transfers.

The Nature of Japanese Markets

Perhaps more controversial than the changes in the nature of the firm, both theoretically and practically, have been the effects of Japan's alliance structures on Japanese market organization. The theory of the firm for several decades now has allowed for accommodations to a range of organizational arrangements and subgoal pursuits.[21] But the theory of markets in perfect competition that continues to dominate economics textbooks presumes conditions that clearly diverge sharply from long-term, complexly nested, socially embedded sets of relationships among buyers and sellers.[22] Knight's definition (1957, p. 78) is a useful point of contrast. In perfect competition, he notes,

> Every member of the society is to act as an individual only, in entire independence of all other persons. To complete his independence he must be free from social wants, prejudices, preferences, or repulsions, or any values which are not completely manifested in market dealing. Exchange of finished goods is the only form of relation between individuals, or at least there is no other form which influences economic conduct. And in exchanges between individuals, no interests of persons not parties to the exchange are to be concerned, either for good or for ill.

This view of market organization has come under increasing criticism both within and outside of the economics profession, as the following chapter indicates, for failing to consider the many relational arrangements that business partners craft to structure their trading. Subsequent chapters demonstrate that, in addition, this model deviates substantially from the empirical reality of Japanese market organization, as measured by behavioral data based on concrete exchange relationships among Japanese firms. Durable cliques of traders in the Japanese economy are far too prevalent across a variety of market types to be viewed as minor anomalies in otherwise arm's-length transactions.

This does not mean that Japan no longer meets the prerequisites of a market economy. But it does require a shift in thinking about the structural underpinnings of those markets. While the belief in perfect competition and the anonymity of exchange may be necessary to equilibrium-based theoretical models, the association between these conditions and the operation of real-world market economies is relatively recent. Classically oriented economists, from Adam Smith to Joseph Schumpeter, have had a very different conception of the way in which market economies work. In their view, markets operate as dynamic systems that adjust production factors by using a logic of decentralized competition and sensitivity to price signals determined by underlying conditions of supply and demand. The focus, then, is on processes of change, not on enduring conditions of a hypothetical equilibrium state among anonymous traders.[23] And when understood in these dynamic terms, Japan operates very much as a market economy.

This suggests that the relationship between market organization and economic outcomes is not a simple one, and that economic efficiency can be defined in a variety of ways. In Chapter 8 the issue of the consequences of Japan's alliance structures for its overall economy is taken up. As an alternative to a single conclusive evaluation, I focus on a set of specific outcomes, which turns out to provide a somewhat mixed picture, although one that is probably on the whole positive: it is difficult to ignore, after all, the reality of Japan's extraordinary rates of growth in productivity, technological innovation, and overall GNP during the postwar period. But it is necessary to point to important problems as well, especially as Japan is increasingly integrated into the world trading system and faces continuing pressures to improve access to its markets for its foreign trading partners.

The first outcome, which is certainly one of the Japanese economy's key strengths, is the effectiveness of its adjustment to external shocks (e.g., the oil price increases of the 1970s and the rapid rise in the value of the yen in the mid-1980s) and to the inevitable fluctuations that occur in any economy. The economic problems attendant on disruptions in ongoing business activities are well-known. As Patrick and Rohlen (1987, p. 379) note, "One of the great costs in macroefficiency of advanced industrial market economies derives from the downswings of the business cycle. The output periodically forgone because of underutilized labor and capital during recessions is huge, far greater than that forgone because of static inefficiencies in resource allocation."

Japan's alliance structures have provided several distinctive mechanisms for coping with these shocks. In some cases these involve highly visible instances of intercorporate assistance, as shown in Sheard's (1986; 1991) detailed research on the role of banks and enterprise groups in restructuring individual companies and industries. In other cases, buffering processes are more ongoing and implicit, as reflected in Nakatani's (1984) analysis of the general stabilization of corporate sales and profitability that results from enterprise group membership and in Osano and Tsutsui's (1986) study of implicit contracts between banks and their corporate borrowers that allow companies to share lending risks by loan interest rate adjustments. As Nakatani suggests, implicit insurance and buffering processes are important in understanding the performance of the Japanese economy as a whole, and the "relatively high capacity of the Japanese economy for adjustment to changed market conditions may thus be closely related to [its] industrial organisation" (p. 244).

A different argument for alliance structures that is not as well developed theoretically, although it is certainly widely believed among Japanese business and public policy leaders, is that these adjustment processes have been accomplished in the absence of—indeed, in marked contrast to—the economic and social dislocations attendant on dramatic restructuring through an active market for corporate control. Stabilization of this market, in this view, has facilitated Japanese firms' planning processes, the making of long-term commitments to workers and other stakeholders in the firm, and the creation of effective interorganizational routines.

Shleifer and Summers (1988) point out that in an economy dominated by takeovers, stakeholders will become reluctant to enter into implicit contracts. Suppliers may refuse to invest in their own businesses without written guarantees from major customers. Company employees, feeling less commitment to their firm, will demand higher wages to compensate for their insecurity and the quality of their work may suffer. And managers may avoid putting time and effort into long-term projects if they are unlikely to survive long enough to reap the rewards. To the extent that this is the case, the benefits of an active market for corporate control (through hostile takeovers and other common features of American capitalism) have been overestimated and the costs underestimated.

A second set of outcomes of Japan's alliance structures for the economy is somewhat more mixed, but probably on the whole positive. This relates to the tendency for the strategic ties between Japanese companies and capital investors to promote high rates of capital investment. Theoretical work within contemporary economics has shown that the nature of the relationship among economic actors is an important determinant of the prices actually paid. Within the financial sector, even relatively small differences in information and monitoring capabilities can have a large impact on questions like the levels of debt, equity, and other financial instruments firms will employ. In this sense, it is not merely the cost of capital that becomes important in understanding Japanese corporate investment behavior, but the quality of information and the effectiveness of the ex post discipline that investors can bring to bear on companies.[24]

It is easy to overemphasize the inefficiency of Japanese capital markets, given the thin volume of trading that takes place among major corporate shareholders. The proof of efficiency ultimately lies in overall market performance, and on this basis Japan's stock markets have done extremely well. Japanese corporations have raised more new capital through equity and equity-related instruments than the firms in any other country during most of the 1980s, with ¥25 trillion raised on the Japanese stock market in 1989 alone (Zielinski and Holloway, 1991, p. 13). Indeed, Carrington and Edwards (1981) find that new issue capital as a percentage of GDP has been greater for several decades in Japan, West Germany, and France than in the supposedly well-developed capital markets of the United States and Britain.

The qualification to an argument for the market's efficiency enters in if the pursuit of growth per se comes to take priority over other economic interests. As suggested earlier, the mechanisms of traditional capitalist control by independent and financially motivated investors have been substantially altered in Japan. To the extent that strategically motivated corporate shareholders have less incentive than purely financially motivated investors to constrain companies to a strict net-present-value criterion, since indirect returns to their business interests are sometimes large enough to offset direct losses to returns on their capital investments, this leads to rates of corporate investment that are disproportionate to companies' own internal capital requirements.

Some writers have suggested that these high rates of capital investment are a source of competitive advantage for Japanese companies (Abegglen and Stalk, 1985). But the benefits that companies enjoy from this do not come without costs to at least some investors and perhaps even to the economy as a whole. By the late 1980s, large Japanese firms had increased their capital stocks to the point where on average they were nearly double the company's own internal requirements when measured by normal business-related investments in plant and equipment (Okumura, 1990). Even as retained earnings and new-issue equity capital increased dramatically, large companies were continuing to take out long-term loans and to reduce their dividend payout ratios.

Spheres of financial concentration have been one result, as reflected in colloquial references to the "Toyota Bank" or the "Matsushita Bank." A substantial share of corporate profits has gone into various forms of speculation (sometimes known as *zai-tech*) in land and financial instruments unrelated to companies' normal business activities rather than being returned to shareholders through dividends. This has also produced structural conditions in which "excessive competition" (*katō kyōsō*) emerges, as Japanese companies seeking to increase their market shares at the expense of domestic and foreign rivals have utilized these resource bases to continue investing in their own businesses beyond a profit-maximizing level.

These consequences have been of sufficient concern to the Japanese government to invite intervention in a number of areas: to cool an overheated property market; to prosecute companies that have overstepped the bounds of legitimate speculation; to manage competition through industrial cartels or informal arrangements; and to negotiate with foreign trading partners threatening retaliation when the effects of excessive competition spill over into their own markets (as in cases of "dumping"). Ironically, then, even as Japan's alliance structures have helped to buffer the effects of macroeconomic uncertainty, they have created new sources of it.

The third consequence of alliance structures for the Japanese economy is certainly the most problematic. This relates to the effects of preferential trading on market access in Japan. The status-quo-oriented character of business relationships that continue to mark Japanese markets have had the net effect of making market entry by newcomers, whether Japanese or foreign, more difficult than in structurally more open markets (Gerlach, 1989; Lawrence, 1991). Market incumbents in Japan enjoy an unusual number of advantages in access to capital and personnel, resulting, as noted earlier, in a tendency for technological innovation and high-value-added production to be carried out by large firms and their affiliates rather than by independent, entrepreneurial startups. Although these disadvantages are partly shared by foreign firms attempting to set up operations in Japan, they are probably less of a barrier to access than the general bias within product markets toward repetitive and reciprocal dealing, as between steel and trading companies or between automobile manufacturers and parts makers.

These patterns are undoubtedly based at least partly on a logic of efficiency, as a number of the researchers discussed earlier have pointed out. But in a global trading system, internal efficiency is only one of several criteria along which economic organization must be evaluated. Preferential trading patterns now expose Japan to serious challenges from its trading partners, who argue that structural asymmetries create problems for an international trading regime in which perceptions of fairness are also important. These patterns were accepted during an earlier period when Japan's economy was small and catching up with the advanced Western economies, but this is no longer the case.

Evaluation of the significance of preferential trading in Japanese markets to trade issues has faced at least two problems. One is theoretical. There remains within orthodox trade theory a bias toward seeing long-term relational contracting as ultimately efficiency reducing and economically stagnating. Since the Japanese economy as a whole does not conform to this image, the conclusion has often been reached that the underlying premise that identity-based trading is pervasive in Japan must be wrong. But this assumes that perfect competition is the ideal state of the world, a view that is increasingly questioned both within new approaches to economic analysis and in discussions specific to Japan. Moving in this direction, new theories of trade have begun to introduce an alternative to perfect competition models that incorporate considerations of real-world industrial organization into their framework (Krugman, 1987).

Even so, a second problem remains—how to measure these effects. What is needed is the ability to augment theoretical and macroeconomic analyses with the detailed study of structures of exchange through which trade is actually organized. In the core empirical chapters of this study, a network approach to the study of intercorporate relationships is developed that seeks to map out relatively precisely the exchange patterns that exist among companies and within enterprise groupings. The results of these analyses bring into doubt the view that cross-national differences in industrial organization within market economies are nonexistent or unimportant. Nor do they provide much evidence that these differences have largely disappeared or that Japanese industrial organization is rapidly moving toward an impersonal market model. However, they also point to the fact that asymmetries in market access affect transactions differentially. The intermarket keiretsu prove to be far more significant overall in the organization of financial capital than they do in consumer product markets. They also prove to be important in certain forms of trade among industrial firms, and for these firms their product market consequences are substantial.

In summary, it is apparent that any overall evaluation of Japanese industrial organization will require both an efficiency evaluation (within single domestic markets) and an effectiveness evaluation (across markets and in conjunction with the factoring in of geopolitical and social costs). Intercorporate alliances in Japan are an important component in the larger explanation of the strategies and structures of the Japanese firm, the resilience of these firms and the overall Japanese economy to external shocks, continuing high rates of capital investment in Japan, and the relative difficulty that market newcomers have in penetrating certain Japanese markets. The dilemma Japan now faces is how to retain those features of its business and economic system that provide real benefits while discarding those for which the costs have come to outweigh the gains. Since in many cases both benefits and costs result from the same systemic factors, this will not be an easy task.

CONCLUSION

The great twentieth-century debate in political economy between decentralized market capitalism and state-planned systems has been fueled by the manifest importance of these choices in a world of cold-war geopolitics. In the contemporary battle of ideas, market capitalism is clearly dominant, especially if Japan is included in the group. And, broadly speaking, Japan should be included: its prices do fluctuate in accordance with changing conditions of supply and demand (over the long term and some more than others), as they will in any "market" economy, while no country has utilized those sine qua non for "capitalist" systems—institutions of private sector capital accumulation and private sector ownership over business organizations—more effectively than Japan.

But the capitalism-communism debate was simplified by the stark contrasts in the alternatives each represents.[25] The intellectual challenge regarding Japan's significance to its Western trading partners lies instead in the nuances of institutional differentiation among market capitalist systems themselves. Along these lines, Herbert Simon has argued, "As economics expands beyond its central core of price theory, and its central concern with quantities of commodities and money, we observe in it ... [a] shift from a highly quantitative analysis, in which equilibration at the margin plays a central role, to a much more qualitative institutional analysis, in which discrete structural alternatives are compared" (quoted in Williamson, 1991, p. 270). What is needed in understanding Japan is a subtle analysis of the particulars of market capitalist organization. This moves us beyond the confines of conventional theory to a consideration of the complex interrelationships within and across market sectors in ways that become more apparent in the following chapter.

Every form of economic organization carries with it a set of benefits and costs, and questions of efficiency or effectiveness must be set in a comparative context.[26] No doubt there will be observers who are uncomfortable with the kind of intertwined linkages of ownership and business that pervade the Japanese economy, seeing these as inevitably leading to forms of informal monopoly. And these concerns are in some respects justified. There are drawbacks to Japan's market capitalist system, among them a lack of transparency and a sense of exclusion experienced by those outside of preferential trading networks.

But it is by no means clear that the changes in Japanese firm structure and motivation or deviations from anonymous markets that Japan's alliance structures have instilled have on the whole been efficiency reducing. Reliance on intercorporate networks has in many ways helped to keep the Japanese firm smaller on average and more focused than its American counterpart while providing many of the advantages brought about by vertical integration. Moreover, the corporate equity holders that predominate in Japanese stock markets have proved far more willing to take long-term investment positions in other companies than have the institutional investors common in the United States. At a minimum, then, intercorporate alliance structures are a core feature of Japanese market capitalism. But they may also represent a form of rational economic organization as yet only poorly understood.

CHAPTER II

Rethinking Market Capitalism

Anthropologists, sociologists, and historians have long pointed to the meshing of social and economic spheres in traditional and non-Western economies: in the village fairs, household production systems, family companies, and informal community networks that dominated much of the daily life. It is widely assumed, however, that this "embedding" was lost during the development of modern market capitalist economies, as economic transactions were disconnected from each other and from other ongoing relationships in the society. The contemporary industrial economy is viewed instead as being driven by the engine of impersonal exchange, the very anonymity of which is the source of its efficiency—or, alternatively, of the anomie that it engenders.

That present-day economies are themselves far from this impersonal ideal is a view gaining prominence within the field in which it has long been most forcefully argued. The new institutional economics (William-son, 1985) now emphasizes that economic theory can and must face up to the limits of atomized, anonymous markets and has set about to explain the institutional forms that have developed in modern economies to overcome these limits. Of particular interest has been the role of long-term contracting and corporate organization as alternatives to competitive price-auction markets. Markets and capitalist enterprises are seen, therefore, not as isolated entities running on a logic of their own, but as complex institutional arrangements embedded in a society's legal order and the basic rules under which actors operate.

This chapter introduces some of the central themes in this debate with the belief that a rapprochement among these perspectives is essential to developing a general theory of economic organization applicable not only to the West but to Japan as well. Even within the context of advanced market capitalist economies, we observe the emergence of significant nonmarket institutions that create efficiency-enhancing order in trading relationships. In this, the institutional economists' critique of perfect competition models is relevant. At the same time, the institutions that create this order extend well beyond formal corporate hierarchies and contractual arrangements defined in well-codified property rights to a wide variety of intermediate and informal forms of coordination and cooperation oftentimes more familiar to noneconomists. Understanding this complex and overlapping network of institutional arrangements is essential to an understanding of economies as *faits sociaux totaux*.

The term "market capitalism," oddly enough, is rarely defined in discussions of comparative economic systems. Indeed, its component words are often used as synonyms. Yet while it is perhaps acceptable to refer to market economies and capitalist economies interchangeably when contrasting systems based on decentralized decision making by private actors with those based on socialist planning, this should not obscure differences in the underlying emphases of each. As we see in this chapter, institutional variations in "market" and "capitalist" arrangements can and do exist, and each has its own independent significance.

Markets comprise the organized circulation of valued goods and services. They represent a form of institutionalized exchange process that, as Hodgson (1988, p. 174) suggests in his broad approach to the question, "help[s] to both regulate and establish a consensus over prices and, more generally, to communicate information regarding products, prices, quantities, potential buyers and potential sellers." Furthermore, because market transactions involve contractual agreement and the exchange of property rights, the market consists as well of "mechanisms to structure, organize, and legitimate these activities." Market institutions, for this reason, concern not only the precise terms of trade (i.e., prices) but also the general dynamics of interaction among the traders themselves and the legal and social context within which exchange takes place.

Discussion of the nature of *capitalism* shifts attention to one particularly important subset of markets. These markets are constituted, of course, by the flow of capital that represents the lifeblood of business operations. But at least as significant as capital per se are the rights to power and influence over how that capital is allocated and, ultimately, to control over contemporary economies' primary decision makers, the corporations.

In the first section of this chapter, we consider the operation of markets as they actually function in Japan and other real-world economic systems, focusing on the limits to impersonal exchange and the separation of social and economic spheres of life that underlie perfect competition models. In the second section, discussion shifts to consideration of the nature of capitalism as a pattern of higher-level control over market assets, and most important, over an economy's capital-allocation and corporate decision-making processes. Linking these component parts, and a key area of difference between market capitalism in Japan and the United States, is the market for corporate control—the social structure of influence relationships between investors and companies.

THE SOCIAL STRUCTURE OF MARKETS

The problems of economic organization are in many ways universal: how to organize exchange effectively among disparate actors whose interests only partially overlap and where conditions are continually changing.[1] But the solutions vary widely across economic systems. In this section, we consider three perspectives on the role of market organization in economic systems. In the first view, represented by Karl Polanyi and his followers in the comparative and historical analysis of economies, impersonal markets are seen as widespread, but only in the context of modern, Western society. A second view, most fully developed by the French historian Fernand Braudel, questions the uniqueness of present-day Western markets and demonstrates that marketlike processes, as measured by the sensitivity of trading patterns to underlying conditions of supply and demand, have been prevalent throughout the world at many points in time. The third view, emerging from within institutional economics, emphasizes that even though market forces may represent an implicit and inevitable "state of nature" (as pointed out by Braudel), truly anonymous exchange even in modern economies is in practice rare and limited to a relatively narrow band of routine transactions.

Karl Polanyi's Comparative Study of Economic Systems

The competitive price-auction market takes as its starting point the assumption that economic relations have been and ought to be separated from other ongoing relationships in society. This perspective has come under increasing criticism by a number of writers in recent years (e.g., Granovetter, 1985; Hodgson, 1988). But it was Karl Polanyi, writing several decades earlier, who argued most persistently against this position, both as a social ideal and as an empirical reality in most parts of the world and at most times in history. Since this influential interpretation relates directly to the issue of the comparative development of economic institutions, it is worth reviewing his basic arguments.

Polanyi's approach was broadly interdisciplinary, using a range of historical and anthropological data to create a system of comparative economics. The basic thesis of Polanyi and his followers was that economic theory applies only to the modern market economy and cannot be used to explain traditional or non-Western societies. Whereas the modern market economy operates under its own internal drive mechanisms through decisions by rationally calculating individuals, economic relationships in premodern societies have been marked by their "embedding" in a larger social system. For this reason, the comparative study of economic systems must begin from the substantive meaning of the term *economic,* not from its formal, or rationalistic, meaning (Polanyi, 1957, p. 243):

1.   "The formal meaning of economic derives from the logical character of the means-end relationship, as apparent in such words as 'economical' or 'economizing.' It refers to a definite situation of choice, namely, that between the different uses of means induced by an insufficiency of those means."

2.   In contrast, "the substantive meaning of economic derives from man's dependence for his living upon nature and his fellows. It refers to the interchange with his natural and social environment, in so far as this results in supplying him with the means of material want satisfaction."

The nineteenth century, Polanyi argued, was a unique period of history when the economy in Europe became separate from the social structure, economic motives were freed from social control, and a process was set in motion whereby economic concerns came to dominate society. "Once the economic system is organized in separate institutions, based on specific motives and conferring a special status, society must be shaped in such a manner as to allow that system to function according to its own laws" (1944, pp. 63–64). Only during this one period did the formal, rationalistic definition of the economy match up with the substantive definition. Polanyi's methodology for getting at these social

structures was through observing the concrete flows of actors and resources:

> In the whole range of economic disciplines, the point of common interest is set
> by the process through which material want satisfaction is provided. Locating
> this process and examining its operation can only be achieved by shifting the
> emphasis from a type of rational action to the configuration of goods and
> person movements which actually make up the economy. This is the task of
> what we will here call institutional analysis. [Polanyi et al., 1957, pp. 241–42]

Recurrent patterns of flows that defined the fundamental institutional
forms of integration in a society gave it unity and stability. While different institutional patterns might coexist in a single economic system,
the societies Polanyi observed were presented as dominated by one type
of economic organization. Three fundamental patterns were observed in
traditional societies: reciprocity, or "movements between correlative
points of symmetrical groupings in society"; redistribution, or "movements towards an allocative center and out of it again"; and exchange,
or "vice-versa movements taking place as between 'hands' under a market system" (Polanyi, 1957, p. 250).[2]

Polanyi left no doubt that his sympathies lay with the first two,
reciprocity and redistribution, but not with market exchange. He was a
utopian who saw no place in utopia for the "higgling-haggling" of the
market or the "obsolete market mentality" (1944). Market trade was
viewed as a marginal activity in most societies, largely incompatible with
the dominant pattern of reciprocity or redistribution. Nonmarket societies sheltered themselves from the divisiveness of market exchange in
various ways. The institution that interested him most was the "port of
trade." This was Polanyi's term for a settlement that acted as a control
point in trade between two societies. These served the function, Polanyi
believed, of isolating market relationships with outsiders from the remainder of society—that is, of creating a buffer between two different
social systems.

Despite the originality of his ideas, Polanyi's Rousseauistic vision of
harmonious, integrated primitive societies (not uncommon among func-
tionalist writers at the time) prevented him from seeing significant elements of market exchange in the societies he was studying and led him to
ignore elements of reciprocity and rule-ordered exchange in modern
market economies.[3] It would be just as easy, for example, to interpret the
port of trade quite differently: as an institutional framework for defining
the rules and ordering exchange among strangers and for creating sanctions where those of the community do not operate. A significant feature

of ports of trade, Polanyi noted, was that they operated under an administration that regulated features within them, confining trade to official
channels and restricting access, requiring that transactions be made in an
approved place and form, and subjecting them to a judicial authority
able to settle disputes on the spot. We find these same features in modern
societies within the quintessential market institutions, stocks and commodities exchanges (Telser, 1980; Leblebici and Salancik, 1982). One
might better argue, therefore, that the first goal of most institutionalized
markets, including stocks and commodities exchanges, village bazaars,
and perhaps even the port of trade, is to facilitate exchange rather than
to buffer the society.

The Great Transformation? Braudel's Critique

Polanyi's study of the embedding of economic relations in preexisting
social structures was an important contribution to the theory of the
organization of economies. He was able to make compelling the notion
of the economy as an instituted process and to develop a comparative
framework for classifying patterns. Still, his position concerning "the
great transformation" in the development of the nineteenth-century
market capitalism—in which an embedded economy existing in a presumed pristine state in an earlier period gave way to a rationalized
economy dominated by self-contained markets—merits critical review,
particularly as we try to understand the conditions necessary for the rise
of market institutions in the West and as we apply this analysis to the rise
of the institutions of Japanese market capitalism. This critique may be
approached from two directions: first, by questioning the absence of
market exchange in traditional and non-Western societies; and second,
by challenging the predominance of impersonal exchange in modern
market economies.

From the first direction, Fernand Braudel's epic trilogy on the development of Western market capitalism, *Civilization and Capitalism,
15th–18th Century,* has much to say. Braudel offers what in many ways
is an extended argument refuting the Polanyian position on the uniqueness of modern-period market institutions. This is most explicit in the
second volume, *The Wheels of Commerce* (1979), in which Braudel
directly challenges Polanyi on the issues of methodology, data, and
interpretation (though perhaps not granting him sufficient credit for his
theoretical insights).

In Braudel's view, Polanyi's historical analysis is subject to methodological criticism in that, rather than follow a single economy through time to observe the persistence and transformation of institutional relationships, Polanyi tries to draw single-point-in-time comparisons across heterogeneous samples.

> There is no law against introducing into a discussion of the "great transformation" of the nineteenth century such phenomena as the *potlatch* or *kula* (rather than, say, the very diversified trading organization of the seventeenth and eighteenth centuries). But it is rather like drawing on Levi-Strauss's explanation of kinship ties to elucidate the rules governing marriage in Victorian England. Not the slightest effort has been made to tackle the concrete and diverse reality of history and use that as a starting point. [Braudel, 1979, p. 227]

As a result, Polanyi on the one hand fails to see inchoate forms of markets in centuries prior to the nineteenth and in places other than Europe:[4] "alongside the 'non-markets' beloved of Polanyi, there always have been exchanges exclusively in return for money, however little. In rather minimal form perhaps, markets nevertheless existed in very ancient times within a single village or group of villages—the market being a sort of itinerant village, as the fair was a sort of travelling town" (p. 228). And on the other, Polanyi ignores the fundamental social element intertwined with the workings of even market economies.

> [The] notion of the "self-regulating market" proposed in this research— which "is" this or that, "is not" the other, "cannot accommodate" such and such a deformation—seems to be the product of an almost theological taste for definition. This market, in which the only elements are "demand, the cost of supply and prices, which result from a reciprocal agreement" is a figment of the imagination. It is too easy to call one form of exchange economic and another social. In real life, all types are both economic and social. [Braudel, p. 227]

This is not merely an idle issue, for it relates to the entire issue of how one interprets the social organization of market economies. If Braudel and not Polanyi is correct, then patterns of economic organization found in nineteenth-century Europe are likely to have made their appearance long before, as well as in other parts of the world. We find in Braudel's *longue durée* not radical discontinuities but slowly evolving mixtures of institutional forms, some of them a kind of primitive market capitalism. In defense of this position, Braudel devotes considerable energy toward presenting statistical and other data to buttress his argument that market forces defined by underlying conditions of supply and demand were in operation centuries before the nineteenth in ways that marked Europe as a market-influenced regional system. He concludes:

Historically, one can speak of a market economy, in my view, when prices in the markets of a given area fluctuate in unison, a phenomenon the more characteristic since it may occur over a number of different jurisdictions or sovereignties. In this sense, there was a market economy well before the nineteenth and twentieth centuries. . . . Prices have fluctuated since ancient times; by the twelfth century they were fluctuating in unison throughout Europe. Later on, this concord became more precise within ever stricter limits. [Pp. 227–28]

Are Contemporary Industrial Economies Really Dominated by Impersonal Markets? The Institutional Economists' Critique

Braudel points to ways in which price-based market processes are observable in pre-nineteenth-century, traditional economies. A different critique of market theory has emerged recently within economics itself, arguing that modern economies, even if sensitive to underlying market conditions, need not be and often are not based on ideal-type, impersonal exchange. A central theme in the new institutional economics is that economic organization varies around a continuum defined at each end by markets and firms. Perfectly competitive markets—impersonal, atomized, arm's length—may actually be quite rare, since various formal and informal arrangements have arisen that bring parties together into relationships that are enduring or governed by other, nonmarket mechanisms. "Much of economic activity takes place within long-term, complex, perhaps multiparty contractual (or contract-like) relationships: *behavior is, in various degrees, sheltered from market forces*" (Goldberg, 1980, p. 338, emphasis added).

The most fully realized development of an economic approach to organization is found in the work of Oliver Williamson (1975, 1985). Key concepts in Williamson's analysis of the limits to markets are (1) transactions costs, or the "comparative costs of planning, adapting, and monitoring task completion" (Williamson, 1985, p. 2) and (2) governance structures, or the institutional arrangements designed to govern transactions and thereby reduce transactions costs. Transactions costs and the search for ways to minimize them are inevitable, Williamson argues, because economic life is inherently complex and because actors can be opportunistic in pursuing their own interests.

Following from Ronald Coase's (1937) original study of the nature of the firm and the business historian Alfred Chandler's (1962) pioneering work on the rise of the modern corporation, Williamson points to the ways in which various forms of internal organization emerge in order to economize on transactions costs prevalent in market exchange. Receiving special attention is the M-form, or multidivisional, firm, in which operating business decisions are decentralized to independent profit centers that are connected through a central strategic capital allocation system. Williamson argues that this form improves on arm's-length capital markets in three important respects. First, it is better able to provide salaries and bonuses that are geared toward cooperative behavior among the profit centers. Second, the records of division managers are subject to review, again ensuring incentives for internal cooperation. And third, the M-form creates a greater depth of information, as opposed to the market's breadth, which allows for efficient cash flow allocation: "This assignment of cash flows to high yield uses is the most fundamental attribute of the M-form enterprise" (1975, p. 148).

With the rise of the modern corporation came changes in the basic character of economic exchange as much of it has moved from the anonymous world of the invisible hand into concrete spheres of planning and coordination. By the 1970s, the largest one hundred firms in Britain constituted approximately 42 percent of manufacturing output in Britain, 33 percent in the United States, and about 28 percent in West Germany.[5] As a result of this shift, Cable and Dirrheimer (1983, pp. 43–44) note, "a significant proportion of western economic activity now takes place within the quasi-autonomous operating divisions of giant enterprises, under strategic direction from a network of central head-offices." This represents, as they point out, "a major departure from the structural conditions of production contemplated by competitive equilibrium."

Coase's original formulation of the firm—as a realm of exchange in which the price mechanism is suppressed—might have proved profoundly disturbing within economics given the empirical importance of firm-based trading in contemporary economies. His article nevertheless received sympathetic treatment, perhaps because, by sharply differentiating between firm and market, it left the latter intact for standard economic analysis.

This pattern of clear differentiation continued in earlier transactions costs formulations as well. But more recent work has increasingly challenged the belief that even nominally market transactions are organized through impersonal exchange. Williamson (1979, 1985) argues that a variety of nonmarket relationships between companies are much more widespread than is commonly recognized. Where trading partners make investments in specialized assets that depend on the actions of others,

they require some form of guarantee, or *credible commitment,* from
their partner that goes beyond the protections that market discipline can
offer. Because the costs of writing and enforcing contracts that cover
every possible contingency can be extraordinarily expensive, partners
often choose instead to negotiate private ordering arrangements that
bind the partners more completely than impersonal market transactions,
but in more open-ended arrangements than contracts allow. Although
the forms of these arrangements can vary widely, among the most important from the point of view of studying alliance structures are *hostage
exchanges,* which include one-way and reciprocal equity investments
that companies make in their business partners to ensure continued
access to important resources.

In this sense, firms are, as Richardson (1972, p. 883) notes, not simply
"islands of planned coordination in a sea of market relations." Interfirm
transactions are themselves often structured in repetitive, informal, and
socially significant relationships. The reality of contemporary market
organization, for this reason, is not a strict disjuncture between markets
and firms but a continuum of relationships, with many constituting a
middle sphere defined by various forms of interfirm cooperation.

In a somewhat different formulation, also relevant to this discussion,
A. O. Hirschman (1970) points to ways in which atomized markets and
arm's-length exchange can suffer from an impoverished repertoire of
governance structures. Sanctions based in the market *exit* option, where
traders disband immediately after completing transactions, fail to convey key information that might be transmitted were the relationship to
be continued. Within the nonmarket, *voice* option, in contrast, a portion
of customers remain loyal to the products or services of the seller—even
where quality is deteriorating. These traders become, in a sense, business
partners, actively participating in quality improvement.

The importance of loyalty and other forms of relational contracting is
particularly evident where exchange is idiosyncratic, complex, or dynamic. In these situations, prices as simplifying heuristics often do not
capture proper values, and exchange is governed instead by an "immense
variety of institutional supports to market processes—such as trust,
friendship, law, and reciprocity" (Teece and Winter, 1984, p. 119). In the
operation of real-world markets, truly impersonal transactions are limited to a small set of routine trades that take place in narrowly circumscribed and highly institutionalized settings, such as stock and commodity exchanges.[6]

And in Japan? Here as well, the firm has become a central locus of exchange, with the largest one hundred nonfinancial firms constituting just over one-quarter of the total assets in nonfinancial sectors in the late 1960s and about 21 percent in 1980 (Uekusa, 1987). These firms have taken the additional step of organizing themselves into coherent and enduring alliance structures, resulting in a highly institutionalized arena of intercorporate cooperation, discussed below. As the share of total economic activity accounted for by Japan's largest firms has gradually declined, the number of companies with identifiable keiretsu affiliations has increased, suggesting an ongoing expansion in the proportion of total economic activity accounted for by interfirm cooperation as opposed to intrafirm control.[7]

Understanding Markets as Concrete Institutions

It becomes apparent from the above that overall economies and specific markets are organized around a wide range of institutional forms of order. Approaches to these forms vary considerably, of course. Institutional economics has focused primarily on the organization of exchange under legal institutions defined in a clearly delineated property rights structure, particularly the formal contract and the modern corporation. Polanyi, Braudel, and other historical and comparative observers, on the other hand, have emphasized the embedding of exchange in the social institutions and structures of traditional societies. The latter viewpoint is useful to keep in mind, for the existence of firms implies not only that markets have failed, but that alternative forms of social governance have too.

Differences also exist in the purposes that forms of nonmarket organization are seen as serving. Institutional economics has been concerned with the ways in which institutions arise to create order in exchange relationships where markets fail, the purpose being to improve economic efficiency.[8] Polanyi and his followers, in contrast, have been more interested in social cohesion and taming the conflict they perceive as inherent in unrestricted market exchange.

These differences, however, should not be overstated. Just as anthropologists have shown that traders in traditional economies personalize or particularize exchange relations (Belshaw, 1965; Geertz, 1978), so too are social considerations rarely absent from even the most rationally calculated business decisions in contemporary economies. A variety of studies over the past several decades have emphasized the long-term, relational character of contemporary industrial markets (e.g., Macaulay, 1963; Richardson, 1972; Macneil, 1974, 1978; Williamson, 1979; Okun, 1981; Granovetter, 1985; and Carlton, 1986). Carlton (1986) finds that the average length of purchasing relationships among industrial firms in his survey was between seven and eleven years. And Macaulay observes that these relationships are frequently mediated informally rather than through reliance on detailed contracts: "Businessmen often prefer to rely on 'a man's word' in a brief letter, a handshake, or 'common honesty and decency'—even when the transaction involves exposure to serious risks" (1963, p. 58). At a theoretical level, Williamson (1975) has introduced into his transactions costs framework the idea of "atmosphere" to account for the fact that people incorporate in their economic decisions information not just about the outcomes of a transaction but also about the process of exchange and the quality of their relationships with their trading partners. To the extent this is the case, characteristics of the overall social order may themselves become important in determining the efficiency of alternative modes of exchange.

When organized within alliance forms, informal relationships are taken a step further and in so doing a context for cooperation is created that is both structurally coherent and socially significant to its participants. In the view of Japanese managers, stable, symbolically identified intercorporate relationships lead to a variety of intangible benefits, among them: increased feelings of trust among the participants; a more personalized and less formal mode of interaction; improved access to the interpersonal relationships that ultimately determine how much of organizational activities in Japanese business are actually carried out; and the ability to conduct long-term decision making among interdependent companies.

The embedding of economic interests in a social context (Granovetter, 1985) does not eliminate rational considerations, however. Certainly Japanese managers tend to explain business behavior in relational rather than instrumental terms, with words like "trust" and "loyalty" appearing repeatedly in accounts of the Japanese company and intercompany cooperation.[9] But trust is a tenuous thing, even in a "high trust culture" like Japan's and even where relationships among partners have continued over decades (Gerlach, 1990; Ramseyer, 1991).

Indeed, the ubiquity of trust as a cultural characteristic of Japanese society is itself by no means universally accepted. In one influential analysis of this issue, John Haley questions the widespread belief that there is "an unusual and deeply rooted cultural preference for informal, mediated settlement of private disputes and a corollary aversion to the formal mechanism of judicial adjudication" (1978, p. 359). Haley claims instead that low litigation rates in contemporary Japan are the product of a range of institutional barriers, among them a substantial shortage of practicing lawyers resulting from sharp restrictions on certification, long delays in obtaining court trials, and the lack of appropriate remedies for litigants.[10] In addition to a discussion of these barriers, Haley also notes two statistical facts awkward to the culturalist argument: data indicating that litigation rates in Japan have declined since the end of the second world war rather than increased, as might be expected with the modernization of Japan; and data showing that, while litigation rates in Japan are much lower than they are in the United States, they are actually higher than those found in several other Western countries.

The lack of reliance on contractual modes of exchange in Japan, therefore, is not simply the product of a deep-rooted cooperative ethic. Haley points in one alternative direction by arguing that noncontractual arrangements are the product of the weakness of the "sheath of justice" in Japan (Haley, 1982) and the resulting inability of individuals and companies to rely on legal recourse in resolving contractual disputes. The result, he continues, has been the widespread adoption of a variety of private-ordering arrangements, including promissory notes, informal mediators, and letters of guarantee.

A different direction to the issue of noncontractual arrangements among businesses is suggested by the fact that these relations are common *across* market economies. In explaining the prevalence of noncontractual relations among the American businessmen he studied, Macaulay (1963) notes a variety of "counterbalancing sanctions" to which sellers have access, including demanding downpayments before delivery, possession of proprietary skills that limit the ability of buyers to switch sources, and the existence of "blacklists" that hurt a company's business reputation. Macaulay's work points out that reputation is not an abstract quality, but a tangible discipline exercised both through formal channels (e.g., the risk of a bad report from credit-rating agencies such as Dun and Bradstreet when buyers fail to pay their bills on time) and through informal networks (e.g., discussions among purchasing and sales agents at trade meetings, country clubs, and social gatherings).

Contractual arrangements, therefore, are often not the preferred mode of coordinating economic activity even where the legal system and court ordering do operate effectively. The theory of incomplete contracting (e.g., Williamson, 1985) has pointed to the impossibility, as a practical matter, of including all contingencies in private contracts. Future

states of the world are difficult to predict and the substantive and procedural requirements necessary to enforce agreements in public courts are
far greater than for private arrangements. Moreover, economic action
requires extensive tacit knowledge that promotes smooth functioning
among business partners but is difficult to codify in precise blueprints of
action (Nelson and Winter, 1982).

Alliance structures deal with these problems in two ways. First, a basic
set of governance mechanisms is established, with shareholding playing
an especially prominent role in the process. Grossman and Hart (1986)
suggest that equity ownership has the advantage of assigning control
over the use of an asset in all contingencies not explicitly contracted
upon. Whereas full-scale vertical integration is the usual application of
this principle, an alternative is mutual shareholding among legally separate companies. Second, this basic structure of rights and responsibilities
serves as the backdrop before which a wide variety of more specific
informal and social ties among specific actors develop. As Zucker (1988,
p. 33) notes, organizations help to resolve conflicts in self-interest that
would exist without formal structures, and in this sense, they "provide
frameworks within which joint action is smoothed by arriving at and
retaining solutions to social dilemmas." Alliance structures create a
similar framework, which in turn allows for the emergence of task-
oriented routines at the interorganizational level.

In conclusion, we may point to a linking theme among the various
writers considered here: a common appreciation of economic organizations as complex institutions to be understood through the observation
of concrete exchange relationships. Polanyi and his followers follow "the
configuration of goods and person movements which actually make up
the economy" (Polanyi et al., 1957, pp. 241–42). Braudel traces the
contours of everyday, material life, "guided by concrete observation and
comparative history" (1979, p. 25). And transactions costs economics
studies the transaction as the basic unit of analysis, which "occurs when
a good or service is transferred across a technologically separable inter-
face" (Williamson, 1985, p. 1) and explores the ways transactions become organized into the complex variety of institutional arrangements
that make up contemporary economies. Markets, therefore, are best
seen less as the reification of an abstract ideal—self-sustaining, self-
regulating, self-functioning mechanisms running on an internal logic
apart from the remainder of society—and more as social inventions that
are embedded in larger institutional structures, both legal and social.

THE SOCIAL STRUCTURE OF CAPITALISM

The analysis of market organization points to a broad range of ongoing trading activities that constitute the economy as a whole. The analysis of capitalism, in contrast, focuses directly on the economy's most central actors: those who control its basic assets, especially its capital and corporations.[11] Among the significant innovations within the capitalist system, two stand out: the joint-stock corporation and the stock exchange. The corporate form, by establishing a division of labor between holders of capital and management and limiting the liability of the first, simultaneously opened up new sources of capital for faster growth, allowed for the specialization of the management function, and diffused risk across a broader set of investors. Development of the corporation also established arrangements whereby ownership interests would be represented, including the board of directors and the general shareholders' meeting. Within the corporation, the invisible hand of anonymous traders was replaced by the quite-visible hand of corporate managers (Chandler, 1977), but the firm itself was to be disciplined externally through these shareholder institutions.

Emerging in conjunction with joint stock corporations were large-scale, regulated stock exchanges. The stock market provided a highly ordered central locus for the trading of shares that corporations issued. Access to the actual trading process was limited to a specific group of exchange members. These traders in turn made their services available to a general investing public, who were granted protection through liability limits (which restricted investor risk to the amount of their investment). Linking these two institutions, the corporation and the stock market, was what is perhaps the quintessential market in capitalist economies: the market for corporate control.

Japan's opening to the West during the Meiji Restoration led to the introduction of both the corporate form and stock markets (Clark, 1979). But Japan has also crafted a distinctive institutional arrangement to mediate between the corporation and the stock market: the intercorporate alliance. Alliance structures retain the advantages of the corporate form of organization, as each of its firms operate as a legally independent entity. Outside capital can therefore be raised, a division of labor maintained, and risk diffused. But the sources of external discipline are changed dramatically, for affiliated financial institutions become an important source of capital, while stockholdings are organized through long-term positions among companies' business partners.

The Managerial Revolution

In discussions of the relationship between the corporate form and the stock exchange, probably no book has had the impact of Berle and Means's *The Modern Corporation and Private Property* (1932). Berle and Means argued that the rise of the large, diffusely held, professionally managed corporation fundamentally altered the nature of the relationship between ownership and control over the firm. They worried that in separating these two functions, organizational behemoths were created that were largely unaccountable to traditional property holders and would pursue their own interests at society's expense. Much of the work in organizational economics and business history over the past two decades has, implicitly or explicitly, been an attempt to address the Berle and Means thesis by providing an efficiency rationale for the managerial bureaucracy (e.g., Chandler, 1962, 1977; Williamson, 1975, 1985; Fama and Jensen, 1983). The reality of the management-ownership separation in the United States, however, is not itself in dispute among these writers.

And in Japan? On the one hand, there are far fewer publicly traded companies in Japan than in the United States and far more privately held firms. These private companies are very often smaller and owner-managed (Patrick and Rohlen, 1987), suggesting the kind of traditional capitalist enterprise that Berle and Means admired. As of 1987, there were more than 24,000 public corporations in the United States, in comparison with less than 2,000 in Japan. Since the number of firms listed on the New York and Tokyo stock exchanges was nearly identical (at 1,647 and 1,634, respectively), the big difference is in the prevalence of smaller, public U.S. firms traded over-the-counter and on smaller exchanges, and their near absence in Japan. Public listing in Japan is limited almost entirely to the oldest, most prestigious corporations. According to one study, nearly half of all public corporations in the United States went public within the first ten years of establishment, in comparison with under 1 percent in Japan.[12]

Among its largest corporations, on the other hand, Japan, like the United States, has progressed far down the road toward managerial capitalism. As of at least the mid-1970s, the ownership of shares in large corporations by their officers in both countries was negligible. Herman

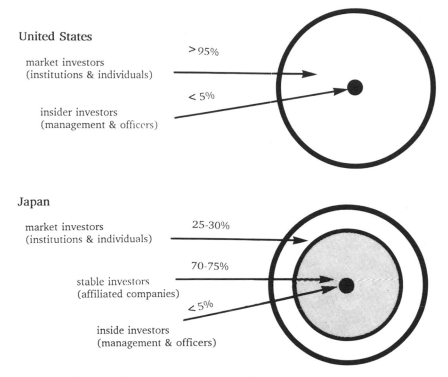

United States

market investors
(institutions & individuals)   >95%

insider investors   < 5%
(management & officers)

Japan

market investors   25-30%
(institutions & individuals)

                                  70-75%
stable investors
(affiliated companies)   < 5%

inside investors
(management & officers)

Fig. 2.1.   Investor Composition in Large U.S. and Japanese Companies.

(1981) finds that in nearly two-thirds of the two hundred largest non-financial firms in the United States, directors owned less than 1 percent of the voting stock. Similarly, Okumura (1983) presents statistics showing that the holdings of corporate officials (directors and auditors) in Japanese firms of over ¥10 billion in assets (around $400 million at 1983 rates) averaged under 1 percent in 1976. In the United States, nearly all the remainder is controlled by independent individual and institutional investors, most often in small, fractional holdings. In Japan, in contrast, a substantial portion of the remainder is controlled by alliance partners, existing in a gray area somewhere between the polarities of Berle and Means's management-shareholder dichotomy. The differences between these two systems of corporate control are depicted schematically in Figure 2.1.

   What does the existence of these distinctive capital relations mean for the interaction between ownership and management in Japan? One perspective that has been taken in financial monitoring models is that it improves the capability of shareholders to learn about and to discipline management in otherwise diffusely held corporations (Jensen, 1989). As relatively coherent shareholder bodies, this argument goes, corporate alliances are able to mobilize collectively in cases of severe managerial malfeasance in order to protect shareholder interests. This is more difficult when shareholders are poorly organized, as in the United States. It should be pointed out, however, that shareholders in diffusely held U.S. corporations enjoy control mechanisms never anticipated by Berle and Means—and largely unused in Japan—including hostile takeovers and proxy contests.[13]

Two other implications are less obvious, but at least as significant. The improved managerial discipline function of corporate alliances noted in the previous paragraph continues to view the interests of affiliate-shareholders as identical to those of other shareholders—albeit, perhaps, with greater means of enforcement and better information. But affiliate-shareholders actually have plural interests. As companies' bank lenders and business partners, these investors are interested in a more complex set of goals than capital market returns. As two observers have pointed out:

> Unlike Western institutional shareholders, which invest largely for dividends and capital appreciation, Japanese institutional shareholders tend to be the company's business partners and associates; shareholding is the mere expression of their relationship, not the relationship itself. [Clark, 1979, p. 86.]

> In most listed companies in Japan, a sizable portion of the stock remains permanently in "safe" hands, thus assuring continued control by management. Shareholdings are fragmented between "insiders" and "outsiders." Insiders are small circles of executives and financiers often connected with the issuer's enterprise group. . . . The insiders are in charge, not by virtue of their positions, but as a product of the multiplicity of their roles in the firm; they are creditors, shareholders, lifetime employees, management and business partners. [Heftel, 1983, p. 165.]

Moreover, they often have their own shares held reciprocally and in complex networks of shareholding among other affiliated enterprises. Companies whose shareholding bodies are dominated by affiliate-shareholders will, quite rationally, consider the interests of alliance partners first before those of independent shareholders when making investment decisions.

In addition to redefining the constraints placed on the Japanese firm, the predominance of affiliate-shareholders also shapes the character of Japanese stock markets. This is not so much through modifications in the basic regulations and rules of operation, for these are similar in most formal respects to those in the United States and elsewhere (although actual functioning differs in several important respects, discussed later). Rather, it is through changes in the dominant players in the market. In both the United States and Japan, an "investor revolution" marked by the rise of large-scale investors has taken place that in many ways is as important to the understanding of twentieth-century capitalist enterprise as the managerial revolution identified by Berle and Means. But whereas the managerial revolution has followed relatively similar trajectories across all advanced economies in the broad sense that corporate decision making moved into the hands of nonowning managers, the investor revolution has not.

The Investor Revolution

The main concern of Berle and Means was the increasing diffusion of ownership in public corporations and the consequent loss of shareholder control, with the result that large corporations were run by professional managers rather than by firms' owners. But this trend has also had an economic rationale. To the extent that large, bureaucratic organizations were able to accomplish the objectives of reducing coordination and transactions costs for complex and capital-intensive economic tasks and smaller firms were not (Chandler, 1962, 1977; Williamson, 1975, 1985), it made sense to establish a division of labor in talent and expertise. Professional managers were to specialize in running corporations while investors specialized in the capital provision and risk-bearing function.[14] This division of labor and the corresponding managerial revolution has appeared in all advanced capitalist economies, and generally in similar industries (Chandler, 1984).

The rise of the large-scale investor represents a second but less well appreciated trend apparent in the United States and in other countries. Traditional owner-founders had interests in their companies over and above the extent of their capital investments. They were members in their business communities, linked their personal interests with those of their companies, and typically passed their companies on to family heirs. The institutional investors of the late twentieth century are instead large organizations run by specialist money managers who are linked to the investment rather than the business community and whose interests in companies are limited to the extent of their (often short-term) capital involvement. They are, in short, professional investors.[15]

The decline in individual investment over time across capitalist economies is shown in Figure 2.2. Focusing solely on this aggregate trend,

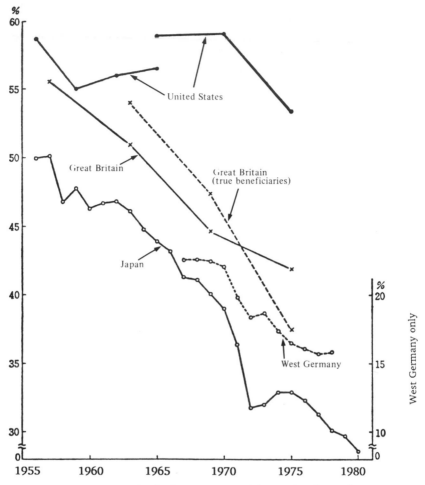

Fig. 2.2.   Decline in Individual Investors in Advanced Industrial Economies.
Source: Futatsugi (1982).

however, obscures important differences in the nature of the trend. First,
countries vary in the extent to which individual investors have been
replaced by other investors. While individual investors still owned over
one-half of the shares in publicly traded U.S. companies in the 1970s,
this figure was under 25 percent in Japan and under 20 percent in West
Germany.[16] The extent of decline in individual investment has proceeded
even further in these two later-developing economies.

    Second, and more important, the nature of the investors that have arisen to replace these individuals varies considerably. In the United States, investors are in significant proportion managers of pension, trust, and other forms of investment funds—that is, true institutional investors. In a 1975 New York Stock Exchange survey, trust and nominee accounts constituted about 40 percent of total market value, and this figure has risen to about two-thirds since then (Aoki, 1984a; *Business Week*, February 4, 1985). These investors are constrained by a set of fiduciary obligations such as the "prudent man rule" and laws that stress safety and the duty to pursue the interests of the pension or trust, creating strong pressures toward acting as arm's-length market investors. As a result, the primary source of institutional investor control over corporations comes not in direct voting control but in indirect effects on share price through stock trading (Herman, 1981). By the mid-1980s, institutional investors accounted for roughly 90 percent of share turnover in American stock markets.[17]

Individual investors in Japan, in contrast, have largely been replaced by other corporations (Okumura, 1975). Figure 2.3 shows how financial firms (banks and insurance companies) and business enterprises (industrial and commercial firms) make up the vast majority of share ownership in Japan. Financial firms controlled nearly two-fifths of all shares by 1985, and business enterprises another one-quarter. Investment trusts, however, controlled only 6 percent of all shares.[18] This difference is important because, as indicated above, Japanese financial and industrial investors use their shareholdings primarily in order to consolidate business relationships for strategic purposes and only secondarily for the kinds of direct (capital market) returns that are essential to investment trusts. In addition, Japanese law grants corporate investors substantial latitude in influencing management on the basis of the investor's own business interests in the company.

Despite their small numbers, however, individuals are not irrelevant to Japanese stock markets. Individual shareholders serve as the speculators that help to "make" markets in the absence of a large number of floating shares, in order for stock prices to be determined—a function similar to that of speculators in commodities markets who fill in the transactional interstices to create flexible markets among the traders that are commodity users. In this capacity, these investors have done quite well overall, at least until recently. Abegglen and Stalk (1985) calculate that among leading firms in twenty-one different industries, the stock market performance of sixteen Japanese firms was superior to that of their U.S. counterparts during the ten-year period 1973–83. Their re-

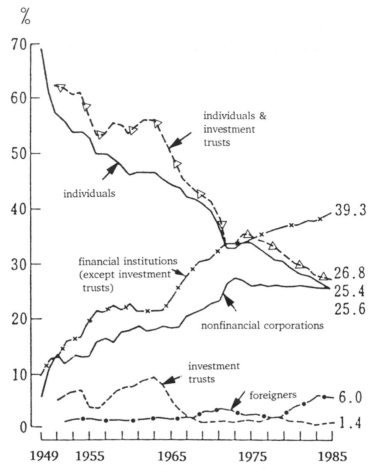

Fig. 2.3. Composition of Shareholding in Japan. Source: Nihon
Keizai Shinbun (1987, p. 53).

turns in much of the latter half of the 1980s, with the rapid appreciation
of share prices on the Tokyo stock market, were at least as impressive.

Stockholders, Stakeholders, and Alliance Structures

Immediately after publication of *The Modern Corporation*, Berle and
Means became embroiled in a debate over whether they had ignored the
importance of constituencies other than shareholders. Perhaps it is not
stockholders alone, this argument went, but firms' collective "stakeholders" that are important. Dodd (1932) took the lead in this attack,

claiming that corporate directors had an obligation to serve as trustees for all constituencies of the companies on whose boards they sat. Others disagree. Oliver Williamson's influential contemporary analysis of the corporation (1985, chapter 12) argues that the unsecured position of equity shareholders' investments puts them logically first in the queue for corporate control, with management granted a secondary position. Constituencies other than these two are better off, Williamson asserts, protecting their business interests by direct contractual guarantees rather than through board representation.

Japan's distinctive capital relations reveal yet another approach. The interests of external constituencies get represented in Japan, as advocated by Dodd and others. But boards of directors are not the primary mechanisms for ensuring this. Rather, these constituents take equity positions in other firms in which they have business interests, creating economic stakes in those companies that serve as legitimate bases for influence, as advocated in the models of Berle and Means and Williamson. In this way, key external constituencies (banks, suppliers, customers, etc.) get represented by becoming legally empowered stakeholders of the firm. These constituents may also sit on the company's board, but Japan has crafted an alternative to the outsider director as well: the multicompany presidents' council, which brings together the top executives of affiliated crossheld companies in periodic meetings to address matters of group-wide concern. (The workings of these councils are discussed in Chapter 4.)

The interests of internal constituencies (primarily, management) are represented in two ways. Managers dominate the boards of their own companies, ensuring a substantial voice in internal decision making. Since corporate shareholding is often reciprocal, at least among large firms, managers are also able to exercise influence over the very external shareholding companies that constrain them. Mutual shareholdings represent an "exchange of hostages" (Williamson, 1985) in which attempts at control in one direction are balanced against reciprocal holdings in the opposite direction.

Perhaps what is most interesting from a comparative institutional perspective about Japanese capitalism, therefore, is the nature of investors themselves. In the United States, these investors have become largely differentiated from the activities of the firms themselves—that is, from their employees, lenders, and trading partners. We find therefore a large constituency of institutional investors that have common interests but little ongoing interest in the firms in which they hold shares. In Japan, in contrast, corporate involvement equity shareholding is so pervasive that, without risking great exaggeration, we can say that Japanese stock markets have been transformed largely into instruments of corporate rather than purely financial interests.

CONCLUSION

Economic systems vary in the social structure of both their market systems and their corporate enterprise in ways that are complexly inter-related. Much of the market activity in advanced industrial societies has been removed from the forces of impersonal competition by organiza-tion within firms, leading to internal labor markets, internal transfer pricing policies, and other forms of exchange that have a substantial administered component. Intercorporate alliance forms in Japan have furthermore merged these organization-level interests with a broader nexus of interests companies have in each other.

In working at a level between that of isolated firms and that of extended markets, these alliances have redefined both. Japanese markets have become organized through close relationships among affiliated firms, creating a finely spun web of business networks in which prefer-ence is given to long-term trading partners over market newcomers. At the same time, these relationships have transformed the business en-vironment surrounding Japanese managers by ensuring that the com-pany's shareholders are its major customers, suppliers, and financial institutions rather than an anonymous body of stock market traders. The constraints Japanese companies face, therefore, are primarily those arising from their ongoing business interests rather than those of inde-pendent capital markets. It is this complex linkage of market relation-ships and the basic capitalist definition of the economy's core players that has given Japanese alliance capitalism its distinctive character and form.

CHAPTER III

The Organization
of Japanese Business Networks

A vast range of business activities in Japan have been "externalized"—moved outside the firm—while being reorganized at the interfirm level. Supply, distribution, and capital allocation functions that are performed internally by vertically integrated firms in the United States are all carried out as intercorporate transactions to a far greater extent in Japan. Consider the following:

1. *Supply Relationships.* Patterns of external sourcing are common in many industries, including automobiles, consumer electronics, and precision machinery. In automobile production, for example, about 80 percent of the costs of a Japanese automobile come from outside suppliers, in contrast to only 50–60 percent in the United States, West Germany, and France (Odaka, Ono, and Adachi, 1988).

2. *Distribution.* The Japanese distribution system works largely through external networks. Within domestic markets, wholesalers (*ton'ya*) are organized into elaborate networks in which products may pass through three or four middle stages before reaching final users.[1] In international markets, over half of all trade in primary materials and overseas goods takes place through only a handful of firms—Japan's nine general trading companies (*Sōgō shōsha nenkan,* 1985).

3. *Capital Funding.* In making capital investments, large Japanese firms have relied considerably more than their U.S. counterparts on funding from external sources rather than from internal cash flows.

During much of the postwar period, this was through heavy borrowing from financial institutions.[2] In recent years, it has come increasingly from bond and equity issues financed through these same financial institutions. In addition, trading companies have long served as an important source of capital for smaller businesses through the extension of trade credit.

While moved outside the firm, these external relationships have themselves been organized at the intercorporate level through complex overlapping webs of business affiliations. Japanese industrial organization contains enterprise groups of varying degrees of coherence and intensity, several basic forms of which are introduced in this chapter.

I begin by outlining general patterns of relationships common to business networks in market economies and looking at how these are reflected in specific alliance patterns in Japan. I then consider some fundamental characteristics of Japanese industrial organization that distinguish it from its American counterpart and demonstrate these empirically through comparative analyses of the basic features of corporate ownership networks in the two countries. These analyses show that ownership structures of Japanese corporations are far more likely than in the United States to be organized as stable relationships that endure over decades, to be reciprocated among mutually positioned companies, and to be embedded in other ongoing business relationships among the firms. This sets the framework for a more detailed study of the organization of relationships among Japan's largest corporations, as seen in the intermarket keiretsu. This alliance form is described briefly in this chapter and studied in more detail in following chapters.

THE WEB OF BUSINESS AFFILIATIONS

The term "network" has taken on dual meaning in the area of organizational theory. On the one hand, it refers to a rigorous, formalized methodology, as reflected in journals like *Social Networks* and sophisticated techniques of structural analysis (e.g., White et al., 1976; Burt, 1983). On the other hand, it has been used to refer to informal social systems which are not easily captured by formal theories of bureaucracy or markets (e.g., Eccles and Crane, 1988; Lincoln, 1989; Powell, 1990). Both the more formal and the metaphorical usages of the network perspective have received increasing attention in the analysis of the industrial organization of East Asian economies. Comparative approaches have looked at how network structures differ across countries and have combined elements of rigorous network data collection with informal theories of "network organization" (Hamilton and Biggart, 1988). Normative approaches (Imai, forthcoming) have provided economic rationales for particular arrangements and have relied primarily on an informal approach to network analysis. The approach taken here combines elements of both the formal and the informal meaning of network.

In the network approach, emphasis is placed on the direct study of how economic and other transactions allocate resources in a social system (Wellman and Berkowitz, 1987). The particular composition of ties among financial, commercial, and industrial firms is seen as determining significant features of an economy's overall organization and its resulting performance. Institutions such as markets, industries, and business groups become defined as characteristic patterns of concrete exchanges among diverse actors within a broader matrix of intercorporate relationships in which they are embedded. Among various archetypal patterns, we consider the following three: industry, the business community, and the intercorporate alliance. Each represents a distinctive social focus (Feld, 1981), with industry set in the context of relationships based in competition within similar market niches, the business community in the loosely coupled structure of interpersonal networks; and alliances in historical ties of obligation among companies.

The importance of industry has been a primary focus of economists and is of increasing interest to sociologists and organizational theorists as well. In network theory terms, industry represents a nexus of critical resource dependencies among an identifiable set of "structurally equivalent" firms—companies that share common patterns of exchange in economic markets (Burt and Carlson, 1989). Pursuit of competitive advantage is an important driving rationale. Corporate ownership, for example, becomes a means of gaining control over critical uncertainties in organizational environments—a tool by which organizations seek to "restructure their environmental interdependence in order to stabilize critical exchanges" (Pfeffer and Salancik, 1978, p. 115). Similarly, mergers and joint ventures arise in order to manage concrete but problematic relationships with other firms (Williamson, 1985). Empirically, the structure of industries has been correlated with various features of firm conduct and performance in the industrial organization literature, including advertising and R & D expenditures, and profits, growth, and diversification rates (e.g., Scherer, 1980).

The business community as an organizing framework can be viewed in several ways. In a social-hierarchy formulation, economies are seen to stratify around firms' statuses. Averitt (1968) argues that this results in a "dual economy" made up of large, technologically sophisticated, multi-market, elite firms at the center and small, less-developed firms at the periphery—a formulation that has long been popular for explaining Japanese industrial organization. Whether developed economies, including that of Japan, can in fact be divided this neatly has been increasingly questioned.[3] Nevertheless, it is clear that the markets for capital and labor, at the least, are affected by a firm's position in a larger social structure. The work on diffuse networks of intercorporate relationships suggests ways in which relationships among firms may be organized to serve interests at the level of a broader business class (Palmer, 1983; Ornstein, 1984). Useem (1984), for example, argues that directorships shared across firms serve not so much the immediate interests of each organization—to monitor and mobilize bilateral pairs of firms—as a resource dependency position would indicate, but rather the interests of an inner circle of business elites.[4]

These archetypes suggest two different, though not incompatible, sets of business relationships. The industry framework focuses primarily on firms' immediate task environments and the ways in which critical resource- and technology-driven dependencies have led to adaptations at the interfirm level to manage them. The business community framework, in contrast , is concerned with the position of corporations in an extended social structure, its stratification, and the ways in which this affects interfirm activity.

A third organizing framework is what I have termed the "intercorporate alliance": relationships based on localized networks of long-term, mutual obligation.[5] In contrast to the broader class-wide interests of an extended business community, alliances are defined by interests among specific subsets of closely connected firms. The most powerful "inner circle" for each firm is made up of the other group companies with which it is affiliated. At the same time, alliances differ from organization by industry in that historical association is as important as immediate task requirements in determining the particular patterns they take. Firms in Japan are linked together over time in relationships that, as we see in the following chapter, involve strong patterns of preferential trading among firms in the same group. These patterns, moreover, occur even where functional transactions (e.g., bank loans or steel trade) could easily take place across groupings.

Industries, Status Hierarchies, and Alliances:
Cross-Cutting Spheres of Japanese Business

The names of Mitsubishi, Mitsui, and Sumitomo are well known as the
remnants of the prewar zaibatsu groupings operating under family-
controlled holding companies. But these represent only a fraction of the
vast complex of elaborate alliances that make up the Japanese economy and bring firms into complex and often overlapping networks of
vertical, horizontal, and diversified relationships. There exists in Japan
no single, universally accepted system for classifying these relationships. Nevertheless, we can differentiate four broad categories of alliance that are typical in Japan, which are referred to here as (1) the
intermarket keiretsu, (2) the vertical keiretsu, (3) small-business groups,
and (4) strategic alliances, including joint ventures and project consortia.

Figure 3.1 depicts these relationships schematically, showing their
representation in different market sectors and their location in the business community. The horizontal axis reflects the diversity of market
sectors in which the group is involved, with a wide span indicating broad
industrial representation. The vertical axis indicates firms' positions
within the structure of firm stratification. The "traditional" sector at the
bottom reflects the central role of local social networks of family, friendship, and community ties, while the "modern" sector at the top reflects
embeddedness in a national network of business elites (the *zaikai*)—the
Japanese social economy is acutely sensitive to company size, and security, status, wealth, and power accrue to the largest.

The Intermarket Keiretsu   Groupings of large firms based around a
major commercial ("city") bank are referred to variously as keiretsu,
kigyō shūdan or kigyō gurūpu (enterprise group). As noted earlier, I
have adopted the keiretsu terminology and have added the qualifiers
"intermarket" and "vertical" to characterize two quite different forms
of group structure. This form of alliance, discussed in considerably
greater detail below, represents loosely structured associations of large
relatively equally sized firms in diverse industries, including banking,
commerce, and manufacturing. The social communities of business that
they represent are the elite in Japan—economically, politically, and
socially.

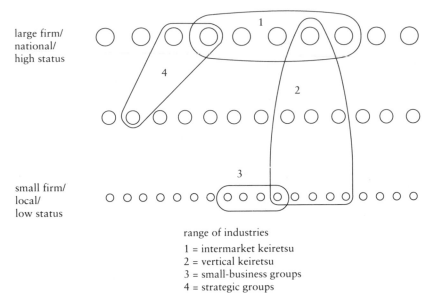

large firm/
national/
high status

small firm/
local/
low status

range of industries
1 = intermarket keiretsu
2 = vertical keiretsu
3 = small-business groups
4 = strategic groups

Fig. 3.1. Cross-Cutting Social Spheres: Industrial Diversity, Status Position, and Alliance Form.

The Vertical Keiretsu   In contrast to the highly diversified character of the intermarket keiretsu, the vertical keiretsu are tight, hierarchical associations centered on a single, large parent firm and containing multiple smaller satellite companies within related industries. While focused in their business activities, they span the status breadth of the business community, with the parent firm part of Japan's large-firm economic core and its satellites, particularly at lower levels, small operations that are often family-run. Most firms in intermarket keiretsu maintain their own vertical keiretsu, leading to an intersection of these two forms, as seen here.

The vertical keiretsu can be divided into three main categories. The first are the *sangyō keiretsu,* or production keiretsu, which are elaborate hierarchies of primary, secondary, and tertiary-level subcontractors that supply, through a series of stages, parent firms. The second are the *ryūtsū keiretsu,* or distribution keiretsu. These are linear systems of distributors that operate under the name of a large-scale manufacturer, or sometimes a wholesaler. They have much in common with the vertical marketing systems that some large U.S. manufacturers have introduced to organize their interfirm distribution channels (Stern and El-Ansary, 1977). A third—the *shihon keiretsu,* or capital keiretsu—are groupings based not on the flow of product materials and goods but on the flow of capital from a parent firm, and are sometimes referred to in Japanese academic writings by the German term *Konzern.* The leading contemporary examples are the railroad groups of Tokyu and Seibu, which have diversified from train lines into real estate, hotels, department stores and distribution, and travel and recreation businesses.

Small-Business Groups Firms of fewer than a thousand employees account for over half of all sales and assets in the Japanese economy but are often overlooked in favor of the more conspicuous large firms. One of the ways that small firms have tried competing with the more efficient large-firm sector is through collaboration. The result is a rich panoply of producers and purchaser cooperatives, traditional and high-technology industrial estates (the last are sometimes known as "technopolises"), and neighborhood associations. I have labeled these collectively as "small-business groups."

Small-business groups involve a considerably greater diversity in the type of interfirm organization represented than do the intermarket or vertical keiretsu. They are sometimes focused on a single industry but also frequently bring together firms across multiple industries, positioned horizontally and organized within a common geographical nexus. Small-business groups trade largely in social currency and are closely tied to the local communities of which they are a part.

Strategic Alliances Strategic alliances include a wide range of interfirm organizations based on relatively focused instrumental needs. They are sometimes called "functional" groups (*kinō-teki shūdan*) though "ad hoc" is probably closer; they include joint ventures, project consortia, and various other forms of cooperation (in Japanese, the popular word *teikei*) that move firms outside their traditional keiretsu groupings into new alliances that bridge industries and utilize new technologies. Strategic groupings cut across all sectors of industry and society, often in diagonal relationships that span diverse market sectors and social positions. Strategic alliances have increased dramatically in frequency in Japan in the 1980s, as they have in the United States. Large firms in Japan, for example, are now establishing relationships with small, high technology firms in an attempt to expand beyond their traditional industries (see, for example, Imai, 1984).

Alliances and the Firm's Institutional Environment

From the Japanese firm's point of view, trade takes place within a set of ordered environments that can be dimensionalized along a continuum from "relational" to "transactional" exchange, as seen in Figure 3.2. Legal theorist Ian Macneil (1978) has characterized transactional exchange as the sine qua non of impersonal market exchange: "A transaction is an event sensibly viewable separately from events preceding and following it, indeed from other events accompanying it temporally—*one engaging only small segments of the total personal beings of the participants*" (p. 893). It is a one-time, arm's-length exchange among anonymous or otherwise unrelated traders, requiring neither structural nor symbolic connection between the parties. In relational exchange, in contrast, actors rely on various forms of implicit assumptions and agreements to organize their relationships: "The fiction of discreteness is fully displaced as the relation takes on the properties of 'a minisociety' with a vast array of norms beyond those centered on the exchange and its immediate processes" (p. 901).

Trade within the firm, at the center of Figure 3.2, is marked by a high degree of relational exchange: actors are embedded in a common arena governed by structurally interlinked resource flows and by a common set of rules and rituals that constitute the firm as a social system. The relationship among organizational members as a whole takes precedence over that of any single transaction. The first ring demarcates the firm's boundaries, and immediately outside of it lies the firm's first-order environment. At the interfirm level, probably the most critical relationship is that between the company and its suppliers. The close ties that exist among Japanese firms and the subcontractors in their vertical keiretsu are an often-noted feature of the organization of industry in Japan (e.g., Clark, 1979). As suggested earlier, these subcontractors perform many of the functions typically carried out in-house by U.S. firms through their own divisions. Within the vertical keiretsu, exchange between the parent and satellite firms is embedded in a dense network of ongoing relationships, as various forms of information, technical and financial assistance, and managerial expertise are provided on a reciprocity basis.

The parent firm, and by extension its satellites, are in turn embedded in a broader set of relationships defined by the intermarket keiretsu. This second-order environment comprises more loosely coupled relationships among dozens of firms in diverse industries. Internal exchange is gener-

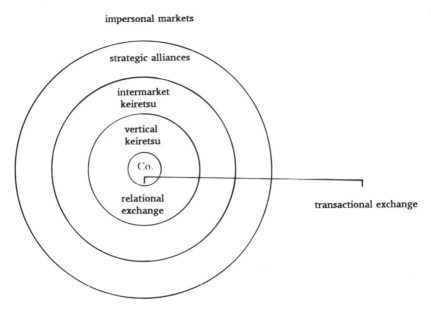

Fig. 3.2. Alliance Form and the Japanese Firm's Institutional Environment.

ally less pervasive than at the firm or vertical keiretsu level, but the identity of the group nevertheless imparts structural and symbolic significance to these exchanges. Strategic groupings represent a third-order environment. These involve exchanges more intimate and durable than those in impersonal markets, but generally without the history, symbolic coherence, or density of exchange networks found in the vertical or intermarket keiretsu. Finally, at the outer level one finds impersonal exchanges among actors that are relatively unconnected structurally or symbolically—for example, a firm's occasional purchases of office supplies from a large number of different retailers. These are "true" market transactions, without intensive ties or enduring obligations.

OVERALL PATTERNS IN JAPANESE
AND U.S. OWNERSHIP NETWORKS

The importance of Japan's overlapping structure of intercorporate relationships is nowhere more evident than in the case of intercorporate ownership networks. As noted in the previous chapter, corporate ownership and the market for corporate control represent fundamental relationships in capitalist systems that define the underlying structure of influence over the basic decision-making units, that is, its corporations.

Herman (1981, p. 101) points out that corporate ownership "has what might be termed an 'omnipresence effect' on managerial purpose and behavior, affecting them at many levels and through a variety of channels."

Corporate shareholding in the United States generally takes the form of a capital market transaction, the primary purpose of which is direct returns on investment. For this reason, financial theories focus on the daily, ongoing patterns of trading that define a circular flow of capital among investors. The buying of corporate shares by investors is seen as based on a profit-maximizing calculus, sensitive to price signals reflected in changing share prices among anonymous traders. To the extent that investors have generally similar access to information and this information gets quickly transmitted in share prices, the market is informationally efficient. At this level, the stock market most closely conforms to its original purpose of raising and allocating capital by corporate stock issuers.

This is not the only significance of the stock market's operation, however. Where investors are other corporations, as is the predominant pattern in Japan, ownership becomes a means for structuring relationships among those corporations in ways that set markets for capital and control in the context of other business interests. This does not imply that the stock market no longer allocates capital or responds to conditions of supply and demand in Japan. Rather, corporate ownership takes on the added feature of being one of the main arenas in which corporations' strategic interests are protected and promoted. This difference is reflected in the concrete pattern of relationships among shareholders, of which we consider the following four: the extent of concentration; stability; reciprocity; and multiplexity, or the overlap with other business relationships.

Concentration of Shareholding

Among the measures of corporate ownership that have received attention, probably none has been more widely discussed than shareholding dispersal. This is in large part due to its prominence in Berle and Means's original argument, which premised a belief in the rise of managerial control on the observation that individual owners in most major corporations no longer hold dominant blocks of stock. Berle and Means reasoned that investors holding only a small fraction of a company's shares would be reluctant to spend the time and energy necessary to

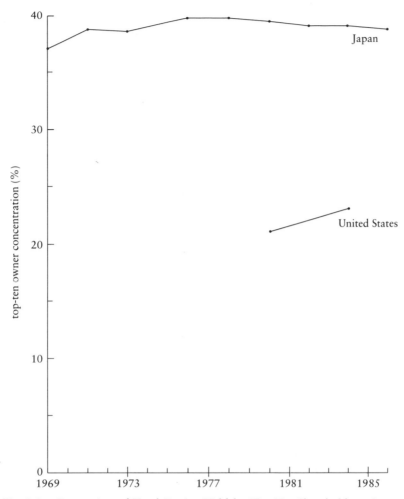

Fig. 3.3. Proportion of Total Equity Held by Top-Ten Shareholders. Source: See Appendix A.

ensure that the company's managers were looking out for shareholder interests.[6]

Since Japanese intercorporate shareholding primarily reflects concrete strategic interests rather than those of portfolio diversification, major shareholders should take more substantial positions in other firms. This is apparent in Figure 3.3, based on data described in Appendix A. Between 1969 and 1986, the top-ten shareholders in Japanese companies held from 37.1 percent to 39.8 percent of total issued equity.

In the United States for the two years of available data, these figures were 21.1 percent and 23.1 percent. Among the leading five shareholders in each country (not reported here), the figures were 27.8 percent and 29.4 percent for Japan and 15.2 percent and 16.6 percent for the United States. Thus, corporate ownership is far more concentrated in Japan than in the United States (although note that the U.S. sample showed a nearly 10 percent increase during the four-year interval covered by the data).

Presented as an overall total, as above, these figures maintain the company-centered focus of managerial theory and provide an overall index of the relative role played by leading shareholders in the capital structure of corporations. Another way of interpreting these figures is as a measure of the "strength" of dyadic relationships between investors and companies. Interpreted in this way, we find that Japanese top-ten equity investors hold an average of between 3.7 percent and 4.0 percent of total issued equity and the top-five alone hold between 5.6 percent and 5.9 percent. In the United States the respective figures are 2.1 percent and 3.0 percent for 1980 and 2.3 percent and 3.3 percent for 1984. Major intercorporate ownership dyads, therefore, are not only more prevalent in Japan, they represent stronger relationships than in the United States.

Stability of Interlocks

There is good reason to believe that the relationship between equity shareholder and firm in Japan will be a highly durable one where shareholders take on the role of a reliable constituency of well-known trading partners. As an executive in Sumitomo Life Insurance, the largest holder of shares in the Sumitomo group, put it: "If group shares go up, we don't sell them off quickly, though naturally we're happy. If the value of a company's shares goes up, that improves the financial condition of all group companies." A survey in the *Nihon keizai shinbun* found that more than 60 percent of publicly traded Japanese companies think it is desirable to have 60–70 percent of outstanding shares held by stable shareholders. The main reason given was that it freed executives from plotting takeover strategies to concentrate on business goals (cited in the *Wall Street Journal,* November 17, 1989). In another survey, fully 660 out of 661 Japanese firms expressed a belief in the importance of the stable shareholder system (Heftel, 1983, n. 46).

Independent estimates of holdings by stable shareholders (*antei kabunushi*) typically fall somewhere around 70 percent of total shares

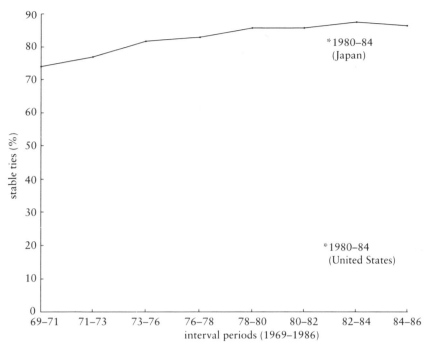

Fig. 3.4.   Proportion of Stable Top-Ten Equity Ties. Source: See Appendix A.

held on the Tokyo Stock Exchange. Indeed, the Ministry of Finance has at various times sought to regulate the extent of stable shareholding by mandating a minimum level of "floating" shares. Since such a proportionately small ratio of firms' shares is actually traded, the belief is that stock prices often do not accurately reflect the market value of the firm.[7] In comparison, U.S. institutional shareholders are seen as extremely active traders in corporate securities—and, by implication, unstable shareholders. It is this ability to exit the relationship, often in mass, that gives institutional investors in the United States their power over corporations. As one business writer states: "In Wall Street, people argue that that is the best way for institutions to influence management. Selling the stock in large blocks pushes the price of the stock down, increasing the company's costs of raising capital, and punishes the management for poor performance" (quoted in Mintz and Schwartz, 1985, p. 99).

These differences should be reflected in overall greater stability of equity interlocks in Japan than in the United States, a prediction explored empirically in Figure 3.4. "Stable" equity relationships are defined in this analysis as top-ten shareholders in one measurement period that remain in the top ten in the subsequent measurement period. Among the American firms in the database, less than one-quarter (23 percent) of the top-ten shareholders in 1980 remained in the top ten in 1984. In contrast, over four-fifths (82 percent) of the top-ten shareholders remained in the top ten for the Japanese sample. It is evident from this that there are dramatic differences in ownership stability in the two countries.

The biannual data available for Japanese firms also shows the trend in stable shareholding during the 1969–1986 period. These results reveal a gradual but detectable increase in stable shareholdings throughout this period, from 74 percent in the first interval to 87 percent in the last interval. There is no evidence, therefore, that stable shareholdings represent a declining proportion of total shareholding in Japan or that equity relationships among corporations are becoming more transitory. The corporate capital structure of the Japanese firm has been and continues to be dominated by investors that maintain a long-term stake in the company.

Extent of Reciprocity

Intercorporate shareholding in Japan is also more likely to be reciprocated than in the United States as a result of the system of *kabushiki mochi-ai,* or stock crossholdings. The term *mochi-ai,* construed narrowly, means "to hold mutually." But it also carries an additional connotation from its other uses of helping one another, of shared interdependence, and of stability. Crossholdings, as Japanese businessmen point out, "keep each other warm"—*hada o atatame-au.*

In the process of holding each other's shares, mochi-ai becomes self-canceling—a *kami no yaritori,* or a paper exchange—thereby removing shares from open public trading. The issue of explaining a self-canceling shareholding system was raised by an executive in the Mitsui group more than twenty years ago: "What's the use of owning two or three hundred shares in related companies? If we had the money, we would put it to better use in equipment or something else" (quoted in *Oriental Economist,* March 1961). No answer was provided by this executive but the question is a good one. Borrowing heavily from financial institutions in order to make equity investments in other firms will rarely make sense from the point of view of narrow economic rationality, for companies are paying interest on that borrowed capital. The reasons for share crossholdings seem to lie instead in their importance in shaping the qualitative relationships between firms. Share crossholdings among group com-

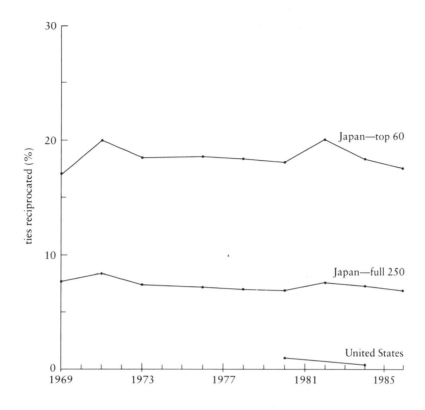

Fig. 3.5. Proportion of Reciprocated Top-Ten Equity Ties. Source: See Appendix A.

panies create a structure of mutually signified relationships, as well as serve as a means of protecting managers from hostile outsiders (Okumura, 1983; Nakatani, 1984).

Reciprocal shareholdings are likely to be far less common in the United States because of the absence of coherent alliances around which to organize and the uncertain legality under antitrust laws of reciprocity where partners also do business together. These predictions are tested in Figure 3.5, where we find some support. Among the intercorporate equity interlocks in Japan, 7 percent are reciprocated in 1980, while this figure is only 1 percent in the United States in 1980 and declines to less than half a percent by 1984.

Although higher than in the United States, these reciprocity figures are lower than were expected for Japan. One possibility is that it is primarily very large companies in Japan that reciprocate ties. Nearly one-third of the sample of two hundred industrial firms in Japan are satellites (*kogaisha* or *kanren gaisha*) of a major parent manufacturer. These firms are unlikely to reciprocate ties since theirs are primarily subordinate relationships. To test this prediction, reciprocated ties solely among the forty largest industrials and twenty largest financial institutions were analyzed. When we limit intercorporate interlocks to these sixty companies, reciprocity rates for 1980 more than double, increasing from 7 percent to 18 percent.[8] Company size, therefore, appears to be a fundamental determinant of the precise character of companies' intercorporate equity linkages.

Multiplexity of Ties

One of the most important measures of the significance of strategic interests in ownership patterns is the extent to which ties in equity networks are "multiplex," or overlap with ties in other networks. Both transactions costs and resource dependence theories view the taking of equity or board positions in other companies as means of managing dependency and gaining control over critical banking and trading relationships (Pfeffer and Salancik, 1978; Williamson, 1985). The Japanese data permit a strong test of the multiplexity hypothesis, since equity crossholdings and board interlock patterns can be compared with the networks mapped by banking and trade. The U.S. data permit a weaker test of the multiplexity hypothesis, comparing information on ties they contain pertaining to equity ownership and directorship interlocks.

The prediction tested here is that shareholding positions in Japan are more likely to become embedded in other ongoing relationships between the firms, as the role of shareholder becomes merged with that of business partner. In the words of one Japanese executive, "there is no sense in holding shares in a company with which business ties are slim." This relationship is especially apparent in relationships among industrial firms and their client banks, where the linking of equity and loan positions indicates a transformation in the nature of each. Credit, in the form of bank loans, has come to resemble equity in allowing creditors flexibility in repayment by deferring interest and principal payments and reducing the "compensating balances" that corporate borrowers need to leave in banks during times of financial adversity. Loans are rolled over as a matter of practice. Furthermore, banks become active participants in the management of their client firms, particularly when the company is in trouble (Pascale and Rohlen, 1983). Common stock, in contrast, seems to take on many of the characteristics Westerners associate with debt. Shareholders demand relatively fixed returns on their investment, in the form of stable dividend payments, but do not ask for active influence over management.

Relatively strong securities regulations in the United States limit the methods by which shareholders can control firms. These legal differences are reflected in the extent of overlap found between the two network variables coded for both countries, equity and directorships. Japanese firms with a top-ten equity position in another firm were about five times more likely to dispatch a director to the same company as were American firms. In total, 10.1 percent of the leading shareholders in the Japanese sample held a simultaneous board position on the same firm, in comparison with 2.1 percent of the leading shareholders in the U.S. sample.

For the Japanese data, we are also able to discern other forms of multiplexity, including debt-equity and trade-equity linkages. Figure 3.6 shows the extent to which equity shareholdings are associated with directorship, debt, and trade ties. In addition to the multiplex directorship relationships just noted, in 7.9 percent of the cases where an equity tie was sent, a trade tie in the same direction was also sent, while in fully 39.0 percent of the cases a debt tie was sent. In total, when we exclude double counting of relationships, we find that in 48.9 percent of all cases where a company is a leading shareholder, we can detect other simultaneous relationships as a top-ten lender, a leading trading partner, and/or a dispatcher of one or more directors.[9]

THE SIX MAIN INTERMARKET KEIRETSU: AN OVERVIEW

The features of the Japanese business network structure outlined above—dense connections of substantive, enduring intercorporate relationships—are pervasive in Japanese industrial organization. Where these take the form of alliances among major financial, industrial, and commercial companies, they often add another feature: organization into identifiable keiretsu.

Among the firms that constitute the intermarket groups are those companies and industries that have historically been most central in the

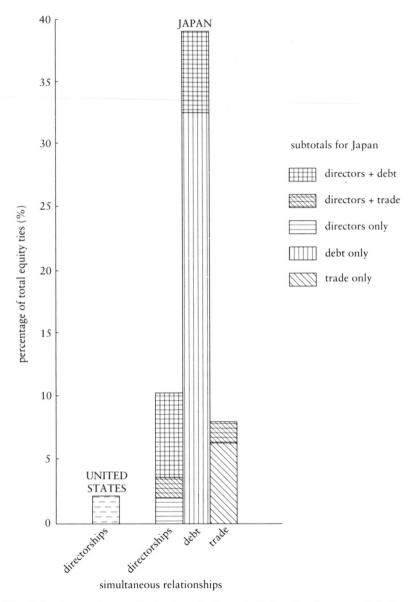

Fig. 3.6. Proportion of Equity Interlocks with Other Simultaneous Relationships (Multiplexity). Source: See Appendix A.

Japanese economy. Within the six main groups, three have clear and direct connections to zaibatsu that dominated the Japanese economy during the prewar and wartime periods: the Mitsubishi, Mitsui, and Sumitomo groups all have at their center most of the companies that were first-line subsidiaries of the zaibatsu holding company, the *honsha*. In addition, the Fuji (or Fuyo) group and the newly emergent Dai-Ichi Kangyo Bank group bring together subgroups of firms that had been associated with other prewar zaibatsu. Fuji takes as its financial core firms in the old Yasuda zaibatsu—including Fuji Bank, Yasuda Trust and Banking, and Yasuda Mutual Life Insurance—while Dai-Ichi Kangyo brings two smaller prewar zaibatsu—Furukawa and Kawasaki—together with a large number of other firms to form a newer grouping still in the process of consolidating. Because of the comparatively weak ties that the Fuji and Dai-Ichi Kangyo groups maintain with these old zaibatsu and because of the centrality of their banks, these two groups are usually classified together with a third group, based on the Sanwa Bank, as "bank groups." The Mitsui, Mitsubishi, and Sumitomo groups are classified as "former zaibatsu groups."

The Characteristics of Keiretsu Membership

Earlier we noted the problem of defining membership in alliance forms, where boundaries are often unclear. This methodological problem can be partially resolved in the intermarket keiretsu by utilizing group presidents' councils in order to identify membership. These councils, which are discussed in detail in the following chapter, have become an institutionalized forum for communication among group firms' chief executives and now publish lists of their participants. This measure of group membership is both unambiguous and empirically correlated with all major features of the keiretsu. Since participation in the council is restricted to those firms most central to the group, what we might call the "core" members, it avoids the problem of including peripheral members or those whose membership might be questioned in the analysis.

The membership lists for the six groups are presented in Table 3.1, which includes all firms that were in one of the councils as of 1989. In overview, we find that the firms affiliated with the intermarket keiretsu are among the largest, oldest, and most prestigious in Japan. The 188 companies listed here (193 formal affiliates less five duplicate entries) represent only slightly over .01 percent of the estimated 1.7 million firms

TABLE 3.1. MEMBERSHIP IN THE SIX MAIN INTERMARKET KEIRETSU (PRESIDENTS' COUNCIL MEMBERS ONLY), 1989

Industry	Mitsui (24 cos.)	Mitsubishi (29 cos.)	Sumitomo (20 cos.)	Fuyō (29 cos.)	Sanwa (44 cos.)	Dai-Ichi Kangyo (47 cos.)
City bank (40.5)	Mitsui Bank	Mitsubishi Bank	Sumitomo Bank	Fuji Bank	Sanwa Bank	Dai-Ichi Kangyo Bank
Trust bank	Mitsui Trust	Mitsubishi Trust	Sumitomo Trust	Yasuda Trust	Toyo Trust	
Life insurance (52.8)	Mitsui Life	Meiji Life	Sumitomo Life	Yasuda Life	Nippon Life	Asahi Life Fukoku Life
Casualty insurance (52.8)	Taisho F&M	Tokio F&M	Sumitomo F&M	Yasuda F&M		Taisei F&M Nissan F&M
Trade & commerce (66.7)	Mitsui Mitsukoshi	Mitsubishi Corp.	Sumitomo Corp.	Marubeni	*Nissho Iwai Nichimen Iwatani Takashimaya	C. Itoh *Nissho Iwai Kanematsu-Gosho Kawasho Seibu Dept. St.
Construction (66.7)	Mitsui Constr. Sanki Engnr.	Mitsubishi Constr.	Sumitomo Constr.	Taisei	Ohbayashi Toyo Constr. Sekisui House Zenitaka	Shimizu Constr.
Real estate (55.1)	Mitsui Real Est.	Mitsubishi Estates	Sumitomo Realty	Tokyo Tatemono		
Fibers & textiles (40.3)	Toray	Mitsubishi Rayon		Toho Rayon Nisshin Spinning	Unitica Teijin	Asahi Chemical

Chemicals (43.3)	Mitsui Toatsu Mitsui Petro-chemical	Mitsubishi Kasei Mitsubishi Petro. Mitsubishi Monsanto Mitsubishi Gas Chem. Mitsubishi Plastics	Sumitomo Chemical Sumitomo Bakelite	Showa Denko Nippon O&F Kurha Chem.	Sekisui Chemical Ube Industries Hitachi Chemical Fujisawa Kansai Paint Tokuyama Soda Tanabe Seiyaku	Denki Kagaku Nippon Zeon Sankyo Shiseido Lion Asahi Denka Kyowa Hakko
Oil & coal (45.0)	Mitsui Mining Hokkaido Coll.	Mitsubishi Oil	Sumitomo Coal Mining	Tonen	Cosmo Oil	Showa Shell
Glass & cement (48.8)	Onoda Cement	Asahi Glass M. Mining & Cement	Nippon Sheet Glass Sumitomo Cement	Nihon Cement	Osaka Cement	Chichibu Cement
Paper (37.7)	Oji Paper	Mitsubishi Paper		Sanyo-Kokusaku		Honshu Paper
Steel (52.7)	Japan Steel Works	Mitsubishi Steel	Sumitomo Metal Ind.	NKK	*Kobe Steel Nakayama St. Hitachi Metals Nisshin Steel	Kawasaki Steel *Kobe Steel Japan M&C
Nonferrous metals (56.0)	Mitsui M&S	Mitsubishi Metal Mitsubishi Aluminum Mitsubishi Cable	Sumitomo M&M Sumitomo Electric Sumitomo Light Metal		Hitachi Cable	Nippon Light Metal Furukawa Co. Furukawa Electric
General & transportation machinery (45.5)	Toyota Motors Mitsui Eng. & Ship.	Mitsubishi Heavy Ind. Mitsubishi Kakoki Mitsubishi Motors	Sumitomo Heavy Ind.	Kubota Nippon P.M. Nissan Motors	NTN Toyo B. Hitachi Zosen Shin Meiwa Daihatsu	Niigata Engnr. Kawasaki Heavy Ind. IHI Heavy Ind. Isuzu Motors Iseki & Co. Ebara Corp.

(continued on following page)

TABLE 3.1. (Continued)

Industry	Mitsui (24 cos.)	Mitsubishi (29 cos.)	Sumitomo (20 cos.)	Fuyō (29 cos.)	Sanwa (44 cos.)	Dai-Ichi Kangyo (47 cos.)
Electrical & precision machinery (39.3)	Toshiba	Mitsubishi Electric Nikon	NEC	*Hitachi Co. Oki Electric Yokogawa Elec. Canon	*Hitachi Co. Iwatsu Electric Sharp Nitto Electric Kyocera Hoya	*Hitachi Co. Fujitsu Fuji Electric Yaskawa Electric Nippon Columbia Asahi Optical
Shipping (58.7)	Mitsui-OSK Lines	Nippon Yusen		Showa Denko	Yamashita-SII	Kawasaki Kisen
Warehousing (33.9)	Mitsui W.	Mitsubishi W.	Sumitomo W.			Shibusawa W.
Other industries (N.A.)	Nippon Flour	Kirin Brewery	Sumitomo Forestry	Nisshin Flour Milling Sapporo Breweries Nichirei Tobu Railway Keihin Railway	Ito Ham Toyo Tire *Nippon Express Hankyu Suntory Orix	Yokohama Rubber Korakuan Stadium *Nippon Express Nippon K.K. Securities Orient

SOURCES: Membership lists are translated and reformatted from tables provided in *Kōsei Torihiki Iinkai* (1983b, pp. 3–4) and *Kigyō keiretsu sōran* (1990, p. 58). The collective share (%) of industry sales is shown in parentheses in the first column. These figures come from *Nihon kigyō shūdan bunseki*, vol. 2 (1980, p. 11). They are calculated as the total sales accounted for by shachō-kai members in the six groups as a percentage of total sales by all companies listed on the Tokyo Stock Exchange.

* Asterisk indicates membership in more than one presidents' council.

in Japan and just over 10 percent of the 1,700 firms listed on the Tokyo Stock Exchange, but their significance extends far beyond what these numbers might indicate. Among the largest 100 industrial firms in Japan, 56 are council members while 34 more are among the next 100. An additional 9 firms are not council members themselves but subsidiaries or affiliates of council member companies.

In total, therefore, among Japan's 200 largest industrial firms, about one-half (99) maintain a clear affiliation with a group, either by direct council membership or through a parent firm that is a member.[10] The importance of group companies is even more striking when considering financial institutions. All five of Japan's largest commercial banks (Dai-Ichi Kangyo, Fuji, Sumitomo, Mitsubishi, and Sanwa) are at the center of their own groups, as are the five leading trust banks, the five leading casualty insurance companies, and four of the five leading life insurance companies.

The industries in which the intermarket keiretsu are strongly represented are among those most central in an industrial economy, including capital, primary products, and real estate. The percentages in the left-hand column of Table 3.1 indicate the extent of total sales in these industries that were held by core group firms in 1980. Natural resources (oil, coal, mining), primary metals (ferrous and nonferrous metals), cement, chemicals, and industrial machinery are all well represented, as keiretsu members control between 43 percent and 56 percent of total sales in these industries. Among financial institutions, group commercial and trust banks control 40 percent of total bank capital, and group insurance companies 53–57 percent of total insurance capital. In real estate, 55 percent of total business is controlled by group members, while in distribution, 67 percent of sales is accounted for by formal keiretsu member companies.

Industries that have weak or no keiretsu participation are more likely to be newer and less central to core industrial operations—what the Japanese sometimes call the "soft" industries. These include publishing, communications, and air travel, in which the keiretsu have no involvement, and the broad category of service industries, in which they constitute less than 5 percent of total sales.

A significant feature of the interaction between industrial and alliance dynamics is what has come to be called in Japanese business parlance the "one-set principle" (*wan setto-shugi*). This is the tendency among the major groupings to have one, and only one, company representing each significant industry. We see in Table 3.1 a high degree of diversification in the six groups, yet with relatively little overlap between the product lines of its member companies. The one-set pattern, described later, is adhered to most closely among the former zaibatsu groups of Mitsui, Mitsubishi, and Sumitomo. Mitsubishi and Mitsui are represented in each major industry listed here, while Sumitomo participates in all but shipping and textiles, both declining industries in Japan. In addition, there are few industrial overlaps among companies within each of these three groups.[11] The membership lists in the Sanwa and Dai-Ichi Kangyo bank groups do not follow the one-set pattern as clearly. While they have representation in most of these industries, there are internal duplications in several— trading and commerce, chemicals, steel, and electrical machinery.

Another important characteristic of membership is the extremely low overlap in participation across groups, as member firms are nearly all identified with just a single council. Out of 193 total memberships in 1989, there were only 5 multiple memberships, which involved four firms: one company (Hitachi) now participates in three councils, while three others (Nissho-Iwai, Nippon Express, and Kobe Steel) participate in two. These reflect historical associations each of these firms has had with multiple group banks. The remaining members are all formally affiliated with only a single group, although some maintain informal ties elsewhere.

The Position of the Groups
in the Japanese Business Community

The share of the total Japanese economy held by the three leading zaibatsu of Mitsubishi, Mitsui, and Sumitomo fell dramatically after the war with the U.S. Occupation-enforced dissolution of the controlling holding companies in each group. Whereas these three controlled 24 percent of total paid-in capital at the end of the war (up substantially from 11 percent in 1937), this share fell to 10 percent in 1955 before increasing several percent in the following decade (Miyazaki, 1976, p. 260). The overall position of the three former zaibatsu groups and of the three postwar bank groups has remained fairly stable since the 1960s. Collectively, the 188 core members in the six groups controlled 23.5 percent, or about one-quarter, of all stocks held in the Japanese corporate sector in 1986, up slightly from 22.6 percent in 1975. This was evenly divided among the former zaibatsu groups, at 11.9 percent, and the bank groups, at 11.6 percent (*Kigyō keiretsu sōran*, 1988, p. 20).

Part of the zaibatsu dissolution statutes called for a ban on use of the names, logos, and trademarks of the former zaibatsu firms. However, this law was rescinded by Japanese authorities in 1952, and firms that had been members in the old zaibatsu soon returned to using their old names. For example, six companies in the Sumitomo group that had historically used the Sumitomo name (including the big three firms of Sumitomo Bank, Sumitomo Chemical, and Sumitomo Metal Industries) readopted the name after the rescinding of the Trademarks Law. Each of these groups also returned to its historical logo, which is still used both by the group as a whole and by individual companies. These are reproduced in Table 3.2 for the three former zaibatsu groups, along with their founding dates.

The group name not only identifies membership to other group companies, but to the world at large. As one Mitsubishi executive put it, "Once a firm grows to this size, it can't afford to be fettered by the group. Still, we can make good use of the internationally vaunted Mitsubishi name, as in our technical cooperation with China and our construction of a plant in Saudi Arabia." At the time, the Mitsubishi group was using as its motto the phrase, "Your Mitsubishi, the world's Mitsubishi." In some cases, the reverse happens: the group name is avoided for fear of besmirching the reputation of other companies should the company fail. This was the case in 1917, when the Mitsui zaibatsu chose to enter the casualty insurance business but to exclude the Mitsui name from the risky venture. The consequently named Taisho Marine and Fire Insurance Co. remained a member of the Mitsui group, but it was not until the spring of 1990 that the decision was finally made for the company—now the third-ranking firm in its industry—to take on the Mitsui name.[12] According to company sources, the reason for the change to Mitsui Marine and Fire was to take advantage of the better-known Mitsui image (*Japan Times,* May 10, 1990).

Each of these groups maintains a somewhat different reputation within the Japanese business community. The keiretsu have become reified and animated in much the same way as do other social collectives, and one may refer to the importance of Mitsui "individualism" (*hito no Mitsui*) in the relatively loose organization of the group and the strength of the individual companies and personalities involved in it; Mitsubishi "organization" (*soshiki no Mitsubishi*) because of its tight quasi-hierarchical structure and the large number of group projects that bring together its member firms; and Sumitomo "cohesion" (*kessoku no Sumi-*

TABLE 3.2.   FOUNDING DATES AND LOGOS
OF THE SUMITOMO, MITSUI,
AND MITSUBISHI GROUPS

Founding Date	Name	Logo	Meaning
1590	Sumitomo		Well-frame
1615	Mitsui		Three wells
1871	Mitsubishi		Three diamonds

tomo), since it has maintained only a small core set of firms and has been the group most reluctant to expand its core membership beyond the original Sumitomo zaibatsu lineage. Similarly, relationships between the groups become part of a wider social competition. The "battle" between the Sumitomo and the Mitsubishi groups, at least in the eyes of some observers (e.g., Kameoka, 1969), is really one between two different business cultures—the rationalistic and commercial orientation of Osaka, where Sumitomo developed, and the social and political orientation of Tokyo, the home of Mitsubishi.

Where detailed analyses are called for in the following chapter, I focus on one of the three former zaibatsu groups, Sumitomo, and one of the three bank groups, Dai-Ichi Kangyo. These represent two extremes in intermarket keiretsu organization. Sumitomo is the oldest of the groups, dating its origins back four hundred years to the start of a copper crafting shop in Kyoto in 1590, twenty-five years before the beginnings of the Mitsui group. It was Sumitomo that most quickly reorganized after the war and is considered, along with Mitsubishi, to be the most closely integrated. It has the smallest nucleus set of firms—the twenty firms in its presidents' council. At the other extreme in age and size is the Dai-Ichi Kangyo group. The Dai-Ichi Kangyo Bank, which serves as the core financial institution in the group, was formed from a merger in 1971 of the former Dai-Ichi Bank—Japan's oldest, dating back to 1871—and Nippon Kangyo Bank. In 1977 Dai-Ichi Kangyo was the last of the six groups to formalize a presidents' council. It is sometimes considered representative of a new type of alliance that may replace the relatively tightly interlinked former zaibatsu—a more loosely organized arrangement, involving an extended and rather motley collection of former independent firms and prewar zaibatsu remnants. These form the largest set of core organizations, with forty-seven firms participating in the group's presidents' council.

Moving beyond Caricature: Alliances as Process versus Pattern

The identifiability of membership in the keiretsu and visibility of the presidents' councils has led at times to an oversimplification of the relationships among affiliated companies. For some, the contemporary groups are not very different from the centrally controlled industrial conglomerates their prewar zaibatsu counterparts are presumed to have been (foreign observers are especially prone to this assumption). Perhaps in response, the opposite argument has also been put forward, namely, that those groups are really nothing more than social clubs and have no real economic impact. The sharing of common names or participation in a group presidents' council or a supplier association is seen as unrelated to companies' actual business relationships. Both of these views caricature reality and overlook the possibility of intermediate forms existing between internal hierarchy or arm's-length markets. Yet this is exactly where the keiretsu must be understood: as a combination of firm-level decision-making units and intercorporate coordination and constraint.

Consider this second view in more detail. The argument that the keiretsu are economically unimportant, which is often heard in response to foreign complaints about "structural barriers" in Japanese markets, generally relies on one of two sources of support. The first is that, because affiliated companies carry out trade with companies in other groups in varying orders of magnitude, alliance identity must not be important to understanding Japanese markets. This is an odd argument. If one were to apply the same logic to the firm, one might very well conclude that because individual companies source a portion of their supplies externally, the firm itself is irrelevant as a unit of internalized exchange. But are the automobile companies introduced at the beginning of this chapter that rely on outside suppliers for 80 percent of the added value in production therefore themselves unimportant in the process? While few would agree with this view concerning the firm, it seems to carry weight when applied to aggregates of firms such as the keiretsu. These are apparently expected to be self-contained. However, the real issue is not whether transactions take place across organizational interfaces (whether at the firm or the keiretsu level), for surely such transactions are inevitable but, rather, how transactions "inside" differ from those "outside."

The reality of contemporary Japanese industrial organization is neither complete openness, nor complete insularity. Instead, it occupies a complex middle ground based in preferential trading patterns that rely on probabilistic rather than deterministic measures and models. While trading within groups is not exclusive, actual empirical patterns are far too biased toward own-group firms to be explained away as minor deviations from otherwise-anonymous market transactions. As I demonstrate in the following chapter, Japanese business networks are strongly organized by keiretsu relationships across three types of ties (dispatched directors, equity shareholding, and bank borrowing) and more weakly organized in a fourth (intermediate product trade).[13]

A second and related argument against the significance of the keiretsu is that, because only a relatively small number of firms are formal members of keiretsu, alliance affiliation does not have important economic consequences. As with the previous argument, this position relies on a false dichotomy, equating the lack of formal affiliation in one of the major groupings with true independence of operation. Research on the keiretsu has been hampered by stylized models of boundaries based on a priori categories of membership. Utilizing instead network data that map relationships across all large public Japanese corporations, I demonstrate in Chapter 5 that network structures characterizing the most formalized keiretsu actually pervade the networks of linkages among other Japanese firms as well. Whether companies "belong" to one of the prominent intermarket groups or not (itself a relative notion), they share the following common characteristics: (1) ties are durable—leading equity and debt ties endure over periods of decades; (2) ties are multiplex—equity and directorship interlocks are linked to debt and trading positions; and, (3) ties are mutual—share crossholdings and other forms of business reciprocity are common among networks of large corporations. Alliance forms are therefore far more prevalent in the Japanese economy than widely acknowledged, and correspondingly more important.

More recently, a somewhat different argument has received attention. This is the view that, even though the keiretsu may have at one time been significant, traditional group structures are now breaking down. Although this perspective does receive some support in the changes occurring in new technology development, capital financing, and internationalization, the idea that this represents a fundamental transformation is greatly exaggerated. Evidence used in support is largely anecdotal; where rigorously measurable relationships are considered, these changes appear far weaker. We do find in the following chapters that Japanese companies are increasing the number of tie-ups with firms outside their traditional groupings. But this is not new: corporate growth through expansion of business partners has long been characteristic of Japanese industrial organization, even during the prewar period; indeed, this represents one of the key differences between Japan's historical reliance on the spinning off of operations and the reliance in the United States on intrafirm divisionalization. Regarding capital market changes, the fact that large Japanese companies are relying on banks less than they used to for loans is true so far as it goes. But this must be balanced against a recognition of the predominance of equity financing during much of the prewar period as well, and of the increased role of banks in equity markets and the "keiretsu-ization" of medium-sized firms that are themselves affiliated to large keiretsu parent companies.

What, then, about the ongoing trends toward internationalization and liberalization of the Japanese economy? Japanese firms have long sought to stabilize their external environment in the face of dramatic shocks and restructuring. If the past is a reliable guide for the future, therefore, these trends could actually have the opposite effect from that predicted. In the market for corporate control, at least, firms have used new threats imposed by hostile outside interests as a rationale to strengthen alliances with selected affiliate-shareholders. The apparent chinks in what seems a formidable wall around Japan's markets for corporate control in the 1980s (these include Merck's acquisitions of the Banyu and Torii pharmaceutical companies and the recent buyout of Sansui Electric by Britain's Polly Peck) have actually proven how formidable that wall remains: these were acquisitions of failing operations, not promising growth companies.[14] In short, as we see in the following chapters, while specific *patterns* of relationships in Japan are gradually evolving, there remains an important continuity in the underlying *processes* of alliance formation.

CONCLUSION

Since organizational actors represent the most stable and powerful participants in contemporary community life and those with the greatest access to resources, economic action in industrialized countries is largely defined by organizational and interorganizational relationships. Where the key decision makers are corporations, as in capitalist systems, this leads to the study of intercorporate networks. This chapter has outlined basic characteristics of business network organization in Japan, as well as introducing the database used in the following chapters through a set of comparative analyses of ownership networks in Japan and the United States. We also considered several social frameworks that organize these networks in Japan, noting in particular the prevalence of intercorporate alliance forms.

The overall richness of interorganizational linkages in Japan reinforces the emerging view that Japan, like its East Asian counterparts, can be usefully thought of as a "network economy" (Hamilton and Biggart, 1988; Lincoln, 1989; Imai, forthcoming). That is, processes that take place at the level of the Japanese firm have been combined with processes that integrate firms at the interfirm level. The basic dynamic in Japanese industrial evolution has been the spinning off of new satellite firms from a central set of operations while organizing these firms collectively under a higher-level capital and control system. In the following chapters, we study in detail how this dynamic works in organizing the large firms that make up Japan's economic core.

CASE STUDY: A BRIEF
HISTORY OF THE SUMITOMO GROUP

In order to provide a sense of the context within which the intermarket keiretsu arose, we consider here in broad overview the history of a single group, Sumitomo.[15] An outline of this history is presented in Table 3.3.

Sumitomo's history is an intertwining of families, political events, and economic development over the course of nearly four centuries. It is a story of both stability and change: change in the form of the growth, development, and transformations of Sumitomo from a tiny shop to a world-class, diversified group; stability in the traditions of the Sumitomo family, as seen in the following passage from the official Sumitomo history, describing a ritual ceremony among affiliated companies that continues even today:

> Every year, on April 25, members of the Sumitomo family and the chief executives of the companies of the Sumitomo Group gather at Hosendō Hall, dedicated to the family's ancestors and past employees, in the city of Kyoto. There they conduct a solemn memorial service for the past family heads and for those who have contributed to the development of the Sumitomo enterprises.

TABLE 3.3.   OUTLINE
OF SUMITOMO'S HISTORY

Date	Event
1590	Soga Riemon founds Izumi-ya, a copper-crafting shop in Kyoto.
Early 1600s	Riemon develops first process in Japan for extracting gold and silver from copper ore. Izumi-ya prospers.
1652	Sumitomo and Soga *ie* (households) fully merge as Riemon's son, Tomomochi, becomes official head of Sumitomo.
1691	Sumitomo buys Besshi mine in Shikoku. This becomes the most profitable mine in Japanese history and the main source of Sumitomo revenue for the next two centuries.
1700s	Sumitomo maintains position as world's largest producer and exporter of copper.
1868	Meiji Restoration. Sumitomo struggles to downplay old ties to the shogun.
1895	Sumitomo Bank is started.
1896	Sumitomo Honten begins as holding company to oversee expanding operations.
Early 1900s	Sumitomo expands into other businesses by starting Sumitomo Steel Casing, Sumitomo Electric Wire, Sumitomo Chemical, as well as other satellites.
1937	Sumitomo Honsha is incorporated.
1948	Sumitomo Honsha is dissolved under Occupation. Sumitomo name is dropped from companies.
Early 1950s	Sumitomo name is readopted by most Sumitomo companies. Hakusui-kai (presidents' council) is formed, and group companies increase their shareholdings in other group companies.
1956	Sumitomo's first major postwar group project, Sumitomo Atomic Energy, is formed.
Present	Sumitomo, now a well-established group with twenty core members and dozens of peripheral members, is involved in a diversity of projects.

Period I. The Early Years (1590–1868)

In 1590, Soga Riemon opened a copper-crafting shop in Kyoto, calling it Izumi-ya. (*Izumi* means spring or fountainhead, and *ya* is a suffix added to shop and inn names.) At this time, Riemon adopted as Izumi-ya's emblem the *igeta,* or well frame, which is typically placed around a spring (see Table 3.2). This symbol was registered in 1885 as the Sumitomo trademark and is still used by the Sumitomo group and its core companies as their logo.

Riemon was not a blood connection to the Sumitomo family, but he was married to one—to the elder sister of Sumitomo Masatomo, a Buddhist priest and the spiritual leader of the family at that time. The ties between the Soga clan and the Sumitomo clan were further strengthened by the adoption of Riemon's eldest son into the Sumitomo clan. In the meantime, the expansion of Izumi-ya (at this time just a small shop) was made possible by Riemon's development in the early 1600s of a process for extracting gold and silver from copper ore. Riemon and his process prospered as he expanded first into copper refining, then later into copper trading and mining. Riemon's son Tomomochi, adopted into the Sumitomo family, started a branch of Izumi-ya in Osaka in 1623. There the family copper-refining business flourished, as Osaka was rapidly replacing Nagasaki as Japan's main center of commerce.

Tomomochi's Izumi-ya eventually absorbed a shop started by Sumitomo Masatomo under the name of Fiji-ya, as well as the original Izumi-ya in Kyoto, which was being run by Riemon's second son. Tomomochi took over as head of the Sumitomo family in 1652. In this way, the two clans—Sumitomo and Soga—fully merged. The copper refinery Tomomochi built in Osaka became the center of Japan's copper industry and remained so throughout the Tokugawa period (1603–1867), though it never grew beyond a peak employment of several hundred workers. The Sumitomo family became quite wealthy and politically influential during this period. Sumitomo and other Osaka copper interests were benefiting from a decree by the shogun that all copper for export had to be refined in Osaka, apparently as a control measure to ensure that the valuable silver was indeed being fully extracted from the ore. Copper mining and production expanded rapidly during this period in Japan as a whole, and Sumitomo grew accordingly. In order to control fierce competition among the increasing number of rivals, the shogunate restricted copper trade to sixteen members of the copper guild. Of these, ten were from Osaka and four were Sumitomo family members. By the 1670s, Sumitomo controlled one-third of Japan's copper export trade, already the world's largest.

Sumitomo's full-scale entry into the copper-mining business came in 1680 with its purchase and rehabilitation of the dilapidated Yoshioka mine in Okayama Prefecture. With its other mining interests, this acquisition made Sumitomo the leading private mining enterprise in the country. In a move a decade later that was to prove perhaps the single most important event in its history, Sumitomo purchased rights in 1691 to a promising mining site in Besshi (Ehime Prefecture, Shikoku). The Besshi mine was to be the most productive mine in Japanese history over the next two-and-a-half centuries, and the continuing lifeblood of Sumitomo's existence.

Period II. The Development of Sumitomo Zaibatsu (1868–1945)

The greatest threat to Sumitomo as an ongoing entity came following the Meiji Restoration in 1868. Sumitomo was closely connected to and privileged by the shogun—its Besshi mine operated on land controlled by the shogunate, and received low-priced rice for its mine workers and special trading concessions. These ties were to prove detrimental in collecting debts from former warlords who had fallen out with the shogun. At the same time, commodity prices were dropping dramatically, and the Sumitomo family discussed selling the Besshi mine to finance their debts. They were swayed away from this, however, by the manager of the mine at the time, Hirose Saihai. Hirose argued, with great prescience, that the mine could, with work, continue to be Sumitomo's core operation (its "cash cow," in contemporary vernacular). Hirose introduced Western technology into the mine and turned what had been a dying enterprise into the mainstay of the expanding Sumitomo group, quintupling output in just over two decades. As a reward, he was made director general of Sumitomo headquarters, becoming the first in a line of nonfamily, professional managers to run the Sumitomo group.

Apart from a venture in the commodity mortgage loan business and several short-lived attempts to enter textiles and camphor, Sumitomo remained during the first several decades of the Meiji period primarily a copper business, focused on its Besshi mine. It was not until Hirose was succeeded by his nephew, Iba Teigo, and Sumitomo was again on solid financial ground, that Sumitomo took advantage of the opportunities the Meiji period afforded for the entrepreneurially inclined and true diversification took place. Iba started the Sumitomo Bank in 1895, among other smaller enterprises. The third professional director general, Suzuki Masaya, presided over Sumitomo's expansion in coal mining, fertilizer manufacturing, and other enterprises during the early 1900s. A succession of professional managers followed in the interim between the two world wars, and with them came aggressive diversification by Sumitomo into life insurance, trust banking, and various manufacturing industries, notably steel, electrical products, and glass. It was during this period that most Sumitomo companies came into existence, as shown in the Sumitomo "family tree" in Figure 3.7.

The Commercial Law of 1890 established three types of company

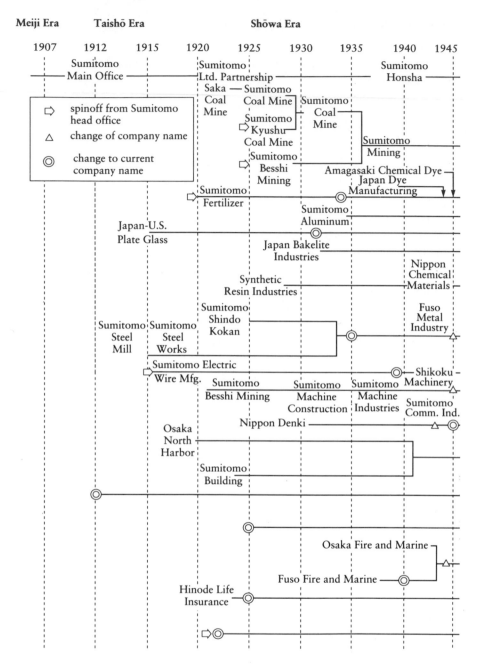

Fig. 3.7. Sumitomo Family Tree. Source: Asano (1978). Note: The chart depicts the evolution of the core firms in the present-day Sumitomo group. Startups are counted from their first listing as stock companies.

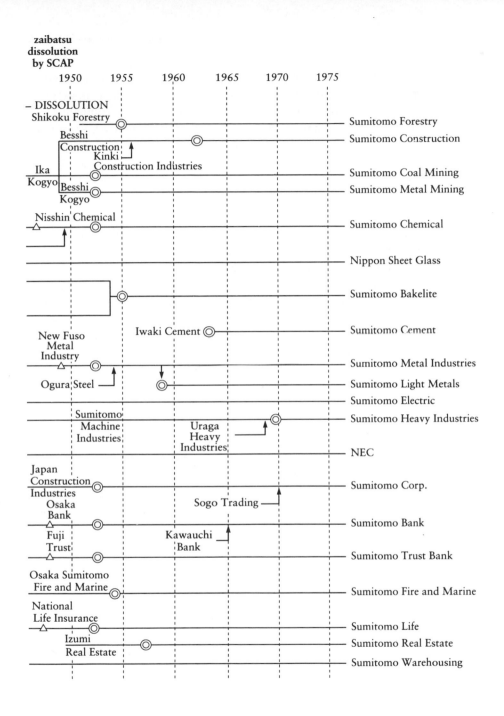

zaibatsu dissolution by SCAP

| 1950 | 1955 | 1960 | 1965 | 1970 | 1975 |

− DISSOLUTION

Shikoku Forestry — Sumitomo Forestry

Besshi Construction — Sumitomo Construction

Kinki Construction Industries — Sumitomo Coal Mining

Ika Kogyo

Besshi Kogyo — Sumitomo Metal Mining

Nisshin Chemical — Sumitomo Chemical

— Nippon Sheet Glass

— Sumitomo Bakelite

Iwaki Cement — Sumitomo Cement

New Fuso Metal Industry — Sumitomo Metal Industries

Ogura Steel — Sumitomo Light Metals

— Sumitomo Electric

Sumitomo Machine Industries — Sumitomo Heavy Industries

Uraga Heavy Industries

— NEC

Japan Construction Industries — Sumitomo Corp.

Osaka Bank — Sumitomo Bank

Sogo Trading

Fuji Trust — Sumitomo Trust Bank

Kawauchi Bank

Osaka Sumitomo Fire and Marine — Sumitomo Fire and Marine

National Life Insurance — Sumitomo Life

Izumi Real Estate — Sumitomo Real Estate

— Sumitomo Warehousing

forms in Japan: the general joint stock company, the limited partnership (*gōshi*), and the unlimited partnership (*gōmei*). The zaibatsu, as a rule, adopted the joint company form for their operating companies and either the limited partnership or the unlimited partnership form for the holding company. In 1896, the Sumitomo family constitution was changed in order to establish a holding company (Sumitomo Honten) assigned the role of overseeing the operating companies. This headquarters was given the form of a limited partnership in 1921 with a total capital of ¥150 million. The titular president of Sumitomo Goshigaisha, as it was now called, was the head of the Sumitomo household, Sumitomo Kichizaemon. Kichizaemon, however, delegated actual management duties to the director general at that time, Suzuki Masaya. The head office required that all companies submit plans for equipment investment and operations to the office annually before the fiscal year began. These were reviewed by the head office and adjusted to take into consideration the entire zaibatsu before being submitted for the approval of the board of directors (*rijikai*). Control was strict. The head office expected monthly and ten-day reports from the operating companies. Detailed regulations were incorporated into the Sumitomo *Kahō* (family constitution and company manual) and later into the *Shasoku* (a revised version of the *Kahō*). The general financial controlling function was performed by the accounting department and the accounts section of the general affairs department of the head office.

The organizational structure of the zaibatsu in the 1920s was comparatively straightforward. The head office collected the surpluses from its operating companies and allocated funds in businesses it thought would be profitable. Where Sumitomo Goshigaisha ran short of funds, it borrowed them from its financial institutions, especially from the Sumitomo Bank. The method of capital allocation within the zaibatsu, therefore, involved loans to and deposits from member companies, directed through the head office.

Perhaps the key issue facing every zaibatsu at the time was how to balance the desire to expand business while maintaining control over the operating companies. Sumitomo only gradually and cautiously transformed its enterprises into joint stock companies. Sumitomo Bank (started in 1895) became a joint stock company in 1911, Sumitomo Metal Industries (1901) in 1915, and Sumitomo Electric (1911) in 1920. However, the shares of most of these companies were not publicly issued, but rather were held by other Sumitomo companies. During the prewar period, only five firms (though among the largest) opened shares to the public—Sumitomo Bank (in 1917), Sumitomo Trust and Banking (1925), Sumitomo Chemical (1934), Sumitomo Metal Industries (1935), and Sumitomo Electric (1937)—and ownership and capitalization were carefully controlled. Other enterprises such as coal mining and sales, copper drawing, and chemical fertilizer remained under direct management of the headquarters. Sumitomo Kichizaemon himself owned 98.7 percent of Sumitomo Goshigaisha in 1927, as well as major portions of six subsidiaries. Operating control, however, was delegated to professional managers hired by the family, who simultaneously served as the board of directors.

Movements to the joint stock form appear not to have been for the purpose of raising outside capital, for nearly all shares were still held by the Sumitomo family and the head office. The system of finance was still closed. Rather, it seems they were a means of gaining control over subsidiaries akin to the purposes of the modern-day profit center. Yasuoka (quoted in Asajima, 1984, p. 113) argues that the joint stock company form in the zaibatsu at the time served to "rationalize the holdings and management of the various enterprises" and to "organize a system that can expand to giant size." Similarly, Masaki (1978, p. 33) suggests that "what the zaibatsu tried to stress was not the capital-raising function but the control-concentrating function of incorporation."

A second advantage of public incorporation was in diffusing public opinion, for the 1930s were marked by periodic public outcries against the zaibatsu and their closed financial system. The increasingly powerful military was dubious about what it perceived as competition for power and pressured the zaibatsu into increasing donations to public works projects. That the zaibatsu were sensitive to public pressure is indicated in the public explanation given by the Mitsubishi zaibatsu for the opening of one of its subsidiaries, Mitsubishi Heavy Industries, to the public in 1934. It stated that it was going public for the purpose of "avoiding monopoly of profit by a few rich families and making the company open to the general public" (quoted in Masaki, 1978, p. 46). Public offerings, then, were one means of diffusing this pressure by opening the group, albeit nominally, to outside capital.

Sumitomo Goshigaisha was incorporated as Sumitomo Honsha in 1937, though its shares were never offered to the public (they remained in the hands of family members). Ironically, given earlier right-wing animosity, the zaibatsu prospered during the next eight years as a result of the military war effort. Sumitomo companies which were benefiting from military demand (Sumitomo Metal Industries, Sumitomo Chemical, Sumitomo Industries, etc.) increasingly needed to rely on sources of funds other than the head office. These were primarily loans from Sumitomo Bank and other Sumitomo financial institutions and external loans from special financial institutions, in particular the Bank of Japan. Funds from other city banks were rarely used. In this way the external funds that were introduced would not disturb the internal control structure of the zaibatsu. It was a system that depended on and was made successful by deposits from the general public and borrowings from government-controlled sources.

Companies also offered equity shares, but again, not for the purpose of gaining outside capital. These tended to be limited to "friendly" shareholders—primarily other subsidiaries and zaibatsu family members. Life insurance companies were important holders since they were expected to have no desire to control other companies. Employees and their relatives were also offered shares. Masaki (1978, p. 46) reports that Mitsubishi was quite explicit that their shares were not a publicly tradable commodity, issuing shares in 1928 with the following proviso: "Since these stocks are offered for a long-term investment, such action as immediately selling them should be abstained from in the light of moral obligation to the company. If it is necessary, however, to sell them, inform the head office beforehand so that we can buy them back at the selling price."

Period III. The Dissolution (1945)

The ownership structure of Sumitomo at the time of zaibatsu dissolution is indicated in Table 3.4. The dominant shareholder of most group subsidiaries was the holding company, Sumitomo Honsha, and the dominant shareholder of the holding company itself was the Sumitomo family (particularly the head of the family, Sumitomo Kichizaemon), which held 83 percent of the shares at the end of the war. In addition, some cross-holdings existed among the subsidiaries themselves (e.g., Sumitomo Bank's 40 percent stake in Sumitomo Trust and Banking).

With Japan's defeat in World War II and the subsequent arrival of U.S. Occupation Forces came a major overhaul of the Japanese economy as a means toward economic democratization. The most important measures from the point of view of the zaibatsu were the dissolution of the holding companies, the elimination of family assets held in the zaibatsu, the removal of many top executives from first-line subsidiaries, and the breakup of a number of leading zaibatsu companies (Hadley, 1970). The

TABLE 3.4.   SUMITOMO GROUP
SHAREHOLDINGS AT TIME OF DISSOLUTION

Shareholder

Issuing Company	Sumitomo Family (%)	Sumitomo Honsha (%)	Sumitomo Bank (%)	Other Sumitomo Companies (%)	Total Sumitomo Holdings (%)
Sumitomo Honsha	83.3				83.3
Sumitomo Bank	11.3	24.1		16.7	52.1
Sumitomo Trust Bank	2.8	1.5	40.2	0.5	45.0
Sumitomo Marine	2.6	17.0			19.6
Sumitomo Metal Mining	53.4	26.6	7.0	14.0	100.0
Sumitomo Metal Industries	4.3	20.9	6.8	8.7	39.7
Sumitomo Electric	4.7	24.3	1.0	8.2	38.2
NEC	2.0	11.1	0.2	6.5	19.8
Nippon Sheet Glass	4.6	19.2		0.4	24.2
Sumitomo Chemical	7.3	17.5	0.5	6.2	31.5
Sumitomo Heavy Industries	7.2	21.0		69.0	97.2

SOURCE: Calculated from data provided in *Nihon zaibatsu to sono kaitai* (reproduced in Futatsugi, 1976, pp. 52–55).

Note: All of the above are current company names.

changes in group structure wrought by the dissolution are depicted schematically in Figures 3.8a and 3.8b. With dissolution, family owner-ship connections to the honsha (as well as its smaller holdings in the subsidiaries) were eliminated. So too were honsha connections to the direct subsidiaries, or *chokkei gaisha*.

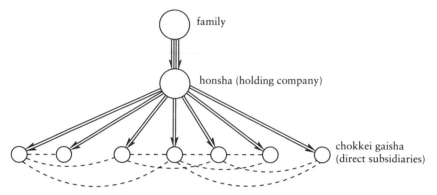

Fig. 3.8a.   Prewar Zaibatsu Pattern of Ownership and Control.

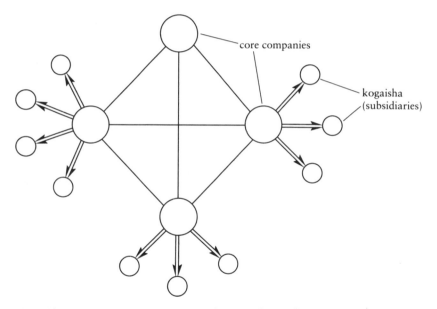

Fig. 3.8b.   Postwar Keiretsu Pattern of Ownership and Control.

This left only intersubsidiary connections intact, but these intersubsidiary crossholdings provided an important infrastructure on which to
rebuild the groups in the 1950s. The subsidiary companies became the
nucleus around which the present-day groups are based, and most have
become substantial enterprises in their own right with their own networks of subsidiaries (kogaisha) and satellite firms ringing their periphery. From the prewar zaibatsu, then, came the beginnings of the postwar
groups.

CHAPTER IV

The Basic Form and Structure of the Keiretsu

Chi wa mizu yori koi
Blood is thicker than water

Onaji kama no meshi o kutta nakama
The group that eats from the same pot

*Sayings used to describe
relationships within
the keiretsu*

The fundamental organizational problem facing the contemporary kei-retsu is that of creating a degree of coherence among its members in the absence of formal structures defining the roles and responsibilities of its participants and clear-cut purposes around which activities are to be focused. It exists not in the legal world as a formal organization (in the classical or Weberian sense) but in the social world of the business community as a loosely organized alliance.

It has nevertheless been able to express itself as a significant form of organization because of the ways it has structured interaction among its members and created an ongoing symbolic framework within which this interaction takes place. This chapter describes in detail three processes by which Japan's business groupings are organized collectively: (1) the creation of high-level executive councils that symbolically identify group members and the boundaries of social unit, as well as providing a forum for interaction among group firms; (2) the structuring of exchange networks—specifically, debt, equity, directorship, and trade networks—that define the position of individual firms in the group and establish group-wide constraints on behavior; and (3) the promotion of group-wide industrial and public relations projects that affirm the existence of the keiretsu as a coherent organizational form.

Of special interest is empirical data across a large number of firms in a

broad spectrum of Japanese industry indicating systematic and continuing patterns of preferential business relationships based on keiretsu
affiliation. For all six major groups, the identity of business partners is
shown to be a fundamental determinant of actual patterns of exchange.
We furthermore find little evidence for the decline of preferential patterns during the 1970s and 1980s in the three capital market measures
studied (debt, equity, and steel transactions). Not that Japan's alliance
structures have been static: a number of important changes since the
postwar period are discussed, including the shift from debt to equity
financing and the declining role played by group trading companies as
mediators of trade where assembly-intensive products are involved. But
these are seen here as largely evolutionary rather than revolutionary
transformations.

DEFINING MEMBERSHIP AND REPRESENTING
GROUP INTERESTS: THE ROLE OF SHACHŌ-KAI

Among the most prominent features of the keiretsu is a layered set of
personnel connections that serve as a conduit for information between
companies and, occasionally, as a source of external discipline. Employee transfers are common among business partners, particularly
among banks and their client firms and large manufacturers and their
subcontractors. Group projects, discussed later in this chapter, are also
important in bringing together personnel from middle and technical
levels of several or more firms.[1]

In addition, firms in intermarket and vertical groupings are linked
through a variety of intercorporate executive councils that serve as a
forum for managers from different levels of the companies involved. The
Sumitomo group, for example, has more than half a dozen different
councils, including not only the group presidents' council but also an
informal OB-kai ("old-boy" get-together) for its chairmen, which is
oriented primarily toward playing golf, as well as a variety of regular
meetings for directors, vice presidents, and buchō (division managers)
for the purposes of discussing corporate planning, public relations, and
other group-wide activities. Recently, each of the big-six intermarket
groups has started its own kenkyū-kai (research councils) to help develop collectively the emerging information technologies. In the case
of the Sumitomo group, two separate councils have been created, one
for buchō-level executives and the other for kachō-level (department)
managers.

While group interaction takes place at many levels, undoubtedly the most prominent of these meetings are the presidents' councils that bring together the chief executive officers from the group's nucleus companies.[2] In Japanese, these are known as the *shachō-kai*, combining the word for company president, *shachō*, with the suffix *-kai*, for meeting, gathering, or association. The shachō-kai is a kind of informal community council, with membership limited to a set of core members.[3]

While the shachō-kai is typically viewed as a postwar phenomenon, it actually traces its beginnings to the prewar period and is a long-standing and widespread feature of interfirm relationships in Japan. The shachō-kai falls under a broader category of associations called in their most general form *kyōryoku-kai*, or cooperative councils. The kyōryoku-kai format is now found within even vertical alliances, bringing together the parent firm (Toyota, Hitachi, etc.) and its first-line subcontractors. The origins of the shachō-kai in the contemporary keiretsu may be traced to councils started by their zaibatsu counterparts.[4] In 1938 the Mitsubishi zaibatsu formed the Mitsubishi Kyōryoku-kai, establishing a forum for executives from the extended Mitsubishi group—the honsha and its first-line subsidiaries. Sumitomo followed this in 1944 with the Sumitomo Wartime Cooperative Council, or Sumitomo Senji Kyōryoku-kaigi (Okumura, 1983, p. 93).

These councils were dominated by the zaibatsu holding company as representative of zaibatsu family interests. The end of the second world war saw the dissolution of the honsha and the removal of its key executives, but not the abolition of personal connections among the executives in the former subsidiaries. As one chief executive in the Sumitomo group put it: "It was natural for me to feel kinship with [other group presidents]. We were all in the old Sumitomo zaibatsu together. After the war, after the zaibatsu was dissolved, we rose together in our separate corporations. But we kept in close touch. We have played baseball together, we've gone swimming together" (quoted in *Business Week,* March 31, 1975).

Informal meetings among these executives continued during the late 1940s (Okumura, 1983). Sometime in 1951, the meetings became organized on a more systematic basis among Sumitomo companies, resulting in formation of the Hakusui-kai, or White Water Club.[5] In its first meeting, all eleven first-line companies in the old Sumitomo zaibatsu participated. Several years later, companies related to the former Mitsubishi zaibatsu formed their own council. Its chairmen and presidents met on the second Friday of the month, leading to the title of Kinyō-kai, or Friday Club.

The other four groups all began their own shachō-kai in the 1960s, taking their lead from the example set by Sumitomo and Mitsubishi. Mitsui, which had been slower than the Sumitomo or Mitsubishi zaibatsu to reform after the war, began a council in 1961 that met on the second Thursday of every month, calling it the Nimoku-kai, or Second Thursday Club. The inchoate bank groups also adopted the shachō-kai format and two followed the Mitsubishi and Mitsui idea of naming it after the day on which the executives met. In the mid-1960s the Fuji and Sanwa groups announced the formation of, respectively, Fuyō-kai (taken from an old group name) and Sansui-kai (Third Wednesday Club). The last group to formalize a council was Dai-Ichi Kangyo, which in 1978 formed the Sankin-kai (Third Friday Club), seven years after the merger of the Dai-Ichi and Nippon Kangyo Banks. The Sankin-kai brought together three councils that had existed under the old banks: the Kawasaki Mutsumi-kai and Furukawa Sansui-kai, both dating from the mid-1950s under the umbrella of the old Dai-Ichi Bank, and the Jūgosha Shachō-kai, begun in 1970 under the old Nippon Kangyo Bank.

From the informality of the early postwar period—a necessity, perhaps, given the strong anti-zaibatsu feelings among economic reformers at the time—the shachō-kai has become an institutionalized feature of the keiretsu. The roster of their participants is released to the public, and some groups now even permit the registration of alternate representatives from member companies if a company's president is unable to attend. As we see below, and later in Chapter 7, the shachō-kai in some ways serves as a functional equivalent for a U.S.-style board of directors by bringing together key external constituencies through regular meetings, though with several distinctive features.

The Basic Format of the Shachō-kai

Presidents' council meetings are held on a monthly basis (or, in the case of the Dai-Ichi Kangyo group, once every three months). In addition to a chairman—a position that rotates every meeting in some groups and is fixed in others—the meetings typically also assign a secretary, whose function is to record the proceedings. These records are not, however, made available to the public, nor are they transmitted formally within the firms. For this reason, information about the internal contents of the meetings and their dynamics is by necessity second-hand and inferential. What follows comes from interviews with a number of executives involved in group councils, both at the shachō-kai and at lower levels. I have also used accounts gleaned from various press reports.[6]

It appears that the shachō-kai in practice is less a command center to determine the policies and practices of individual companies than a forum for the discussion of matters of mutual concern. It simultaneously (1) establishes an identity for the group and its participants, signifying relationships among firms, and instilling a sense of coherence; (2) creates a setting in which issues of group-wide concern may be negotiated, including protecting and promoting the group name and, less often, arranging for assistance for companies in trouble, resolving conflicts among members, or disciplining deviant group companies; and (3) enhances the group's position in the larger business community by presenting the image of a powerful and historically prestigious collective.

More often than not, the executives remarked, nothing of particular note is discussed and the meeting is merely an opportunity to exchange views with other chief executives and to socialize. (Even in Japan, it appears, it is lonely at the top.) Often the meetings revolve around a theme—say, "Information in the Twenty-first Century"—and a guest speaker is invited to address the assembly, providing a basic focus for discussion. Companies often report on new products and technologies that they are developing, decisions to open new subsidiaries in foreign markets, and general conditions in their own industry. Periodically, special matters of group-wide interest come up, including projects that the group is engaged in as well as various charitable activities. Infrequently, topics arise that require special attention—intramural conflicts or group companies that are having financial difficulties. The atmosphere, as it was described to me, is one of camaraderie rather than of a formal meeting with a defined agenda. Nevertheless, the shachō-kai is considerably more than a quaint business custom, for it serves both to signify membership in the group and to provide a common arena for the expression of the strategic interests group firms have in one another. As such, it is significant both for its symbolism and for what it reveals about the dynamics of keiretsu membership.

Externally, the shachō-kai serves as a signal to the larger business community that a relationship exists. This confers on the member company a degree of status resulting from being associated with the name of Mitsubishi, Sumitomo, and so on. How much status depends on the position of the group itself, leading to various forms of intergroup competition for prestige. From the 1950s until the 1970s, Mitsubishi was held as probably the most prestigious group with which to be affiliated, as it was perceived as the most powerful, progressive, and cohesive. More recently, the Sumitomo group has taken the lead in the prestige rankings, leading to talk in the Japanese business press of a "Sumitomo Boom" (*Shūkan asahi,* April 5, 1985). Though smaller than Mitsubishi, Sumitomo has been growing faster and has several members at the leading edge of high technology—particularly NEC in computers and telecommunications and Sumitomo Electric in optical fibers and compound semiconductors. Council membership also sends signals that get picked up by managers in the purchasing and finance departments of their respective companies, tilting decisions in favor of other group firms when there are no compelling reasons to go elsewhere. As we shall see below, membership is closely associated with patterns of banking, trade, and other business relationships involving group companies.

The Shachō-kai as Political Arena

Behind the shachō-kai's passive and harmonious external surface, companies and their representatives compete with one another on a subtly curtained stage. The Japanese are fond of pointing out the duality of social relationships residing in the *tatemae,* the pleasant exterior constructed to maintain ongoing social relationships, and the *honne,* the darker, emotion-laden reality that lurks inside. That the honne is so rarely openly expressed in the shachō-kai is a reflection of the effectiveness of the structures of constraint on individual firm action, as well as the importance to the group of maintaining a useful front of coherence with which to compete with other groups. The power the council maintains is implicit rather than formalized into statutes governable by laws and stems to an important degree from the embeddedness of firms in group-wide exchange networks, discussed below. Because of the high degree of ambiguity in the precise roles and functions of the shachō-kai, influence is a continually negotiated process, determined through the interaction of the characteristics of the individuals attending and of the positions of their firms in the group.

Among the characteristics of powerful leaders, the two that stand out are seniority and personality. Several informants mentioned that presidents who had been in their positions longer were likely to have more influence over group decisions. This seems to reflect the senpai-kōhai relationship that pervades social relationships in Japan—that those who have been in a position longer are deferred to by virtue of this fact.[7] Personality is also a factor that was mentioned frequently. Charismatic leadership by the long-standing president of Sumitomo Bank in the 1950s and 1960s was widely credited for bringing the Sumitomo group together at that time, while a change in leadership at Sanwa Bank in the 1960s also led to a new strategy of group consolidation. Similarly, the lack of this kind of leadership in the Mitsui group was cited in explaining the slower process of Mitsui consolidation.

Power derived from personal attributes, however, is set within the context of the company's position in the group. The tenure of companies is a factor, particularly in the older ex-zaibatsu where associations with the group's past confer an honored position on some firms. In the Sumitomo group, this is particularly true of Sumitomo Metal Mining, the descendant of a three-hundred-year-old copper mining operation that was for two centuries the life-blood of Sumitomo operations. Several managers from other Sumitomo companies talked about the "special feeling" they had for Metal Mining, a feeling born from its historical significance. Sumitomo Corporation, in contrast, although the largest nonfinancial company in the group when measured by sales, was formed after the war through the efforts of other core companies in the group and has not fully risen above its image of a company formed out of (and therefore under) another.

However, most important in determining power within the group is position in its constituent exchange networks. The two firms most likely to have significant linkages with all keiretsu companies are the group bank and the group trading company. These constitute the network "bridges" (Granovetter, 1973), with common connections to all group members through their control over capital and intermediate product markets. These same two firms, and particularly the bank, have been the most active in reorganizing the keiretsu during the postwar period and are widely considered to be the most central group members. Manufacturing concerns, in contrast, have been more likely to try to maintain a degree of independence. The resulting internal dynamics of the group reflect a balancing of the competing interests for group-level control and company-level independence. In the words of one executive, "The keiretsu have to move both centripetally and centrifugally. While holding together, they have to expand their outside ties (*gaibu to no kankei*). Too strong a push for control by the group bank and the delicate balance of power in the group is threatened."

There has been some discussion in recent years of the waning power in the group of banks and trading companies, as industrial companies have developed their own sources of capital and trading networks. In part, this reflects the increasing size of the groups and the dispersal of shareholdings across a larger number of companies—though the network analyses below raise doubts that these changes are as striking as they are sometimes presented. More important in the shifting balance of power, however, has been the changing positions of companies in the larger business community. The restructuring of Japanese industry away from heavy industries toward high technology industries has also altered roles within the groups. Several informants noted, for example, the rising status of NEC (involved in the computers and communications industries) within Sumitomo.

The interaction of personalities and company positions over time has led to some variation in the dynamics of the different councils. Mitsubishi's Kinyō-kai is perhaps the most formalized and centralized of the councils. Its chairmanship has traditionally rotated among Mitsubishi's leading firms, which constitute the core group's inner circle, known as the Sewanin-kai (mediator's club). First among equals, however, has been the group bank. In a nice quote that simultaneously captures his leadership position and its symbolic manifestation, a president of Mitsubishi Bank in the 1970s, Wataru Tajitsu, described his position as the Kinyō-kai chief as follows: "My role is akin to that of a Shinto priest. I take on any and all squabbles and problems within the group and pronounce a benediction. If that does not do the trick, I draw my sword . . . unfortunately with a blade of bamboo and not steel" (*Oriental Economist*, May 1974).

If Mitsubishi is the most centralized council, then Sumitomo's Hakusui-kai is perhaps the most decentralized. There is no formal position of leadership. Rather, the chairmanship of each meeting rotates regularly among the presidents of all twenty companies. Since there is no assigned seating arrangement, attendees try to come early to get the best seats. It is also the most restrictive of the councils, as attendance is limited to the company presidents, and neither company chairmen (a largely honorary position in Japan) nor proxy representatives are allowed.[8] The president of Sumitomo Bank, Isoda Ichirō, reported on the internal dynamics of the Hakusui-kai a number of years ago as follows:

> There are no specific representatives to the Hakusui-kai, it is true. At the beginning, I used to sit at the center of the table but I stopped this practice after six months or so. As seats start to fill from the corners, you have to sit in the center when you join the group late. So I make it a practice to go to the meetings rather early and take a corner seat. . . . In times of real crisis, leadership will naturally emerge on its own on the basis of the ages of the presidents represented and the history, real prowess, and social positions, etc. of the corporations involved. [*Oriental Economist*, May 1981.]

The Mitsukoshi Incident

The vaguely defined but widely acknowledged role of enterprise group-ings and their leadership councils is evident in the "Mitsukoshi Inci-dent," an event that took place in 1982 and received extensive publicity within the Japanese business community. Mitsukoshi is a venerable institution—the largest, oldest (founded in the seventeenth century), and most prestigious of Japan's remarkable department stores. But from the late 1970s until the incident reached its finale, Mitsukoshi was rocked by a series of scandals, including an investigation by the Japan Federal Trade Commission into allegations of illegal sales pressure exerted by Mitsukoshi on its suppliers.

These problems became more serious in the early 1980s when inven-tories of unsold items began to pile up in Mitsukoshi's warehouses, and it turned out that much of this excess inventory had been sold to the department store through companies with questionable ties to its presi-dent, Okada Shigeru. Okada had long been romantically involved with Takehisa Michi, the proprietress of a group of firms that imported and distributed foreign-made products. This special relationship had helped Takehisa to expand sales to the department store, and her companies were enjoying large profits even at a time when the department store's sales and profits were weak. Takehisa's influence within Mitsukoshi through her association with Okada reached a point where she was sometimes referred to as the empress (*jotei*) of Mitsukoshi. Her "reign" resulted in bad press for Mitsukoshi and substantial disruption in the ranks. It was widely believed that the directors had not reported to Okada the extent of the inventory problem for fear of the consequences if they crossed Takehisa.

The final stage in Okada's undoing came in August, 1982, when Mitsukoshi put on an exhibition of Persian antiques in its gallery, selling a number of them at very high prices to wealthy customers. This is a common practice among leading department stores, but it was dis-covered shortly thereafter that some of these "antiques" were in fact fakes that had been manufactured no further away than the suburbs of Tokyo. Exacerbating the problem was Okada's refusal to resign to take blame for this problem. Under normal circumstances, a blossoming scandal of this magnitude is dealt with under Japanese business etiquette by the resignation of the CEO and by a round of public apologies by various company officials to those affected and to the general public.[9] But Okada denied any association with wrongdoing and continued in his position as president. This presented the board of directors of Mitsu-koshi with a delicate problem, since nearly all members were full-time employees of Mitsukoshi who worked under Okada, the very man they were in a position to have to remove.

As a member of the Mitsui group, however, Mitsukoshi had long-standing associations with other group companies, and particularly with Mitsui's financial institutions, a number of which were among Mitsu-koshi's leading shareholders. While Mitsukoshi continued to decline in the public eye, the latent power of the group became increasingly apparent. Rumors began to circulate that group companies would refuse to buy gifts during the year-end gift-giving season in Japan, a major source of revenue for Japanese department stores. A senior member of the group, Edo Hideo, who was also chairman of Mitsui Real Estate, was quoted at the time as saying, "We can no longer stay clear of the situation. . . . [T]his is smearing mud on the history of Mitsui" (*Shūkan asahi*, September 24, 1982). The scandal was coming to affect Mitsui's own good name (as well, not incidentally, as its companies' financial positions in Mitsukoshi).

The Mitsui group's interests were expressed through Koyama Goro, a retired chief executive of Mitsui Bank who sat on Mitsukoshi's board. As a former leader in Mitsui's presidents' council, the Nimoku-kai, and as an advisor to the bank, Koyama's support was considered critical because of his high position and influence within the Mitsui group. Several top executives and corporate auditors approached Koyama to see whether he would provide external support for the removal of Okada at a forth-coming board meeting. Before the meeting, Koyama arranged to meet with Okada to confront him directly with Mitsukoshi's problems. On September 7, Koyama arrived at Okada's office. According to several accounts, the meeting was a disaster, as Okada accused Koyama of meddling in affairs that were none of his business (*Shūkan asahi*, October 8, 1982; *Yomiuri nenkan*, 1983).

At this point, there was no turning back. Okada's behavior entered the agenda of the group's Nimoku-kai, where it was decided that Okada would have to be eased from power. Mitsukoshi's board meeting took place on the morning of September 22. After other items of business were completed, a senior executive on the board took the floor and proposed the dismissal of Okada as president. With the exception of Okada, all directors on the board, each of whom had been carefully solicited before the meeting, stood up in support of the proposal. Okada cried out, "What for!", to which Koyama responded, "Since you're the one on the agenda, you have no right to speak." Even after the board

meeting was finished, Okada remained in the conference room be-
seeching other directors to reconsider. But Koyama had the last word,
coolly informing Okada, "The meeting's over. . . ." (*Shūkan asahi,*
October 8, 1982; *Yomiuri nenkan,* 1983). Thus ended what was reported in the Japanese press to be the first time a chief executive had been
forced out of office by his own board of directors.

THE STRUCTURE
OF INTERCORPORATE NETWORKS

If the shachō-kai serves to define membership and express group interests, then flows of resources are the concrete manifestations of these
interests in the ongoing life of each firm's interactions with its affiliated
enterprises. In the structure of these flows we find clear indications of the
significance of the keiretsu in organizing intercorporate exchange in
Japan. Ostensibly bilateral linkages are themselves organized into alliance networks of varying densities. These represent collective structures, both in the ways in which transactions signify relationships (e.g.,
establishing trading relationships by taking an equity position), and in
the creation of exchange networks whose overall structures become
important determinants of relationships within the keiretsu.

In the following sections, we look at the patterns of interfirm exchange
networks established through (1) loans from group financial institution,
(2) share crossholdings, (3) outside directorships, and (4) trade in intermediate products. Within the group, these exchanges are closely intertwined with other ongoing relationships among group members. Each
apparently discrete transaction (e.g., one firm's equity position in another) is itself embedded in a joint social construction—the group.

The analyses below rely on the following measures of network structure. The first is *density,* defined by Mitchell (1969) as the proportion of
linkages completed in a network as against the number of total potential
linkages. More useful for determining the extent of preferential trading
is the *transaction matrix.* This matrix provides a detailed breakdown of
the share of ties by both sending and receiving firms according to alliance
affiliation. Through the device of the transaction matrix and a set of
related network measures, we are able to demonstrate relatively precisely the extent to which nominal classifications of groupings determine
concrete patterns of intercorporate linkages. In so doing, we also demonstrate just how far Japanese business networks deviate from hypothetical
market anonymity.

The transaction matrix yields two derivative measures of substantive

interest. One of these is *internalization,* defined here as the proportion of
alliance firms' total (or top-ten) interfirm linkages that take place with
firms in their own keiretsu. The other is the *preferential transaction
ratio,* an index of the exclusiveness of each group. The preferential
transaction ratio is calculated as the proportion of ties that take place
among firms within the same keiretsu divided by the average number of
ties these firms have with other major keiretsu. Where internalization
puts the group in the perspective of the entire business network (including independent and subsidiary firms that maintain no formal group
affiliation), the preferential transaction ratio assesses the importance of
each alliance only against other keiretsu. Complete neutrality in dealings
with other companies results in ratios of 1 : 1, while deviations from this
are interpreted as preferential patterns in the network. The stronger the
patterns, the farther these intercorporate relations are deviating from
pure market anonymity.

JAPAN'S FINANCIAL SYSTEM

In studying the significance of the keiretsu in structuring Japanese capital
markets, it is essential to consider the distinctive patterns of corporate
finance as they have evolved over time in Japan. The central role during
the prewar period in capital allocation among zaibatsu subsidiaries was
played by the holding company. During the postwar period, with the
dissolution of the holding companies, this role was largely taken over by
financial institutions and especially by large city banks as major lenders
of capital. This created the conditions in the critical wartime and early
postwar period within which more extended alliances organized around
lead banks emerged. More recently, as a result of capital market liberalization and a slowing in the overall growth of the Japanese economy,
there has been a proportional shift in the sources of external capital
among large Japanese companies away from long-term debt toward
equity and bond financing.

   Despite these changes, certain underlying characteristics of Japanese
capital market relationships have continued since the postwar period
into the present day in modified form. These include the fundamental
importance of large financial institutions in mediating between household savers and corporate users of capital; capital allocation through
closely administered ties between these financial institutions and their
industrial clients, even where financing takes the form of securities-based
capital; and strong preferential patterns of capital supply in both debt

and equity capital markets among affiliated enterprises. As a result, when the position of banking, insurance, and securities companies are considered as a whole, we find far less change in the capital allocation process than is often believed.

The Historical Role of Financial Institutions

The financial function was already well developed in the Tokugawa economy with the large merchants playing an especially important role. Modern banking and life insurance companies, however, were not introduced until the 1870s, as an import from the West. The Japanese government encouraged the banking system in various ways but left the actual role of financing Meiji development largely to private financial institutions. These banks, particularly the large-scale city banks, emerged in close conjunction with the development of manufacturing operations and never achieved the independent status that they did in the United States. Each inchoate zaibatsu of the Meiji period started its own bank for the purpose of funding the activities of its group companies. As Lockwood (1968, p. 222) points out,

> Big banks and trust companies were securely tied into each major combine by intercorporate stockholding, interlocking directorates, and the "interrelated solvency" of these institutions and their combine affiliates. They held the deposits of affiliated companies (as well as individual depositors) and were at the same time their chief source of capital.

Those banks that had begun independently, such as Dai-Ichi Koku-ritsu Bank (the forerunner of the contemporary Dai-Ichi Kangyo Bank), found it necessary to develop close relationships with a subset of dependable client firms that relied on them for the bulk of their external capital needs. Even the smaller, specialized zaibatsu (e.g., Nissan) developed their own internal financial arms for the same purposes. This supporting role is evidenced in the term that described them—*kikan ginkō*, or "organ banks." Less often, the reverse pattern occurred, with entrepreneurs focusing primarily on developing financial enterprises and later extending these to the building of industrial empires. The Yasuda zaibatsu was representative of this pattern.

In the 1930s, as the Japanese economy was rapidly expanding to meet Japan's wartime needs, banks increasingly replaced the honsha and the zaibatsu families as the main sources of working capital for the group companies. Since banks were not prohibited from holding equity, they became significant shareholders in their client firms, increasing their share of all nongovernment securities from about one-fifth to about one-half between 1930 and 1945. Banks also provided, through loans, over half of Japanese companies' total external capital. In total, four-fifths of all debt financing and two-fifths of all external corporate funds came from banks during this period (Goldsmith, 1983).

The close connections between financial institutions and their clients that have dominated the Japanese postwar period were, therefore, already well in place by the end of the war. This was reinforced when banks managed to escape postwar dissolution and benefited further by the freezing of bank deposits held by the zaibatsu families, releasing the banks' deposit liabilities. Industrial firms themselves were growing rapidly and had extremely high external capital requirements that could not be met by the relatively undeveloped equity market, so they turned increasingly to the banks. The postwar period was marked by a dramatic increase in reliance on bank borrowing, with stock financing declining from two-fifths of total funds in 1934–36 to less than one-tenth in 1945–53, and loans and discounts increasing from less than one-tenth in 1934–36 to considerably over one-half in 1946–53 (Goldsmith, 1983, pp. 142–43).

During much of the postwar period, relationships among the government, banks, and large corporations have been maintained through a kind of administered interdependence (Suzuki, 1980). Since capital was in chronic short supply, the government was able to ration credit among preferred institutions. Government-bank ties were reinforced through the practice of "overloans," in which banks themselves borrowed heavily from the government Bank of Japan in order to gain access to capital, which was then lent to large firms. Out of this emerged "window guidance"—moral suasion over amounts loaned by the banks to the banks' customers resulting from the Bank of Japan's position of power. The capital shortage naturally shaped banks' relationships with their corporate clients, as firms interested in expanding were forced to maintain tight business relationships with their banks by "overborrowing"—that is, borrowing beyond the company's current needs and depositing the surplus in the banks as a kind of side payment known as "compensating balances." Although financial deregulation in the 1970s and 1980s has changed these relationships in certain respects, as discussed below, this long period of interaction has institutionalized a general pattern of cooperation among capital suppliers and large corporate capital users that has remained in modified form to the present day.

The importance of large financial institutions has come not only in providing capital but also in looking out for the wide range of business interests of their industrial clients. Japanese businessmen put great emphasis on the main bank relationship. Status as the number one lending institution for a company carries with it the expectation that the bank will not only provide a significant portion of the firm's capital but will also look after its interests in a variety of ways. The main bank sends a signal to other banks about the financial health of the company, a role that Horiuchi, Packer, and Fukuda (1988) have termed a "delegated monitor" function. The main bank also ensures that the company is able to gain loans from other banks as well—a process known as "pump priming," or *yobi-mizu*. In 1975, for example, the Sumitomo Bank and the Mitsubishi Bank agreed to extend loans of ¥2 billion (somewhat over $5 million at the time) to the largest manufacturing companies in the other's group, Mitsubishi Heavy Industries and Sumitomo Metal Industries, on a mutual basis. This was reported to be a way to circumvent regulations enacted by the Ministry of Finance the previous year placing limits on the amounts banks were able to lend to a single customer (Okumura, 1983).

Bank assistance extends as well to helping its clients find business customers. A Sumitomo Bank executive explained as follows: "Sumitomo Metal Industries docs a lucrative business now selling sheet steel to the Matsushita companies, the Nissan companies, and Toyo Kogyo, among others. They enjoy this business because the bank provided a large part of the financing for these companies and acted as go-between to get this business for them. There are many, many arrangements such as this in the group" (quoted in *Business Week,* March 31, 1975).

Where the company does get involved in financial problems, the main bank is expected to come to its client's rescue. An example of this was provided by a manager formerly affiliated with Akai Electric, a major video and audio tape-deck manufacturer. Akai had during the early 1980s run into financial difficulties and was under financial reconstruction with bank support. It was Akai's main bank that took the lead in its reconstruction. This was Mitsubishi Bank, which owned 8 percent of Akai's shares and was the lender of 16 percent of its borrowed capital. As part of the assistance, Mitsubishi sent three people to Akai—the chief secretary to the president, the department manager in charge of international business operations, and the department manager for international finance—as well as extending additional loans to the company.[10]

In addition to their role as lenders, Japanese banks also maintain an additional source of influence over their client companies not enjoyed by U.S. commercial banks: the ability to take equity positions in other companies on their own account. Unlike banks in the United States, which are restricted by provisions of the Glass-Steagall Act, Japanese banks typically maintain holdings of several percent of most of their main client companies' stock.[11] The fact that banks have been able to both lend capital and hold equity positions has reinforced their central positions in Japanese capital markets, and they have aggressively expanded their client base while promoting internal coordination through joint councils and projects.

The capital market relationship is reciprocated from company to bank, as firms maintain a significant portion of their own capital in their banks in the form of deposits and equity shareholdings. Hamada and Horiuchi (1987) report that Japanese nonfinancial corporations held over 30 percent of their financial assets in the form of bank deposits during the period studied, 1954–83. Companies furthermore typically hold shares of the banks that lend to them, which they are able to use as collateral on their loans. The relationship between bank and client company extends even to employee accounts, as corporate customers often have employee wages automatically transferred to an account opened for each employee with the bank in lieu of cash payments. This practice has intensified recently with the emergence of firm banking— electronic data transmission systems between banks and their client firms.

As a result of these intertwined forces, there emerged during the postwar period what one set of observers aptly term a kind of "banking-industrial complex" in Japan, with transactions in capital taking place largely through close and longstanding business associations between banks and their clients rather than through impersonal capital markets: "At the risk of oversimplification, we may characterize the American financial system as a market-oriented system. The Japanese system had more administrative or organizational aspects to its capital allocation mechanism, and in some cases the line of demarcation between 'the company' and 'the market' was rather blurred" (Flaherty and Itami, 1984, p. 158).

Capital Markets and the Keiretsu

The maintenance of the central position of the group banks was ensured by the postwar economic reforms pushed by the U.S. occupation, which broke up the zaibatsu holding companies but not the zaibatsu banks. As a result and in conjunction with the Japanese government's policy of allocating scarce capital to the city banks through its own financial organs, these city banks reinforced their importance as the leading sources of capital for group companies and were in a position to give preference to their own long-standing clients. Groupings formed around these banks as companies were willing to forego a degree of independence in order to gain access to scarce-but-needed capital, particularly during the economic resurgence in the mid-1950s. Today we find that the large city banks associated with the six big intermarket keiretsu are the main banks for virtually all of their group companies, while other group financial institutions play an important secondary position. Figures 4.1 and 4.2 depict these relationships for the leading companies in two groups, Sumitomo and Dai-Ichi Kangyo Bank.

While the existence of close banking relationships is readily apparent in these figures, it is possible that strong banking ties exist among keiretsu firms and financial institutions in other groups as well. In order to evaluate this possibility, a transaction matrix was created for the two hundred industrial firms in our sample, based on the percentage of capital coming from firms' top-ten lenders broken down by group affiliation. These results are reported in Table 4.1 for the year 1986.

The boldface figures along the diagonal show the extent of internalization of borrowed capital to financial institutions in the same group. As we see here, intra-group capital proportions range from a low of 23.3 percent for Dai-Ichi Kangyo industrial firms to a high of 42.8 percent for Mitsubishi firms and 42.4 percent for Sumitomo firms. Most of the remaining debt capital for each group firm comes from "independent" financial institutions—an amalgamation of smaller commercial banks and insurance companies, as well as long-term credit banks. Capital linkages to financial institutions in other keiretsu account for a much smaller share of the total in each group. No single group is the source of more than 10 percent of the total capital borrowed by any other group, and in the case of Sumitomo group borrowing, the figure is zero in three cells (i.e., none of these ten companies count a Fuji-, Sanwa-, or Dai-Ichi Kangyo—affiliated financial institution among its top-ten creditors). It becomes quickly apparent from the transaction matrix that the hypothesis of substantial across-group ties in the loaned capital market does not hold for the shachō-kai firms in the sample.

The extent of bias toward affiliated financial institutions can be understood through a simple derivative measure, the preferential transaction ratio. This is calculated by dividing the share of same-group transactions

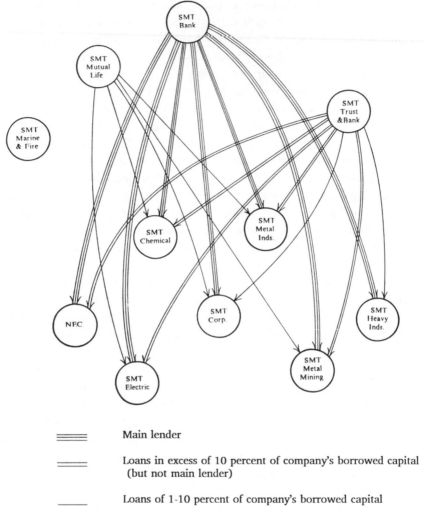

Main lender

Loans in excess of 10 percent of company's borrowed capital
(but not main lender)

Loans of 1-10 percent of company's borrowed capital

Fig. 4.1.   Intragroup Borrowing Dependency of the Leading Companies in the
Sumitomo Group. Source: Data from *Industrial Groupings in Japan* (1982).
Note: SMT = Sumitomo.

by the average for those in each of the other five groups. While internalization points to the absolute proportion of borrowing coming from
one's own group, the preferential transaction ratio looks specifically at
intra- versus intergroup relationships and the possibility not only that
firms prefer to borrow from their own group but also that they prefer to
use banks outside the other keiretsu (e.g., the Industrial Bank of Japan)

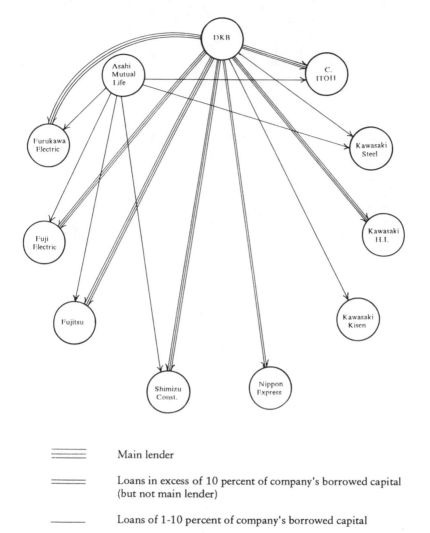

Fig. 4.2.   Intragroup Borrowing Dependency of the Leading Companies in the Dai-Ichi Kangyo Bank Group. Source: Data from *Industrial Groupings in Japan* (1982). Note: DKB = Dai-Ichi Kangyo Bank; H.I. = Heavy Industries.

for their nongroup capital. In total, firms in the six big keiretsu are about 15.1 times more likely to borrow capital from financial institutions in their own group than from those in another group. What this ratio makes clear is that the identity of keiretsu affiliation is itself important in defining patterns of transactions.

Next we consider the role of the keiretsu in organizing Japanese

TABLE 4.1. TRANSACTION MATRIX FOR BORROWED CAPITAL, INDUSTRIAL FIRMS, 1986

Affiliation of Industrial Borrower

Affiliation of Lending Institution	Mitsui (12)	Mitsubishi (12)	Sumitomo (10)	Fuji (13)	Sanwa (17)	Dai-Ichi Kangyo Bank (20)
Mitsui (3)	39.5	1.9	1.0	1.8	2.5	7.1
Mitsubishi (3)	1.0	42.8	2.9	4.3	4.8	4.5
Sumitomo (3)	3.0	3.5	42.4	5.3	1.6	4.2
Fuji (4)	0.5	0.7	0.0	26.6	8.9	3.2
Sanwa (2)	1.0	0.5	0.0	3.0	32.2	6.8
Dai-Ichi Kangyo Bank (2)	5.8	4.0	0.0	8.1	4.9	23.3
Other Banks (29)	49.2	46.5	53.8	51.0	45.0	50.9
Total	100.0%	100.0%	100.0%	100.0%	100.0%	100.0%

SOURCE: See Appendix A.

Note: Figures represent percentages among the top-ten lenders only. Number of sample companies is given in parentheses. Owing to rounding, columns may not add up to 100%.

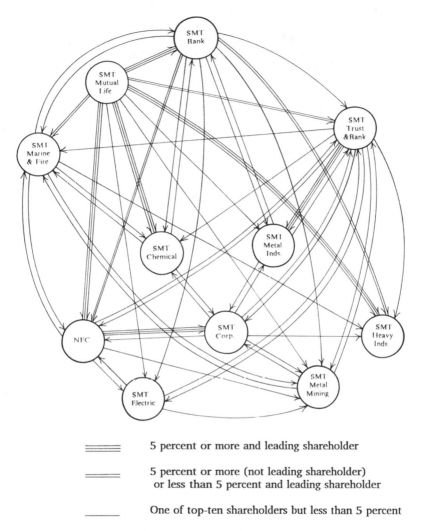

5 percent or more and leading shareholder

5 percent or more (not leading shareholder)
or less than 5 percent and leading shareholder

One of top-ten shareholders but less than 5 percent

Fig. 4.3. Stock Crossholdings of the Leading Companies in the Sumitomo Group (Top-Ten Shareholdings Only). Source: Data from *Industrial Groupings in Japan* (1982). Note: SMT = Sumitomo.

equity markets. Specific patterns of share crossholdings are shown in Figures 4.3 and 4.4 for the leading companies in the Sumitomo and Dai-Ichi Bank groups. The network of crossholdings among the eleven Sumitomo firms shown here is extremely dense, with 71 percent of the possible connections actually constituted.[12] At least four of the top-ten shareholders among each of these firms are other companies in the

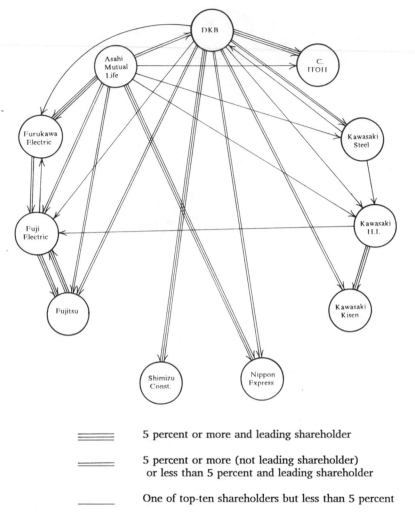

Fig. 4.4. Stock Crossholdings of the Leading Companies in the Dai-Ichi Kangyo Bank Group. Source: Data from *Industrial Groupings in Japan* (1982). Note: DKB = Dai-Ichi Kangyo Bank; H.I. = Heavy Industries.

group. The pattern that emerges for the Dai-Ichi Kangyo group is substantially different. Historical connections across the group as a whole have been largely through a single firm, Dai-Ichi Kangyo Bank. The current group is the amalgamation of several smaller groups that had associations with the former Dai-Ichi and Nippon Kangyo banks. Asahi Mutual Life, Furukawa Electric, Fuji Electric, and Fujitsu were all part of the smaller prewar Furukawa zaibatsu and maintain within the larger Dai-Ichi Kangyo group a subset of close relationships, with five of the six possible connections completed. Among the three firms associated with the Kawasaki zaibatsu—Kawasaki Steel, Kawasaki Heavy Industries, and Kawasaki Shipping—two of the three possible connections are completed. Overall density of the group is 40 percent.[13]

The leading eleven companies[14] within the other two zaibatsu groups, Mitsubishi and Mitsui, have densities of 69 percent and 58 percent, respectively, while the density in the Fuji group is 49 percent and that in Sanwa 45 percent. These findings conform to popular accounts of the cohesion of the various groups. Sumitomo is widely viewed to be, along with Mitsubishi, the most cohesive of the groups. Conversely, the three bank groups are all viewed as more loosely organized than their zaibatsu counterparts.

Table 4.2 shows the transaction matrix for shareholding among the financial and industrial firms in our sample in 1986. Internalization to own-group firms among companies' top-ten shareholders is over 25 percent for all six keiretsu and over 50 percent in the three zaibatsu groups. Shareholdings across keiretsu, in contrast, are generally small or nonexistent. Among shares issued by Sumitomo group companies, for example, less than 3 percent are held by Mitsui, Mitsubishi, Fuji, or Dai-Ichi Kangyo group firms. Equity control is, to a large extent, located among shareholders in the same group. Not surprisingly, preferential transaction ratios are also high. In total, companies in the six groups are 12.8 times more likely to have their shares held by other firms in the same group, a figure nearly as high as for bank borrowings.

It appears from these results that the keiretsu continue to be a major source of both debt and equity capital for their affiliated firms. As recently as 1986, these data demonstrate, shachō-kai member firms and particularly those in the ex-zaibatsu rarely cross boundaries to establish major equity or borrowing positions with firms in other groupings.

Continuity and Change in Japanese Corporate Finance

Over the past two decades, capital market liberalization in Japan has made available financial instruments not previously available to corporate borrowers. Firms are now free to raise investment funds through a variety of equity, bond, and hybrid mechanisms, and in both domestic and overseas markets. Many large Japanese companies have taken advantage of these opportunities, and the result has been a substantial decline in the proportion of external corporate capital coming from traditional sources such as long-term debt.

Observers now talk about the "dis-intermediation" of Japanese capi-

TABLE 4.2. TRANSACTION MATRIX FOR EQUITY SHAREHOLDINGS, FINANCIAL AND INDUSTRIAL FIRMS, 1986

Affiliation of Company Holding Shares	Affiliation of Company Issuing Shares					
	Mitsui (15)	Mitsubishi (15)	Sumitomo (13)	Fuji (17)	Sanwa (19)	Dai-Ichi Kangyo Bank (22)
Mitsui (15)	51.4	2.3	2.1	0.7	4.4	5.3
Mitsubishi (15)	1.6	63.4	0.9	4.0	4.7	4.4
Sumitomo (13)	1.6	2.2	63.9	3.7	3.9	2.8
Fuji (17)	0.0	1.5	2.2	38.1	4.8	4.4
Sanwa (19)	10.1	8.8	9.1	11.1	28.0	10.2
Dai-Ichi Kangyo Bank (22)	1.3	3.1	0.9	10.4	12.8	31.6
Other Cos. (137)	33.7	19.0	21.0	34.7	42.4	42.0
Total	100.0%	100.0%	100.0%	100.0%	100.0%	100.0%

SOURCE: See Appendix A.

Note: Figures represent percentages among the top-ten shareholders only. Number of sample companies is given in parentheses. Owing to rounding, columns may not add up to 100%.

tal markets with the rise of "direct" (securities-based) financing. More colloquially, the phrase *ginkō banare* is sometimes heard, implying the weaning of companies from their banks. The assumption is that these changes represent the elimination of the traditional role of financial institutions as conduits through which capital flows from household savers to corporate borrowers and the rise of more marketlike patterns of corporate finance. Just how extensive are these changes? And to what extent do they represent fundamental and long-term shifts in the underlying character of relationships between financial and nonfinancial corporations in Japan?

One way of measuring the effects of these changes is by looking at the relative share of external capital being provided by own-group financial institutions. Figure 4.5 shows time-lines for capital internalization among shachō-kai members based on data compiled by the Japan Federal Trade Commission and the data used in the present study. The JFTC studies have measured the extent of borrowing and shareholding since the late 1960s and show keiretsu relationships based on overall percentages of capital sourced within groups. The database used to compile the above figures is based on leading (top-ten) lenders and shareholders, and covers data from 1969 to 1986. Each of these sources, therefore, emphasizes somewhat different characteristics of the network. The JFTC data put financial sourcing in the context of firms' aggregate positions, and therefore include a large number of smaller lenders and shareholders. The database used for this study focuses only on major lending and shareholding positions (presumably those investors best able to form effective voting coalitions to influence corporate management) and has the advantage of including data on relationships *across* groupings.

Both measurement methods indicate that equity internalization is now substantially higher than debt internalization. The JFTC data report that this is part of a trend dating back at least to the mid-1960s. Since that time, firms have borrowed a declining share of their capital from financial institutions in their own group but relied on firms in their own group for an increasing proportion of equity capital. The two curves appear to have crossed sometime around 1970, the period at which our own sample data begin. The much higher internalization figures for both debt and equity in our sample when compared with the JFTC results reinforce the point that affiliated firms constitute a disproportionate share of leading capital positions. The percentages found in this sample also do not show a significant decline when compared with the 1970 period, nor do they indicate any increase in across-group

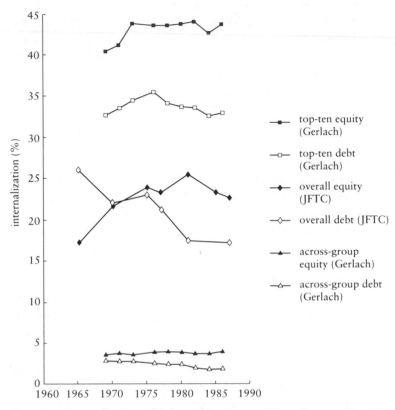

Fig. 4.5.   Internalization of Debt and Equity over Time. Sources: Kōsei Torihiki Iinkai survey data (various years); for information on other data, see Appendix A. Note: Across-group figures are taken as a weighted average.

holdings during this period. Although the JFTC data suggest some decline in equity internalization since the early 1980s, the figures for 1988 are still higher than those fifteen years earlier.

These findings indicate that keiretsu affiliates continue to be an important source of external capital for Japanese firms. They also suggest that financial liberalization in Japan has not had the effect of increasing the proportion of external capital coming from financial institutions affiliated with other groups. What, then, is one to make of the changes occurring in Japan's financial structure?

The widespread view that Japanese corporate finance has moved from "indirect" to "direct" financing is based on the traditional perspective within financial economics that household savers channel capital to corporations either directly, by entering the stock or bond market, or indirectly, by depositing it in banks that lend to companies. The reality in contemporary Japan is that even securities markets are mediated by large institutions linked through a complex set of strategic relationships with corporate users of capital. An actual revolution from indirect financing to direct financing would involve the discontinuation of the historically configured flow of money through indirect financing that tightly links corporations and financial institutions, and the advent of direct supply of savings (personal capital) to industry without passing through financial institutions.

That this has not been the case is evident in analyzing the actual pattern of the flow of funds rather than the mechanisms through which those funds travel. The ratio of individual shareholding in Japan has continued to decline and less than one-quarter of all shares in Japan are now held by individuals. Banks and insurance companies, in contrast, have continued to be net purchasers of securities (buying about 18 trillion shares and 16 trillion shares during the 1980s, respectively) and together now control nearly one-half of all publicly traded shares in Japan.[15] For this reason, when we examine the flow of capital through the Japanese economy, the vast majority continues to be mediated by financial institutions, as shown in Table 4.3. Although securities-based financing accounted for 44.2 percent of the total flow of funds through the corporate sector in 1987, all but a small fraction of this passed through financial institutions rather than being channeled directly from household savers or investment trusts into stocks and bonds. Together with credit-based financing that accounts for most of the remaining flow of funds, over 90 percent of total capital flows continue to be mediated by financial institutions into the late 1980s.

This gradual change in financing methods might have great significance if these financial institutions as purchasers of securities behaved quite differently than they do as financial lenders—for example, by becoming unstable stock market investors rather than stable lead banks. However, as empirical results in Chapter 3 demonstrated, equity ties among financial and nonfinancial companies continue to be structured in long-term relationships that reflect a complex set of strategic interests among the parties involved. These, therefore, continue to be administered rather than impersonal market transactions. Further indicating the continued role of keiretsu capital is the finding, reported in Figure 4.5, that the internalization of equity capital within the same group is now actually higher than for bank capital. Shifts toward equity capital

TABLE 4.3.   "INDIRECT" FINANCING
THROUGH THE JAPANESE SECURITIES MARKET—
EVIDENCE FROM FLOW OF FUNDS

	Flow of Funds		
	"Indirect" Financing		
Year	Total	Securities Investments	"Direct" Financing
1975	93.1%	22.3%	7.1%
1980	86.1%	25.9%	8.5%
1985	87.0%	29.0%	6.5%
1987	90.7%	37.5%	6.7%

SOURCE: *Securities Market in Japan 1990*, p. 3.
Notes: "Indirect" financing refers to funds raised through financial institutions. "Direct" financing refers to funds raised through non-mediated securities investments, including those raised through investment trusts. Foreign capital markets account for the remaining flow of funds in each year. These figures were −0.2% in 1975, 5.4% in 1980, 6.5% in 1985, and 2.6% in 1987.

would therefore seem actually to be working toward one of the *strengths* of the intermarket groups.

This is not to say that the shift in the nature of capital financing is unimportant. With the decreasing proportion of total capital allocation channeled through the traditional prime rate system, the Ministry of Finance and the Bank of Japan are no longer able to exercise the same degree of control over financial markets that they once could. It is also true that, with the new reliance on securities-based finance, Japan's major securities companies are now more important in financial markets than in the past. Furthermore, even as banks and other financial institutions account for an increasing share of securities-based capital, the ability of highly profitable industrial firms to fund their investments through retained earnings has reduced their overall external capital dependency and shifted the balance of bargaining power with lending firms in their direction.

However, the overall effects of these changes on the internal cohesion of Japan's intermarket groups are not nearly as dramatic as they might at first appear. Even as they retire their own debt, large firms continue to rely on banks to provide loans for their affiliates. For example, Mitsubishi Motors, which was spun off from Mitsubishi Heavy Industries in 1970 with the equity participation of Chrysler Motors, continues twenty years later to use the same financial institutions as its parent company. Among the top-ten lenders to Mitsubishi Heavy Industries, eight are also among Mitsubishi Motors' top-ten lenders, and both firms use the same main bank, Mitsubishi. Even for smaller companies, parent companies serve as an important source of bank capital by introducing and guaranteeing their bank borrowings. In an analysis of satellite firms affiliated with major electronics producers, for example, I found that 68 percent used the same main bank as their parent company (Gerlach, 1992b).

Japanese securities companies are themselves linked through long-term relationships with their industrial clients. Although not generally as closely identified with well-defined keiretsu as the city banks or as widely recognized, these affiliations are not unimportant. Among the Sumitomo group's twenty core companies, for example, all but four rely on Daiwa Securities as their lead underwriter as of 1989, and all but one of these companies has done so for the past two decades. Daiwa Securities is linked in turn into the Sumitomo group by virtue of the fact that its two leading shareholders and reference banks are Sumitomo Bank and Sumitomo Trust and Banking.[16]

In addition, the "securitization" of Japanese capital markets has actually been in the interests of Japan's commercial banks in at least one important respect. Since the mid-1980s, Japanese banks have been under new regulatory pressures, especially in order to meet BIS requirements for minimum capital ratios.[17] These requirements have forced the banks to raise new equity capital, and they have been among the most active participants in stock issues. During the six years from 1984 to 1990, Japan's twenty-three largest banks raised ¥13.5 trillion in equity capital, an amount that represented a substantial fraction of all new equity capital raised in Japan during this period (*Wall Street Journal,* March 18, 1991).[18] Moreover, the basic pattern of interlocking shareholding has continued, with nonfinancial firms utilizing approximately 30–40 percent of their own new capital to purchase bank equity issues and maintain their stable crossholdings (*Nihon keizai shinbun,* October 24, 1989). In this way, the demands for equity-based financing have served both nonfinancial and financial interests while limiting disruption to traditional ownership relationships.

In short, because of their central role as providers of both loan-based and securities-based capital, Japanese banks remain the main source of external capital for most major Japanese corporations. Even those firms that have retired their debt and rely heavily on internal profits to fund investment activities continue to have these financial institutions as leading shareholders, granting them the attendant rights to vote shares and monitor management. Moreover, insofar as debt continues to be channeled to the affiliates of these corporations, the total dependency of vertical keiretsu chains of suppliers and distributors on these banks in most cases is still very high. Indeed, Japan's banks actually increased their loans in the 1980s at a rate that was higher than the growth rate of the economy as a whole, and by the end of the 1980s, most of the world's largest banks were Japanese.[19] This suggests a different interpretation of the changing nature of the keiretsu: what may be happening is not a breaking down of bank-led groupings so much as an expansion of these groupings across a broader spectrum of Japanese industry; their increasing organization within elaborate hierarchical structures around local centers of power (the parent companies); and their linking through securities-related instruments of finance and control.

THE FLOW OF DIRECTORS

Among the most studied areas of interorganizational relationships in the United States has been that of interlocking directorates—connections among firms in business networks through the sharing of executive position holders. Applying this same approach in order to induce alliance structures in Japan presents a number of interesting and different features that shed light on the nature of corporate control over the Japanese firm and the ways in which it is embedded in interfirm networks. These features may be summarized as follows: First, directorships in Japan are associated with a broader system of interfirm personnel flows known as *shukkō*, or employee transfers. Instead of serving as part-time directors, executives moving from one firm to another typically take up full-time positions in the recipient firm. The pattern of movement of personnel between firms indicates that the dispatching process serves to reinforce specific relationships between firms rather than the more general interests the firm might have in monitoring its environment. Second, the dispatching of directors most often expresses a vertical relationship, with the flow of directors moving unidirectionally from one organization to another. Three vertical relationships predominate: government-company, parent company–satellite, and bank-client. Third, as a result of the first two features, outside directorships among keiretsu firms are limited largely to other group firms, but the overall intragroup network is sparse in comparison to what we might expect from the dense patterns of equity crossholdings.

Interfirm Personnel Connections in Japan:
Outside Directorships versus Employee Transfers

In the prewar zaibatsu, an important source of control by the honsha over its subsidiaries was through directors sent out to those firms. By 1945 Mitsui honsha held twenty-one directorships in its subsidiaries, Sumitomo fifty-one, and Mitsubishi eighty-five, or an average of about two to four directors per first-line subsidiary (Miyazaki, 1976). With the postwar democratization of large-scale enterprise in Japan came the belief that boards should represent interests other than those of capital and, in particular, of the families that controlled and benefited from the zaibatsu. Changes in the Commercial Code in 1950 allowed nonshareholders to become directors, and this has evolved into a system whereby directors are full-time executives of the firm with interests like those of management rather than those of representatives of external shareholders. Clark (1979) notes in his case study of a Japanese firm that

> the board has much more the look of a senior management meeting than of the convocation of the representatives of the shareholders. Most of the directors have responsibility for running part of the company, and are not in an ideal position objectively to review the performance of a management which includes themselves and their senior and junior colleagues. . . . Becoming a director, therefore, was a precondition of future progress in the standard ranks, rather than the acquisition of a new role, entirely different from that of an employee. [Pp. 100, 108.]

Over 90 percent of the boards of large Japanese firms are now composed of full-time managers (Ballon et al., 1976; Bacon and Brown, 1978) and better than two-fifths of all firms have no outside directors. The result is a system in which the board of directors takes on largely ceremonial functions (see Chapter 7) instead of serving as a forum for the representation of owner interests.[20] The following comment by one board member was typical: "Not that much is discussed at the board meeting. It is after the meeting that we talk about various things."

But the predominance of full-time managers as directors is also significant because not all of them began their careers in the same company. A large portion have moved from one firm to another by mutual agreement. Inohara (1972, p. 5) reports that an average of more than three hundred employees in each of the three large companies he studied (all had more than five thousand employees) had been sent to other firms. Most involved younger employees and were only temporary transfers. These typically lasted for two years, during which the dispatching firm guaranteed the employee's salary. But a smaller fraction of the total were employees in their early fifties who were unlikely to be promoted to the director level in their own firm before retirement. When upper-level executives are dispatched to other firms, it is usually on a permanent basis with the employee taking on an executive position in his new firm. Where these employees become officers or directors of the recipient firm, they are known as *haken yakuin*, or dispatched directors. As a result of transfers, about one-third of the directors of Japan's major corporations now come in from the outside, compared to the United States where outside directors constitute over two-thirds of the total.[21]

The distinctive feature of this form of directorship is that, in contrast to the U.S. model in which the director is truly "outside"—that is, the directorship is a part-time position and connections to another organization are maintained—the dispatched director in Japan becomes a full-time employee in the receiving firm. These generally represent long-standing and multistranded interorganizational linkages and serve the interests of management in two firms at once as part of an ongoing relationship between the firms. Nearly all dispatching firms—86 percent in one study (Kōsei Torihiki Iinkai, 1983b)—are simultaneously among the recipient firm's top-ten shareholders. This relationship is further supported by the efforts dispatching firms make to maintain connections with their transfers. Inohara (1972, p. 18) reports that one company maintained a special consultation room open to transferees in its own office, continued to invite them to the company's "friendship organization" (*kōyū-kai*) and other activities, and sent them regular information about the company, as well as congratulatory and condolence messages.

Dispatched Directorships as an Expression of Vertical Interfirm Relationships

In addition to reinforcing ongoing relationships among firms, the dispatched directorship system in Japan is also distinctive in the predominant type of relationship which it expresses. This is a vertical one between two asymmetrically positioned firms, typically between one of three sets of organizations: government-corporation, parent company–satellite, and bank-client. This contrasts sharply with the image in the United States of interlocks across horizontally positioned firms for the purposes of diffusing information or reinforcing broader community- or class-wide interests (Useem, 1984).

According to figures provided in *Industrial Groupings in Japan* (1982, p. 23), of the 2,980 outside directors moving to a firm that is listed on the Tokyo Stock Exchange, 30 percent came from government, 35 percent came from manufacturing concerns and from trading companies, and 35 percent came from banks. Outside directors coming from government are generally from one of the government ministries and organizations most closely associated with a firm's own business—the Ministry of International Trade and Industry (MITI) for manufacturing concerns, the Ministry of Finance (MoF), the Bank of Japan for financial institutions, and so on. The process of moving from government agency to corporate position is referred to as "descending from heaven" (*amakudari*). These officials are required to retire formally from their government position, then spend a two-year grace period before being adopted into their new position. Informal connections with their old organization, of course, typically remain.

Directorship connections between firms are most likely to involve parent companies and their satellites and banks and their clients. Within the large vertical keiretsu, representative directors are usually dispatched from the parent manufacturer to its subcontractors. Toyota Motors, for example, sends an average of three to six representative directors to each of its first-line satellites, as do Nissan, Hitachi, Matsushita, and other large parent industrial concerns (from data in *Industrial Groupings in Japan*, 1982). Banks are less likely to send more than one director to a company, unless the company is undergoing restructuring with bank assistance. They do, however, send directors to a wide range of companies and are the firms most likely to dispatch directors to large companies. Nearly half of all outside directors among these companies come from their group bank (Kōsei Torihiki Iinkai, 1983b, p. 12). As a result of the vertical relationship implied in these directorship interlocks, it is the largest firms in the Japanese economy that are overall most likely to be the dispatchers. The *Oriental Economist* (December, 1982) found that the 182 shachō-kai member companies at the time sent over one-half of the dispatched directors among the 1,600 firms listed on the Tokyo Stock Exchange.

The Keiretsu and Directorship Networks

The distinctive features of directorship connections outlined above have resulted in group directorship networks with two main structural features. First, the fact that directors typically become full-time employees in the recipient firm and reinforce ongoing relationships between firms rather than more general interests in the wider business community has made the identity of sender and receiver a particularly critical issue. Since ongoing relationships are more likely to be with other firms in the same group, outside directorship connections are heavily internalized and there is a strong bias toward one's own group. At the same time, the hierarchical relationship implied by directorship connections in Japan has resulted in relatively few directorship connections among large firms in favor of connections vertically from larger to smaller firms. Within the intermarket groups, which are composed almost entirely of larger firms, this has meant sparse patterns of connections in comparison with the dense patterns found in equity interlocks.[22]

One source, *Nihon kigyō shūdan bunseki* (1977, vol. 1, pp. 124–26), provides a detailed list of outside directorships for the extended Sumitomo group that indicates both original positions of directors and their positions in the recipient firm. An analysis of these directorships indicates that of the total of 160 directorships among Sumitomo companies, 122, or 76 percent, were dispatched from a shachō-kai member firm to a satellite firm in the group—sometimes in the position of president or chairman of the satellite—while only 38, or 24 percent, moved from one shachō-kai member to another.[23] Specific patterns of interlocks are shown for the Sumitomo and Dai-Ichi Kangyo groups, in Figures 4.6 and 4.7. Intragroup networks in the Sumitomo group are particularly sparse, while linkages within the Dai-Ichi Kangyo group are primarily through the bank.

Although directorship interlocks are infrequent among large firms, Table 4.4 makes evident that, when outside directors are brought in, they are most likely to come from another firm in the same group. Altogether, over one-half of outside directors come in from other companies in the firm's own group. Of the remainder, nearly all are amakudari directors from government. In only five cases overall, and only one among the three zaibatsu groups, do outside directors come from a company in another group. For this reason, the preferential transaction ratio is very high, averaging 21.9 times among those firms that have outside directors. In short, outside directorships are infrequent among the largest

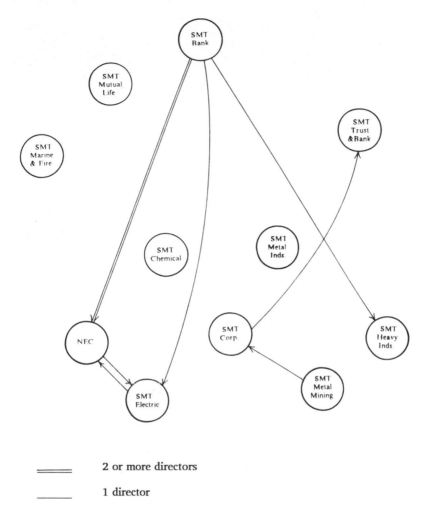

═══	**2 or more directors**
───	**1 director**

Fig. 4.6. Dispatched Directors of the Leading Companies in the Sumitomo Group. Source: Data from *Industrial Groupings in Japan* (1982). Note: SMT = Sumitomo.

firms, but where they exist they are most likely to involve other firms in the same group.

INTERMEDIATE PRODUCT MARKETS

No doubt the most controversial issue in understanding the role of keiretsu organization in the Japanese economy is its impact on product market trade. Given the strong preferential patterns demonstrated ear-

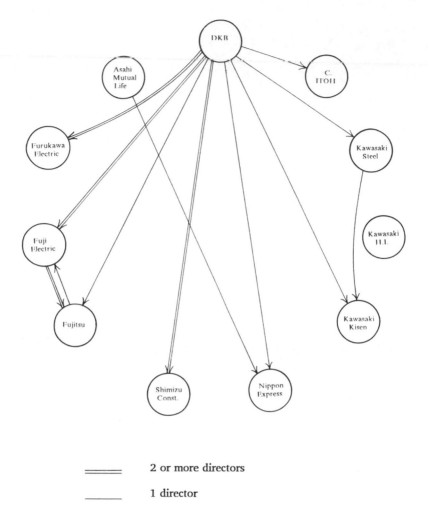

                    2 or more directors

                    1 director

Fig. 4.7. Dispatched Directors of the Leading Companies in the Dai-Ichi Kangyo Bank Group. Source: Data from *Industrial Groupings in Japan* (1982). Note: DKB = Dai-Ichi Kangyo Bank; H.I. = Heavy Industries.

lier in networks of borrowed capital, corporate ownership, and director-ships, it should not be surprising if the keiretsu are also involved in structuring linkages within intermediate product markets. As we see below, however, internalization tends to be lower in product trade than in other relationships and varies substantially according to the type of company involved. Nevertheless, the overall pattern is clearly not one of trading neutrality. In this section, we consider the extent of keiretsu structuring of product trade through direct purchases and sales (e.g., a

TABLE 4.4. TRANSACTION MATRIX FOR DISPATCHED DIRECTORS, 1980

Affiliation of Sending Company	Affiliation of Company Receiving Director(s)					
	Mitsui (5)	Mitsubishi (15)	Sumitomo (8)	Fuji (13)	Sanwa (13)	Dai-Ichi Kangyo Bank (16)
Mitsui (15)	48.0	0.0	0.0	7.7	0.0	0.0
Mitsubishi (15)	0.0	60.4	0.0	0.0	0.0	3.6
Sumitomo (13)	0.0	6.7	67.1	2.6	0.0	0.0
Fuji (17)	0.0	0.0	0.0	25.9	0.0	0.0
Sanwa (19)	0.0	0.0	0.0	7.7	36.2	0.8
Dai-Ichi Kangyo Bank (22)	0.0	2.2	0.0	4.1	23.6	38.7
Other Cos. (137)	52.0	30.7	11.5	46.4	40.3	53.7
Govt. Orgns.	0.0	0.0	21.4	6.1	0.0	1.0
Total	100.0%	100.0%	100.0%	100.0%	100.0%	100.0%

SOURCE: See Appendix A.
Note: Number of sample companies is given in parentheses. Owing to rounding, columns may not add up to 100%.

steel company's purchase of a mining company's coal), and in the next section we expand the analysis to include collaborative group projects among affiliated companies.[24]

The main actor in the organization of product market relationships of both kinds has been the group trading companies. The sōgō shōsha are to the keiretsu trading network what banks are to its capital networks— the most centrally positioned firms, with direct linkages to most other companies in the group. For the majority of intermediate product manu-facturers in a keiretsu, they are the leading overall supplier and customer. Moreover, they are important as an organizer of small- and large-scale group projects.

The sōgō shōsha have been critical in the historical development of the Japanese economy. By 1900 Mitsui Bussan alone handled about one-third of Japan's foreign trade. As was the case with banks, the emergence of trading companies was closely tied to that of the zaibatsu themselves:

> The general trading companies developed best when they were part of a *zaibatsu*. Those that were started independently of the *zaibatsu* either did not succeed or remained small. The *zaibatsu* was a system that provided them with ample capital and security as well as with room for initiative. And the name of the *zaibatsu* assured them also of qualified personnel because of the prestige and power the *zaibatsu* name involved. [Hirschmeier and Yui, 1975, p. 192.]

A more recent example of this interdependent development can be seen in the case of a postwar start-up, Sumitomo Corporation. This general trading company was begun in the mid-1950s by the Sumitomo group from the fragments of a small prewar trading company in order to provide an alternative to the dominant position in international trade held by the huge trading houses of Mitsui and Mitsubishi. It grew dramatically thereafter through the advantages it enjoyed in the Sumi-tomo group, including large loans from Sumitomo Bank and preferential trade with other group companies. In a thirty-year period, it moved from an insignificant position in the economy to the fifth-largest firm in Japan as measured by sales (and sixteenth-largest when measured by assets).

Even today, the sōgō shōsha are Japan's *sekai kigyō*, or "world corpo-rations." They handle a significant portion of domestic trade[25] and are the leading intermediary in international trade. In the mid-1970s they exported over 70 percent of all Japanese iron and steel products and 70 percent of machinery products and handled nearly half of machinery imports (*Wall Street Journal*, July 18, 1983).

There have been periodic reports of the impending decline of the sōgō shōsha since the early 1960s, when Misonō Hitoshi published an influential article, "Is the Sun Setting on the Sōgō Shōsha?" ("Sōgō shōsha wa shayō de aru-ka," *Mainichi Economist,* May 1961). More recent concerns were expressed in the early 1980s when the Japanese business community began talking about "the era of winter," after the title of a bestseller at the time which predicted severe difficulties in the years ahead for the trading companies. As evidence of this, percentages of sales handled by the sōgō shōsha had declined by 10 to 20 percent in a number of major industries. But a revival seemed well under way by 1985, when sales of all major trading companies were up and four of the six leading sōgō shōsha reported record profits (*Japan Times,* May 25, 1985).

Nevertheless, while reports of its demise appear exaggerated, the role of the trading firm is changing with the ongoing restructuring of Japan's economy away from heavy, industrial, and capital-intensive products toward lighter, consumer, and knowledge-intensive industries. The proportion of group trade conducted by the sōgō shōsha and group companies involved in heavy and industrial versus light and consumer product markets is shown for the Mitsubishi and Mitsui groups in Table 4.5. The companies that are involved in newer fields (particularly Toshiba, Toyota, Mitsubishi Electric, and Kirin) have gained on their own the overseas experience and networks that have been the trading company's advantage. Moreover, these products depend less on another of the historical strengths of the sōgō shōsha: trading in large volumes and capitalizing on small price differentials across markets.

Instead of moving into newer industries as trading agents, the sōgō shōsha are increasingly shifting their attention toward global information acquisition, representing client firms in multiparty negotiations, and arranging projects among group companies. The information-center role was outlined by an executive in the Sumitomo Corporation as follows: "Ultimately, the sōgō shōsha should become a sort of multinational corporation with its subsidiaries and affiliates operating in widely diversified industries throughout the world. It should play the role of a satellite: gathering, relaying and transmitting necessary information on economic and human activities, as well as money, goods and resources." The satellite metaphor is a good one, as the sōgō shōsha have recently been taking a leading role in arranging projects involving telecommunications and satellite technology. Two of the leading sōgō shōsha, Mitsubishi Corporation and Mitsui and Co., have teamed up with other companies in their respective groups to enter NASA's space program (*Japan Times,* October 11, 1983) and have been leading organizers of intragroup communications networks and information systems.

The sōgō shōsha are now involved in a wide range of functions that

TABLE 4.5.   PERCENTAGE OF GROUP TRADE
CONDUCTED THROUGH THE GROUP TRADING
COMPANY FOR SELECTED COMPANIES
IN THE MITSUBISHI AND MITSUI GROUPS

	Sales	Purchases
Heavy Industries		
Mitsubishi Heavy Industries	55	27
Mitsubishi Oil	25	35
Mitsubishi Metals	22	38
Mitsubishi Chemicals	26	41
Mitsubishi Aluminum	75	100
Mitsui Shipbuilding	75	18
Mitsui Petrochemicals	65	50
Hokkaido Colliery	68	55
Mitsui Metal Mining	33	31
Component-Assembly and Consumer Industries		
Mitsubishi Electric	20	15
Nippon Kogaku (Nikon cameras)	7	11
Kirin Beer	0	23
Toshiba	15	5
Sanki Electric	9	4
Nippon Flour Milling	28	1
Toyota Motors	1	1

SOURCE: Data from Okumura (1983, p. 138).

facilitate interfirm trade: searches for and negotiations with trading and joint venture partners, equity participation in resulting projects, ongoing import, export, and other sales business, and post-import financing for final sellers. For example, C. Itoh, which served in the late 1960s as mediator in negotiations for the partial acquisition of Isuzu Motors by General Motors, then teamed up with these two firms through an equity investment to form a new company for the manufacture of automobile speed variators and gas turbines. Within the keiretsu, the sōgō shōsha are the leading organizer of intragroup cooperative projects. As part of an extended annual review of the activities of each group, *Keiretsu no kenkyū* provides a summary of major projects involving two or more firms from the same group. Considering only the Sumitomo group, we find that of twenty-five projects involving Sumitomo group companies in the years 1982–84, the group's trading company, Sumitomo Corporation, was a major participant in seventeen.

Intermediate Product Trade in the Keiretsu

Determination of the role of the keiretsu in intermediate product trade is more complicated than for the other business relationships studied here. Accurate statistics on overall intragroup patterns of trade are difficult to obtain because companies often consider this information to be sensitive or proprietary. In addition, the extent of internalization varies substantially among firms, with vertical keiretsu or other relationships of far greater importance for many companies than the intermarket keiretsu, particularly for those firms involved in complex-assembly industries.

There is certainly abundant anecdotal evidence that preferential trading does take place. One early source, the *Oriental Economist* (July 1959), reported that in the late 1950s Sumitomo Metal Mining (the direct descendant of Sumitomo's main Besshi mine) sold 60 percent of its copper output to Sumitomo Electric Industries and Sumitomo Metal Industries, while Sumitomo Electric filled 80 percent of its copper requirements with supplies originating from Sumitomo Metal Mining. In the 1970s, an article in *Business Week* (March 31, 1975) said that Sumitomo Metal Industries continued to rely on Sumitomo Corporation to sell 47 percent of its output and quoted Sumitomo Metal Mining's president as saying that 39 percent of his companies' products were going to other Sumitomo group companies that year.

The preference group companies give to others in their group has sometimes been a source of problems in joint ventures with foreign partners. One case where this came up, which was related by a consultant who had been part of the negotiations, involved a foreign manufacturer and a partner in the Mitsubishi group in a dispute over the pricing policy for supplies in their automobile parts joint venture. The Japanese managers in the venture wanted to use Mitsubishi group companies wherever possible to supply steel, plastics, and other materials, whereas the U.S. manager wanted to buy on the open market. A resolution was finally effected through the intervention and personal influence of the Japanese head of the joint venture—a distinguished retiree from another Mitsubishi group firm—who went directly to the Mitsubishi companies and was able to influence them to come down to competitive rates. The

TABLE 4.6.   TRADE
IN INTERMEDIATE PRODUCTS

	Zaibatsu Groups	Bank Groups	Total
Internalization	12%	6%	10%
			11% (a)
			16% (b)
Preferential transaction ratio	7	1.7	3
			3 (a)

SOURCES: Figures are calculated from data provided in Imai (1982, p. 59), using percentages of tie-up contracts. Other figures are calculated from data provided by (a) Rotwein (1964, p. 66), for trade measured by principal transaction partners, and (b) Sakamoto (1983, p. 153), for trade measured by estimated total sales and purchases.

purchases would still come through the same affiliated firms, only they would reflect something closer to the prevailing market price.

A number of studies have tried to utilize more rigorous measures of intragroup trade, as reported in Table 4.6. Estimates of the overall internalization of trade using data from the three sources cited here vary between 10 percent and 16 percent. Preferential transaction ratios can be calculated from data provided in two of these studies; both show that group companies are about three times more likely to engage in trade with companies in their own group than with those in other groups. Similar results are arrived at by using the data in this study on the identity of leading trading partners. These are derived from information on companies that serve as major suppliers and customers to other companies. Information on these companies is provided in *Kaisha nenkan*, based on firms' annual reports and other records. From these data, we are able to create a transactions matrix of major business relationships, as shown in Table 4.7. Overall internalization is again low in comparison with the earlier network relationships analyzed, ranging from 6.4 to 15.2 percent. Preferential transaction ratios are about 2.8 times, close to those found in other studies.

These results can be misleading, however, when we are trying to understand the overall importance of intercorporate affiliations in Japanese product markets. This is for two reasons. First, major companies in assembly- and service-intensive industries, such as motor vehicles and electrical appliances, rely on their own network of smaller upstream

TABLE 4.7. TRANSACTION MATRIX FOR
LEADING TRADING PARTNERS, 1980

Affiliation of Trading Partner	Affiliation of Industrial Company					
	Mitsui (11)	Mitsubishi (10)	Sumitomo (10)	Fuji (9)	Sanwa (18)	Dai-Ichi Kangyo Bank (20)
Mitsui (15)	**14.3**	3.2	2.8	2.7	3.9	5.3
Mitsubishi (15)	3.5	**15.2**	5.4	7.1	4.7	5.7
Sumitomo (13)	1.5	2.2	**12.8**	1.9	2.9	2.6
Fuji (17)	4.4	2.5	4.6	**8.4**	6.6	3.4
Sanwa (19)	4.0	1.7	2.2	3.2	**6.4**	4.3
Dai-Ichi Kangyo Bank (22)	6.2	10.3	6.5	9.0	8.2	**13.2**
Other (137)	66.1	64.9	65.7	67.7	67.4	65.5
Total	100.0%	100.0%	100.0%	100.0%	100.0%	100.0%

SOURCE: See Appendix A.

Note: Number of sample companies is given in parentheses. Owing to rounding, columns may not add up to 100%.

suppliers and downstream distributors for the bulk of their product market transactions. Affiliated firms are typically organized within vertical rather than intermarket keiretsu and are classified as "independent" companies in the studies cited above. Second, the figures reported here refer to direct trade among companies and exclude the role of the sōgō shōsha.

Kotabe (1989) presents detailed data on the sales and purchasing activities of a major electronics firm, disguised in his study as "Takeshita Kogyo." Kotabe finds that this firm relied on shachō-kai firms in its own intermarket group for only 1.6 percent of its total purchases, most of these from the group trading company and several raw material and heavy equipment producers. Total sales to these firms were 1.9 percent, the majority to the group financial institutions and steel company. In contrast, about 40 percent of its total purchases came from affiliated supplier firms and fully 90 percent of its semiconductor sales passed through two captive distributors in its vertical keiretsu. As we see in Chapter 6, high levels of internalization within vertical keiretsu relationships are also typical in the automobile industry.

Preferential trading within the major groupings is far more prevalent among sōgō shōsha and other types of companies, especially those in intermediate product markets. Estimates of the overall share of sales among the zaibatsu successor companies that is channeled through the group trading firm range somewhere between 20 and 30 percent.[26] More precise information can be obtained for relationships between the sōgō shōsha and major steel companies from a series of volumes, entitled *Sōgō shōsha nenkan,* published annually between 1972 and 1985. The results of a series of analyses utilizing these data are reported in Figures 4.8 through 4.10.

Figure 4.8 shows the extent to which trading companies manage the transactions of the steel companies with which they are most closely affiliated. As these figures demonstrate, the extent to which supply and sales representation is identified with affiliated companies varies greatly. At one extreme, over 90 percent of the steel involved in domestic transactions managed by Sumitomo Corporation is supplied by Sumitomo Metal Industries, and over 70 percent in overseas transactions. At the other extreme, C. Itoh relies on Kawasaki Steel to supply only 20 percent of the steel that it sells in both markets. This appears to reflect, once again, the relatively weak coherence of firms affiliated with the Dai-Ichi Kangyo Bank group. Preferential transaction ratios (calculated from transaction matrices not reported here) also vary, but in most cases are

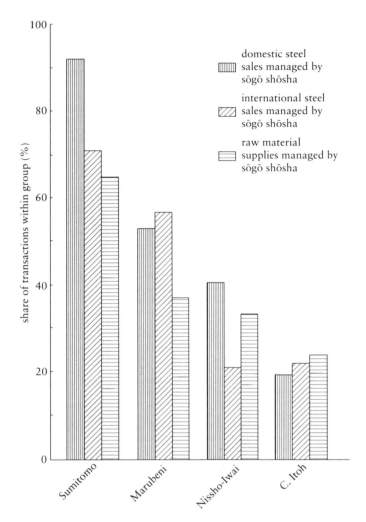

Fig. 4.8. Sōgō Shōsha Sales and Purchases from Affiliated Steel Companies, 1983. Source: *Sōgō shōsha nenkan* (1985).

over 3 : 1. On average, the trading companies are about five times more likely to handle raw materials for their affiliated steel companies and about fifteen times more likely to manage the steel output of those companies.

These figures also indicate two other points of significance. First, the sōgō shōsha/steel company relationship is of nearly equal importance in both domestic and international transactions. This reflects an important consideration in understanding the internationalization of the Japanese

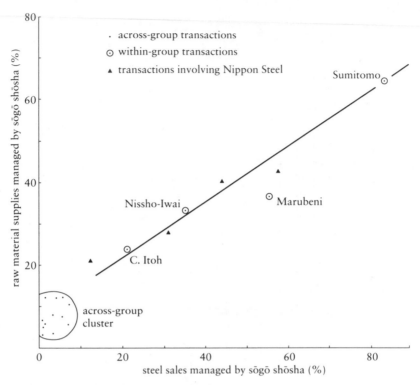

Fig. 4.9. Business Reciprocity Between Sōgō Shōsha and Steel Companies, 1983. Source: *Sōgō shōsha nenkan* (1985).

firm: *overseas business relationships follow patterns of domestic relationships.* Second, supply and sales representation relationships move together, with close ties in upstream markets associated with close ties in downstream markets. That is, *business transactions are based on clear patterns of reciprocal trading.*

Further evidence that supply and sales representation relationships are reciprocally linked is provided in Figure 4.9. These data report trading patterns among all five of Japan's major steel companies and the same four trading companies. In the far upper right-hand corner, Sumitomo Corporation relies on Sumitomo Metal Industries as a customer for about 65 percent of its raw material (iron ore and coking coal) sales and as a supplier for over 80 percent of its steel. Figures for the other three trading companies and their affiliated steel companies are, respectively, 37 percent and 55 percent for Marubeni and NKK, 34 percent and

31 percent for Nissho-Iwai and Kobe, and 24 percent and 21 percent for C. Itoh and Kawasaki. In contrast, both supply and sales representation relationships are minimal across groups, as indicated in the cluster in the lower left-hand corner. That this pattern of reciprocal trading also takes place among "non-keiretsu" firms is evident in the business relationships of Nippon Steel, Japan's largest and most independent steel company. As with other steel manufacturers, when Nippon Steel's purchases of raw materials for a trading company increase, so too does its use of the same company in managing its domestic and overseas sales.

Figure 4.10 shows how keiretsu-based trading relationships among these companies have evolved over the period in which the *Sōgō shōsha nenkan* volumes provide data. With the exception of a proportional drop in sales representation of Kawasaki Steel by C. Itoh in the late 1970s, the share of sales has proven strikingly stable. Throughout this period, the average share of across-group transactions (the dotted line at the bottom) has remained quite low. Once again, the results indicate that long-term, preferential relationships represent a durable and continuing characteristic of Japan's intercorporate network structures.

GROUP-WIDE ACTIVITIES: THE SYMBOLS AND CEREMONIES OF ALLIANCE

Symbolically significant group-wide activities within the keiretsu serve to establish a framework within which group interaction can take place. These both establish a sense of coherent identity for group members and, just as important, position the group as a whole within the larger business community. The presidents' council represents one important symbolic framework within which group cohesion is created, but in addition, each of the keiretsu has moved into a variety of industrial, public-relations, and social activities that bring together group companies as a collective social unit.

The Symbolic Role of Industrial Projects

Where joint projects involving group firms expand to include most or all of the core companies in the group, their significance extends beyond a smaller subset of companies to take in the group as a whole. Among the twenty-five projects involving the Sumitomo group cited in *Keiretsu no kenkyū* for 1982–84, nearly half involved more than three group companies, and some brought together most or all of the core group mem-

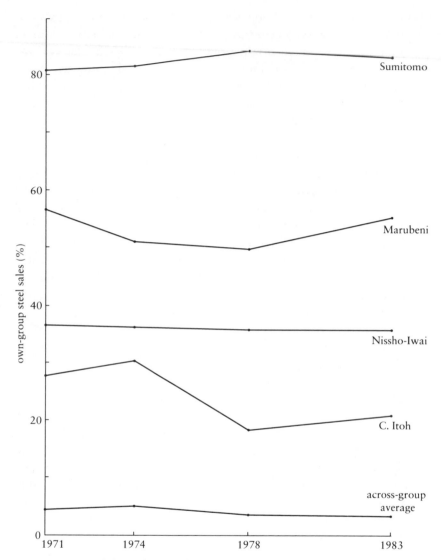

Fig. 4.10. Durability of Sōgō Shōsha–Steel Company Transactions. Source: *Sōgō shōsha nenkan* (1972, 1975, 1980, 1985).

bers. While the symbolic content of group-wide activities is perhaps more readily apparent in other group activities, even ostensibly instrumental business projects such as joint industrial investments often appear to be more important for establishing the position of the group within the larger business community than for pursuing their immediate economic interests.

The evidence for this is found in the fact that group-wide industrial projects, even in major industries such as atomic energy and overseas petroleum development, have nearly all remained limited in size and scope. Within the Sumitomo group, for example, the largest joint project, Sumitomo Atomic Energy, employs only thirty people, and its asset value (¥ 2.3 billion) puts it at well under 1 percent of the total asset value of any of its core investing Sumitomo companies (data from *Industrial Groupings in Japan,* 1982). Rather than grow into large operations in their own right or produce breakthrough technologies, group industrial projects tend to serve as a focus for the resources and technologies already existing among group firms.

The symbolic importance of collaborative projects in the status competition among groups is further evident in the way in which group projects have tended to spring up almost simultaneously in highly visible and currently popular fields. This is seen in the project waves that marked the period 1957–73, shown for the three former zaibatsu groups in Table 4.8.

The first wave of group projects began in the late 1950s, when Japan was seeking alternatives to imported oil as a source of energy and each of the three groups moved into the field of atomic power. This was an important event in the postwar history of the groups, as it was the first time since the dissolution that the companies involved had cooperated as a group on a systematic task. The intragroup ownership structure for Sumitomo's atomic energy project as of 1980 is shown in Figure 4.11.

After a series of smaller ventures in the information industries in the late 1960s, the groups moved into the next major wave in the early 1970s in domestic and overseas development projects. Mitsubishi was the leader this time, starting Mitsubishi Development in 1970 to celebrate its centennial anniversary, with thirty-two companies participating. This was a decade of heady growth for Japan, as seen in then Prime Minister Tanaka Kakuei's plan to "remodel the Japanese archipelago," with the resulting need to build industrial centers in sparsely settled areas of Japan. With the stimulus of economic potential and, perhaps more important, the challenge posed by the Mitsubishi group, the Mitsui and Sumitomo groups started projects the following year with thirty-four and fifteen companies, respectively. Among the bank groups, companies affiliated with the old Dai-Ichi Bank were the first to enter, joining Mitsubishi in the same year with a twenty-seven-company project. The Fuji and Sanwa groups started their own projects in 1972 with twenty-eight and twenty-nine companies, respectively.

TABLE 4.8. PROJECT WAVES INVOLVING THE MITSUBISHI, MITSUI, AND SUMITOMO KEIRETSU, 1957–73

Year	(Group)	Project Name	Capitalization (million yen)	Share Held by Council Members
1957	(SMT)	Sumitomo Atomic Energy	1,590	80.0%
1958	(MTB)	Mitsubishi Atomic Power Inc.	4,500	97.9%
1958	(MTS)	Japan Atomic Energy	3,250	72.4%
1967	(MTS)	Mitsui Information Devt.	500	61.0%
1969	(SMT)	Japan Information Service	600	95.0%
1970	(MTB)	Mitsubishi Research Inst.	1,000	61.0%
1971	(SMT)	Sumitomo Business Consulting	200	44.5%
1970	(MTB)	Mitsubishi Development	2,500	87.8%
1971	(MTS)	Mitsui City Development	1,000	63.0%
1971	(SMT)	Sumitomo City Development	1,000	100.0%
1967	(MTB)	Western Japan Petro. Devt.	13,600	56.8%
1968	(MTB)	Middle East Petroleum	7,570	41.2%
1969	(SMT)	Sabah Overseas Petroleum	2,780	42.4%
1969	(MTS)	Mitsui Petroleum Devt.	6,980	74.1%
1972	(MTB)	Mitsubishi Petroleum Devt.	7,000	81.1%
1973	(SMT)	Sumitomo Oil Development	5,000	78.9%

SOURCE: Futatsugi (1976, p. 64).
Notes: MTB refers to the Mitsubishi group, MTS to the Mitsui group, and SMT to the Sumitomo group.

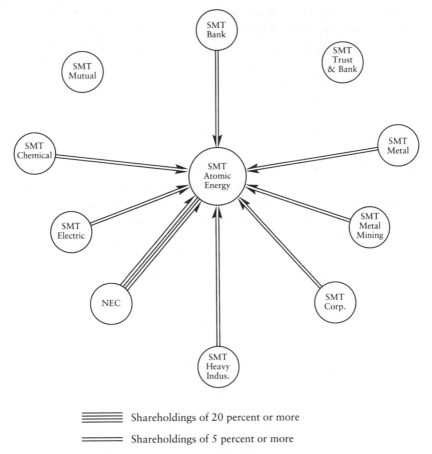

Fig. 4.11. Sumitomo Atomic Energy Industry, Ltd. Source: Data from *Industrial Groupings in Japan* (1982). Note: SMT = Sumitomo.

Large-scale overseas petroleum projects were also highly visible during this period, but were unusual in that they also brought in a number of important nongroup companies. Mitsui began in 1967 with its Iranian petroleum complex, which involved its trading firm, Mitsui and Co., as main sponsor (holding 45 percent of equity) and also included Mitsui Toatsu and Mitsui Petrochemicals, as well as the outside firms of Japan Synthetic Rubber and Toyo Soda Manufacturing. Mitsubishi's project in Saudi Arabia began with Mitsubishi Corporation and brought in other group companies (most visibly Mitsubishi Petrochemicals). However, they were able to position themselves as a national project, receiving

45 percent of capital in Overseas Economic Assistance money from the Japanese government, by bringing in outside steel, automobile, and other non-Mitsubishi companies. In total fifty-nine firms were involved. Sumitomo's oil project in Malaysia brought in outside companies for the same reason as Mitsubishi's—in order to qualify for government assistance as a "national project."

The 1980s have seen the proliferation of projects in all six major keiretsu in new and high technology industries, particularly in what the Japanese business community has called the "C&C industries"—computers and communications. Mitsubishi formed the Mitsubishi C&C Kenkyū-kai in 1981, a study team bringing together forty Mitsubishi companies to develop technologies related to high-level data transmission that will link firms through electronic firm banking, producer-sales agent data exchanges, and other forms of interfirm communication. Mitsui followed in 1982 with the Mitsui Jōhō Shisutemu Kyōgi-kai, with thirty-nine Mitsui companies participating in projects in value-added networks and other telecommunications-related technological fields. In 1983 ten more firms were added, including several large firms that maintain close connections with the Mitsui group but do not participate in its council—Sony, Ito Yokado, and Tokyo Broadcasting System.

The Mitsubishi and Mitsui groups have escalated the battle by introducing foreign competitors into their alliances. This began with a tie-up involving Mitsubishi Corporation, Cosmo 80 (a Japanese software company), and IBM in a venture business in the computer software and communications field. The Mitsui group followed by establishing an arrangement with AT&T to introduce the latter's large-scale enhanced information networks into Japan. Recently, IBM's relationship with Mitsubishi has been extended to the formation of a partnership with Mitsubishi Electric in which IBM Japan will supply the key technologies of some of its most advanced mainframe computers in return for Mitsubishi sponsorship of IBM sales in Japan (*Japan Times*, April 28, 1991).

The implications of these trends are important in at least two ways. First, they suggest that foreign firms positioning themselves in the Japanese market are also subject to the same dynamics of alliance formation that affect the positions of Japanese firms. This must therefore become an element in foreign firms' market entry strategies. Second, the network technologies themselves will undoubtedly affect the nature of interfirm relationships, since decisions about the organizations with which one establishes information networks will set the framework within which other ongoing business transactions are carried out. If, for example, direct orders can be made between companies by computer, a key factor in determining sales patterns will be the presence or absence of computer and data transmission connections between firms. Choices about communications networks will become an increasingly important part of firms' alliance strategies.

Public Relations and Social Activities

The importance of collaborative projects in symbolizing group coherence is clearly seen in the groups' public relations activities. Osaka's Expo '70 attracted pavilions for the five major keiretsu existing at the time as well as for several vertical groups. These pavilions brought together not just core firms but the broader group, including satellites of core companies and companies in the group periphery. Altogether, Sumitomo's pavilion involved forty-seven companies, Mitsubishi's thirty-five, Mitsui's thirty-two, Fuyo's thirty-six, and Sanwa's thirty-two (Miyazaki, 1976, p. 229). These five groups were also included more recently at the 1985 Tsukuba Science and Technology Exposition. Each had its own pavilion, the contents of which involved displaying various technologies and products of member firms, as well as presenting the group as a whole as a progressive force for the future.[27]

Group projects have even moved into the social sphere, including facilitating marriages among employees of different member companies through group-wide marriage advisory centers, or *kekkon sōdan-jo*. In the case of the Fuji group, for example, prospective brides and grooms go to a special office with small rooms and red velvet sofas and fill out questionnaires about their lives, interests, and requirements for a mate. Applicants pay a service charge for registration and an additional charge if the registrant gets engaged.[28]

Perhaps the most elaborate set of activities is found in the Sanwa group, now formalized into a separately chartered organization called the Midori-kai and involving an extended membership of 154 corporations. The functions of this association are summarized in the *Oriental Economist* (September 1982) as follows:

> Twice a year the Midori Kai sponsors a special invitation bazaar for discount sale of a wide range of merchandise to member-company employees and their dependents. Tennis tournaments, baseball games, and other sports events are organized as are competitions in *go, shogi* (Japanese chess) and other indoor pastimes. There are also study groups, art classes, and cultural and topical

seminars as well as beer parties and other recreational gatherings. Also maintained are a health care center, clinics, a wedding hall and dining rooms for nuptials and various social functions. In short, the Midori Kai takes care of virtually all needs in food, clothing and housing as well as in health, medical care, travel, insurance, consumer credit, leisure, and recreation. Taking advantage of the services and facilities offered are close on a million people when employee families are included. . . . The Midori Kai projects the Sanwa image of caring for people and their immediate needs.

The Fuji group also maintains a set of facilities for group-wide use, though it is not on the scale of Sanwa's. At the "F-kai," group-wide events include sports tournaments and beer parties where the middle-level managements of group firms can interact. Among upper-level executives, the prime forum for social interaction, apart from the golf course, is typically the hostess club. Accordingly, Fuji group companies have invested together in a downtown Tokyo club dubbed the Fuyo Ginza Club.

The keiretsu also have their own group publications, of which Sumitomo's English-language magazine is representative. Called the *Sumitomo Quarterly,* a typical issue includes interviews with one or two executives in Sumitomo group companies, news of various group projects, events involving individual group companies such as new technology development, as well as several articles of more general interest. The front cover of one issue, which shows the outside of Sumitomo's 1985 Tsukuba pavilion, is reproduced in Figure 4.12. Other publications are also issued by the Sumitomo group, including the group's official history and a book of general information on group companies. All of these are published through the group's trading company, Sumitomo Corporation.

SUMMARY

We have seen in this chapter how the keiretsu serves as an important organizing framework for market relationships in Japan. The presidents' council identifies core membership and acts as a forum for interaction within the group. The existence of the keiretsu as a coherent social unit is furthermore affirmed through collaborative projects, events, and publications. Perhaps the strongest evidence for the importance of the group, however, is in the ways in which it has structured exchange among member firms. Table 4.9 summarizes earlier findings on the effects of group participation on interfirm networks.

Fig. 4.12.   Sample Cover of the Sumitomo Group's Quarterly Magazine. Reprinted by permission of Sumitomo Corporation.

Debt, equity, directorship, and trading networks are all significantly determined by keiretsu membership. This is most striking in the case of the networks of corporate ownership. The density of ownership connections among group firms, the proportion of shareholdings internal to the group, and the patterns of preferential trade are all quite high. As suggested earlier, ownership plays an important symbolic function in signifying ongoing, durable business relationships, but other advantages to intragroup shareholdings are also important—particularly the role of crossholdings in constructing stable institutional environments for group firms and their managers (see Chapter 7). No density figures were calculated for debt networks, since the only ties likely to be constituted

TABLE 4.9.   SUMMARY TABLE,
SIX-GROUP AVERAGE

Network Measure	Type of Tie			
	Debt	Equity	Directorships	Trade
Density	—	16.2%	4.1%	3.4%
Internalization	34.1%	43.7%	45.5%	11.5%
Preferential transaction ratio	15.1	12.8	21.9	2.8

Note: Internalization and preferential transaction ratios are calculated from Tables 4.1, 4.2, 4.4, and 4.7 and are weighted by the number of companies in each group. Debt and equity ties are for 1986. Directorship and trade ties are for 1980.

were between financial and industrial firms. However, both internalization and preferential transaction ratios show values in the range of those for directorship and equity networks, indicating strong keiretsu effects in this market as well.

While density figures for equity networks are high, those for directorships are quite low. This results from the nature of interfirm directorship networks in Japan. Dispatched directors are largely the expression of vertical relationships, particularly between parent companies and their satellites. Since member firms in the keiretsu are large parent companies in their own right, their relationships are more nearly horizontal and outside directors are few. When outside ties do exist, however, they are largely with other firms in the same group, as shown in the internalization and preferential transaction measures.

Of the business relationships analyzed, product market ties are the least strongly organized by group affiliation. As noted earlier, there are data and methodological difficulties in accurately describing these patterns, so these results should be viewed with caution. Relying on studies that exclude the sōgō shōsha and looking only at direct relationships among manufacturers, we find that network measures of density, internalization, and preferential transaction ratios are all lower than for other types of ties. Nevertheless, group membership is not irrelevant, as firms are approximately three times more likely on average to trade directly with other industrial firms in their own intermarket keiretsu than with those in each of the other groups. Including vertical keiretsu relationships and the sōgō shōsha would certainly increase keiretsu effects substantially.

The implication of these analyses is that the keiretsu do, in fact, reflect important features of the organization of markets in Japan. These markets are constituted by real alliances among financial, commercial, and industrial organizations in which the identity of those organizations is of central importance. These structures have proved remarkably durable, surviving through both regulatory and industrial changes, indicating that the keiretsu is not simply a fragile legacy of the past, but a continuing and fundamental feature of Japanese economic organization.

CHAPTER V

Patterns of Alliance Formation

The keiretsu represents a coherent, durable form of social organization that is significant, as we saw in Chapter 4, both in the ways it has structured interaction among its members and in the ways it has created an ongoing symbolic framework within which this interaction takes place. In this chapter, we move from an analysis of internal relationships among alliance members and definitions of boundaries to an analysis of the overall patterns of affiliation in the Japanese economy. We explore processes of group expansion and the evolution of group affiliations over time, commonalities among "keiretsu" and "independent" firms, and factors associated with group membership.

It is in the interaction of strategic interests and institutionalized structures that specific alliance patterns in Japan have developed. Strategically, Japanese firms have sought to improve their positions in larger business networks by creating collective interorganizational structures. Firms seek a range of economic and social goals, including business profits, sales growth and market share, enhanced prestige in the business community, production stability, and managerial security.[1] They act on these interests by their positioning in a range of essential markets that are essential for their survival—labor, capital, raw materials, component goods, technology, etc. Markets therefore are arenas of strategic action within which various institutional arrangements, including intercorporate alliances, are constructed.

Over time, these relationships take on a life of their own, resulting in membership patterns in which historical connections are as important as the immediate needs of any given transaction. Alliance formation, therefore, is not merely a matter of companies "joining" groups in response to immediate strategic needs, in the same way that we might think of a consumer choosing among products in a supermarket. Rather, the keiretsu result from the long-term balancing of a complex set of interests as firms singly and collectively move through broader business networks.[2] The institutional arrangements that result from this strategic pursuit become interesting owing to three important features of the alliance formation process: (1) the market opportunities actors seek to appropriate are continually changing; (2) actors' network positions and resulting market power differ considerably; and (3) network structures take on a life of their own, becoming institutionalized features of the economic landscape.

THE APPROPRIATION OF CHANGING MARKET OPPORTUNITIES

The importance of appropriating changing market opportunities has been central in various views on modernization, industrialization, and development, particularly in those of Joseph Schumpeter (1934, 1950). For Schumpeter, it is the continual pursuit of new markets by entrepreneurs that most clearly characterizes the process of capitalist development. Far from being an unfortunate by-product of the workings of otherwise viable markets, Schumpeter argues, monopolies and the profits they generate are necessary in order to reward entrepreneurs and are therefore the driving force of economic development. Even though monopoly profits are necessary, they are also typically short-lived, Schumpeter believes, as other entrepreneurs emerge to take advantage of these opportunities by creating new and better products.

Schumpeter's interest in market appropriation has been taken up by the contemporary literature on corporate strategy and the means by which companies create and protect rent streams in their business activities. In one set of perspectives, associated with the "competitive strategy" literature (e.g., Porter, 1980; Abegglen and Stalk, 1985), the focus is on the pursuit of market share and the creation of entry and mobility barriers through the differentiation of product lines and early positioning in markets to gain experience and production-volume advantages over competitors. Another perspective, more in the spirit of Schumpeter's original emphasis on organization as the source of economic rents, emphasizes the importance of the diverse array of means by which firms set the boundaries of their operations in order to foster the generation of productive knowledge of diverse types and to appropriate the rent streams thereby created. In keeping with this "resource-based" view of strategy, Teece (1986) argues that a key factor influencing technological innovation is the ability of firms to capture the returns from their research-and-development investments. Various institutional devices, including contractual arrangements and vertical integration, exist in order to improve the appropriability of returns to the innovator.

As we see later, the logic of rent-creation activities applies as well to interfirm networks. No firm is an island, and all rely heavily on outside sources of supply. Where firms are particularly dependent on certain sources, they seek to craft stronger mechanisms for ensuring a steady supply. Firms are in this sense relational entrepreneurs, as isolated transactions or linkages become organized into larger and more durable relationships. Just as Schumpeterian entrepreneurs put together the factors of production in new ways in order to earn profits, relational entrepreneurs craft specific arrangements with other economic actors in order to improve their positions in overall business networks. Diversified intercorporate alliances are one strategy, exclusive alliances a second, and full-scale merger or acquisition a third. Profits on direct lines of business is one of a number of goals, which include as well the reliable acquisition of resources for other corporate activities and for organizational stability.

DIFFERENCES IN NETWORK POSITIONS AND MARKET POWER

While economic actors seek to appropriate changing market opportunities, the nature and range of those opportunities are themselves shaped by the network positions actors hold, for these determine actors' abilities to gain access to critical resources. The importance of what we might call "network power" is evident in the theoretical models of Burt (1983) and Marsden (1983). Burt has shown how firms' market positions (defined by the constraints placed on them by suppliers' and buyers' positions) and patterns of interlocking directorates are important determinants of their profitability. At the same time, Marsden notes how networks tend to close in on themselves, restricting the access of others to that portion of the network. This process results, Marsden argues, from ideological similarity and embeddedness in preexisting social networks. As a result, mechanisms limiting contact of actors with one another create a network of access relationships, and an actor's position in such a network defines a set of potential exchange partners (Marsden, 1983, p. 690).[3]

Market sectors are themselves organized hierarchically. In a passage that applies no less to Japan than to the Western economies on which it was based, Collins (1986, p. 139) argues that the financial system has emerged as a "superordinate market," which is the "command center of the economy" through its control over the central resource of capital:

> Business enterprises are linked to particular sources of capital. The large corporations are tied to the big banks, whereas small businesses get their funds from smaller "country" banks. Regionally powerful lead banks organize consortiums to finance large-scale loans—not only to business but also to municipalities at home, and entire states abroad. . . . The business world is tied together hierarchically through the size of the financial institutions upon which each enterprise can draw.

Within Japan, financial institutions' preeminent business positions have been reinforced by concentration and state influence in the commercial banking industry and by the important role that banks and insurance companies have played as shareholders. These financial institutions became the center around which the postwar groupings emerged. Recently, industrial changes have pushed technology- and information-oriented firms to more central positions in the groups. As we see later in this chapter, even though there are many commonalities in the network relationships among large Japanese firms, there are also interesting differences among certain firms related to the types of markets they serve and their positions in those markets.

THE INSTITUTIONALIZATION OF NETWORK STRUCTURES

Specific organizational forms emerge, disseminate, and become durable features of business networks. In this way, network patterns over time become institutionalized structures, with the importance of total relationships superseding that of single, constituent transactions. The development of these structures is largely an evolutionary one in the sense of "the cumulative effect of a long string of happenings stretching back into the past" (Winter, 1988, p. 178). Economic organization, therefore, is the result not simply of rational action within immediate contexts, but of the learning of entire routines of action that are embodied in long-term patterns of intrafirm and interfirm coordination.

As specific relationships become institutionalized, corporate positioning that may have begun "externally" in the initial stages (i.e., choices
over whether and with whom to affiliate) increasingly becomes "internal"
(positioning within affiliations already formed). Through their continual
reenactment, these relationships create a structure of reality that defines
what has meaning and determines the possible constraints on actions
(Zucker, 1983). Relationships in their entirety come to take priority over
their component exchanges and become durable features of the network.
And as they develop a taken-for-granted character, history becomes a
fundamental determinant of particular patterns of interaction.

Institutionalization also takes place at the level of larger organizational networks, fields, or populations, with the issue here becoming explaining how particular patterns of organizational forms develop within
this broader context and how these forms become similar or different
over time.[4] This is seen in the emergence of particular models of appropriate keiretsu form, discussed in the previous chapter, including the
shachō-kai, main bank relationships, and group-wide projects. As these
models have developed and evolved in Japan, patterns of intercorporate
relationships have come to take on common characteristics that make
network patterns among large Japanese firms—whether formally affiliated with a group or not—far more similar to each other than they are to
their American counterparts.

In sum, firms seek to appropriate changing market opportunities
through independent and collective action but are constrained both by
their network positions and by the institutionalization of particular
arrangements. In the following sections, we consider empirical patterns
of alliance formation through a series of quantitative and qualitative
analyses of group membership patterns. As we shall see, although there
are firm- and group-specific instrumental considerations at work, these
are oriented not only toward generating rent streams in specific lines of
business but also toward maintaining a reliable framework of exchange
among group members across diverse and interrelated business activities
and toward improving firms' positions in overall business networks.

HISTORICAL DETERMINANTS OF
CONTEMPORARY MEMBERSHIP PATTERNS

Important as the Occupation-induced dissolution of the zaibatsu was, in
retrospect it is clear that it was far from the kind of universal overhaul of
the Japanese economic system that its initiators had intended. The dis-

solution successfully eliminated the position of the zaibatsu families, dissolved the zaibatsu honsha (holding companies), broke up the trading firms and large manufacturing operations, and swept top management clean in the subsidiary companies. These proved, however, to be only a portion of the networks of connections that held together the various elements constituting the group, and important connections to the past remained. A new generation of executives was selected to replace those who had been forced out, but these people came from middle management in the old subsidiaries and had developed and maintained ongoing personal connections with managers in other subsidiaries extending back to the war and prewar years. Moreover, many were chosen for their new positions by the top executives being removed.

Similarly, while the leading manufacturing and trading houses of the group were broken up (most later regrouped), the group banks were not. These banks had already taken up a position during the wartime period as leading financiers to the group. In his study of financing in the Sumitomo group, Asajima (1984, pp. 109–10) finds that after the mid-1930s, the group commercial and trust banks replaced Sumitomo Honsha and the Sumitomo family as primary sources of external funding, accounting for 32 percent of total funds during the 1937–43 period in comparison with under 1 percent coming from the honsha.[5] After the war, these banks—still intact—took on the role of filling the power vacuum left by the dissolution of the holding company, a position enhanced considerably by the scarcity of capital during the postwar period.

Another form of continuity was the significant equity interlocks subsidiaries had maintained even before the war. Table 3.4 above, which outlines intragroup holdings in Sumitomo at the time of dissolution, indicates that Sumitomo Bank held 40 percent of the shares of Sumitomo Trust & Banking, as well as 7 percent of the shares of Sumitomo Metal Mining and Sumitomo Metal Industries. Other zaibatsu subsidiaries held significant positions in the Sumitomo Bank itself, as well as Sumitomo Metal Industries, Sumitomo Metal Mining, Sumitomo Electric, Sumitomo Chemical, Sumitomo Heavy Industries, and Nippon Electric—all of the major subsidiaries that were to constitute the core of the newly formed Sumitomo group. Unlike honsha and family holdings, these shareholdings were not eliminated after war and served as a structure around which the groups began reforming. By the mid-1950s, over 15 percent of the shares of core Sumitomo companies were in the hands of other group companies. An executive in the Sumitomo group explained at the time,

If one looks for stable and trustworthy shareholders, one naturally turns to former Honsha subsidiaries. It is not that any specific plan was followed in going ahead with interlocking ownership. It would be more correct to say that things happened in this way out of the desire, among brother-companies, to help each other. [*Oriental Economist*, April 1955.]

The family metaphor was also used by another executive: "Because one's parents are dead, one is not prevented from continuing as before with one's brothers and sisters. What could be more natural than the brothers and sisters of a family helping each other to keep going as a group?" (*Oriental Economist*, January 1959). We find the keiretsu emerging out of the structure of existing exchange networks, facilitated by the emerging dominance of the bank as financier to group operations. Thus, when Sumitomo began meeting again in the early 1950s, all eleven of its old first-line subsidiaries, now each independent operations, took part in the first meeting.

Patterns of Expansion

The membership roles of the six big intermarket groups expanded rapidly during the 1960s and 1970s, before leveling off in the early 1980s. Core membership, as defined by shachō-kai participation, increased from 137 to 193 for the period 1966–89. This net gain of 56 participant represents an increase of 41 percent over this twenty-three-year period. If we include six firms that were eliminated due to intragroup mergers, then 62 new memberships in total were actually created during this period. A listing of new members is shown in Table 5.1, by group.

The newer bank groups of Dai-Ichi Kangyo and Sanwa were far more aggressive at expanding than the other four groups, accounting for more than two-thirds (68 percent) of total new core memberships. Growth in the Dai-Ichi Kangyo group was accelerated by the consolidation of the group bank under the 1971 merger bringing together the Dai-Ichi and Nippon Kangyo. Both groups have been less limited by historical, and particularly zaibatsu, connections and have actively sought to grow to a scale comparable to that of their competitor groups.

The complete list of membership initiates from 1966 to 1989 is shown in Table 5.2. What all sixty-two companies on this list have in common are extensive and longstanding ties with their group before becoming official members. Prior to joining the shachō-kai, each had group financial institutions (especially the group bank) as a leading source of capital,

TABLE 5.1.   NEW MEMBERSHIPS
IN PRESIDENTS' COUNCILS, 1966–89, BY GROUP

	Mitsui	Mitsubishi	Sumitomo	Fuji	Sanwa	Dai-Ichi Kangyo	Total
Old ties	8	3	3	4	22	20	60
Spinoffs		2					2
Reductions through mergers	<1>	<1>			<1>	<3>	<6>
Net gain	7	4	3	4	21	17	56

SOURCES: Lists taken from *Keiretsu no kenkyū* (1967, pp. 11, 53–68) and *Kigyō keiretsu sōran* (1990, p. 58).

had group companies among its leading shareholders, or, most frequently, had both.[6]

Of the twenty companies for which *Keiretsu no kenkyū* provides detailed information, all retained the group as a leading source of capital before joining. An average of 25 percent of the capital borrowed by these firms in 1966 came from financial institutions in the group each eventually entered.[7] In addition, 13 percent of the shares of these same companies were held by other companies in the same group. Several huge enterprises that had strong associations with the prewar zaibatsu but have developed relatively independently since the war decided during this period to participate in meetings of the newly reformed groups— notably Toyota and Toshiba of the Mitsui group.

In several cases in which ties to the group had previously existed, ties to another group were equally strong if not stronger. This is uncommon and is a sensitive situation for firms to negotiate. The working rules of alliance in Japanese business custom are clear on the point that old relationships are not readily dropped. After joining the new group, therefore, these companies maintained some form of association with their old groups. The following three examples illustrate the point:

1.   The Sumitomo group has collectively remained a more important source of borrowed capital for Kubota than has the Fuji group, on whose shachō-kai it currently sits (13.8 percent as opposed to 11.9 percent, according to *Industrial Groupings in Japan,* 1982), though loans from

TABLE 5.2. NEW PRESIDENTS' COUNCIL MEMBER COMPANIES, 1966–89

Mitsui	Mitsubishi
Mitsukoshi Dept. Store	Mitsubishi Construction
Mitsui Construction	Nikon
Onoda Cement	Mitsubishi Motors
Oji Paper	Mitsubishi Aluminum
Toyota Motor Co.	Mitsubishi Cable Industries
Toshiba	
Mitsui-OSK Lines	
Nippon Flour Mills	

Fuji	Sumitomo
Kureha	Sumitomo Forestry
Yokogawa Electric	Sumitomo Construction
Canon	Sumitomo Bakelite
Kubota	

Sanwa	Dai-Ichi Kangyo
Nichimen	Taisei Fire and Marine Insurance
Toyo Construction	Nissho-Iwai
Sekisui House	Shimizu Construction
Sekisui Chemical	Asahi Chemical
Hitachi Metals	IHI
Hitachi Cable	Ebara
Hitachi Chemical	Hitachi Corporation
Tanabe	Shibusawa
Zenitaka	Orient
Suntory	Kyowa Hakko
Kyocera	Kawasho
Hoya	Isuzu Motors
Nisshin Steel	Chichibu Cement
NTN Toyo Bearing	Japan Metals & Chemicals
Iwatani	Isehi
Fujisawa	Asahi Optical
Shin Meiwa	Lion Corporation
Iwatsu Electric	Showa Oil
Sharp	C. Itoh
Nitto	Kobe Steel
Ito Ham	
Oriental Lease	

SOURCES: See Table 5.1.

the Fuji Bank have risen so that they now constitute the identical amount as those from Sumitomo Bank.

2. C. Itoh, which has gradually been shifting toward the Dai-Ichi Kangyo group, has also maintained its financial ties with the Sumitomo group as a whole. While C. Itoh now uses the Dai-Ichi Kangyo Bank as its single largest creditor, Sumitomo Bank retains the number-two position as equity holder and number-three, after Sumitomo Trust and Banking, as lender.

3. Kobe Steel has also become a new member of the Dai-Ichi Kangyo Bank group but has maintained its membership in the Sanwa group and continues to use Sanwa as its leading source of borrowed capital. Like Kubota, Kobe Steel has equalized its loans from its two main banks, increasing borrowing from Dai-Ichi Kangyo to the point of parity with those of Sanwa Bank.[8]

In a number of cases, new members are closely linked as affiliates of existing member firms. This is most strikingly seen in the case of a trio of firms affiliated with the Hitachi subgroup—Hitachi Chemical, Hitachi Metals, and Hitachi Cable. Each has 51–56 percent of its shares held by Hitachi, Ltd., as of 1990 and each has followed its parent concern into the Sanwa group. Other examples of satellite companies becoming formal members under the aegis of a parent company are Mitsubishi Motors (26 percent owned by Mitsubishi Heavy Industries), Sumitomo Bakelite (21 percent owned by Sumitomo Chemical), Sekisui House (21 percent owned by Sekisui Chemical), and Kawasho (25 percent owned by Kawasaki Steel).

The Permanence of Core Positions

In no cases have companies that are presidents' council members left their council for any reason, except for mergers and resulting company dissolvements. This indicates an extraordinarily high degree of stability in core group membership, as these positions become de facto permanent seats for their occupants. In part this stability reflects the prestige associated with affiliation, which firms are unlikely to want to give up. But it also reflects strong pressures within the larger business community to maintain "loyalty" toward one's alliance partners even if it is not in one's immediate interest to do so. The durability of memberships also implies something else: group companies rarely fail. That not one of these nearly two hundred firms has left its group because of bankruptcy is a striking record and points to the important protective function the group plays for its members, discussed later in this chapter.

In its longevity, the keiretsu conforms to the image of alliances that comes out of anthropological field studies suggesting long-term social relationships that link kinship groups over generations (e.g., Dumont, 1957). This image is quite different from that of another social science metaphor, the coalition, as it has developed in contemporary game theory (Schotter, 1981) and organizational theory (Cyert and March, 1963). Coalitions, particularly in their game theory formulation, are viewed as a relatively fluid set of relationships established and reestablished among actors in a continual search for advantage, responding to the logic of strategic self-interest. Self-interest is evident too in the alliance but is tempered by the central role played by group history—ties of mutual obligation as they have developed over extended periods of interaction. More transient coalitions may, of course, arise within alliances—as, for example, when some firms push for a group-wide project that other group members oppose—but these are set within the context of a basic acknowledgment of the group as a perpetually ongoing social unit.

This view of the keiretsu stands in contrast to that provided in some other accounts of the alliance formation process in Japan. Clark (1979), for example, claims, "It is this mutability of the relations between companies, the formation of and disengagement from alliances, and the gain and loss of independence, that most conspicuously differentiates any of these groups from the centralized conglomerate" (p. 87). Although this view might accurately capture certain strategic alliances among Japanese firms in areas such as high technology development, it does not for the kind of keiretsu relationships studied here. Unlike many large firms in the United States, which actively buy and sell business units in response to perceived profit opportunities or changes in corporate strategy, the keiretsu has proved to be a remarkably durable institution.

THE PREVALENCE OF ALLIANCES AND THEIR VARIATIONS

Shachō-kai participation represents only the most visible indication of alliance relationship, and many firms that are not formal council participants nevertheless maintain close arrangements with their banks and trading partners. Relying on a more liberal classification scheme based

TABLE 5.3.   THE "KEIRETSU-IZATION"
OF THE JAPANESE ECONOMY, UTILIZING
KEIRETSU NO KENKYŪ CLASSIFICATION

	1970	1980	1990
Number of companies	371	536	577
Percentage of total assets	65.8	75.7	68.8
Percentage of total sales	71.2	78.5	75.9

SOURCE: *Keiretsu no kenkyū* (1970, 1980, and 1990).

on stable capital affiliations, *Keiretsu no kenkyū* finds the number of affiliates among the firms listed on the first section of the Tokyo Stock Exchange to have increased from 371 in 1970 to 577 in 1990, and the share of total assets and sales of all first-section firms to have increased to about 70 percent and 75 percent, respectively. These figures are reported in Table 5.3. Although their share of total assets and sales dropped somewhat from a peak in 1980, the overall image that emerges from this source is one of an ongoing "keiretsu-ization" (*keiretsu-ka*) of the Japanese economy at least well into the 1970s.

Some writers have criticized this source as too liberal in its membership classification (e.g., Hadley, 1984). However, the real problem is not so much an overly inclusive definition but how to set boundaries in what are largely socially and structurally rather than legally defined entities. The criterion of stable ties to banks used by *Keiretsu no kenkyū* is a reasonable one for some purposes, such as the identification of main bank relationships. For other purposes, such as the performance analyses reported later in this chapter, more restrictive definitions might be preferred. In still other cases, such as the measuring of stable shareholding relationships, alliances are even more pervasive than the figures suggested here. There is no single measure that can unequivocally be considered the best measure of affiliation for all purposes.

In addition to formal shachō-kai participation, we can distinguish at least two broad patterns of looser alliance. These are termed here quasi-affiliations and multiple-affiliations. The significance of these patterns is that they reflect the more pervasive reality of alliance in the Japanese industrial organization. As we show in this section, intercorporate relationships that are long-term, reciprocal, and multiplex are common among a large part of the population of major firms in Japan.

Quasi-affiliations

Quasi-affiliates are in many ways similar to group member companies except that they do not formally participate in the presidents' council and are overall somewhat less clearly integrated into the group. Quasi-affiliation divides broadly into one of two categories. The first are those firms that are subsidiaries or satellites of one or more firms that are themselves core members of the group. Typically these firms operate within the framework of a vertical keiretsu relationship, with the parent firm acting as the company's sponsor in various matters (e.g., procuring loans from the group bank). Most are relatively small operations whose size and status prevent them from becoming full-fledged members in the group's council. The second type, and the one that shall concern us here, are those nonsatellite firms that maintain close relationships with one or more group firms, particularly the group bank, but are not in the formal group council. These quasi-affiliates are large entities in their own right. This category includes many firms, such as Sony, Honda, and other nominally independent companies that actually maintain primary affiliations with a major group. In the case of Sony, Mitsui Bank has served as its main bank for the past three decades, while in the case of Honda, Mitsubishi Bank has played the same role.

Estimates of the number of quasi-affiliates in Japan vary by source. *Keiretsu no kenkyū* classifies total membership in the six main keiretsu in 1980 at 536 firms out of 838 companies studied, or 64 percent. Of these 536 firms, 354 did not formally participate as part of a presidents' council, so they may be considered quasi-affiliates. In total, therefore, core firms constituted about 22 percent of the firms studied, quasi-affiliates about 42 percent, and independent firms about 36 percent.[9] A second source, *Industrial Groupings in Japan*, is more conservative in its attributions of memberships.[10] Including all 1,734 companies listed on the stock exchange and an additional 16 shachō-kai members that are not listed on the exchange in its analysis of membership in 1982, it classifies 182, or 10.5 percent, as core members; 440, or 25.4 percent, as quasi-affiliates; and the remaining 1,112, or 64.1 percent, as independent.

Quasi-affiliations of the nonsatellite, large-firm variety have been particularly important for the three former zaibatsu, for these groups have limited core membership largely to the descendants of prewar zaibatsu subsidiaries. Quasi-affiliate status has been a way of keeping a "purity of the bloodline" (*junketsu*) while expanding membership.

Quasi-affiliates of this type represent the group's periphery and are strategically important as an intermediate condition between full-scale membership and independence. The Sumitomo group has an extended network of quasi-affiliates owing to an active policy by the Sumitomo bank of expanding its own set of clients beyond those in the original zaibatsu lineage. This is often done by offering assistance in times of need: Toyo Kogyo moved considerably closer to the group after Sumitomo Bank assisted it in the 1970s when it was having trouble selling its rotary Mazda automobiles, and Asahi beer was protected by Sumitomo group purchases of its shares during an unusual hostile takeover bid in the 1960s. A third company, Meidensha, is a large, old electrical equipment manufacturer that had financial difficulties during the early 1960s. Although it had maintained comparatively weak connections with the Sumitomo group before 1960, it had become involved in the Sumitomo atomic energy project. This provided the catalyst for closer ties to develop as Meidensha faced increasing losses, including about ¥600 million (just under $2 million) in 1964. Following the usual custom, a quid pro quo was established whereby Meidensha gave up a degree of its independence—accepting directors from Sumitomo Electric and Nippon Electric, and later from Sumitomo Corporation and Sumitomo Bank—in return for loans from and stock purchases by Sumitomo financial institutions (Kameoka, 1969, p. 50).

The degree of formalization of quasi-affiliation varies considerably by group. Within Sumitomo it is acknowledged only by the inclusion of a number of companies in the membership descriptions provided in group publications, by their participation in group-wide activities such as Sumitomo's pavilion at the Tsukuba Science Exposition of 1985 and the Osaka Flower Exhibition of 1990, and in other informal ways. The drinking of Asahi beer, for example, is de rigueur at Sumitomo group functions and company executive lounges. In contrast, two other groups, Mitsui and Sanwa, have formalized their quasi-affiliates into secondary councils. Mitsui has a second presidents' council, the Getsuyō-kai (Monday Club), which brings together both the chief executive officers of Mitsui's core 24 firms and those from 44 other companies in the extended Mitsui group. Three firms that are now members of the elite Nimoku-kai began in the Getsuyō-kai before being promoted—Mitsui Construction, Mitsui-OSK Lines, and Nippon Flour Mills. Sanwa has an even more extended group involving 155 companies known as the Midori-kai, which has been formalized into a separate legal entity that itself has become a participant in the group's core shachō-kai (*Industrial Groupings in Japan*, 1984).

TABLE 5.4.   THE EXTERNAL CAPITAL STRUCTURES
OF CORE SUMITOMO COMPANIES
VERSUS QUASI-AFFILIATES, 1982

	Debt		Equity	
	Core Members	Quasi-Affiliates	Core Members	Quasi-Affiliates
Proportion of total held by Sumitomo companies	33.6%	30.2%	29.9%	15.5%
Average proportion held by companies in other groups	1.2%	3.4%	0.6%	1.2%
Preferential transaction ratio	28.0	8.8	49.8	12.9

SOURCE: *Industrial Groupings in Japan* (1982).
Note: Equity includes only shares held by the top-ten shareholders. In contrast to Table 4.2, they are taken as a percentage of the company's *total* outstanding shares.

The interfirm exchange networks for quasi-affiliates are structured around the group in ways similar to those of core members, though they are not as exclusively group-centered. Table 5.4 compares the structures of banking and ownership of the 19 listed members of Sumitomo's Hakusui-kai with those of the 19 largest quasi-affiliates, as classified in the 1982 volume of *Industrial Groupings in Japan*.[11]

While orientations toward the group are somewhat stronger among the core companies, the quasi-affiliates also show a clear group-based pattern. Quasi-affiliates are particularly likely to use group financial institutions as their main source of loans—a percentage almost equal to that of the core group firms (30.2 percent compared to 33.6 percent of total borrowed capital). They also have a substantial proportion of their total shares held by other group companies, though it is only about one-half of the internal holdings of core companies (15.5 percent compared to 29.9 percent). That quasi-affiliates also show high preferential transaction ratios (8.8 for debt and 12.9 for equity) confirms the importance of group affiliation for these firms.

Multiple-affiliations

Both group member and quasi-affiliate firms tend to be most clearly linked with a single group. Other Japanese firms, in contrast, have developed alliances with two or more groups simultaneously. The intensity of the relationships forged within these multiple-affiliations varies considerably. Four firms are formal council members in two or more of the big-six keiretsu. These are Hitachi Ltd. (which is a council member in the three groups of Fuji, Sanwa, and Dai-Ichi Kangyo), as well as Nissho-Iwai, Kobe Steel, and Nippon Express, each of which is in both the Sanwa and Dai-Ichi Kangyo groups. Other firms in this category maintain only informal associations with their alliance partners. Yet even though their relationships may be less intense, the basic alliance form remains.

This is perhaps best seen by example. Table 5.5 compares the external capital structures in 1985 of a multiple-affiliation firm with that of a single-affiliation firm in the same industry. Nippon Steel, Japan's largest steel manufacturer, has diversified its alliances across a number of groups but is a formal member in none. In contrast, Sumitomo Metal Industries, third largest in the Japanese steel industry, has maintained close relationships only with other Sumitomo companies and is a core member of Sumitomo's council, the Hakusui-kai.

Nevertheless, the relationships they maintain with their shareholders share three features: they are *reciprocal,* they are *embedded* in other ongoing business relationships, and they are *long-term.* Among seven leading shareholders, excluding the three mutual life insurance companies whose shares cannot be held, Nippon Steel holds reciprocal top-ten positions in four. Similarly, among its six leading shareholders, again excluding mutual life insurance companies (as well as Bisch Company, for which data were not available), Sumitomo Metal Industries maintains reciprocal shareholdings in four, including all three non-life-insurance Sumitomo companies. These equity positions are not only linked with each other but also with other financial relationships among the firms. Most of the financial institutions and all of the commercial bank shareholders also extend a significant portion of loans to the two companies. In the case of Nippon Steel, 31 percent of all borrowed capital came from its top-ten shareholders, while this figure was 51 percent for Sumitomo Metal Industries.

The long-term stability of both of these external capital structures can be seen in Table 5.6, which compares the 1985 figures with those from fifteen years earlier. The top-five shareholders in 1985 for both companies were the same in 1970, as were most of the top-ten shareholders. While there was some variation in the rank orders among these investors and fluctuations in the percentages of shares held, the stability of equity positions over this fifteen-year period is remarkable. The same can be

TABLE 5.5.   THE EXTERNAL CAPITAL STRUCTURES
OF NIPPON STEEL AND SUMITOMO METAL
INDUSTRIES, 1985

% of Equity Shares	Shareholder	Shareholder Affiliation	% of Steel Co.'s Total Borrowing
Nippon Steel—Independent			
3.4[a]	Industrial Bank of Japan		9.5
3.0[b]	Nippon Life	Sanwa	1.9
2.0[b]	Meiji Mutual Life	Mitsubishi	1.8
1.8[b]	Dai-Ichi Mutual Life		1.6
1.8[a]	Fuji Bank	Fuji	4.8
1.7[a]	Sumitomo Bank	Sumitomo	4.4
1.6[a]	Sanwa Bank	Sanwa	4.4
1.6	Tokio Marine and Fire	Mitsubishi	
1.6	Sumitomo Marine and Fire	Sumitomo	
1.6	Dai-Ichi Kangyo Bank	Dai-Ichi Kangyo	2.3
Sumitomo Metal Industries—Sumitomo Group			
5.5[a]	Sumitomo Trust and Banking	Sumitomo	10.0
4.5[b]	Sumitomo Mutual Life	Sumitomo	2.9
4.2[b]	Nippon Life	Sanwa	1.6
3.9[a]	Sumitomo Bank	Sumitomo	12.6
2.6[c]	Industrial Bank of Japan		9.2
2.4	Long-Term Credit Bank		7.8
2.1[b]	Taiyo Mutual Life		1.3
1.8[a]	Sumitomo Corporation	Sumitomo	
1.7	Nippon Credit Bank		6.4
1.5[b]	Bisch Company		

SOURCES: *Keiretsu no kenkyū* (1987); *Kaisha nenkan* (1986); *Kigyō keiretsu sōran* (1986).
[a]Steel co. holds a reciprocal top-ten equity position.
[b]Reciprocal position is unknown or impossible (e.g., where the shareholder is a mutual life insurance company).
[c]Steel co. holds a reciprocal top-twenty equity position.

TABLE 5.6. THE STABILITY OF EXTERNAL CAPITAL STRUCTURES—NIPPON STEEL AND SUMITOMO METAL INDUSTRIES, 1970–85

Shareholder	% of Equity Shares 1970	% of Equity Shares 1985	% of Steel Co.'s Total Borrowing 1970	% of Steel Co.'s Total Borrowing 1985
Nippon Steel—Independent				
Industrial Bank of Japan	2.6	3.4	14.3	9.5
Nippon Life	2.2	3.0	2.2	1.9
Meiji Mutual Life	1.8	2.0	2.4	1.8
Dai-Ichi Mutual Life	1.7	1.8	1.4	1.6
Fuji Bank	1.9	1.8	4.9	4.8
Sumitomo Bank	1.7	1.7	3.7	4.4
Sanwa Bank	1.7	1.6	3.6	4.4
Tokio Marine and Fire	1.7	1.6		
Sumitomo Marine and Fire		1.6		
Dai-Ichi Kangyo Bank[a]	1.5	1.6	2.2	2.3
Sumitomo Metal Industries—Sumitomo Group				
Sumitomo Trust and Banking	3.9	5.5	10.5	10.0
Sumitomo Mutual Life	4.4	4.5	6.7	2.9
Nippon Life	3.7	4.2	2.9	1.6
Sumitomo Bank	5.3	3.9	15.8	12.6
Industrial Bank of Japan	2.3	2.6	8.6	9.2
Long-Term Credit Bank	2.3	2.4	6.7	7.8
Taiyo Mutual Life		2.1	2.3	1.3
Sumitomo Corporation	2.2	1.8		
Nippon Credit Bank[b]	1.3	1.7	4.8	6.4
Bisch Company		1.5		

SOURCES: *Keiretsu no kenkyū* (1971, 1987); *Kigyō keiretsu sōran* (1973).

[a]Figures are for 1972, following the mergers of Dai-Ichi Bank and Nippon Kangyo Bank in 1971.

[b]Nippon Credit Bank was called Nippon Fudosan Bank until 1977.

said for each company's sources of borrowed capital. The composition of top lenders in 1985 did not change from 1970, and the proportion of total loans, particularly in the case of Nippon Steel, is extremely stable. These findings support at the individual company level observations made earlier that corporate shareholders are bound in durable relationships with the companies they hold. Furthermore, this extends to firms' borrowing from financial institutions. In short, the external capital structures of large Japanese corporations, both single- and multiple-alliance, share the features of mutual equity holdings, close linkages to other business arrangements, and long-term stability.

What differentiates these two firms, and single- from multiple-alliance firms in general, is the affiliation of the corporate shareholders. Whereas the ownership of Nippon Steel is dispersed across financial institutions in different groups, ownership of Sumitomo Metal Industries is concentrated largely within the Sumitomo group (the sole representative of another keiretsu being Nippon Life, loosely of the Sanwa group).[12]

Further Evidence of Similarities in Network Patterns

That the similarity of patterns is not unique to Nippon Steel is provided further support by comparing network relationships among the entire sample of 250 industrial and financial enterprises in Japan. Firms were divided into shachō-kai members and non-shachō-kai members and compared along the same set of dimensions. Figure 5.1 shows that the stability of equity interlocks over time has been almost identical for both groups of firms, with less than 20 percent of the leading shareholding positions "broken" in any two-year period since 1969. Over the four-year period 1980–84, 81 percent of the top-ten shareholders remained stable in the shachō-kai firms and 83 percent in the non-shachō-kai firms. In comparison, as shown in Chapter 3, only 23 percent of the leading shareholding positions were stable in the 250 firms in the U.S. sample.

Table 5.7 demonstrates that multiplex ownership relationships are also common across Japanese business networks. Among non-shachō-kai firms, 47.5 percent of the top-ten shareholding positions involved identifiable relationships across other types of ties, just below the 50.6 percent figure for shachō-kai firms. In over 10 percent of the cases for both groups, these involved simultaneous directorship positions, a number much higher than that found in Chapter 3 for the firms in the U.S. sample (2.1 percent). These results indicate that important characteris-

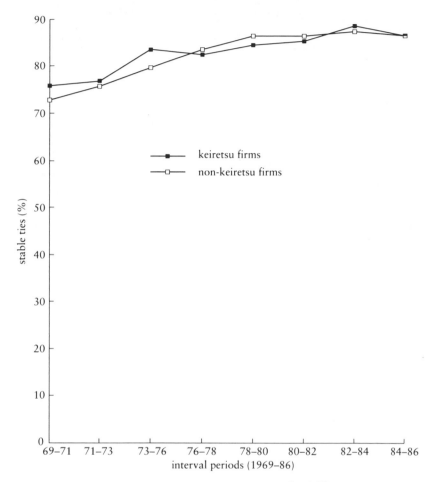

Fig. 5.1.   Proportion of Stable Top-Ten Equity Ties, by Affiliation. Source: See Appendix A.

tics of network structure are common among both shachō-kai and non-shachō-kai firms, suggesting a high degree of institutionalization in these overall patterns in Japan. In contrast, major differences appear to exist in network structures in the United States and Japan.

THE DETERMINANTS AND OUTCOMES
OF SHACHŌ-KAI MEMBERSHIP

What then, if anything, distinguishes shachō-kai member firms from other large Japanese corporations? And what does this tell us about the

TABLE 5.7.   MULTIPLEXITY
OF EQUITY INTERLOCKS, 1980

Interlocks	Shachō-kai (%)	Non-shachō-kai (%)
Equity only	49.4	52.5
Multiplex ties		
Equity + Directors	1.7	2.0
Equity + Directors + Debt	7.1	6.3
Equity + Directors + Trade	1.3	1.8
Equity + Directors + Debt + Trade	0.1	—
(*Equity/Directors Subtotal*)	(10.2)	(10.1)
Equity + Debt	33.0	31.9
Equity + Trade	7.2	5.5
Equity + Debt + Trade	0.1	—
(*Subtotal of all multiplex ties*)	(50.6)	(47.5)
Total	100.0	100.0

SOURCE: See Appendix A.

overall function of the contemporary keiretsu in the Japanese economy? A number of researchers have attempted to infer the functions of business groupings from the characteristics of their constituent firms. Firms that are strongly affiliated with particular keiretsu are compared with those that are not. To the extent these two sets of firms differ systematically along certain measures, such as company performance, these differences are presumed to explain the strategies of the companies involved.

Among the most interesting and influential of these studies is that of Nakatani (1984), who finds in a series of regression models that independent firms have higher rates of profitability and sales growth than firms classified with one of the major six intermarket groups, but also higher rates of variance in profitability and sales and lower levels of employee compensation. Nakatani interprets these results in terms of an implicit insurance scheme in which managers in affiliated enterprises sacrifice profits and sales in favor of risk sharing and external stability. Since Japanese managers cannot diversify their own risks resulting from job loss in the same way that shareholders are able to diversify a stock portfolio, he argues, they have created a structure for reducing it—the keiretsu. Joint stock crossholdings, loans from group banks, and intra-group sales create a stable firm environment and shelter managers from external pressures, including hostile takeovers and company failures. In this way, the group represents "an ingenious solution to the problem of the non-existence of contingent markets for 'management risks'" (p. 229).

Although Nakatani's results have been widely cited, several caveats to his interpretations should be noted. First, the overall performance differences between "keiretsu" and "non-keiretsu" firms in his sample, while in a consistent direction, were quite small across most variables, with profit rates and sales growth averaging less than 2 percent lower for most of the six groups and profit and sales variance less than 1 percent.[13] Second, results in several other studies fail to demonstrate equally consistent performance effects. An earlier study by Caves and Uekusa (1976) finds negative correlations between group membership and company profitability, although the absolute differences are even smaller than those shown by Nakatani and only occasionally reach statistical significance. In more recent studies, Cable and Yasuki (1985) are unable to demonstrate significant group effects on profitability for most of their measures, while Roehl (1989) shows that group effects on stock returns vary over time.

The relatively small differences observed in all of these studies and the inconsistency of the results suggest that caution should be exercised in extrapolating findings to a general theory of the function or origins of the keiretsu. Important issues remain unresolved in understanding the consequences of groups for company performance, including the effect of different classifications of membership, the effects of these classifications on other factors that shape and define corporate strategy and performance, the possibility that performance effects will vary with the time periods studied, and the type of performance measures tested. As demonstrated above, large Japanese firms vary far less along important dimensions of intercorporate relationships than is often assumed. Whether formally affiliated with a group or not these companies hold in common long-term, reciprocal, and multiplex network ties that make them far more similar to each other than to most American firms. Moreover, the central role of history in the alliance-formation process means that particular patterns of relationships will be determined to a large extent by path-dependent causeways rather than the immediate interests of the companies involved.

This is not to say that Japanese firms or their alliance patterns are entirely identical. At a minimum, social perceptions of firms often differ substantially, with ex-zaibatsu firms widely perceived as more conservative than their postwar counterparts (e.g., more recent start-ups such as Sony or Honda). As we see in this section, shachō-kai and non-shachō-kai firms also differ in other interesting ways across a range of factors. These differences become important, for we find in later performance analyses that it is variations along these dimensions, rather than group membership per se, that explain profitability among large Japanese companies.

Characteristics of Shachō-kai Members

Among the 200 industrial firms in our sample, 89 participated in at least one shachō-kai as of 1982 while the remaining 111 did not. Since these firms do not appear to differ substantially in the basic relationships they have with equity shareholders, are there other factors that help to define distinctive characteristics of the two groups? We consider here the following variables related to firms' positions in product markets, capital markets, and the overall business community:

1. Product market position.
   a. *Industry type*—whether a firm is in a producer or a consumer industry.
   b. *Market dominance*—the extent to which a firm holds a dominant position in its primary product line.
   c. *Export ratio*—the share of a company's total sales accounted for by overseas markets.
2. Capital market position.
   a. *Debt-equity ratios*—a company's capital structure.
   b. *Ownership structure*—the extent to which the firm has a dominant owner (individual, family or parent company).
   c. *Main bank relationship*—the share of a company's borrowing coming from its top lender.
3. Business community position.
   a. *Company age*—the company's tenure in the business community.
   b. *Company size*—as measured by total assets.

Table 5.8 presents overall means for shachō-kai and non-shachō-kai firms along each variable, as well as statistical significance tests of differ-

TABLE 5.8.   A COMPARISON OF SHACHŌ-KAI
AND NON-SHACHŌ-KAI MEMBERS
AMONG JAPAN'S 200 LARGEST INDUSTRIAL FIRMS

Variable Description	Means		
	SK-member	Nonmember	t-Statistic
Product market position			
Product line composition (% of products in consumer markets)	22.4	44.9	3.81***
Industry dominance (% of firms with dominant position in main market)	5.6	15.4	2.32*
Export ratio (% of sales in overseas markets)	16.4	13.8	1.16
Capital market position			
Debt-equity ratio (total debt/shareholders' equity)	3.12	1.67	3.06**
Dominant owner (% of firms with dominant owner [> 10 percent of shares])	18.0	41.8	3.81***
Main bank relationship (% of borrowed capital from leading lender)	16.9	22.4	3.03**
Business community position			
Postwar founding (% of firms founded after WWII)	11.2	23.6	2.35*
Company size (total assets, in billion yen)	525.6	238.9	4.00***

SOURCES: See text and Appendix A for information on coding of data.
   * = p < .05, two-tailed test.
  ** = p < .01.
 *** = p < .001.

ences. As this table indicates, the two groups of firms do indeed differ significantly, and on all but one of these variables. Some explanations for these findings are offered below.

Product Market Position   Discussion in Chapters 3 and 4 indicates that intermarket keiretsu members are disproportionately represented in producer-oriented industries and intermediate product markets. That is, these groupings constitute what we might call the "industrial core" of the Japanese economy in the sense that they are predominantly alliances of industrial manufacturers, their financial backers, and their commercial representatives. Their structure is that of a partially internalized trading system among firms specializing in raw materials, metal, chemicals, and machinery industries, supported by group financial institutions, and working through the group sōgō shōsha.

In contrast, firms in consumer-oriented markets are organized within the quite different vertical keiretsu that bring together a single large manufacturer and elaborate networks of medium and smaller firms that extend backward into subcontracting and forward into distribution, retail sales, and the final consumer. The parent firms in these industries organize production and marketing functions and serve as conduits through which products flow from components to final markets. In selling highly differentiated products, these firms have taken the strategy of controlling their own distribution networks rather than working through a large trading company. This suggests that the incentives for affiliation might be lower among firms oriented toward consumer markets than among firms oriented toward industrial markets, since group membership will open fewer trading doors for them. Alternatively, as we see below, group membership may be important as a means of accessing capital, and this will be especially important for firms in capital-intensive industrial sectors.

In order to test for the impact of industry type on membership patterns, all 200 firms were classified by the share of sales accounted for by product-lines that were either producer-oriented or consumer-oriented. Market orientation was coded according to the proportion of a firm's products sold mainly to other industrial firms (i.e., producer-oriented) versus nonindustrial users, such as distributors and individual consumers (i.e., consumer-oriented).[14] Product-line proportions for each firm were determined from the 1980 volume of the *Japan Company Handbook*. We see support for the importance of industry type as a variable in that among the 111 non-shachō-kai firms, average product composition was 45 percent consumer-oriented, while for the 89 shachō-kai firms it was only 22 percent, a statistically significant difference.

Although gaining market access may drive producer-oriented firms into keiretsu, these same alliances may constrain other market opportunities. For this reason, firms that maintain a clearly dominant position in an industry may have less incentive to develop clear affiliations than those with more modest positions. By remaining independent, market-dominant firms are in a position to sell to companies in all groups, as well as to other independent firms. Each is treated on a more equal basis and the widest market can be served.[15] These firms are furthermore less likely to seek the security and prestige associated with group affiliation, since these same features accrue already from their strong market-leadership position.

The 200 industrial firms were classified dichotomously as either dominant or nondominant in their industry. Industry sales and market shares were calculated from data provided in the 1982 volume of *Industrial Groupings in Japan* and the 1980 volume of the *Japan Company Handbook*. Dominant firms were defined as those in which the firm was the leader in its industry and moreover controlled a share of industry sales in its primary product lines more than double that of its next leading competitor.[16] By this definition, 23 of the 200 firms were industrially dominant. Among these 23 firms, 6 were group members and 17 were not, representing 7 percent of all group firms and 15 percent of all nongroup firms, also a statistically significant difference.

Another way of measuring the market constraint hypothesis is by looking at the share of total sales by shachō-kai and non-shachō-kai firms going toward overseas markets. If the first are more constrained in domestic markets, we would expect these firms to have a greater incentive to export than independent firms. An alternative interpretation of the same results, and one more positive in its view of group functioning, is that these firms are better able to export for reasons of financial or logistical group support in their home markets. Results for export ratios, taken from the *Japan Company Handbook* (1980), indicate that both shachō-kai and non-shachō-kai firms obtained the vast majority of their revenue from sales within Japan itself. Only 16 percent of total sales of shachō-kai firms and only 14 percent of non-shachō-kai firms came in overseas markets. These differences are statistically insignificant.

The overall image that emerges from the analysis of the product-market positions of the two sets of firms is that shachō-kai membership is more likely among firms in industrial markets but that membership does not appear to be associated with a strong market position, either domestically or internationally. While it is not surprising that core group members tend to be in producer sectors of the Japanese economy, the finding that it is non-shachō-kai companies that are most likely to have dominant market positions runs counter to much of the writing on Japan's business groupings, which sees them as manifestations of market power (e.g., Miyazaki, 1976). Understanding this finding requires acknowledging the dual consequences of alliance as opportunity and constraint, discussed later in this chapter.

Capital Market Position   The second set of variables concerns the position of companies in markets for capital and corporate control. In a series of carefully crafted studies, Hoshi and his colleagues have argued that strong financial linkages allow the keiretsu to play an important role in Japanese capital markets (Hoshi, Kashyap, and Scharfstein, 1990a, 1990b, 1990c). Following other recent observers (e.g., Sheard, 1986; Horiuchi, Packer, and Fukuda, 1988), they argue that main banks may serve as corporate monitors who pay the costs of becoming informed about their client firms, thereby ensuring that the managers of these firms take efficient actions (Hoshi, Kashyap, and Scharfstein, 1990a). Taking the models of Myers and Majluf (1984) and others as their starting point, they posit certain information problems in the capital market and predict that firm-level "liquidity" will be positively related to investment, since managers are privately informed about the value of investment. In results that are strongly supportive of this hypothesis, they find that (a) the marginal effects of liquidity on independent firms' investment is nearly ten times as large as the effect for affiliated firms' investment; and (b) firms that have reduced the amount of borrowing from their main bank are increasingly liquidity-constrained (Hoshi, Kashyap, and Scharfstein, 1990b).

Further support for the role of the keiretsu in reducing liquidity constraints is provided by comparing the debt-equity ratios of shachō-kai members with other firms. Nakatani measured the rate of own capital to total assets for the firms in his sample and found the rates to be 4–9 percent higher for firms with close ties to the six major keiretsu. These findings are reinforced in Table 5.8, based on calculations utilizing the NEEDS corporate financial database. Derived from a somewhat different measure from Nakatani's (i.e., total debt to shareholders' equity), the figures here show shachō-kai firms to have nearly twice the debt-to-equity ratios of non-shachō-kai firms. The keiretsu, therefore, appear to be serving as an important source of external capital for these firms when compared with their non-shachō-kai counterparts.

While supportive of the view that the keiretsu serve as collective monitors, thereby permitting higher debt-to-equity ratios and reducing liquidity constraints on member firms, these results must also be considered in light of the performance consequences of group membership. Studies of corporate profitability, noted earlier and discussed further below, show that companies with close group affiliations perform no better than other firms, despite the prediction that monitoring will effectively discipline the managers of these companies. However, it is also possible that other monitoring devices are serving as substitutes for the keiretsu.

Under one monitoring alternative, a dominant owner controls an extensive portion of a company's total shares. This might be a single individual, a family, or another firm. Using a 10 percent minimum to define effective control and borrowing from the shareholder listings in the *Japan Company Handbook* (1980), I classified the 200 industrial firms in the sample dichotomously as either owner-dominant or non-dominant.[17] Sixty-three were classified on the basis of the 10 percent criterion as having dominant owners. Of these 63 firms, 17 were group members and 46 were not, or 18 percent of all shachō-kai and 42 percent of all non-shachō-kai firms. Thus, group member firms are much more likely to be diffusely held.

Under a second monitoring alternative, a substantial portion of total loans is extended by a single, "delegated" main bank. Using the *Keiretsu no kenkyū* data provided earlier in Chapter 4, the strength of the main bank relationships was calculated for each industrial firm in the sample based on the absolute share of borrowings from a company's leading creditor. The figures reported in Table 5.8 suggest that non-shachō-kai firms actually borrowed on average a higher percentage from their leading banks than did shachō-kai firms (22 percent versus 17 percent). Although somewhat surprising in light of the close banking relationships found within groups, these results may reflect the process described in Chapter 4, whereby core firms use their affiliations to "prime the pump" for multiple bank loans. This process opens access to capital from other financial institutions both within and outside their own group, leading to high ratios of debt to equity but smaller proportionate borrowing from any single lender.

The results overall are consistent with the view that groups, dominant owners, and dominant banking relationships represent alternative structures of capital allocation and governance. That is, shachō-kai firms rely on a partially internalized but diffuse set of shareholding and banking relationships, while non-shachō-kai firms are more likely to have strong ties to a single, dominant shareholder or bank.

It should not be forgotten, however, that there is a strongly strategic element to the relationships among corporate managers and financial monitors that make their interaction more complex than a simple substitution effect suggests. For example, in the ongoing positioning among these groups for corporate control, the power that can be exercised by a dominant shareholder is maximized by having external capital as diffusely spread and poorly organized as possible. Alliances, in contrast, are coherent governance structures that typically control over one-third of the leading shareholding positions and maintain a forum, through their executive councils, in which to act in concert if necessary. Group membership, therefore, involves a partial relinquishing of control, a fact that can have significant implications for a company's flexibility in forging other business relationships. Where firms are still under the leadership of a founder or other major owner, they may be less likely to give up control unless the group offers compelling advantages over independence. For this reason, among satellite firms controlled by large parent companies, membership only occurs in cases where the parent concern is also a group member (e.g., Mitsubishi Motors under the auspices of Mitsubishi Heavy Industries or Sumitomo Light Metals through the support of Sumitomo Metal Industries).

Business Community Position   While the preceding variables reflect a company's position in the markets, a third set of variables reflects more general considerations regarding a company's overall social and economic position. Company age reflects the firm's tenure in the business community. The former zaibatsu groups, and to a lesser extent the bank groups, have reemerged with their prewar predecessor firms as nuclei. Even those older firms that were not part of the original zaibatsu are more likely to have built up the network of connections necessary to be invited to participate in a presidents' council.

The two hundred industrial firms were classified dichotomously as either a prewar or a postwar firm based on company-founding information provided in the 1986 volume of *Kaisha nenkan*. When a firm's history as a corporation could be traced to the period prior to Japan's defeat in the second world war, it was coded as a prewar firm, while those that were started after the war were coded as postwar. Among the two hundred industrials, thirty-six firms are postwar firms. Among these thirty-six, nine are shachō-kai members and twenty-six are nonmembers, or 10 percent of all group firms and 24 percent of all nongroup firms, a statistically significant difference.

Although company size is partially controlled for by limiting the sample of companies studied to Japan's two hundred largest industrial firms, there is still the possibility that within these companies, size may be a significant determinant of membership. To test this, companies' total assets were also measured. Data came from the 1980 volume of the *Japan Company Handbook*. As Table 5.8 shows, shachō-kai members were more than twice as large, with average total assets of ¥525 billion in comparison with only ¥239 billion for nonmember firms.

Shachō-kai Membership and Corporate Profitability

The above results suggest a number of differences in the characteristics of shachō-kai and non-shachō-kai firms. How, then, do these differences, including keiretsu membership itself, relate to the financial performance of Japanese corporations? While previous studies have found negative (or zero) correlations between group membership and company profitability, it may be that these results are confounded by other factors of the kind shown above to covary with group membership. These factors, of course, are an important source of information about the nature and purposes of the keiretsu. But it is also worth exploring the effects of these factors on company performance directly, for they may provide independent information.

Table 5.9 reports results from several models of returns on assets (ROA) for the two hundred industrial firms in the sample. The first column shows the basic performance model in which group membership is included, along with a set of control variables comparable to those found in Nakatani's study (1984).[18] The data were from a more recent time period (1976–85) than that used by Nakatani (1971–82), while the same pooled cross-sectional approach to analysis was employed. The sample was split according to both Nakatani's classification system and the much more conservative measure of shachō-kai membership.[19] Interestingly, performance results were very similar for both samples, with the shachō-kai definition able to recreate the negative returns found in the earlier study. Findings reported here refer to runs based on shachō-kai membership, in keeping with analyses earlier in this chapter and in Chapter 4. Shachō-kai members as a whole have profit rates that are lower by about 1.9 percent than non-shachō-kai member firms, in the range of those shown by Nakatani.

In the second column of the table, two capital structure variables that were shown in Table 5.8 to covary with shachō-kai participation have been added to the model. Both of these variables, dominant ownership and main bank share of total loans, prove significantly and positively correlated with company profitability. At the same time, the negative

TABLE 5.9.   REGRESSION ANALYSES
OF DETERMINANTS OF PROFIT RATES
FOR LARGE INDUSTRIAL FIRMS, 1976–85

Independent Variable	Model		
	(1)	(2)	(3)
Constant	0.0716***	0.0549***	0.0383***
	(0.0081)	(0.0089)	(0.0092)
Nominal GNP Growth	0.0104	0.0132	0.0569
	(0.0016)	(0.0550)	(0.0563)
Average Wages	−0.0053	−0.0139	0.0158
	(0.0013)	(0.0196)	(0.0203)
Total Assets	1.3×10^{-9}	7.9×10^{-9}	8.3×10^{-9}*
	(3.0×10^{-9})	(3.3×10^{-9})	(3.5×10^{-9})
Group Member	−0.01940***	−0.0147***	−0.0130***
	(0.0029)	(0.0031)	(0.0031)
Dominant Owner		0.0117***	0.0077*
		(0.0035)	(0.0036)
Main Bank		0.0005***	0.0005***
		(0.0001)	(0.0001)
Debt-equity			−0.0001*
			(3.9×10^{-5})
Industry Dominance			0.0031
			(0.0054)
Postwar Founding			0.0235***
			(0.0040)
Adjusted R-square	0.325	0.474	0.416
F	54.859	51.190	48.157

SOURCES: See text and Appendix A.
Notes: Industry dummies were also included in the models, but are not reported here.
The upper figures for each variable are coefficients and the lower figures are standard errors.
    * = $p < .05$, two-tailed test.
  ** = $p < .01$.
*** = $p < .001$.

coefficients for group membership decline in this model, yet remain statistically significant.

The positive coefficient for dominant ownership is interesting in light of the earlier discussion of the possibility that this might serve as a substitute for group membership in the monitoring of corporate performance. In theory, concentrated shareholding should result in an investing body with greater incentives to watch over managerial performance and greater ability to effect changes in the management team if needed. Empirical tests of the effects of ownership structure on company performance in the United States have provided mixed results, with some studies finding that firms with strong owner control outperform diffusely held corporations and other studies finding no effect (cf. Larner, 1966; Demsetz and Lehn, 1985). The results reported here suggest some support for the view that concentration of ownership in Japan is associated with performance improvements, as measured by returns on assets.

It is possible that concentration in bank loans will have a similar effect. Empirical tests of this hypothesis in the United States have been lacking, however, in part because the necessary data on banking ties have not been available. This makes the results reported here especially interesting, since the strength of ties to a lead bank are tested directly. The positive and statistically significant effect on profitability of borrowing a substantial share of total loans from a single main bank is consistent with a bank monitoring hypothesis.

While these results suggest support for the argument that dominant shareholders and banks in Japan monitor corporate managements in the interest of improving profitability, the monitoring argument also faces the anomalous finding that group membership continues to be associated with somewhat poorer profitability. Is the implication therefore that groups as a whole are ineffective in evaluating and influencing the managements of their member firms? This interpretation seems doubtful in light of the extensive mechanisms keiretsu companies have to influence poorly performing members (discussed in Chapter 4 and again in Chapter 7). An alternative, and I believe more plausible, interpretation is that group membership is associated with a variety of business interests, some of them not directly related to corporate profitability.

As pointed out in the earlier discussion, shachō-kai membership may open up access to resources in diverse markets, but this access also comes at some cost to firms. Evidence of higher debt-equity ratios and the results of other studies suggest that membership reduces the constraints on firms' capital liquidity. At the same time, the smaller proportion of group firms with dominant positions in their own product markets shown earlier in Table 5.8 reflect the difficulties firms with strong affiliations have in expanding their across-keiretsu sales.

The final model in Table 5.9 explores the effects of these two variables, as well as company founding date, on company performance.[20] The negative coefficient shown here for debt-equity ratios is interesting in light of several arguments suggesting that their relationship to profitability should be positive. Jensen (1986) proposes that high leverage eliminates companies' free cash flow, thereby reducing the discretion managers have to pursue their own (non-profit-maximizing) interests. In extending this discussion to Japan, Jensen (1989) suggests that high ratios of debt to equity are a source of competitive advantage for Japanese firms, an effect that ought to show up in performance improvements with increased leverage. It also seems reasonable that highly leveraged firms will be riskier, and will therefore require a higher payout to reward investors.

On the other hand, the negative results are consistent with the view that bank borrowing opens channels to capital that is used for investment projects not intended simply for direct returns. As Aoki (1984b, 1988) points out, banks that serve as companies' equity investors may accept lower shareholding profits if they enjoy a substantial loan business with those firms. Higher rates of borrowing by companies may also reflect "insurance premiums" that they pay in return for protections offered by their main banks should they face financial difficulties (Caves and Uekusa, 1976; Nakatani, 1984; Hoshi, Kashyap, and Scharfstein, 1990c). Nevertheless, these results should be interpreted with some caution. Considerable uncertainty remains regarding the origins and outcomes of corporate capital structure, and the proper balancing of debt, equity, and other capital sources depends on many factors (Myers, 1984; see also Chapter 8).

The industry dominance variable in this model attempts to capture the consequences of a firm's position in its primary market. Although detailed data on firm-level market share is beyond the scope of this study, this variable represents a partial proxy by considering whether the lower profitability of shachō-kai members is a function of the fact that, as noted earlier, few of these firms have strong positions in their primary markets. The effect of this variable, however, appears to be negligible in this model.

More important in predicting profit rates is the company founding date, the final variable included in the model. The positive coefficient identified here indicates that firms founded after the second world war have profit rates over 2 percent higher during the time period studied here than firms founded before the war. This finding seems to mesh with general views in Japan that it is the younger, postwar companies that have performed most impressively in the past two decades.

In sum, what can be said about the group membership–company

performance relationship? Insofar as the effects of the group dummy variable on corporate profitability remain negative in all models, formal group membership would not appear simply to be a profit-maximizing strategy. As suggested earlier, group membership reflects a complex set of strategic considerations that determine both patterns of membership and resulting organizational outcomes in ways we are only beginning to appreciate. Corporate profitability itself is a function of a wide variety of considerations, including a company's ownership structure, the strength of its banking relationships, its debt-equity ratios, and its age.

Although the overall results suggest that the two sets of firms differ somewhat in their overall profitability, the values for group coefficients are sufficiently small (1–2 percent here, as well as in Nakatani's study) that it seems unlikely that performance differences are the main reason behind affiliation patterns in Japan. As discussed earlier, there is a strongly institutional character to patterns of alliance in Japan. Large firms share many features of ownership and other networks, while specific patterns often reflect the distinctive evolution of particular relationships. Even relatively independent firms craft various governance structures in their intercorporate networks. Many firms outside the shachō-kai, for example, maintain strong main bank relationships, and these may prove to be important sources of capital or of introductions to new business opportunities. It should not be surprising for this reason that similarities in performance linkages are also found: where overall network patterns tend to be isomorphic and where history is the main determinant of specific ties, strong performance differences among firms along a single (and possibly crude) dimension like "group membership" are unlikely.

GROUP-LEVEL DETERMINANTS OF MEMBERSHIP PATTERNS: THE ROLE OF THE ONE-SET PRINCIPLE

Just as firms seek to position themselves advantageously in their industry and in the broader business community, so too do groups as a whole. This is perhaps clearest in the processes by which groups have sought to regulate their membership. Through control over participation, the group acts to enhance its position in the business community vis-à-vis other groups while controlling internal competition by limiting firms in overlapping industries.

Together, these twin goals have led to the one-set membership pattern, in which groups strive to have in their core one company involved in each major industry, but only one company (Miyazaki, 1976). The working rules of alliance membership captured in this phase are twofold. To borrow from the terminology that anthropologists have used to describe patterns in kinship alliances (e.g., Levi-Strauss, 1969), I will call these the positive or inclusionary rule, and the negative or exclusionary rule. The positive rule is an affirmation of the need for external connections—exogamy as a positive process of establishing politically and economically useful outside relationships. The normative requirement is that the group be included in all major industries—"from soup noodles to missiles," as Mitsubishi's trading company puts it.[21] The negative or exclusionary rule—the prohibition against endogamy—states that, furthermore, no more than one company in the same industry should be a member, because this would create conditions that lead to internecine competition.

It is perhaps in the one-set principle that the interaction of alliances, industries, and positions in the wider business community is clearest. The overall pattern in the keiretsu, as we have seen, is one of wide diversification into most major financial, commercial, and industrial markets. Industrial gaps are filled in one of two ways. They may be filled through the initiation of group-wide projects, leading to project waves of the sort discussed in Chapter 4, as groups seek to emulate each other in the competition for prestige. More important, expansion into other fields may be carried out through the addition of new member firms already involved in those fields. The new shachō-kai participants added during the 1966–89 period (listed earlier in Table 5.3) have been heavily weighted in favor of five industries: trade and commerce, construction, chemicals, general and transportation machinery, and electrical and precision machinery. Whereas these five industries represented only 52 of the 137 total shachō-kai memberships in 1966, or 38 percent, 42 of the 62 total new memberships over the next 23 years, or 67 percent, were added in these areas. Total membership in the five industries expanded by 81 percent during this period, in comparison with an expansion of only 24 percent in the other 14 sectors.

Yet while new memberships have been added primarily within these few industries, most of this expansion has involved the introduction into the group of firms that compete against firms in other groups rather than within the same group. Among the four groups of Mitsui, Mitsubishi, Sumitomo, and Fuji, none of the new members is in industries that overlap significantly with existing group members. Within the chemical area of the Fuji group, for example, while Showa Denko is a petrochemical specialist and Nippon Oil and Fats focuses on oil-based paints and chemicals, a new member, Kureha, is involved primarily in pharmaceuticals. The Sanwa and Dai-Ichi Kangyo groups, which are more loosely structured, have been more willing to expand into competitive overlaps. Several executives in the Dai-Ichi Kangyo group emphasized the relative independence of companies in the group and the reluctance to adhere too closely to a one-set pattern. Both have been active in expanding during this period, with Sanwa adding twenty-two new members and Dai-Ichi Kangyo twenty, a number of them direct competitors with other group companies. Sekisui Chemical and Hitachi Chemical, both new members in the Sanwa group, are each leading producers of synthetic resins, while Fujisawa and Tanabe Seiyaku both compete in several lines of pharmaceuticals. Overall, however, new members come primarily from industrial fields not yet represented in the group.

Exogamous Expansion: The Inclusion Rule

In anthropological alliance theory (Dumont, 1957; Fox, 1967; Levi-Strauss, 1969), the positive role of alliance states that exchange outside one's immediate kin group has value to the group in establishing relationships with other parties that can be called on in times of need or for protection of one's own group. Translated into business group terms, the positive rule is a policy of establishing linkages with a wide range of critical industries, with a resulting structure of inclusion, the breadth of which is the source of its strength. By expanding to include group-level representation in a broad variety of fields, the alliance simultaneously preempts market opportunities, enhances its prestige in the larger business community, and diversifies risk across a spectrum of industries.

The rapid expansion in the industries of trade and commerce, construction, chemicals, and machinery reflects the industrial orientation of the groups and the rapid development in these industries over the past two decades. Commercial operations are the core around which expanding Japanese trade depends. Construction has been at the center of the industrial building boom that has occurred over the past two decades. Chemical and machinery industries are also core fields, though, interestingly, expansion in these areas has been oriented as much toward the growing Japanese consumer markets as it has toward industrial markets. Among the new members in chemical industries, three are in pharmaceuticals while a fourth is in cosmetics. Among machinery makers, three are automobile companies and three others are camera makers.

The pattern of expansion of the groups corresponds to the development of Japan as a world power in these industries. And with power goes prestige. Affiliation by prestigious corporations enhances the position of the entire group, since attractive membership roles make the group more appealing to prospective business partners and improves its status in the larger business community. Affiliation opens doors to trade with other group members, and with the trading partners those firms have. There is a widespread belief, for example, that Japan's most profitable bank, Sumitomo, has been facilitated in finding new trade by the success of its client firms in the Sumitomo group, such as rapidly growing NEC and Sumitomo Electric. The fortunes of group companies are in this way intertwined.

Over the past decade a number of "honorary" memberships have been extended to certain prestigious firms that were formerly reluctant to ally themselves too closely with a group. Toyota's and Toshiba's entrance into Mitsui's shachō-kai in the 1970s is a prominent example. With their entrance, the image of the Mitsui group within the Japanese business community, which was declining relative to Mitsubishi's and Sumitomo's in the 1950s and 1960s, improved substantially.

In addition to market preemption and prestige enhancement, expansion of the group into new fields also serves to distribute group risk. The spreading of risk across partially uncorrelated social sectors has been an important explanation for a wide variety of forms of organization, including the conglomerate firm (Amihud, Dodd, and Weinstein, 1986), implicit labor contracts (Akerlof, 1983), extended kinship groups (Posner, 1980), and certain forms of primitive reciprocity (Sahlins, 1972). Since managerial security and overall organizational stability are important considerations in the strategy of alliance, discussed below, representation in a broad set of industrial sectors buffers the group in a dynamic economy both from short-term economic fluctuations and from the dislocations involved in long-term industrial restructuring and the decline of some industries. By linking firms in multiple industries, a performance decline in some firms (which may require additional capital infusion from the bank or a location to send excess workers that would otherwise have to be laid off) can be counterbalanced against the performance of firms that are still in good financial health. Breadth, in this sense, distributes gains and losses across firms and becomes a kind of insurance policy against possible future problems. In addition, breadth confers on the group self-sufficiency across an extended network of "safe" intragroup trading partners. Petroleum companies, for example, were reported to favor other companies in their own group during the oil shortages in the mid-1970s.

Internal Limits on Membership: The Exclusion Rule

If the positive rule of membership states the group should expand to create key external linkages, then the negative rule states that this expansion should take place without the duplication of similar members. In part, this pattern can be explained as a function of the peculiar history of the former zaibatsu groups. These groups reconstituted themselves largely around the core subsidiaries of the old honsha, each of which was in a different industry, and this division of labor has been maintained in the decades since the zaibatsu dissolution. As these groups have brought in new members, however, the pattern of industrial exclusivity has been maintained.

The keiretsu is a socially rather than legally constructed form and cannot rely on the same enforcement of rights as corporations enjoy. For this reason, it is particularly sensitive to the quality of the relationships among its member firms. When, for example, group firms are asked to come to the assistance of another group firm in trouble, the primary obligations for assistance are moral ones. The rule of exclusion reduces the possibilities for internal conflict by avoiding competitive overlap. It is a means of creating a closer, more cohesive social system. Firms that are core group participants have a de facto first claim on that industry against infringements by other current or prospective members—a kind of rule of primogeniture. By maintaining only one firm in an industry, internal sources of competition are thereby reduced.

This is not simply a process of choosing fields to be in and picking members accordingly. It also involves internal political battles among existing group members over representation in different industries. These rarely become public, but when they do, they provide clear evidence of group processes at work. One of the most important challenges to the one-set pattern occurred in the early 1970s within the Sumitomo group, the most exclusive of the groups. Sumitomo Light Metals, a subsidiary of Sumitomo Metal Industries, decided to enter the aluminum industry in order to integrate backward into aluminum production. Sumitomo Chemical, however, was already involved in aluminum production and protested before the Sumitomo shachō-kai that this would be a "duplicate investment" for the group. The council agreed but was unable to convince Light Metals or its parent, Metal Industries, to abandon the project. In 1972 the president of Sumitomo Light Metals announced plans for an aluminum smelter to be completed by 1975. At this point the Japanese Ministry of International Trade and Industry intervened, claiming that this would result in excess capacity in the Japanese aluminum industry. Moving back to the group level, a compromise was reached whereby Sumitomo Chemical's existing smelter was spun off as a separate company, Sumitomo Aluminum Smelting, jointly owned by Sumitomo Chemical and Sumitomo Metal Industries.

Mergers are another means of reducing intragroup competition. Mergers within groups have been common since the 1950s and are often carried out at the urging of the group bank for the purpose of eliminating divisive industrial overlaps. This is a delicately negotiated process, as the firms to be merged themselves have to be convinced. During the early 1970s, the Sanwa Bank strongly pushed on its two main trading firms at the time, Nissho-Iwai and Nichimen, to merge in order to create a single firm that could represent the group on the same level and scale as the leading sōgō shōsha in the other five groups. The executives in both firms refused with a public vehemence unusual in Japan. Nissho-Iwai's president at the time, Tsuji Yoshio, commented to the press, "There is nothing realistic about the idea of one trading company per bank. Consequently, there would be no compelling reason for insisting that we must merge with Nichimen" (*Oriental Economist,* November 1972). Nichimen's president, Kobayashi Masanori, was even more blunt: "There will be no merger. We will rather go into liquidation."

THE STRATEGY OF ALLIANCE: A SUMMARY

Affiliation is a matter of degrees rather than a clear in-or-out decision. Some firms maintain close connections with a single group, while other firms balance their associations among more than one group in a multiple-affiliation strategy. The considerations that move firms in one strategic direction or another covary, as we saw, with certain features of product market position, capital market position, and business community position. Firms in producer markets are more likely to be shachō-kai members, indicating the central role of these groups in core industrial sectors that produce intermediate goods. More likely to be independent are firms with dominant owners or a strong single bank, firms with low debt-equity ratios, newer firms, and smaller firms.

These considerations are not entirely determinative, however. There remains a degree of strategic flexibility, as both group member firms and those that are not maneuver through business networks, slowly moving toward new alliances and/or away from old alliances and manipulating the extent of their involvement in each. What are the fundamental strategic considerations that drive these choices?

The primary importance of the group appears to be in creating and maintaining a stable, ongoing framework for interfirm exchange. Through alliances, firms gain access to reliable sources of capital and trade within the group, as well as a degree of collective security. Haitani (1976, p. 125) has referred to groups as "mutual help societies," Kobayashi (1979, p. 63) has used the term "life lines" (*inochi tsuna*), and Sheard (1989, p. 308) describes groups as a "quasi-insurance agency." One way security is offered, as we shall see in Chapter 7, is by buffering alliance firms from the potential threat of outside shareholders through the creation of stable stock crossholdings.

A second way is by providing assistance to group firms in times of trouble. The Sumitomo group, for example, has been called upon to help out member companies in a number of important cases in the postwar period. In the 1954 salvation of the nearly collapsed Sumitomo Machinery, Sumitomo Bank arranged for an extension of loans from itself and Sumitomo Trust and Banking and sent down a number of leading executives to rehabilitate the firm; Sumitomo Corporation cut its margin in half on its trade with the company; and other Sumitomo group companies agreed to maintain their shareholdings in Sumitomo Heavy Industries and to give the firm priority in its purchases (Atsuta, 1979; for more recent examples, see Sheard, 1991).

The importance of alliance relationships for assistance in times of need, even among firms not formally in a group, has received more rigorous empirical support in a study by Suzuki Sadahiko (1980). Suzuki investigated fifty-two Japanese firms facing company failure to see what features distinguished those that were assisted back to solvency by banks from those that were not. What he found was that the leading determinant of firm salvation was the strength of the firm's main bank relationship. The strength of this relationship was measured by the size of the loans from bank to company, the extent of bank equity involvement, and the existence of personnel connections between bank and company. Firms that had strong connections to a single bank were the ones most likely to be assisted. A second positive determinant was the company's "social importance" (defined by sales and number of employees), suggesting that larger firms were more likely to receive support than smaller firms. Interestingly, he found that traditional financial accounting measures, which might be used to make "rational" decisions over which firm to support—equity ratio, interest coverage, and cash flow coverage—were uncorrelated with salvation probabilities.

But in gaining security and stability, firms give up a degree of independence. Alliances become institutionalized as social and business relationships bound in complexly interwoven patterns of exchange. Affiliation is therefore not simply the establishing of bilateral relationships, but the marrying into an extended family of firms. With this marriage comes its attendant advantages—the stability, security, and status it affords. But it also comes with disadvantages—the loss of a degree of flexibility in maneuvering within business networks.

This tradeoff was explicit in the policies of Omron Tateishi, a fast-growing advanced-technology-oriented firm interviewed for the study. This company had specified in its corporate precepts that it would remain independent of formal linkages with any group. The chief executive explained that the basic choice was one of growth (*chōsei*) versus security (*anzen*). By remaining independent, he said, his firm had been free to pursue any perceived market opportunities, unfettered by the constraints of a group. Independence brought for this firm a measure of freedom.

In summary, then, we may outline the following two basic strategies: (1) in the strategy of single, close alliances, firms choose to gain access to reliable and stable sources of capital, ownership, and trade despite the inevitable dependency on the group this entails; and (2) in the strategy of multiple, loose alliances, firms choose to forgo stability and security in favor of the relatively more open unhindered pursuit of diverse business opportunities.

The difference in impact between these two strategies was brought home in the highly publicized failure of one of Japan's leading independent firms, Sanko Steamship, in the fall of 1985. When Sanko reported bankruptcy, it was the largest company failure in Japanese history. Sanko had been the quintessential independent firm—widely characterized as the "lone wolf" of the shipping industry and alienated from the larger Japanese community in the early 1970s by its highly unusual attempted hostile takeovers of several Japanese firms. In keeping with this independent posture, Sanko had long balanced its financial relationships across three different banks—Daiwa, Tokai, and the Long-Term Credit Bank. This balancing complicated the determination of which one was Sanko's "main bank" and would therefore lead the restructuring and provide the most extensive support. Daiwa Bank eventually took charge, but attempts at restructuring floundered on difficulties in convincing the other banks to carry their proportionate share of the financial burden. The Long-Term Credit Bank acquiesced after lengthy negotiations, but Tokai Bank resisted and the effort eventually failed.

Compare this with the attitude of Sumitomo Bank when leading the reconstruction of Toyo Kogyo. Toyo Kogyo, the maker of Mazda automobiles, faced near-bankruptcy in the 1970s from problems with its rotary-engine cars and a decline in sales. Although it was not a shachō-kai member in the Sumitomo group, Toyo Kogyo was considered an important quasi-affiliate with longstanding relationships to Sumitomo Bank. As a result the bank provided new loans for the company, ensured that other companies would hold on to their shares, sent several top executives to oversee the turnaround, arranged for discounted sales of steel and other supplies, and encouraged other Sumitomo managers to buy their cars from Mazda (Pascale and Rohlen, 1983). Although perhaps overstated, a comment made by the president of Sumitomo Bank a number of years ago in reference to his bank's leading clients is nevertheless of interest: "We are always prepared to help out whenever [Sumitomo] group companies are in trouble. We won't allow any group member companies to go into business failure" (*Oriental Economist*, October 1981). The strength of alliance ties, therefore, determines concomitant obligations.

CHAPTER VI

New Venture Development and Technological Innovation in Japan

Among the extraordinary facets of Japan's postwar economic growth, perhaps none has been more dramatic than its move from technological follower to technological leader. During the 1950s, nearly half of total research and development expenses in Japan went toward payment for foreign technologies, a figure that was down to less than one-sixth by the 1970s. Since then, Japanese inventors have become second only to U.S. inventors as holders of U.S. patents. In those patent classes recognized by the U.S. Patent and Trademark Office where American firms still maintain a strong position, the vast majority (over 80 percent, according to one study) are now marked by a steady deterioration vis-à-vis Japanese firms when measured by rates of new patent awards (Wakasugi, 1984; Frame and Narin, 1990). Clearly, Japan has moved beyond imitation, proving to be an extraordinarily innovative economy in its own right.

The steep curve of this developmental trajectory, however, raises important questions concerning how we understand the relationship between economic organization and technological change. Following from the previous discussion, I argue in this chapter that a significant competitive characteristic in the evolution of the Japanese economy has been the strategic forging of linkages among innovators, providers of risk capital, and users of new technologies. Corporate expansion and diversification has taken place through intercorporate alliances that combine many of the governance and coordination advantages of vertically integrated firms with the flexibility, internal cohesion, and entrepreneurial focus of smaller companies. This basic strategic dynamic—expansion and diversification through external networks—has evolved in a number of ways over the past century but has nevertheless remained a core feature of Japanese industrial structure.

THE SOURCES OF TECHNOLOGICAL CHANGE

Classical economists such as Adam Smith and Karl Marx—both witnesses to the Industrial Revolution—focused on the central role played by market and industrial organization in technological and economic development. Thus, Smith explored the intertwining of market expansion, the division of labor, and productivity growth, while Marx was concerned with the "increasing organic composition of capital" (Dosi and Orsenigo, 1988, p. 14). Joseph Schumpeter picked up on these themes much later in his critique of the rise of economic models of perfect competition that focus on allocative efficiency within static equilibrium and treat technical change as exogenous to the economic system. For Schumpeter, economic growth and development are inevitably linked to technical and institutional change, for these are products not of small adjustments in factor prices but of the creation of entirely new combinations of those factors. Static equilibrium models are largely irrelevant to economic development in market systems, he argued, because price competition is not the primary source of innovation:

> In capitalist reality as distinguished from its textbook picture, it is not [price] competition which counts but the competition from the new commodity, the new technology, the new source of supply, the new type of organization (the largest-scale unit of control for instance)—competition which commands a decisive cost or quality advantage and which strikes not at the margins of the profits and the outputs of the existing firms but at their foundations and their very lives. [Schumpeter, 1950, p. 84.]

The precise relationship between market structure and technological innovation, however, has remained elusive. Whereas early Schumpeter, in his *Theory of Economic Development* (1934), focused on "heroic" individual innovators, later Schumpeter, in his *Capitalism, Socialism, and Democracy* (1950), recognized the increasing reality of large-scale organization and the role of "routinized" innovators. These themes have reappeared more recently in debates concerning the vitality of high-technology sectors of the American economy and the special role played by its smaller firms and venture capital markets. For some, small-firm entrepreneurial innovation is the well-spring of U.S. competitive strength, as reflected in the role of Silicon Valley in the development of the electronics industry. George Gilder (1988, p. 54), a representative of this view, writes,

> The secret of the U.S. success [in computers and semiconductors] was the very venture system that the critics condemn. It counteracted high capital costs by efficiently targeting funds, released energies that were often stagnant in large companies, attracted a crucial flow of inventive immigrants, and fostered a wildfire diffusion of technology that compensated for the lack of national coordination.

For others, this position is panglossian, for the technological and capital requirements of new product and process development have surpassed the scale of single firms, and especially small firms, to promote sustained innovation. Charles Ferguson (1988, p. 57) responds directly to Gilder's viewpoint by arguing,

> Japanese, Korean, and even German competitors seem not to share America's passion for fragmentation and entrepreneurial zeal. U.S. industry falls victim not to nimble, small companies but to huge, industrial complexes embedded in stable, strategically coordinated alliances often supported by protectionist governments—exactly by the kind of political and economic structures that, according to the free-market entrepreneurship argument, give rise to stagnant cartels.

In Japan itself, the balance of opinion on this issue has shifted over the past ten years. The early 1980s saw a spate of white papers, academic treatises, and popular writings extolling the virtues of Silicon Valley start-ups, bewailing their absence in Japan, and advocating policies to rectify the situation. But by the latter half of the 1980s, emphasis was increasingly placed on technological "fusion" and the advantages large firms and interorganizational collaboration seemed to play in this process (e.g., Kodama, 1986).

Empirical analyses of the link between market organization and innovative activity have yielded mixed results. The variety of studies that have tested these relationships have failed to show consistent evidence for a systematic correlation between market structure or firm size, on the one hand, and rates of technological innovation, on the other (see, for example, Kamien and Schwartz, 1982; Mowery, 1986). However, aggregate measures, such as industry concentration ratios or firm size, mask more subtle relationships that define the innovative process and the incentives and constraints under which entrepreneurs actually operate.[1] The relationship between industrial organization and technological innovation may not be a linear function of firm size because decentralized, entrepreneurial firms and large-scale bureaucracies are each good at different things and the interaction among these advantages is complex.

Technological evolution and economic change in Japan has long been marked by the dynamic attempt to balance the advantages of firms and interfirm cooperation, as is increasingly the case in the United States with the proliferation of alliance forms. In rapidly changing environments, often what is needed is not only for firm-level organization to supplement atomized markets, but for interfirm-level organization to supplement firms. The importance of an ongoing interaction and an intimate familiarity among technology collaborators, as well as the peculiar public-goods character of information, raises the transactions costs associated with relying on arm's-length markets to govern transactions. At the same time, the uncertainties born of technological discontinuities in many sectors have ensured that no single firm can expect to be master of more than a fraction of its production inputs, and the diffuse demands of contemporary technological and market development have surpassed the capability of single firms to accomplish the required coordination of interdependent processes on their own. The tension between these considerations has been reflected in Japanese industrial development in the ongoing effort to combine the administrative benefits of larger firms and the entrepreneurial and flexibility benefits of smaller firms, as discussed below.

THE CONTINUING ROLE OF ALLIANCES IN JAPANESE INDUSTRIAL DEVELOPMENT

When Japan's doors were forcibly opened by the West over a century ago, subsequent industrialization took place in the context of the pervasive feeling of external threat and the urgent need for technological development. The political economy of Japan was rapidly revamped from one oriented toward maintaining the social status quo (the Tokugawa legacy) to one marked by a heavy emphasis on fostering development of special skills and capabilities needed in order to compete on equal terms with its Western counterparts. This new reality was captured in the well-known Meiji period phrase, *wakon yōsai* (Japanese spirit, Western technology). The goals of national security took priority, resulting in a set of institutional arrangements whose primary purpose was to promote rapid industrialization (Johnson, 1982).

The pattern marking the strategy of the contemporary intermarket groups—expansion into widely diversified markets through complex external alliances—had its beginnings during this period. Starting from a relatively primitive base during the early Meiji period, Japan was forced to develop capabilities across a wide variety of industrial fronts at once. As Gerschenkron (1962) points out, the more backward a national economy is, the more diversified the areas are in which it is forced to start industrializing simultaneously. Lockwood (1968, p. 227) makes the same point in his economic history of Japan:

> One difficulty facing any country on the threshold of industrialization is the fact that a venture in any single big enterprise may be attractive only if the simultaneous development of other industries is undertaken. Investment to build an electric power industry, for example, is encouraged by the simultaneous development of electric light and equipment industries. But the individual promoter looking at the power enterprise as a single venture may be deterred from going ahead by uncertainty as to whether these complementary industries will in fact develop and thus make profitable what would otherwise be a dubious undertaking. If complementary enterprises are joined in a single program of development—whether at the hands of the government or of a private group—this reduces the risk estimates all around. It makes it more likely that interrelated innovations will proceed simultaneously, each creating the profit expectations of the other.

The entrepreneurs of the Meiji and prewar periods diversified their activities in order to gain returns, Lockwood notes, from a range of complementary businesses. Coordination of complementary investments refers to those cases where, as Richardson (1960, p. 72) explains, "their combined profitability when undertaken simultaneously, exceeds the sum of the profits to be obtained from each of them, if undertaken by itself. . . . Investments may be complementary either because the costs of one are reduced when the other is undertaken, or because the demand for the output of one of them rises with the increased availability of the output of the other." Organizational and technical skills in Japan were scarce, as were capital and political connections, and an effective way to utilize them was to apply them across a set of interrelated, but continually evolving, markets.

The resulting pattern in most industries was the aggressive pursuit of business opportunities by a range of zaibatsu, each of which strived for representation in a variety of industries, with specific diversification strategies depending on the groups' own financial and technical resources. Thus, while the zaibatsu were active across a range of industries, this rarely led to monopoly of markets by single producers, as is often assumed. Lockwood (1968, p. 223) writes,

Despite the concentration of control evidenced in giant combines, there were few cases of outright monopoly by a single seller of a product or group of allied products. In other words, the combination movement in Japan followed a pattern distinctly different from that in the United States at the turn of the century. Here such trusts as U.S. Steel, Standard Oil, American Tobacco, American Sugar Refining, and United Shoe Machinery came to control 65% to 95% of the capital and output in their respective fields.[2]

In part, this was because Japan's need to import raw materials from abroad prevented the kind of concentration in oil and other resource industries found in the United States. But it also reflected early patterns of one-settism in which the zaibatsu tended to move together into new markets in competition against each other, keeping industrial concentration in check. Far from reducing competition, therefore, these alliances may actually have increased competition by creating several viable competitors in industries where only one would otherwise have existed.

Also contrary to common perception, the prewar zaibatsu were neither completely integrated companies nor exclusive trading systems. The *bantō* who managed the zaibatsu subsidiaries were often granted a large degree of autonomy to pursue entrepreneurial interests outside of the group. As Allen (1940) writes, "A *bantō* who had been placed in charge of a firm where he enjoyed considerable freedom from control would be expected in an emergency to come to the aid of the parent concern. . . . Among the *bantō* themselves there were groups in rivalry one with another" (quoted in Imai, 1989b, p. 9). Moreover, owing to the historical pattern of one-settism, firms in the prewar zaibatsu were generally not actively involved in same-industry cooperation with other members in their own group, for the simple reason that there were few enterprises in a zaibatsu that happened to be in the same industry. When collaboration among affiliated firms did take place, it tended instead to focus on those areas that crossed industrial boundaries.

Trading among zaibatsu-affiliated enterprises was far from exclusive, as historical research is now making evident. William Wray's (1984) analysis of the evolution of the Mitsubishi group's flagship company, Nippon Yusen Kaisha (NYK), is one such example. Wray shows that from its beginning, NYK consciously balanced the interests of the larger zaibatsu with its own strategic concerns. Among its shareholders and creditors over time were Mitsui, Yasuda, and Dai-Ichi banks, and in the prewar period it felt sufficiently independent to terminate contracts it had held with Mitsubishi Shipbuilding. Indeed, Wray attributes much of the success of the NYK during its early years to strategic relationships outside its own zaibatsu. He refers to these as "business alliances" involving importing firms, trading companies, shipping firms, industrial producers, and banks: "The company's major innovation prior to World War I, the opening of the lightly subsidized Calcutta line, demonstrated the key to further expansion to be the business alliances in which the N.Y.K. joined with other Japanese firms in quest of their corporate goals" (p. 516).

From Zaibatsu to Keiretsu

For over a century, Japanese industrial organization has been characterized by rapid rates of change in market conditions and technological capabilities and an ongoing evolution in government policies and industrial structure. Earlier zaibatsu arrangements emerged within this context. The zaibatsu represented a compromise between the simultaneous needs to retain control over scarce resources, on the one hand, and to exploit expanding economic opportunities, on the other. Japanese firms expanded not only through the kind of elaborate internal hierarchies that dominated business development in the United States (Chandler, 1977), but through subdivisions into quasi-independent units. In addition, through the zaibatsu these firms diversified far more completely than their corporate counterparts in the United States. By the 1930s Japan's economy comprised a range of competing zaibatsu of various sizes, each increasingly decentralized in its day-to-day operations albeit subject to ultimate control at the top, in varying degrees, by the family-dominated honsha. With the postwar Occupation came the removal of this last element, setting the stage for the emergence of the postwar keiretsu.

Although the contemporary Japanese economy is increasingly located at the industrial frontier across a wide variety of sectors, the basic reality of technological and organizational uncertainty largely remains. In relative terms, Japan since at least the Meiji period has been at its own high technology frontier because it has been forced to learn new production methods rapidly and to invest in new processes with which it was unfamiliar. While its corporations may no longer look to the West to the same extent for their models, new forms of uncertainty and change born of being a technological leader have continued the underlying reality that no single firm has the resources to carry out all of its objectives.

Thus, the search by firms for new business opportunities has long characterized the evolution of the Japanese industrial organization. Although the demands of present-day business activities often require that companies look outside their own keiretsu for special technologies and new market opportunities, the prewar zaibatsu also faced rapidly changing industrial structure and technologies (primitive though they may seem in the present day) and forged new alliances in order to pursue these interests. The keiretsu, like the zaibatsu before them, have proved flexible in accommodating changing technical and market conditions and have expanded to include new members in promising growth areas. The process of overall alliance formation in Japan, therefore, has been one of increasing scale and complexity in group structures. The evolution of alliances has not been a wholesale replacement of old forms of organization with new firms, but a laying of newer and often higher-level structures on top of preexisting, perhaps even primordial, social forms, with the new combination coexisting with other groups serving other organizational purposes.

INNOVATION AND THE LIMITS TO HIERARCHY

The dynamics of technological innovation and economic change pose special problems for industrial organization. Because the innovative process inherently involves the creation of new combinations, standard routines that define well-known production functions and markets are largely absent (Nelson and Winter, 1982). Entrepreneurs operate in a world of uncertainty regarding the preferences of consumers, the possibilities of new technologies, and the prospects of their activities. Moreover, the inchoate nature of innovative activities means that developed customer markets (and often markets for key inputs) are lacking, making it difficult to specify contracts and monitor performances (Teece, 1986). These factors lead to what we might refer to as the information problem created by uncertainty and complexity and the governance problem created by small numbers bargaining (Williamson, 1975).[3]

Internalization of economic activities into vertically integrated firms provides a partial resolution to these problems, one that has received by far the most theoretical and empirical attention. This is not surprising, for capitalist development in most advanced economies has gone hand-in-hand with the increasing scale and scope of industrial enterprises. But vertical integration introduces its own distinctive shortcomings, and the result can be a loss in the kind of entrepreneurial initiative that drives new combinations and creates the energy that characterizes the innovative process in market capitalist systems.

The historical pattern in Japan for much of the twentieth century has been in the opposite direction, away from vertical integration. The share of the total economy accounted for by the largest firms actually declined during the crucial prewar years (Takafusa Nakamura, 1983) and has continued to decline during much of the postwar period. This trend accelerated following the oil shocks of 1973 and 1979 and led to the rise of a new era of *genryoku keiei,* or "weight-reduction management" (Uekusa, 1987). As Japanese firms have gotten smaller during the post-war period, however, the extent of "keiretsu-ization" of interfirm relationships has accelerated (Aoki, 1988). As suggested in the preceding discussion, these two trends are actually part of the same phenomenon, for the development of effective systems of interorganizational coordination and control has set the preconditions within which the shrinking of individual firms became possible. In order to understand why this is so, we need to consider in more detail the nature of economic organization and the costs and benefits of market, hierarchical, and cooperative (alliance) forms.

Creating Small-Firm Advantages in New Venture Development

The highly vertically integrated corporation, with control over the entire production process from primary materials to final user, has realized its most developed form throughout industrial economies in economic sectors with large-scale manufacturing capabilities and significant mass markets: automobiles, steel, chemicals, etc. (Chandler, 1984). These represent very-large-scale, but nevertheless relatively focused, business endeavors with a high degree of control over a predefined set of interdependent activities. Activities are interdependent in the sense that stages in the production process rely on close coordination with other stages and with a technical and sales staff, the benefits of which are lost if any part of the process is broken. The corporate form creates a relatively reliable and stable governance structure not possible in arm's-length markets, where terms of trade may be subject to the hazards of frequent renegotiation (Williamson, 1975).

As the firm grows in scale and scope, however, it begins to lose its business focus, bureaucratic coordination problems arise, and economies of scale that result from the interfirm division of labor are lost. The introduction of other business activities increasingly peripheral to the firm's core businesses and distinctive competencies may cause a loss in corporate focus. In addition, the development of internally generated new ventures may limit access to new supply relationships (upstream) and new markets (downstream) as other firms with similar developmental strategies are reluctant to trade with potential competitors and to make heavy investments where future revenue streams are uncertain. Furthermore, companies become captive to their own preexisting production and organizational patterns, and the larger the firm the more difficult it is likely to be to overcome this inertia. The economic problem, therefore, becomes one of the limits to organization as much as the limits to markets.

This poses companies with a problem: promising new business opportunities may exist that require a high degree of internal control in order to benefit from transaction-specific investments, but full-scale vertical integration into these areas—either through internal expansion or external acquisition—may be impossible or undesirable because of resource constraints, coordination problems, and motivational losses. One resolution to this dilemma is to expand through external alliances that combine elements of both decentralized, focused firms and vertical integration. In interfirm alliances, business operations are only partially integrated within each company's administrative hierarchy, preserving a degree of autonomy and focus for the separate enterprises.

Viewed as a whole, Japan has done remarkably well at creating the virtues of a small-firm economy: spawning high rates of new venture formation, instilling a sense of entrepreneurism among the managers of those ventures, and nesting this in the context of strong patterns of competition. New organizations are spun off to develop emergent market opportunities, nurtured by preexisting firms in those industries, yet they face the possibility of disappearance if unsuccessful. The result has been an economic environment marked by ongoing and multiple sets of organizational "experiments"—the kind of environment that many students of innovation and organization now consider to be central to the evolutionary process (Nelson, 1981; Hannan and Freeman, 1989; Eliasson, 1990).

Perhaps a recent (albeit extreme) example will help to illustrate this process. Nippon Telephone and Telegraph (NTT) was partially privatized in January 1988, in accordance with a government plan to gradually deregulate significant portions of the telecommunications service industry in Japan. As a result of this changed regulatory regime, NTT faced a major set of new competitive challenges in its traditional markets, as well as new opportunities in markets heretofore closed to it. Among the most striking features of its subsequent strategy was the creation of new business ventures across a wide variety of business lines. By June 1989

NTT had eighty-one new subsidiaries in which it owned in excess of 50 percent of the shares and another fifty-six affiliated companies in which it controlled between 20 percent and 50 percent of the total shares (*Jōhō tsūshin nenkan '90*, p. 257). These new enterprises had a total capitalization of ¥67 billion (over $400 million at ¥150/$1)—a figure large enough to represent a major new sector of venture funding if it were so defined. In addition, NTT dispatched several thousand of its own employees to these companies.

The entrepreneurial opportunities facing the independent company go beyond those available to the corporate division. Corporations are restricted by their own internal pay and promotion systems in how fully they can recreate the kinds of incentives that independent entrepreneurs enjoy. In part, this reflects internal rigidities created by fixed reward structures. In addition, those incentives that can be offered tend not to be as effective since they are masked by the "noise" inherent in larger organizations that make managers less able to control the consequences of their own activities.

Many of the incentives offered in entrepreneurial units are nonfinancial. Since growth in organizational size in Japan goes hand in hand with a wide variety of other benefits, firms that are successful will improve not only their profitability but their production output, employment, and corresponding stature in the business community. In addition, the social and the economic become intertwined as the characteristics of the parent company–spin-off relationship—as defined in patterns of equity, directorship, and other connections—move from the unidirectional to the bidirectional. In extreme cases, the spin-off may even become more prominent than the original parent company—something corporate divisions are unlikely to experience. Perhaps the most famous case of this is Toyota Motors, spun off from Toyota Automatic Loom Works (a company rarely heard about these days).

New venture formation is only half of the Schumpeterian process of creative destruction, however. In addition to an ongoing process of experimentally recombining factors in new ways, there must be an equally powerful dynamic allowing for unsuccessful combinations to fail. Indeed, acknowledgment of the possibility of failure constitutes one of the main incentives for spinning off operations by parent firms: to (partially) protect their own name in ventures that are not central to their operations and where the probabilities of success are uncertain. Perhaps surprisingly, given the predilection to focus on risk avoidance and risk sharing when explaining Japanese managerial motivations, rates of business failure have historically been nearly double in Japan what they are in the United States per capita. Major business failures (defined as those with a debt of over ¥10 million) ranged between 15,000 and 21,000 annually between 1976 and 1985 (Ramseyer, 1991).

INNOVATION AND THE LIMITS TO MARKETS

Despite the entrepreneurial incentives enjoyed by smaller firms, the reality of many economic operations is that they require the large-scale integration of a wide variety of activities. To the extent this takes place within transactional markets of independent firms, new problems are introduced related to the coordination of exchange across disparate actors, the setting of terms of trade, and the ensuring of effective compliance with those terms. Intercorporate alliances provide what has been a common solution to these problems in Japan. These represent an organizational technology in many ways of comparable importance to the product and process technologies that they have spawned.

Key linkages have been established by Japanese firms across different sets of relationships in a way that has simultaneously promoted a high degree of entrepreneurial incentive among firm managers and provided many of the benefits of larger firms. Among the latter include access to capital and other critical resources upstream and quick commercialization of market opportunities downstream. These broad linkages have proved especially adept at coordinating complex investments and production processes among industrially dispersed actors of the sort that characterize the development of wholly new markets ("fusion innovation").

Figure 6.1 presents a basic model for understanding three key relationships involved in the organization of the innovative process. The first connects investors to innovators in order to ensure funding for new ideas. The second connects innovators and the chief beneficiaries of innovation (the users) in order to ensure a smooth flow of information transfer. The third completes the circle by determining the ways in which connections between both innovators and beneficiaries are merged back into the interests of investors. We discuss each of these separately below. However, it is important to remember that overall effectiveness comes not at the level of separate linkages. It is in the total coordination and governance of the innovative process, and its dynamic evolution over time, that Japanese economic organization and its technological consequences must be understood.

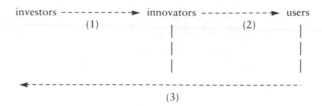

Fig. 6.1.   Key Linkages in the Innovative Process.

The Linkage Between Capital and Innovators

Among the most important linkages in the innovative process is that between investors (as sources of capital) and entrepreneurs (as sources of ideas). Investors ultimately determine, through the capital markets, which projects will be funded and what the expected rate of return will be. By creating credit, as Schumpeter points out, the banker makes savings flexible in order that they can be adjusted to investment: "He makes possible the carrying out of new combinations, authorises people, in the name of society as it were, to form them. He is the ephor of the exchange economy" (1934, p. 74). Through this power, the banker also defines the shape and scope of an enterprise's activities.

Yet this connection is problematic, for the world of capital is different from that of the entrepreneur. The investor bears the financial risks of new projects yet continually seeks to hedge those risks in a changing environment by moving quickly and freely with shifting opportunities. As Braudel (1979, pp. 433–34) points out, the "unlimited flexibility" of capital in its search for profit establishes

> a certain unity in capitalism from thirteenth-century Italy to the present-day West: One's impression then . . . is that there were always sectors in economic life where high profits could be made, *but that these sectors varied.* Every time one of these shifts occurred, under the pressure of economic developments, capital was quick to seek them out, to move into the new sector and prosper.

The entrepreneur, in contrast, is the wellspring of ideas and the source of energy behind the large-scale projects that animate economic development; he cannot easily hedge his bets about where success will lie. In his famous argument on the "animal spirits" that drive the enterprise builder, Keynes (1936) writes,

> Business men play a mixed game of skill and chance, the average results of which to the players are not known by those who take the hand. If human

nature felt no temptation to take a chance, no satisfaction (profit apart) in constructing a factory, a railway, a mine or a farm, there might not be much investment merely as a result of cold calculation. [P. 150.]

[A] large proportion of our positive activities depend on spontaneous optimism rather than on a mathematical expectation, whether moral or hedonistic or economic. Most, probably, of our decisions to do something positive, the full consequences of which will be drawn out over many days to come, can only be taken as a result of animal spirits—of a spontaneous urge to action rather than inaction, and not as the outcome of a weighted average of quantitative benefits multiplied by quantitative probabilities. . . . If the animal spirits are dimmed and the spontaneous optimism falters, leaving us to depend on nothing but a mathematical expectation, enterprise will fade and die. [P. 161.]

The ability to bridge these two worlds—the worlds of the risk-taking innovator and the risk-avoiding investor—is a central goal in capitalist economies. Today's winners may be tomorrow's losers. As a result, the financial system faces the same dilemma as the entrepreneur, that of balancing revealed experience with "heroic trust" in unexplored opportunities. "In this respect, the 'optimistic irrationality' of the Schumpeterian entrepreneurs requires a symmetric counterpart amongst 'bankers'" (Dosi, 1990, pp. 307–8).

One such bridge, fundamental in the funding of new technologies in the United States, is the venture capitalist. A good idea without capital is just that—an idea. The venture capitalist mediates between institutional sources of capital and entrepreneurial sources of ideas, often providing not only equity but operating and strategic advice to the venture as well. But there are limits to the effectiveness of this system. The greater share of venture capital now comes from pension funds, university endowments, and wealthy individuals. Most of these investors are poorly informed about the firms and technologies in which they are investing. While they may rely on better-informed "gatekeeper" venture capitalists to screen projects and monitor performance, this introduces pressures toward short-term returns in what are inherently long-term businesses.

Even if venture capitalists do prove to be effective monitors, their relatively detached position from the businesses they are funding makes it difficult for them to create strategic benefits to innovation.[4] Venture capitalists reside primarily within a single market, that of capital. While they may at times be able to provide market information or managerial assistance, their ability to provide key linkages in other markets—most important, with upstream suppliers and with downstream users of technologies—is limited. This becomes a problem where the benefits to innovation are largely captured by related industries rather than by the innovators themselves, a pattern that characterizes many inventions.

Linkages Between Innovators and Users

Innovation is not simply the product of the corporate R & D laboratory, nor do new technologies emerge full-blown. Most product and process innovations are the result of a long series of "feedback loops" at various stages of the innovative process both within and between firms (Kline and Rosenberg, 1986). Among the important but underappreciated linkages along the way are those between the inventors and the users of technologies. Von Hippel (1988) documents the existence of extensive information sharing through informal engineering networks in the mini-mill steel industry of the United States. Technology users in this way become important sources of ideas and improvements for inventors. Those economies in which information flows freely across firms, he argues, will have lower transactions costs, hence will "out-innovate" other economies.

Bringing the users of technologies on board early imparts advantages to both sides. It can facilitate input into the design process, making products more user-friendly and getting the "bugs" out early. As an executive in IBM's Tokyo headquarters put it, "the closer you can get your customer to development, the shorter the cycle." In addition, it allows users the chance to develop advance familiarity with important new products and processes. When products are further downstream, close vertical linkages can also provide an important base of initial customers to help new products at a critical time for financial success of the innovation.

Given the close connections common between suppliers and customers in many industries, it is not surprising that these vertical linkages are especially important in Japan. A survey by the Industrial Bank of Japan (1983, esp. p. 51) found that the leading source of ideas for new technologies among Japanese firms was technology users. While nearly half of the firms, 47 percent, cited users as sources, only 37 percent cited the second leading source, firms' own research laboratories.

Further evidence of the significance of these vertical linkages is provided in studies by Asanuma (1985, 1989) on the Japanese automobile industry. The closeness of these relationships is suggested by the fact that Nissan relies on the core firms in its supplier association for 90 percent of its purchases. And their durability is evidenced by the fact that only three firms left Toyota's association over the twelve-year period studied. In explaining these relationships, Asanuma borrows from Aoki's (1988) idea of "relational quasi-rents," or the benefits that flow from the effective coordination of long-term supplier relationships. Manufacturers and incumbent suppliers develop "relation-specific skills" that allow them to respond quickly to the special needs of the other. These skills require intensive interaction, and firms work hard to develop the ability to coordinate activities with other firms effectively: "Formation of this skill requires that learning through repeated interactions with a particular core firm be added to the basic technological capability which the supplier has accumulated" (Asanuma, 1989, p. 21). The benefits of these relationships will be most fully realized where significant coordination is required. In keeping with this prediction, Asanuma finds that longstanding relationships among firms tend to be denser where customized parts and idiosyncratic business transactions are involved.

Completing the Circle: Linking Innovators and Users Through Joint Investment

The benefits of successful innovation can be enormous, but they are often captured by other firms and industries rather than by the inventor (Kline and Rosenberg, 1986). Given the highly uncertain nature of the innovative process, it is difficult to quantify *ex ante* these returns. Yet if sufficient benefits do not accrue to the inventor to reward the risks taken, the rate of innovation will suffer. Teece (1986) points to the problems this creates for smaller firms that have been the source of valuable technologies but have failed to commercialize those innovations successfully because they did not possess the necessary complementary assets for full-scale development. Under conditions where patent or process protection is weak—conditions that characterize many innovative industries, such as electronics—the merging of innovators and users in a joint investment structure ensures greater commitment by both innovators and users than would otherwise exist: "If an innovator owns rather than rents the complementary assets needed to commercialize, then it is in a position to capture spillover benefits stemming from increased demand for the complementary assets caused by the innovation" (Teece, 1986, p. 295).

Whereas full-scale vertical integration is one option, there are a wide range of intermediate governance mechanisms available as well: through joint ventures, minority equity stakes, personnel and directorship inter-locks, and other complex forms of investment and corporate control. Companies with an abundance of investment opportunities can limit external capital funding requirements if they are willing to forgo a degree of control over specific operations by providing only a portion of total capital investment, while crafting more effective governance structures than would be possible in pure contractual relationships.

The extensive networks of partial ownership that characterize the Japanese automobile and electronics industries demonstrate how this depth-breadth tradeoff is put into practice. In the automobile industry, for example, parent companies hold large positions in "affiliated" parts-makers, generally defined as those in which the automaker has over 20 percent of total equity. These are most often "manufacturers of high value added key component parts and interior furnishings which are closely related to car design" (Mitsubishi Research Institute, 1987, p. 5)—that is, those suppliers that are directly involved in the technol-ogy- and innovation-intensive areas of the automobile parts supply industry.

Parent companies have also been an important source of technologi-cal upgrading of their own affiliates through a variety of other forms of capital assistance. In addition to arranging for bank loans for their key affiliates (see Chapter 4), parent firms have offered trade credit to these firms during this period as well as loaning or selling production facilities, such as machine tools, at nominal prices (Odaka, Ono, and Adachi, 1988). The results have been impressive, as the total investment by Japanese automobile parts suppliers in tangible assets over net value added has, with the exception of several years during the 1975–79 oil shock recovery period, exceeded 20 percent in every year from 1957 to the late 1980s.

THE EVOLUTION OF JAPANESE INDUSTRIAL STRUCTURE

Far from being the remnants of outmoded ways of organizing, Japan's intercorporate alliance structures have been of central importance in understanding its technological development. Economies and industries that are undergoing initial and rapid development face serious problems of coordination and governance in the learning process. These condi-tions marked Japan as a whole for much of the post-Tokugawa and postwar periods and continue to characterize its innovative sectors today. This introduces a fundamental innovation dilemma. On the one hand, there is the need to promote the "optimistic irrationality" and "animal spirits" of the entrepreneur through high-powered local incentives. On the other, the requirements of overcoming coordination and contracting problems associated with undeveloped markets, their attendant small numbers, as well as poorly developed routines, pushes toward degrees of internalization and linkage through complete or partial integration of operations. Japan has crafted a set of organizational alliance forms that combines elements of both.

The actual alliance-formation process as it unfolds over time relies on a two-stage process. First has been the spinning off from a central set of operations of new satellite firms with parent company support, resulting in vertical keiretsu of varying degrees of breadth and complexity. An alternative path to membership has been the bringing in from the outside of previously independent, small-scale firms through a partial integration of operations, a process sometimes referred to as keiretsu-ization. In the cases of both spin-offs and consolidations, a formal separation is seen both as imparting a stronger spirit of independence of operation than would complete internalization within a corporate hierarchy, and as maintaining a degree of de facto control for the parent company through equity, management, and other linkages.

The second stage comes where these ventures are successful. Success breeds greater independence, as the companies develop new lines of business, sources of capital, and internal technological capabilities. It is this ability to become increasingly separate from the parent that perhaps most clearly differentiates the affiliated company from divisions of a firm: the corporate division, no matter how successful, is ultimately subject to the formal governance of the head office. The general pattern in Japan is not to move to full-scale independence, however. Rather, it is for the former satellites to become embedded in a higher-level and more complex capital and control system that includes both the former parent company and that parent company's banks and other affiliates. Often, these satellites grow to a point where they become major shareholders in the parent companies themselves.

The prewar zaibatsu, like their postwar keiretsu counterparts, emerged from this dynamic interplay. The zaibatsu grew both through internally generated diversification and by bringing in from the outside other companies that meshed with their strategic goals (see the Sumitomo case study at the end of Chapter 3). In general, the spinning-off process has resulted in relationships that are closer and more durable, even as satellite business gains increasing autonomy. In this sense, history continues to matter in that even as new ties are created, old ties rarely disappear. The second stage, in which a higher-order control structure develops, primarily characterizes the postwar period and is a direct function of the dismemberment of the zaibatsu holding companies, which created new pressures to stabilize corporate ownership and to link ownership with complementary business activities.

In conclusion, it is clear that Japan's move from technological follower to technological leader has changed the balance of power among keiretsu affiliates. Within each major grouping, technology-oriented firms have increasingly replaced old-line industrial operations as the largest and most important manufacturers. But this is not to say that the alliance formation process itself is in decline. For much of Japanese economic history, enterprise groupings have been at the forefront of new industries. These groups have faced the demands of technological innovation with a convenient preexisting structure to share information, finance their activities, and carry out interindustry collaboration. For this reason, even as Japanese firms forge new alliances with other Japanese and with foreign firms, they continue to find it to their advantage to organize a substantial proportion of their innovative activities through long-term relational contracts with their own keiretsu affiliates.

CHAPTER VII

The Japanese Firm in Context

In all of the attention that the Japanese firm has received in recent years, surprisingly little has been paid to the firm's institutional environment, and in particular to its joint development with intercorporate alliance structures.[1] As the previous chapter pointed out, extensive cooperation across firm boundaries has enabled the Japanese company to limit its size and scope while maintaining some of the advantages of the integrated firm in promoting technological development. In addition, these relationships have been a precondition for other characteristics of the Japanese firm, including the development of its internal organizational systems. Accolades for Japanese-style management and prescriptions for Western adoption of permanent employment and other internal practices must, for this reason, consider the essential context-dependence of these policies.

Perhaps the most systematic attempt to date to understand this interconnectedness is found in the work of Masahiko Aoki. In a variety of papers and books over the past decade, Aoki (1984c; 1987; 1988) has developed a "corporative managerialist" model of the Japanese firm based on the view that employees of Japanese firms are a constituency of equal importance as shareholders, with management acting as mediator between their interests in the policymaking process. This dual structure stands in marked contrast to the predominant shareholder-oriented focus of the American firm, in which management is presumed to serve the interests of owners passively, and has freed the Japanese firm from the institutional setup of classical capitalist control:

I argue that labor market imperfections (the establishment of the internal labor market) and the relative illiquidity of corporate shareholdings (because of the formation of corporate groups) are twin prerequisites for, as well as twin consequences of, the kind of management that has developed in Japan. The imperfect labor and capital markets reinforce and complement each other. [1987, p. 264.]

This chapter considers in more detail the relationship between the Japanese firm's environment and its internal organization. Although I concur with Aoki's assessment regarding the importance of capital market structure, I place much greater emphasis than he does on attempts by managers to reduce or eliminate the role of independent shareholders in the firm's governance structure. Where investors do influence management, I argue, it is largely a result of their simultaneous roles as bankers and trading partners. Equity investments are not unimportant, for they help to reinforce firms' business interests, but it is their business rather than capital-market function that is of primary concern.

Alliance structures have in turn transformed the respective positions of the firm's key constituencies—owners, managers and other employees, and trading partners—and therefore who controls the firm itself. The result is a form of corporate economy in which the mechanisms of corporate governance operate significantly differently from those in the United States, both in the market for corporate assets and in the institutions of shareholder representation. The chapter concludes with a case study of the transformation of corporate governance in a Japanese firm, showing these processes at work in the Mitsubishi group's buyout of foreign shares in Mitsubishi Oil.

CAPITAL-CENTERED MODELS OF CORPORATE OWNERSHIP

Berle and Means (1932) argued in *The Modern Corporation and Private Property* that with the rise of the large, diffusely held corporation and the dispersion of ownership to thousands of smaller shareholders, the relationship between shareholders and corporate managers has changed and de jure control vested in ownership has given way to de facto control exercised by professional managers. Much of the work on corporate control since then has attempted to address the Berle and Means thesis. Two more recent approaches to the corporation, agency theory and transactions costs theory, focus on the role of the "market for corporate control" in bridging the gap between ownership and control. Through this market, the holders of capital in the capitalist economy—the share-holders of the firm—are granted the formal rights to control the corpo-ration, and these rights are freely tradable in the stock market. Within both approaches, the joint stock corporation is conceived of as a system divided into shareholders, top managers, and internal operating units. Each of these positions is discrete but related through a linear chain of command defining the organizational hierarchy. This image is depicted in Figure 7.1.

The economic theory of agency (Jensen and Meckling, 1976; Fama and Jensen, 1983) focuses on the top half of Figure 7.1, wherein share-holders serve as "principals" who hire managers as their "agents" to actually run the business. Incumbent managers, agency theorists argue, are limited in their ability to exercise discretion at the expense of the organization because of the external discipline of the market for corpo-rate control. Shareholders govern firms through the potential replacing of ineffective management by tender offer (Manne, 1965) or proxy contests. Competition is conceived of as taking place among different sets of managers, some within the firm and some outside. In the arena of the stock market, management teams compete for the right to control corporate resources.[2]

The transactions costs approach most closely associated with the work of Oliver Williamson shifts attention to the bottom half of Figure 7.1. Williamson emphasizes the abilities of internal organizational inno-vations to mitigate the control problems Berle and Means first identified. "In a general sense, the most severe limitation of the capital market is that it is an *external* control instrument. It has limited constitutional powers to conduct audits and has limited access to the firm's incentive and resource allocation machinery" (Williamson, 1975, p. 143). Fore-most among these internal mechanisms is the multidivisional or M-form organizational structure: "The organization and operation of the large enterprise along the lines of the M-form favors goal pursuit and least-cost behavior more nearly associated with the neoclassical profit maxi-mization hypothesis than does the U-form [functionally structured] or-ganizational alternative" (Williamson, 1975, p. 150, italics deleted). The decomposition of firms into semi-autonomous profit centers, in this argument, introduces incentives within the firm's internal structure to generate division profit as a check on managerial discretion.

In capital-centered resolutions to the corporate control dilemma, then, agency theorists focus on discipline brought about through exter-nal market forces while transactions costs theorists emphasize discipline

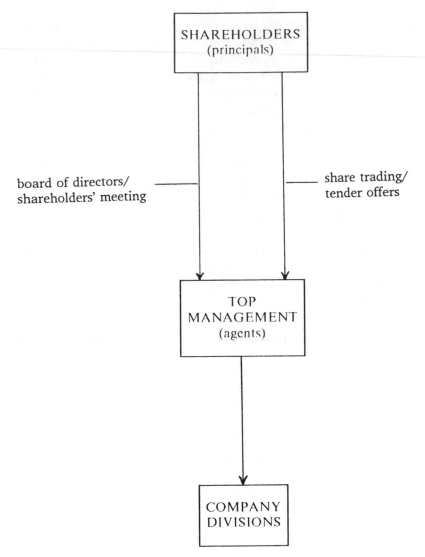

Fig. 7.1.   Capital-Centered Models of Corporate Governance: One-Way Control Exercised by Independent Shareholders.

brought about through adaptations in internal organization. However, both views, along with Berle and Means', share an orientation toward corporate governance in which shareholders, managers, and firms are viewed as differentiated positions with control moving vertically downward along a linear pathway in which capital is the primary constituency of interest.

A STRATEGIC (INTERORGANIZATIONAL) MODEL OF CORPORATE OWNERSHIP

For many investors, the capital-market–centered model accurately conveys how they see their relationship with the companies in which they hold shares. In the United States especially, the ideology of shareholding as corporate ownership is strong among both individual and institutional investors, leading to a wide range of shareholders' rights associations and advocates. Capital is seen as hiring managers who in turn hire workers.

But stockholding can also be used to express a second set of strategic (interorganizational) interests—that is, as a means of consolidating business relationships rather than for direct returns on investment. This is a direction that recent work within the transactions costs perspective has started to move, by placing increased emphasis on intercorporate relationships and the means by which "credible commitments" can be created across organizational boundaries through the mechanism of partial equity investments (Williamson, 1985; Teece, 1986). When this pattern of relations is extended to the broader community, as it is in Japan, the result is a view of corporate ownership different from both capital-centered and purely managerial models: neither the exercise of clearly defined, vertical control by independent shareholders over managers (as suggested in capital-centered theories of the firm), nor the removal of managers from the competitive pressures of external interests (as managerial control theories suggest), but the merging of shareholder and managerial positions into complex networks of overlapping intercorporate interests. This image is depicted schematically in Figure 7.2.

Investors in Japan are embedded in social and business relationships among the top executives in affiliated companies (e.g., through the presidents' councils of the keiretsu and other collective activities) and are often tied together in mutually controlling relationships. The distinction between shareholders' roles as "principals" and managers' roles as "agents" blurs, as corporations become interlocked in complex sets of overlapping ownership and business relationships. Chapter 3 compared Japanese and American stock ownership patterns and found substantial empirical differences in the following areas:

1. *Concentration of Ownership.* Diversification of a portfolio of stocks for the purpose of risk diffusion is a more important goal for U.S. investors and the establishment of concrete intercorporate relationships a more important goal in Japan. This difference results in much larger

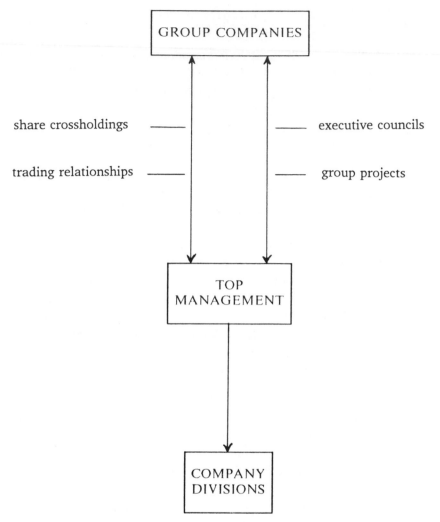

Fig. 7.2.   An Interorganizational Model of Corporate Governance: Reciprocal Control Exercised Through Business Networks.

average investments by major shareholders and more concentrated over-all ownership in Japan than in the United States.

2.   *Stability.* Ownership of corporate shares in Japan is carried out primarily not through anonymous securities markets of fluidly moving individual and institutional traders, but through networks of corporations whose identities are known and whose relationships are durable. Leading shareholders, therefore, take stable positions in other companies.

3. *Reciprocation.* The distinction between owners and owned in Japan breaks down as shareholders lose identity as a discrete constituency. Managers serving as agents of owners in their own firm become themselves "owners" over other firms by virtue of their firm's equity positions. This is seen most clearly in the prevalence of reciprocal share crossholdings.

4. *Embeddedness.* The position of capital, as defined through corporate ownership, furthermore loses meaning in Japan as investments are embedded in ongoing business transactions among firms and cannot be separated from other facets of the interfirm relationship. Ownership becomes part of a larger, multiplex set of business interests.

While distinct interests are clearly observed in the Japanese business community (e.g., in conflicts between securities houses and banks, and between export- and domestic-oriented companies), the kind of fundamental and pervasive tension that exists between management and shareholders in the United States (Coffee, Lowenstein, and Rose-Ackerman, 1988) is largely absent in Japan. But the Japanese resolution to the shareholder-management problem is not so much to make managers act more like shareholders, as Berle and Means and many others have proposed for the United States. Rather, it is the opposite: to make shareholders act more like managers. The Japanese firm's leading share holders are themselves other business firms run by career managers who have had to work their way up competitive internal corporate hierarchies. Corporate financial officers use their companies' shares to promote their company's business interests and are constrained by the fact that their company's own shares are often held reciprocally. The result is an economy in which the role of professional managers is great, both in running their own companies and in influencing the decisions of others, and the role of professional investors correspondingly small.

THE RISE OF JAPAN'S
MANAGERIAL ECONOMY

Japanese alliance structures developed hand-in-hand with changes in the Japanese corporation itself. The postwar period witnessed the removal of top executives from the leading zaibatsu subsidiaries, leaving salaried managers to run what was left. These managers saw their role primarily as professionals, a fact reinforced by changes in Japanese corporate law in 1950 that eliminated the requirement that managers must be shareholders in order to sit on boards of their own companies. This put in place a new generation of managers who rapidly pushed Japan's reconstruction:

> Freed from the control of the holding company and from stringent govern-
> ment regulations that had constricted Japanese industry for almost a decade
> and a half, the long-pent-up energies of these young men found fresh outlets.
> Despite the generally conservative character that Zaibatsu had acquired
> toward the end of the prewar era, many of these younger executives were
> endowed with an entrepreneurial spirit. Thus, within two or three years after
> their ascendancy, these men had established a firm control over the enter-
> prises they managed. [Yoshino, 1968, p. 87]

It was in this context that the contemporary permanent employment system developed. While managers of large firms during the prewar period had enjoyed a relatively high degree of job security, it was not until after the war that this security became more broadly institutional-ized and extended to factory workers (Taira, 1970; Koike, 1983). Yet, by turning companies' personnel from a variable cost in production to a fixed cost, internal labor markets forced firms to stabilize their external relationships by gaining reliable access to critical resources—capital, raw materials, component supplies, and distribution channels—in order to ensure steady employment.

Alliance structures promoted close ties to banks, the main source of capital in the postwar economy, as well as to the large trading firms. They also internalized shareholder relationships, protecting firms' em-ployees from hostile outside interests, something that became increas-ingly important with the gradual but inevitable liberalization of Japa-nese capital markets. As internal labor markets were becoming an in-stitutionalized feature of Japanese business, share crossholdings within the groups rose substantially.

Thus, with the dissolution of the zaibatsu during the postwar period and the democratization of the Japanese economy came the belief that it was not the zaibatsu families but the firm's employees and other key constituencies whose interests should be served by the company. The late 1940s and early 1950s saw the increasing extension of permanent em-ployment privileges to all core employees, and this was facilitated by the simultaneous consolidation of the groups, which created a stable institu-tional environment for these developments to take place. Alliance de-velopment in Japan was therefore set in the context of the special charac-teristics of the Japanese firm, and vice versa.

ADMINISTERED MARKETS
FOR CORPORATE CONTROL

While the intercorporate alliance has become the key link between the Japanese firm and key external constituencies, it has done so in ways that alter the nature of each. In the market for corporate control, anonymous or arm's-length shareholders—notably large institutional investment trusts seeking portfolio returns—are replaced by a closely connected community of mutually positioned, long-term financiers and trading partners. As a result, it is largely an administered market in which mergers and acquisitions take place among parties closely familiar with one another and hostile takeovers are virtually nonexistent.

Mergers and Acquisitions

Among the striking features of the merger and acquisition market in Japan is the great emphasis placed on gaining the approval of key constituencies. The process of merger is a long, time-consuming one that resembles an extended courtship. A Japanese consultant who had arranged several acquisitions by foreign firms of Japanese companies described it as follows: "Price is only the last item of discussion, in contrast with the U.S. approach. Instead, we emphasize the advantages of the company itself. In particular, we show them how the acquiring firm can help their company expand into international markets and gain new access to new technologies." Another consultant said: "At first the Japanese owner can't accept the fact that he is selling his company, and so we talk about the foreign company taking a percentage of equity. . . . Most important, the sellers want guarantees that they and their people are not going to be dismissed."

The most important and most difficult constituency to appease is the company's employees, and particularly its enterprise union. A number of important mergers have been postponed or canceled because this approval could not be obtained. One early postwar case involved the Asahi and Sapporo breweries. Although they had been split up after the war, the chief executives in each company wanted to remerge. However, the employees of Sapporo objected, since the head of Asahi was widely known as a "despotic leader," and the merger talks were abandoned only two days after the plan for the merger was announced to the press (Nakane, 1972, p. 59).

The firm's external affiliates—its trading partners—are also important. They were, for example, a major source of problems in the merger proposed in the late 1960s between Dai-Ichi Bank and the Mitsubishi Bank. Dai-Ichi's customers were worried that the larger Mitsubishi Bank would favor its own customers, particularly Mitsubishi group members, after the merger and that Dai-Ichi's customers would be overlooked. They pressured Dai-Ichi to cancel merger plans, and Dai-Ichi later merged with a bank of its own size, Nippon Kangyo. Similarly, in the ill-fated merger attempt between Sumitomo Bank and Kansai Sogo Bank in the mid-1970s, both employees and affiliated firms joined forces to oppose the merger. Together, the employees, branch offices, and customers of the much smaller Kansai Sogo bank formed the Kansai Bank Preservation Association (Kansai Sōgō Ginkō o Mamoru-kai) with the intention of frustrating merger plans, again over concerns that they would be relegated to second-class status. This group carried out a campaign widely picked up by the Japanese media, which played on themes of Sumitomo's social responsibility, on the importance of the preservation of smaller companies, and even on the necessity of maintaining the employees' *ikigai* (their purpose or meaning in life). Sumitomo eventually abandoned its merger efforts.

One of the consequences of the importance of external constituencies is that mergers across alliances are quite rare. One of the few large intergroup mergers took place in 1964 and involved Mitsui Senpaku and Osaka Shosen (of the Sumitomo Group), forming Mitsui-OSK Lines. At the time, this led to a belief among some in the business community that outside mergers (*keiretsu o koeta gappei*) would become more common. However, this has not happened. Okumura (1983, pp. 68–69) provides data on large-scale mergers (post-merger size of greater than ¥1 billion) from 1953–81. Of the ninety-nine mergers listed, fifty-three were between group firms, thirty-one between independent firms, and only fifteen between group firms and outside firms. Certainly the most important within-group merger was that of Shin-Mitsubishi Heavy Industries, Mitsubishi-Nippon Heavy Industries, and Mitsubishi Ship-building in 1964, re-creating the old Mitsubishi Heavy Industries concern that had dominated heavy industry in the prewar and wartime period and had been broken up by Occupation authorities following the war. Also important was the merger in 1969 of Kawasaki Heavy Industries, Kawasaki Airplane, and Kawasaki Heavy Vehicles into a reunited Kawasaki Heavy Industries. In both cases, longstanding informal ties among managers had been maintained before the remerger.

Why would top management bother to consider the opinions of employees and trading partners if they had decided a merger makes rational economic sense? In large part, this is because core employees of large firms come packaged with the companies involved. This is the case both in the stricter sense that Japanese firms make strong commitments in their internal labor markets with informal employment guarantees, and in the looser sense that firm and employee share a kind of social co-destiny. A large part of business activity in Japan is carried out through relationships among people based on social frameworks developed over long periods of interaction, rather than through formal definitions of roles and responsibilities. These frameworks are not easily meshed, as suggested in the following observation:

> In Japan the use of financial power to take over what other corporations have laboriously created is considered to run counter to good business morality. But perhaps the more pragmatic reason is the virtually insurmountable difficulty of merging two close exclusive communities into an efficient business organization. [Hattori, 1984]

Problems in trying to mesh different social systems have arisen in a number of recent mergers and acquisitions in the United States as well, but these are if anything even more severe in Japan. The predominance of relationally based interaction means that it is difficult to place a money value on the worth of the company since it depends so much on the successful completion of intangible, informal, person-dependent routines. Moreover, potential efficiencies or synergies are more difficult to capture. As a consequence of permanent employment, merged firms cannot eliminate overlapping positions easily. Company directors and others must be guaranteed of their position until they retire. In addition, under *nenko joretsu* employees are assigned positions and compensation based heavily on their seniority status within the firm.[3] There are also social considerations based on the respective statuses of the two firms. It is often thought within the Japanese business community that mergers among similarly sized companies, a "marriage of equals" (*taitō gappei*), are most likely to succeed. In the words of one executive who had been involved in several mergers, "As in marriage, if one partner is too beautiful, it won't last."

The importance of relational statuses in these marriages has resulted in the widespread use of a *nakōdo*, or go-between. As in the *o-miai* (arranged) marriages still prevalent in Japan, one firm approaches its main bank or a business leader who knows both parties well, who then quietly contacts the other party. This is no guarantee, however, that negotiations will flow smoothly, as revealed in the bank-arranged marriage in 1976 of the Ataka and C. Itoh trading firms. At the time C. Itoh was thriving while Ataka was nearly bankrupt owing to various bad deals it had made and to general mismanagement. The merger arrangements were unexpectedly delayed for nearly one year over a deadlock in the negotiations on the merger terms between C. Itoh and Co., on the one hand, and Sumitomo Bank and Kyowa Bank, the two main correspondent banks of Ataka, on the other. Issues dividing the parties included which company would take responsibility for Ataka's bad debts (Sumitomo eventually took the bulk of the responsibility) and what the status would be of Ataka's unprofitable divisions (they were excluded from the agreement). The go-between may facilitate the process of merger, but it remains a complex and difficult process in Japan because of the intertwining of firm and alliance interests.

Hostile Takeovers

Easily the most dramatic event in the market for corporate control is the hostile takeover, a microcosm of the multiple forces that define the firm and its key constituencies. The tender offer has achieved the status in economic theory of guardian over the modern corporation. Since Manne's (1965) pioneering article, the threat of takeover has been considered an important means of disciplining management, even in problematic situations where ownership and management are separated. The fundamental idea is that discipline is achieved through competition among management teams within the area of the stock market, and incumbent management is thereby driven to operate the firm efficiently.

However, hostile takeovers of the kind prevalent in the United States are virtually nonexistent in Japan, and this fact reveals as clearly as any the degree to which the "market" for corporate control takes place not among arm's-length traders in impersonal capital markets but among firms that maintain longstanding relationships with each other. The factors affecting the merger and acquisition market in Japan, described above, apply a fortiori to takeovers.

In the mid-1970s, for example, an investment group made up of Japanese doctors (and therefore independent of the conventions of the Japanese business community) had acquired about 30 percent of the shares of Asahi Breweries. Asahi's share of sales in the beer industry was declining and its overall performance had been poor. Asahi's main bank was Sumitomo, which arranged for Asahi Chemical (no relation) to pick up part of Asahi Breweries' operations. In addition, the bank sent down a number of its own executives to serve as officers in the company, including the new president of the company. Most important, it negotiated with the investment consortium to sell out its shares to the bank and to other "friendly" companies, including other Sumitomo group members (Okumura, 1983, p. 214).

Japanese firms view the intentions of foreign firms with particular suspicion. Foreign ownership of Japanese stock has increased substantially over the past two decades and accounted for about 5 percent of total shareholding in the mid-1980s, up from only 1.4 percent in 1961. Because of the tendency of Japanese institutional investors to hold onto their shares, foreigners, although holding only 5 percent of total shares, account for about 20 percent of all trading on the Tokyo Stock Exchange (*Business Week,* October 15, 1984). In 1969 Isuzu and General Motors announced that the latter would buy shares of the former. MITI, under pressure, at this point raised the limit of foreign capital participation to 35 percent (from 25 percent) on the condition that a substantial portion of the shares be held by stable shareholders. An executive of Fuji Heavy Industries was reported to say at the time of Fuji's break with Isuzu Motors: "I think it is advisable for our company and Isuzu Motors to continue holding each other's shares in spite of their liquidation of ties, so that we can remain each other's stabilized shareholders. Also it is desirable that the automobile firms as a whole hold one another's shares regardless of group affiliations, in order to defend native capital" (quoted in Ballon, Tomita, and Usami, 1976, p. 22). Since this time, Toyota and Nissan have been particularly aggressive in buying shares of their supplier parts companies to preempt foreign corporations.

In 1971 the Finance Ministry revised the securities exchange to allow foreign takeovers of Japanese companies. However, despite this liberalization, there have been almost no major transactions in corporate assets involving foreign firms in Japan. In 1985, for example, a British-U.S. investment group attempted a hostile takeover of the Japanese company Minebea. This attempt was defeated, however, when the investors found Japanese corporate shareholders unwilling to sell their shares. The market is in principle open but in reality internally regulated by the parties involved.

In addition to structural ownership barriers, the business community has established informal sanctions against threats to the internally determined promotion system of the firm (Ramseyer, 1987). Corporate managements and unions work together to expel outsiders in the philosophy of *jibun no shiro wa jibun de mamore,* "protect your own castle." The colloquial term for takeover, *nottori,* is the same word used to refer to an airline hijacking, and the obvious image has been one of illegitimately attempting to control somebody else's property. Similarly, *kaishime,* or buying shares in a company confidentially with the intention of reselling it to management at a substantial premium, retains an image of questionable business practice perhaps even more dubious than the American practice of "greenmail." In an effort to appear more progressive, imported words such as *TOB* (takeover bid) and *M&A* (mergers and acquisitions) have gained greater currency in recent years. These activities have gradually become more widely accepted, at least where Japanese acquisitions of foreign firms are involved and where the acquisition is friendly. But under other circumstances, the image to the vast majority of the Japanese business community remains a negative one.

THE REDEFINITION OF CORPORATE GOVERNANCE

With the transformation in the market for corporate control has gone a symbolic redefinition of the nature of corporate governance itself. Although the legal trappings of the joint stock corporation are maintained, they have been transformed into pro forma rituals intended primarily to satisfy the requirements of procedural legitimacy but largely devoid of real substance. This is most strikingly evident in the operation of two traditional institutions of shareholder control—the general shareholders' meeting and the board of directors.

Shareholders' Meetings

The general shareholders' meeting (*sōkai*) is, along with the board of directors, the primary institution within which owners can, in principle, pass on the performance of the management they have "hired." The Japanese Commercial Code establishes an ambitious agenda for the meeting: the election of directors, approval of the balance sheet and income statement, as well as determination of dividends. The reality, however, is that it is a legal formality—a ceremony, the significance of which lies not in what gets communicated between shareholders and managers but in what it indicates about control over the firm and in the ways it satisfies demands for legitimacy in the larger business community. Large, stable shareholders do not typically bother to show up. In nearly 80 percent of the firms, those attending meetings account for less than 20 percent of the company's shares (Heftel, 1983, pp. 169–70).

The ceremonial character of the sōkai reached perhaps its extreme expression in the first shareholders' meeting ever of Nippon Telephone and Telegraph (NTT) in September 1986. As part of its privatization, NTT must now operate under the formal practices of a public stock corporation rather than as an arm of the Ministry of Posts and Telecommunications. During its first meeting, its only shareholder was the Ministry of Finance, which still held all of NTT's stock. However, dutifully keeping with its new status, NTT went through the motions of a shareholders' meeting, rented a meeting room, and lined up its key executives on one side. At the other end of the room was a single individual—the representative from the Ministry of Finance—who approved everything that was offered at the brief meeting.

Since the sōkai is the company's face to the outside world, Japanese executives are particularly sensitive to the image they convey during the meeting. A group of racketeers, the sōkai-ya, have emerged to take advantage of this situation. These investors are in some ways caricatures of those management gadflies in the United States, such as the Gilbert brothers, who advocate increased shareholder democracy. Many sōkai-ya establish "economic research centers" or similar establishments as a front for their blackmail operations. For the price of a small block of shares, they are allowed to attend companies' shareholders' meetings. Sometime before the meeting, the sōkai-ya visit the responsible executives and threaten to divulge to the public at the meeting company problems or scandals involving its officials—in the early 1970s, pollution issues were common—unless they are paid off. Management, fearful of bad publicity, has typically acquiesced. While expensive, this practice has had the advantage for executives of turning the sōkai-ya into advocates of management. The paid-off sōkai-ya attend the meetings and keep dissident shareholders in line through intimidation. In this way, sensitive proxy contests and other forms of shareholder protest are avoided.

The annual meeting has been dubbed shan-shan sōkai, after the onomatopoeic term for the unison clapping that closes festive occasions like weddings and companies' year-end parties. Management makes several brief opening remarks, offers a teishoku kōsu (set menu) of decisions and policies to be approved, then seeks the approval of those attending in what used to be known as a "Soviet-style election." If all goes well and the sōkai-ya have been mollified in advance or do not show up, the meeting should last about ten to twenty minutes.[4] Well over half of all listed companies have their meetings on the same day of the year—the final Friday of June—and this has increased significantly in the past several years. This appears to be a way for companies to minimize sōkai-ya impact—by all having meetings on the same day and at the same time, it makes it more difficult for the sōkai-ya to attend more than one meeting.

In October 1982 the government passed new laws designed to alter the management-shareholder relationship.[5] These were intended to make it more difficult for sōkai-ya to buy one or a few shares in a company and use them to strong-arm either management or other shareholders, their effects are still uncertain. In the first year after enactment, a number of companies faced what the Japanese media termed "marathon sōkai." Sapporo Beer's sōkai lasted for 7 hours, Isuzu Motor's for 6, Komatsu's and Kirin Beer's for over 5, and Kajima Construction's, Nippon Carbon's, and Mitsubishi Oil's for better than 4. The longest of all was Sony, consuming an embarrassing 13½ hours. Overall, the average length of meetings increased from 15 to 50 minutes. In the marathon sōkai, shareholders asked pointed questions about company social-expense accounts, the independence of the company's auditors, directors' compensation, and other potentially controversial issues that had formerly been suppressed.

Yet despite these attempted changes, the special shareholder-management relationship found in Japan largely remains. The corporate investors that predominate as shareholders of large Japanese firms still leave management to determine firms' internal operations and external strategies. Influence, where exerted, takes place through other means, such as the presidents' council. While this leaves the door open for opportunistic individual shareholders like the sōkai-ya to dominate the shareholders' meetings, the goals of the sōkai-ya are not to maximize returns on investment, as one would expect from traditional investors in the U.S. model, but to receive compensation in other forms (i.e., hush money). They may be a nuisance, but the sōkai-ya exercise little influence over how managers actually run their companies.

The Board of Directors

In Chapter 4, we discussed the peculiar characteristics of the boards of directors of large Japanese firms in comparison with their U.S. counterparts. These boards almost entirely comprise full-time managers in the firms they "direct." Some of these managers have been dispatched by other companies in the group to take up full-time positions in the receiving firm, but most are career employees. Thus, despite the close connections that alliance partners share with one another, interlocking directorships are relatively scarce among major corporations.

The U.S. conception of corporate officers is largely absent in Japan, and as a result, the board of directors' meeting has the flavor of a top-level executive meeting. The *jōmu-kai* (meeting of top executives) has replaced the *torishimariyaku-kai* (board meetings) as the de facto locus of control. As one indication of this, we can look at the function of the company's auditor, who is in charge of supervising the management track record set by the directors. The shareholders of the company are granted the legal authority to appoint this position. However, these positions are almost universally filled by career employees rather than by outsiders, and the job serves primarily as a rubber stamp for the board (which is itself largely internal). The job is often so insignificant that the term for auditor, *kansayaku,* is sometimes facetiously referred to as *kansanyaku,* "officer of leisure" (Heftel, 1983).

This is not to say that the Japanese firm is undisciplined by its external constituencies, however, for the shachō-kai, main bank relationships, and other external monitoring arrangements are indeed capable of con-straining firm management. Among these, the case of the shachō-kai is perhaps most interesting. It has little power of direct control over its companies (a fact that clearly distinguishes the postwar councils from their prewar counterparts). Budget and personnel decisions are consid-ered in all but exceptional circumstances (e.g., when a group company is undergoing bank-organized restructuring) to be under the jurisdiction of the firms themselves and their management. Companies' new products and technologies may be discussed at meetings but are not dictated by the group. Even were the shachō-kai to be considered a legitimate forum for the exercise of control over individual companies, it is extremely unlikely that this could be accomplished within the short time in which the group meets or within its highly informal structure. In the words of one Sumitomo executive, "We are a big company now and cannot be run even from the president's office. How could the Hakusui-kai or some other Sumitomo grouping do it?"

Rather, the shachō-kai serves as a forum for the representation of a complex nexus of interests among a coalition of affiliated financial lenders and trading partners. In some ways, it serves as a substitute for the corporate board in a system where outside directors representing nonmanagerial interests are lacking. However, the shachō-kai represents these interests in a way that is different for the board of directors in at least two respects.

First, unlike members of a board, who retire, die, or leave for other reasons, members of a presidents' council participate in an ongoing social collective that outlasts the tenure of any one individual. The apparently ad hoc manner in which board directors who exit are replaced in the U.S. (e.g., Palmer, 1983) suggests that board participation in the United States is a sporadic process, and perhaps one that serves to link firms not to any specific set of external constituents but to the broader community of corporate leaders (Useem, 1984). The shachō-kai, in contrast, consists of a predefined set of highly visible actors with which the firms have historically carried on a variety of lines of business.

Second, the shachō-kai is an informal institution in which the monitoring function is diffused. There is no defined or legally binding governance relationship between the council and its firms, and as a result, influence is negotiated between relatively equally sized firms based on internal group relations rather than on formal authority vested in law. Associated with this is the fact that governance within the shachō-kai occurs within a known and controllable set of actors. Membership in the group is carefully defined, and control inside takes place among mutually positioned firms in a kind of community-based form of governance—as both governor and governed.

CONCLUSION

The redefinition of the firm in Japan raises what appears to be a paradox: managers have largely removed themselves from competitive markets for corporate control and in the process have reidentified the interests of the firm as their own. Yet at the same time, they have given up a considerable degree of autonomy in the embedding of their firms in external networks of other firms. It is in the resolution of this apparent paradox that the role of the contemporary Japanese manager is given meaning. For just as managers have become agents of other firms on which their own companies depend, so too have they become principals whose interests are to be served in those firms. The two roles have merged into a broader constituency that includes both financial institutions and their customers, shareholders and their managers. Unidirectional relationships based on simple flows of equity capital have been replaced by reciprocal relationships based on complex flows of trade in capital, goods, and personnel. The pressures they face from external constituencies come from those over whom they, in turn, have influence. The seemingly crisp categories of principal and agent become fuzzy as the managers of one firm become the owners of another, and in turn are held by managers of that firm. It is less that management has been separated from control, therefore, than that control has been merged into management. These relationships are then embedded in other business relationships, and ownership ceases to be a separate constituency.

As a result, the nature of ownership and corporate control is transformed. Transactions in corporate assets through mergers and acquisitions among large firms are greatly reduced and require the approval of employees and trading partners, while hostile takeovers are all but nonexistent. Moreover, the institutions of shareholder representation—the board of directors and general shareholders' meetings—lose importance except to satisfy legal and normative requirements in the business community. Ownership is important as much for symbolic as for legal reasons. One manager described an equity position as "working like a kind of engagement ring"—once engaged, influence takes place through the dynamics of the relationship as it develops over time rather than through formal shareholder positions.

CASE STUDY: CORPORATE CONTROL
AND THE MITSUBISHI OIL BUYOUT

News hit Japan in the spring of 1989 that T. Boone Pickens, a well-known Texas oilman and player in the American takeover movement, had acquired a substantial block of shares in Koito Manufacturing Co., an auto parts supplier affiliated with the Toyota group. In conjunction with the 21 percent of Koito's shares that he had reportedly acquired, Pickens claimed the right to three board seats, a figure equal to those of Toyota Motors with 19 percent of Koito's stock. Koito rejected Pickens' claim, arguing that Pickens was merely a short-term shareholder and knew nothing about the automobile industry. For two years the two sides attacked and counterattacked in a full-scale public relations war.[6] Finally, in the spring of 1991, Pickens dropped his claims and abandoned the offensive, asserting exhaustion in trying to deal with "exclusionary" relationships in the Japanese economy.

Extensive media attention and the fame (or notoriety) of its chief protagonist, together with the suspense of the annual shareholders' meetings where Pickens and Koito's top management faced off, lent a certain soap-opera quality to this affair. Despite the drama, the reality is that very little of substance actually happened in the relationships among the principals during the time period involved. The reason is that the script had already been written well before Pickens stepped in, and there was little to be done to change it. Koito's relationship with Toyota and its other leading shareholders had been consolidated many years earlier. Koito's strategy, which ultimately prevailed, was simply to wait out an impatient (and possibly politically motivated) American shareholder activist while trying to win the public relations war. It was, in short, a trench war with the battle lines drawn.

This raises the issue of just how those battle lines are formed in the first place. More specifically, how are large-block stable shareholdings in Japan established; how do they evolve over time; and what does this tell us about the nature of corporate control in Japan?

In order to understand these considerations, it would be useful to observe relationships at work in a dynamic setting. A good candidate for this task is the case of Mitsubishi Oil, which was partially consolidated within the Mitsubishi group in 1984. Analysis of the specifics of this case makes evident the strategic character of major shareholding relationships in Japan, both in gaining control over flows of critical resources and in overcoming the unwanted solicitations of foreign firms. In addition, it demonstrates in some detail the ways in which closely affiliated companies interact to determine corporate ownership structures in Japan. In the buyout of Mitsubishi Oil's shares, it was its own corporate group, and especially its lead bank and trading company, working through the group presidents' council, that was central.

The Mitsubishi Oil affair began in January 1984 when it appeared that Texaco was going to acquire Getty Oil, which for many years had held 50 percent of Mitsubishi Oil stock. If Texaco succeeded in buying Getty, there was a high probability that the stock held by Getty would be released. Texaco itself had reasons to make a quick sale in order to help finance its purchase of Getty Oil. In addition, the leadership of Texaco had not shown interest in the past in the low-profit refining and sales divisions that constituted Mitsubishi Oil's main business activities. Should Texaco choose to unload these shares, bidding was expected to be competitive because Texaco, cash-strapped with its recent purchase, would seek a high price.

Mitsubishi Oil executives became concerned that, unlike Getty Oil, which had exercised little influence on Mitsubishi Oil, a new owner might be tempted to be more involved in internal management. These concerns were shared by the Mitsubishi group as a whole. According to a managing director in Mitsubishi Bank at the time, the group's chief worry was that any Getty stock in Mitsubishi Oil that might be released would wind up in what was described as *hen na tokoro,* or a "strange place" (*Nihon keizai shinbun,* January 25, 1984). Important negotiations between Texaco and the Mitsubishi group began in April and agreement was reached in May of that year that the group would buy the Texaco-Getty interest in the company. As a result of this transaction, Mitsubishi Oil's ownership structure became dominated by other Mitsubishi group firms.

Before the Mitsubishi group stepped in, Texaco had considered selling its shares either to Caltex (a joint venture of Texaco and Standard Oil of California) or to a third party from Kuwait. The acquisition by Texaco of Getty's position in Mitsubishi Oil came right at the time of the restructuring of the oil industry in Japan, which involved several tie-ups and mergers brought on by a crisis in the oil industry resulting from overcompetition, high costs, inefficiency, and red ink. Mitsubishi Oil was a key player and whoever they tied up with would become the leader in the oil industry.

A sale to Caltex represented an unappealing option in the context of the intricate network of linkages that existed among the oil companies themselves at the time. The most pertinent of these are depicted in Figure 7.3. The danger was that Nippon Oil and Texaco, which had close business ties with each other, would gain the upper hand at a time when negotiations for a Nippon Oil–Mitsubishi Oil sales tie-up were being put forth as part of a government-sponsored restructuring of the petroleum industry in Japan. Nippon Oil was linked with Texaco's affiliate, Caltex, through Nippon Oil Refining, a refining operation that was 50 percent financed by Caltex. In addition, Nippon Oil received its crude oil supply from Caltex.

With Texaco's purchase of Getty Oil came a problem of the handling of the Mitsubishi Oil stock held by Getty. If left as is, it was inevitable that the influence by Texaco on Mitsubishi Oil would increase dramatically. According to one industry source at the time, "Nippon Oil, borrowing strength from Texaco, may set about on a takeover [*kyūshū*

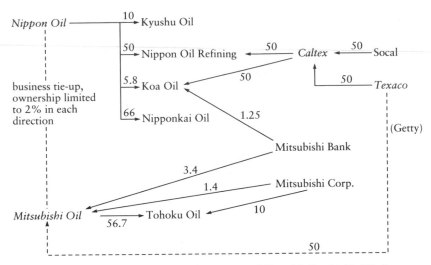

Fig. 7.3. Relationships Between the Nippon Oil and Mitsubishi Oil Groups. Source: *Nihon keizai shinbun*, May 29, 1984. Note: Arrows show direction of investment and numbers show percentages of ownership.

gappei] of Mitsubishi Oil, which is what Nippon Oil is said to have in mind" (*Ekonomisuto*, February 7, 1984).[7]

The sale of shares to an independent party was also a possibility. Early in 1984, the Kuwait Petroleum Corporation probed MITI for approval to obtain Texaco's 50 percent stake in Mitsubishi Oil. On the basis of price, there was a strong likelihood that Texaco would sell to these investors. Texaco told executives in the Mitsubishi group that, with concrete offers in hand, it wanted the final answer on what Mitsubishi was willing to pay no later than May 7. However, MITI intervened in this process by announcing that it would not allow sale of Mitsubishi Oil stock from Texaco to Kuwaiti interests, prohibiting the transaction by means of the Foreign Exchange Act (*Nihon keizai shinbun*, April 25 and 29, 1984).

This left the Mitsubishi group itself as the most promising large-block purchaser of the Mitsubishi Oil shares. Mitsubishi group interests in the purchase reflected in part a desire to protect the group name and logo. As an executive in Mitsubishi Corporation, the group trading company, put it, "We wanted to keep the three diamonds on gasoline stands through-out Japan" (*Business Week*, September 24, 1990). In addition, group companies were seeking to protect the business relationships they had in each other. Negotiations were under way at the time, for example, to use 4,500 Mitsubishi Oil gasoline stations around Japan as a point of sale

TABLE 7.1. BREAKDOWN OF THE PURCHASERS
OF TEXACO'S SHARES IN MITSUBISHI OIL

Purchaser	% of Total Shares
Kinyō-kai members (27 companies, not including Mitsubishi Oil)	about 30%
Major agents (20+ companies with special contractual relationships)	about 7%
Companies with customer relationships with Mitsubishi Oil	about 13%

SOURCE: *Nihon keizai shinbun*, July 6, 1984.

for automobiles produced by Mitsubishi Motors, with the aim of selling 50,000 cars per year this way (*Nihon keizai shinbun*, May 31, 1984).

Among all Mitsubishi group firms, the company with the largest business interests at stake (other than Mitsubishi Oil itself) was Mitsubishi Corporation. This trading firm was the leading importer of overseas energy products in Japan and about 40 percent of this business was connected with Mitsubishi Oil. Mitsubishi Corporation came out aggressively for groupwide acquisition of Mitsubishi Oil stock in order to avoid being placed at a strategic disadvantage. According to one Mitsubishi executive at the time, "It's because Mitsubishi Corporation was fearful of the loss of commercial rights. This was a case where, if Texaco were to continue to retain indefinitely its 50 percent share of Mitsubishi Oil, it would have to buy just Texaco Oil. With that, Mitsubishi Corporation's oil business would be dealt a serious blow" (*Zaikai*, September 4, 1984).

Still, given the large amounts of money likely to be involved, it was not expected to be an easy transaction and had to be carefully coordinated. This job fell to the leadership of the Kinyō-kai, the Mitsubishi group presidents' council. The primary figures involved in organizing the deal were Ōtsuki Bunpei, chairman of Mitsubishi Mining and Cement, who was concurrently chief executive (*sewanin daihyō*) of the Kinyō-kai, Nakamura Toshio, chairman of Mitsubishi Bank and assistant chief executive of the Kinyō-kai, Yamada Keizaburō, vice chairman of Mitsubishi Corporation, and Ishikawa Kiyoshi, president of Mitsubishi Oil. In addition to his role as chief negotiator, Nakamura of

TABLE 7.2.   LEADING SHAREHOLDERS
OF MITSUBISHI OIL AFTER BUYOUT,
AND THEIR BUSINESS RELATIONSHIPS

Company	Equity %	Major Business Relationships
*Mitsubishi Corp.**	20.0 (1.4)	Holder of commercial rights to Mitsubishi Oil's output
*Tokio Fire & Marine Ins.**	5.0 (3.5)	Leading casualty insurance underwriter for Mitsubishi Oil
*Mitsubishi Bank**	5.0 (3.4)	Main bank and lender of 30.7% of Mitsubishi Oil's loans
*Mitsubishi Trust**	3.2 (2.8)	Manager of Mitsubishi Oil's marketable securities and lender of 8.7% of its loans
*Meiji Mutual Life**	2.8	Leading life insurance underwriter for Mitsubishi Oil
Nihon Shōken Kessai	2.7	—
*Chiyoda Engineering**	2.7	Major contractor for Mitsubishi Oil
*Mitsubishi Heavy Ind.**	2.0	Major supplier of equipment to Mitsubishi Oil
*NYK**	2.0	Leading shipper for Mitsubishi Oil
Industrial Bank of Japan	2.0	—

SOURCES: *Kaisha nenkan* (1986), *Japan Company Handbook* (1986), and journal sources.

Notes: Equity percentages in parentheses refer to pre-buyout figures. Firms marked by a "*" are members in the Mitsubishi Kinyō-kai.

Mitsubishi Bank also took charge of obtaining the necessary financing of the stock purchase. Later, after the buyout was completed, Ōtsuki retired from his leadership position at the Kinyō-kai and Nakamura replaced him.

The negotiations were complicated by speculation in the Tokyo Stock Exchange which raised the price of Mitsubishi Oil stock from just over ¥300 per share in mid-December to an all-time high of ¥550 per share on January 24, 1984. As a result of this increase, price became a sticking point between the two parties. Texaco demanded ¥90 billion for the 150 million shares that it owned, based on the current market price of the shares plus a small premium for its large-block interest. The Mitsubishi Group countered with an initial offer of ¥40 billion, based on the per share price just before the turn-of-the-year appreciation began. Eventually, the two sides settled on a price of ¥77 billion ($335 million at ¥230 yen to the dollar), or about ¥513 per share. The actual transaction took place in July 1984 (*Nihon keizai shinbun,* May 2 and 12, 1984).

The ownership structure of Mitsubishi Oil was changed dramatically after the buyout. The majority of the Texaco-Getty shares were purchased by Kinyō-kai members, as shown in Table 7.1. The remaining shares were sold to other investors with business interests in Mitsubishi Oil, primarily leading sales agents and large customers not formally associated with the Mitsubishi group.

Among Kinyō-kai-member firms, Mitsubishi Corporation, with the most to gain or lose, was the largest buyer of shares, increasing its equity stake from 1.4 percent to 20 percent and moving from the number six to principal shareholder. In return for its investment, it placed one of its own energy specialists, Matsuda Tadao, in a specially created position of vice chairman in Mitsubishi Oil's top management. As Table 7.2 indicates, other Mitsubishi firms with business interests in Mitsubishi Oil also became major shareholders. With an increase from 3.4 percent to 5.0 percent of the shares, Mitsubishi Bank not only helped to finance the share acquisition; it also lent nearly one-third of the company's total borrowed capital. Serving as leading shareholders were Mitsubishi Oil's main insurance underwriters, while leading contractors, equipment suppliers, and shippers—all within the Mitsubishi group—also bought major positions. As a result of this ownership change, total shares held by closely affiliated companies increased from about 20 percent to about 50 percent, consolidating Mitsubishi Oil's role as an intimate part of the group.

CHAPTER VIII

Alliance Capitalism
and the Japanese Economy

Economic organization and performance are a function not merely of a country's preexisting resource endowments but of how those endowments are put together. Societies develop through institutional innovations that supplant older forms of economic organization, a process Schumpeter aptly termed "creative destruction." Capitalism was itself a major innovation, the most important feature of which was the dramatic expansion in and transformation of the role of capital and its allocation in the economy. Productive activities broadened in scale in conjunction with their increased reliance on external sources of capital. Indeed, so important were outside investors to this process that Schumpeter defined capitalism as "enterprise carried out with borrowed money" (quoted in Collins, 1986, p. 135).

In the process of institutional evolution, however, the issue of what the ideal economic system would look like is very much a hypothetical one. As G. B. Richardson (1960, p. 222) points out, "We can hope to find which arrangements are optimal only by taking account continuously of different circumstances and by weighing up different requirements, the variety and conflicting nature of which exclude the possibility of a tidy, clear-cut solution." The distinctive patterns of market organization and capitalist relations discussed in this volume are important to the extent they have real and significant consequences for the Japanese economy. Rationalized markets have long been considered efficiency-generating institutions, yet the Japanese economy has out-performed any other major industrial economy for much of the postwar period. If, as I have argued, Japan's alliance structures of industrial organization represent clear deviations from textbook models of market organization,[1] the question becomes whether the Japanese economy has performed as well as it has despite these deviations or because of them.

What follows is the bringing together of arguments developed at various points earlier in the book. The linking theme is the belief that intercorporate alliances have set the framework within which other institutional characteristics of Japanese market capitalism operate. As a result of the way in which they have defined the basic players in the game and their interrelationships, these distinctive relations have established important structural differences in Japanese corporate and market organization. A corollary is that to the extent that these underlying structures remain unchanged, ongoing transformations in the environment of the Japanese economy—as a result of government liberalization measures, currency realignments, and other forces—will have smaller effects on economic outcomes than widely predicted.

We consider in this final chapter three broad characteristics of the Japanese economy: a high degree of resilience in the face of dramatic economic change; impressive rates of long-term corporate investment that remain even in the 1980s substantially higher than in most Western economies; and a market structure with substantial barriers to entry to newcomers, especially in high value-added industrial sectors. The relationships between these characteristics and the alliance structure of Japanese industrial organization can be summarized very briefly in the following points:

1. Resilience in the face of rapid economic growth results to an important extent from the role of intercorporate alliances in stabilizing certain key business relationships, notably in the market for corporate control, while allowing for dynamic adaptation in other areas.

2. High rates of corporate investment have been promoted by Japan's distinctive capital relations, which facilitate monitoring by major corporate investors and which create secondary (strategic) benefits for these investors apart from direct (market) returns.

3. Structural barriers to entry for market newcomers in core industrial sectors are a product of preferential trading patterns as well as the overlap between companies' financial interests and their business interests.

Together, these features of the Japanese economy represent a balancing of benefits and costs that become increasingly important to understand as Japan takes center stage in the global trading community. Although Japanese industrial organization has continued to evolve in significant ways, certain features remain intact even as Japan continues the ongoing process of internationalization that marks the industrial societies of the late twentieth century. The final section of this chapter considers the implications of Japan's economic system for its relationships with its major trading partners.

STABILIZATION OF RELIABLE
BUSINESS RELATIONSHIPS

The Japanese business system has been challenged by dramatic economic and social transformations during the postwar period: the rate of industrial restructuring for much of the period since the 1950s has been the highest in the world (Imai, 1982), while important external shocks affecting all industrial nations (particularly the oil-price increases in the 1970s and the exchange rate fluctuations of the 1980s) have hit Japan particularly hard. Yet despite these pressures, Japan's business system has proved itself both resilient (where change was not necessary) and adaptable (where it was).[2] A major source of this resilience, I believe, lies in the ways in which intercorporate alliances have stabilized critical business relationships, notably the basic governance structure of the firm, while freeing companies to make adjustments in those areas where change is most urgent, including bringing production costs down, introducing new product lines, and focusing on quality improvements.

In order to understand the significance of stability in the face of ongoing change, we need to reconsider the role of uncertainty and complexity in social life. Economic and organizational systems depend for growth not only on the allocative efficiency of their arrangements— the distribution of the resources that maximize joint welfare—but also on the reliability of those arrangements. While the reliable performance of functions is essential in complex systems in which errors can be catastrophic—for example, in nuclear power and air traffic control (see Perrow, 1984; Weick, 1986)—it is also important in the daily life of all organizations. Uncertainty complicates decision making, since complex contingency planning on how to deploy resources in an uncertain future is limited by the bounded rationality of decision makers. As James Thompson (1967, p. 159) points out, "uncertainty appears as the fundamental problem for complex organization and coping with uncertainty is the essence of the administrative process."

Despite the connection between reliability and uncertainty, there is surprisingly little consideration given in economic theory to its importance in trading systems. Reliable business transactions have been considered an exogenous factor that sets the basic parameters within which partners establish prices, rather than an endogenous part of exchange relationships themselves. Among the most important exceptions to this view is Hirschman (1970), who argues that an essential feature of smoothly functioning economies is their willingness to tolerate "repairable lapses" in the performance of individual economic actors without disrupting the overall economic system. Customer persistence in the face of temporary quality declines protects firms from minor disruptions in order to allow them to recuperate sufficiently to deal with the major ones. Hirschman criticizes the image of the "relentlessly taut economy" that predominates in normative economic thought. The taut economy, he observes, is a paradox: "Society as a whole produces a comfortable and perhaps steadily increasing surplus, but every individual firm considered in isolation is barely getting by, so that a single false step will be its undoing" (p. 9).

In reality, social systems need a degree of "slack" or "loose-coupling," in order to operate efficiently. As Schumpeter (1950, p. 83) pointed out long ago, "A system—any system economic or other—that at *every* given point of time fully utilizes its possibilities to the very best advantage may yet in the long run be inferior to a system that does so at *no* given point in time, because the latter's failure to do so may be a condition for the level or speed of long-run performance." Keynes also recognized this, for he writes in various places that uncertainty raises the cost of capital and discourages investments, resulting in a permanently lower level of output than would otherwise be possible (Meltzer, 1988).

Many of the leading sources of uncertainty in the contemporary American economy result from challenges to the basic operations and integrity of the large corporation. Consider this point in terms of the market for corporate control, and the role of the stock market in shaping the industrial structure of U.S. industry in the 1980s. A cover story in *Business Week* (November 24, 1986) on "Deal Mania" begins with the following dramatic pronouncement:

> It's called Restructuring, a late-1980s version of Monopoly played in fast forward: a frenzied blur of buybacks and spinoffs, mergers and acquisitions, LBOs and recapitulations. The rules call for discovering hidden troves of

"undervalued assets" and raiding the powerful corporate fiefdoms that control them. The winner? The first person to succeed in scrambling and redeploying these assets to enhance shareholder values. But don't include Restructuring on your Christmas shopping list. This game is for real, and the stakes are as high as you get—the future economic prosperity of the U.S.

By almost any standard, the transformation of the stock market in the United States during the 1980s—and the resulting reallocation of resources in the overall economy—was remarkable. Several trends are now clearly evident. First, the market for corporate assets is increasingly dominated by institutional investors operating with sophisticated electronic data systems that allow for trading in far larger quantities of stock than was earlier possible. Whereas professional investors could handle only twenty or thirty stocks at a time just a decade ago, now trading is typically in multiples of hundreds or even thousands. In addition, new forms, such as basis trading, have emerged.[3] As a result, the volume of overall trade in shares on all major U.S. stock exchanges has increased dramatically. The New York Stock Exchange now handles well in excess of 100 million share transactions per day, in comparison with less than 30 million shares per day a decade ago.

The market has increased not just in volume but also in volatility. The most dramatic recent example of this, of course, was Black Monday (October 19, 1987), when the market had its largest single-day drop in history. It is not surprising, therefore, that individual investors are getting out of the market. U.S. households have been selling hundreds of billions of shares more than they have bought in recent years. Many are turning to financial intermediaries to handle their portfolios—roughly half of all individual shareholders now own stock through mutual funds, thereby becoming indirect shareholders.

However, more important than the volatility in share trading or prices has been the increased volatility in who manages and who is accountable for the corporation itself. The market for corporate control is now virtually complete. With the emergence of new financial instruments and sophisticated investment syndicates, few if any firms are immune to the threat of takeover. Whereas before, size was a company's best defense, since banks would lend only with dollar-for-dollar collateral behind it, this no longer works against financial instruments like junk bonds.[4] As a result, corporate raiders are able, through leverage, to finance the takeover of even the largest firms by investing only 10–20 percent of their own capital.[5]

The result has been a radical restructuring of U.S. industry—both as a result of takeovers and takeover attempts and in preemptive defenses against them. Among the main tactics in a takeover defense is the trimming of organizational units by selling off parts of one's business and the cutting of staff and other costs in order to maintain profitability and thereby share value.[6] In 1986, four thousand companies spent $200 billion in transactions in assets in order to transform themselves, four times the amount three years earlier.[7] Nearly half of all large firms underwent some form of restructuring during the mid-1980s (Coffee, Lowenstein, and Rose-Ackerman, 1988).

Just what this stock-market-induced restructuring means for the overall long-term performance of the U.S. economy has been an issue of heated debate. On one side are those who point out how restructuring has led to the breakup of unwieldy bureaucracies in some industries (e.g., Jensen, 1986). This is perhaps clearest in the oil industry, where companies grew enormously during the oil-price rise in the 1970s and diversified widely into areas about which they knew nothing (e.g., Exxon's ill-fated attempt to enter the office automation business). T. Boone Pickens almost single-handedly returned these firms to businesses "closer to the knitting" through his own direct takeover attempts or through the implicit fear he has instilled in other oil industry executives.

Proponents of this optimistic view argue that stock-market-induced restructuring may be the United States's own peculiar form of "reindustrialization policy." Leaner, more focused companies are seen as a result. The CEO of the newly "deconglomerated" Gulf and Western, for example, says, "We're out of the deal business, and we're into the operating business." A merger and acquisition consultant echoes this: "We've seen a reversal of the professional-management syndrome" (quoted in *Business Week,* November 24, 1986).

On the other side are those who argue that in firms' preoccupation with buying and selling assets to find small earnings edges, they have ignored making the investments that will promote their long-term competitive viability. In looking over their shoulders toward corporate raiders, this view says, management has been concerned with protecting itself rather than with making the investments necessary to make U.S. firms competitive in the world economy.[8]

In addition to a potential "managerial myopia" (Stein, 1988), restructuring has had other consequences, including widespread employee lay-offs, that impose social costs but are not included in the corporate-level efficiency calculus. In the first few years of the most recent merger and acquisition wave, nearly one-half million people were asked to leave their firms—sometimes through early retirement, and sometimes more bluntly (*Business Week,* November 24, 1986). Direct costs to these layoffs are borne by society through lost income-tax revenues and the payment of government unemployment benefits. Moreover, there are various hidden costs associated with the alienation of employees who had "implicit contracts" with their firms (Shleifer and Summers, 1988).

And Japan? At a minimum, Japan shows that an active market for corporate control is not a precondition for effective overall economic performance. The Japanese stock market has historically been relied upon neither as a major source of external capital nor as a source of discipline on corporate management. The first is now changing, as the high share value of Japanese firms led many companies in the 1980s to tap the securities markets. But the role of stock markets in consolidating and breaking up corporations in Japan has shown few if any signs of increase, even during the post-1985 restructuring in response to the yen's sharp rise. Stock-market-based influence by independent and institutional investors is replaced by a closely connected community of mutually positioned, long-term trading partners. The system of mutual shareholding establishes an implicit hands-off policy in managing the internal affairs in other group companies and precludes the kind of gaming in the stock market common in the United States—as captured in the vernacular of corporate raiders, white knights, shark repellents, greenmail, golden parachutes, ambushes, scorched-earth policies, and poison pills (Hirsch, 1986).

More to the point, the lack of a volatile market for corporate control is an essential component of the stability found at Japan's economic center and, indeed, of its entire business structure. Reliance on stable, outside business partners buffers Japanese firms from the normal fluctuations of the business cycle, as banks provide a steady source of capital to their close affiliates and external subcontractors provide a reliable source of production to buffer firms from economic swings. In addition, companies' affiliated firms provide external assistance in times of duress, since company survival—and that of networks of hundreds of smaller, dependent subcontractors and distributors—is linked to the fate of other firms.[9] In the United States, this kind of reliability has declined significantly with the unpredictability of new industrial arrangements. The president of a large Japanese tool manufacturer, for example, pointed out to me that an American partner of his had gone through three ownership changes over the past decade. "We never know whom we are dealing with" was one of his comments—hence, how to manage their relationship. This was a complaint I heard a number of other times as well from Japanese executives interviewed for this study.

The forging of stable external relationships in Japan has gone hand-in-hand with the development of stable internal relationships, allowing Japanese firms to focus on product market competition, technological innovation, and the development of employee skills. Perhaps the most important product of this external stability is the permanent employment system. Managers of large Japanese companies are sheltered by their affiliate-shareholders from the pressures facing U.S. managers for radical labor cost reductions when earnings are down. Where staff reductions are necessary, voluntary leaves and long-term phasing out of positions are preferred. And in extreme circumstances, alliance partners offer a last-resort source of employment for group firms in trouble. Under what has been called a "Japanese-style layoff system," employees in firms in depressed industries (e.g., aluminum) may be transferred to firms in growth industries (e.g., consumer electronics).

AGGRESSIVE CORPORATE CAPITAL INVESTMENT

The aggressiveness of Japanese firms in pursuing market share, in expanding capacity even in economic downturns, in improving product quality and diversity, and in moving into higher-value-added fields is well-known (e.g., Abegglen and Stalk, 1985) and is evident in a wide range of industries from steel to semiconductors. Nowhere is this aggressiveness more evident than in the high rates of capital investment that have marked the Japanese economy during the postwar period. Patrick and Rosovsky (1976) place special emphasis on this point. In their overview of Japanese economic development into the 1970s, they note that Japan's capital stock grew during the postwar period much more rapidly than its supply of labor, and at twice the average rate for the Western industrialized countries. Much of this growth came in the form of corporate investment:

> Real gross domestic investment, private and public, increased by an average of 12.9 percent a year between 1952 and 1973, and private business plant and equipment investment increased by 14.4 percent. This meant that in real terms gross investment, about 20 percent of GNP in the early 1950s, has composed close to 40 percent of GNP since the mid-1960s, and the share of business plant and equipment investment has increased from about 10 percent of GNP to more than 20 percent. This is the most impressive investment performance ever achieved in any peacetime, democratic, market economy;

no other such industrialized nation has voluntarily plowed back such a high
share of output into further expansion. [P. 18.]

More recent figures for the 1980s show that Japan continues to invest a
higher portion of GNP than Western economies.[10] In addition, there is
evidence that Japanese firms have been able to retain a far larger share of
earnings than have U.S. firms, as seen in Figure 8.1. These internal funds
permit expansion plans without having to go to external capital markets.

The reasons for these high rates of corporate capital retention and
investment remain obscure, however. In part, this is because we do not
understand well the causes and consequences of specific private sector investment decisions. There has yet to emerge from the corporate finance area a widely accepted, broadly applicable theory of corporate investment. Even basic questions concerning the operation of corporate
capital structures—how real-world firms actually set the level of debt,
equity, and other financial instruments used in funding their various
internal projects—have proven conceptually different in the formal theory of finance (Myers, 1984).

Abegglen and Stalk (1985) place great emphasis on corporate capital
investment rates in their analysis of the competitive strategy of the
Japanese firm, particularly for firms in emerging markets: "It is in the
high-growth sectors like semiconductors, and indeed in the whole range
of microelectronically driven new technologies, that the differences in financial policies become critical. It is precisely in these critical competitive
sectors that the growth-driven financial policies of the [Japanese com-
pany] differ most greatly from those of their Western competitors. Japanese in these high growth businesses most often employ financial policies
considered reckless and unmatchable by Western executives" (p. 154).
Abegglen and Stalk admonish managers in Western companies for their
apparent ignorance or timidity in the face of the investment policies of
their Japanese counterparts. But this ignores important structural features of Japanese capital markets that set the context within which
managers set their policies. Rather than merely understanding the "competitive fundamentals" better, as Abegglen and Stalk suggest, Japanese
managers actually face a capital environment that is different in fundamental ways from that facing U.S. managers, and this leads to different
patterns of rational investment.

We consider in this section three sets of structural perspectives: a
traditional view based on direct cost of capital; a newer set of views
that emphasize the role of information and alternative contracting and

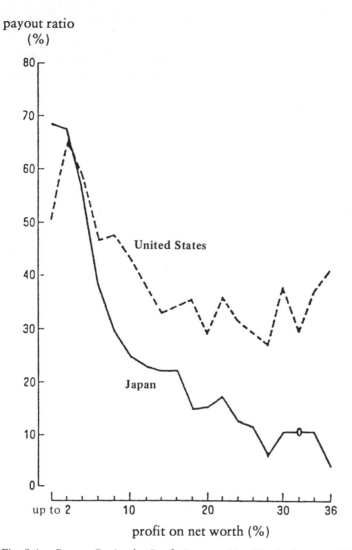

payout ratio
(%)

United States

Japan

up to 2   10   20   30   36

profit on net worth (%)

Fig. 8.1.   Payout Ratios by Profit Rate on Net Worth. Source: Okumura (1988, p. 36). Notes: Payout ratio = dividends/profits. "0" symbol indicates no companies actually exist at this particular point.

governance structures; and a view that focuses on the strategic interests of investors. While there remains doubt regarding the direct cost of capital advantages for firms in Japan, I argue that Japanese firms enjoy very different relationships with investors, as seen in the structured quality of information they receive, their ability to act on that information, and the nature of incentives that link companies with their capital suppliers.

The Cost of Capital

In the first of the three structural explanations for Japan's high investment rates, Japanese managers and the Japanese stock market are seen as facing an abundance of promising investment opportunities and acting accordingly by funding them. One reason for the relatively high rates of investment, this view continues, has been that Japanese corporate and market investors enjoy lower costs of capital, making even less promising investment opportunities viable. Lower returns can be accepted because they are still sufficient to cover original capital costs.

This explanation is intuitively appealing given Japan's high savings rate over the past several decades, a large portion of which has been channeled into productive, long-term corporate investment. Nevertheless, there remains considerable debate over how widely available outside capital has been for Japanese firms and how much those firms actually paid for it. For many U.S. managers in capital-intensive industries, such as semiconductors, the high cost of capital in the U.S. is viewed as a major source of competitive disadvantage. Several studies in the early 1980s that found a substantially lower cost of capital in Japan fueled this concern. As a result, reducing capital costs has been cited as an important area on which to concentrate U.S. public policy for enhancing industrial competitiveness, for example, by lowering the capital gains tax or otherwise increasing the amount of savings channeled into investment.

Defining corporate costs of capital is not a simple affair, however. Subsequent studies that employ different samples and alternative procedures have provided mixed evidence of a Japanese corporate capital cost advantage (for a recent review, see Hodder, 1991). While overall interest rates have surely been lower in (noninflationary) Japan, this has been countered by the fact that corporate borrowers have historically been required to keep a portion of debt as deposits with their lending banks in the form of compensating balances (Hamada and Horiuchi, 1987). These low-interest deposits have had the effect of redistributing benefits back to the banks, neutralizing at least a portion of whatever cost advantages these borrowers would otherwise enjoy.

A different source of capital cost advantage is attributed to the high debt-equity ratios common to large Japanese corporations, offering certain tax advantages to borrowers.[11] But with leverage also comes risks, for companies are obliged to meet their interest payments on a larger number of loans. Studies that have considered this risk factor (e.g., Baldwin, 1986) have found that it largely cancels out capital cost advantages that would otherwise exist for Japanese firms.

The question of outside financing through debt versus equity is not merely one of direct capital costs, however, but one of the institutional arrangements by which capital is allocated. The risks that banks bear in corporate lending vary considerably depending on their relationships to their corporate customers. Osano and Tsutsui (1986) find, for example, that Japanese banks transfer a portion of the lending risk back to large borrowers through implicit contracts concerning the terms of loan interest rates. According to their study, this mutual risk sharing is a better predictor of loan interest rate arrangements than were credit rationing explanations based on the power of banks to choose their customers. They conclude, "Our estimation reveals that risk-bearing between banks and firms through interest rate arrangements is a predominant phenomenon in the Japanese commercial loan market" (p. 434).

Hodder (1991) also emphasizes the special characteristics of the capital allocation process in Japan. After concluding his review of cost of capital studies by noting the lack of evidence for a consistent and systematic advantage for Japanese firms in their risk-adjusted cost of funds from the capital markets, he goes on to discuss the nature of the relationship that exists between capital providers and capital users. Hodder argues that the extent of risk in leveraged Japanese firms is overstated because Japanese financial intermediaries are well positioned to monitor and control their corporate clients as a result of the close working relationships that have evolved over time. Even though firms that are able to finance their expansion plans through internal capital may be better off in the short run doing so, it can still make sense over the long term to build reliable creditor relationships for those occasions when internal cash flow is no longer sufficient.

In sum, it is not clear whether Japanese firms enjoy a capital cost advantage over U.S. firms, and if so, how much. Several recent trends suggest that whatever advantages may have existed are of declining importance. Financial liberalization has opened foreign capital markets to Japanese corporate borrowers. That many firms are now availing themselves of these opportunities suggests that financial markets are now sufficiently global to have at least partially eliminated national origin as a consideration in direct capital costs. The recent move by Japanese companies toward paying off their external debt is also difficult to explain if high debt-equity ratios are still a major source of capital cost advantage. In the following two sections, we pursue further the view that it is the nature of capital relations, rather than capital costs per se, that is most important to understanding the corporate investment process in Japan.

Information and Governance

Several new perspectives on corporate investment have emerged in the areas of financial and organizational economics over the past decade that argue that capital costs as a practical matter are intimately inter-twined with other features of the investment relationship itself. Corporate investment strategies, therefore, will reflect not only the basic prices companies pay for capital but also the quality of the information on which investment decisions are made and the ability of investors to oversee those investments effectively (see Fama and Jensen, 1983; Myers, 1984; Williamson, 1988). In this way, the economics of uncertainty associated with the pioneering work of Hayek, Arrow, Simon, and others is merged with the concerns of Berle and Means over the problems of governance when ownership and control are separated. The result is what are now known as agency and transactions costs theories of organization.

Agency theorists have made as their intellectual centerpiece the separation of ownership and control (see Chapter 7). The principal-agent relationship, in which managers (the agents) make decisions over the allocation of other people's money (the principals), is intrinsically fraught with conflict as a result of information and incentive asymmetries. The basic problem is that managers have more information about how investors' funds are being utilized but less incentive to utilize those funds in the investors' best interests.

Yet despite the problems associated with agency, the argument continues, the separation of principals and agents has itself developed to take advantage of a division of labor between the provision of capital and decisions over its use. Some people specialize in allocating funds to different corporations, while others specialize in managing the firms themselves. In addition to a specialization in skills, this division also allows for the diffusion of risk. Unlike the owner-entrepreneur relationship in which principal and agent are one and the same, in the shareholder-manager relationship, the managers of public corporations need not risk both their careers and their capital by "over-investment" in the firms that they manage. The task of the modern corporate economy, then, is to take advantage of this division of labor while minimizing the resulting agency costs.

Oliver Williamson, the leading proponent of the transactions costs perspective, is more inclined to be skeptical of the ability of external capital markets to discipline firms effectively. While outside investors may have a broad knowledge of the stock market, he argues (1975) they lack deep knowledge of the companies themselves, and for this reason a variety of organization-based means of governing exchange have emerged. Following this line of argument, a number of researchers explain Japan's business groups in terms of the ways in which they internalize transactions in order to capture the benefits of (quasi) internal organization (e.g., Goto, 1982; Imai, 1989a).

The quality of information that alliance partners have at their disposal is clearly different from that available to outside investors. These are what Clifford Geertz (1978) has termed clientelized relationships: "Clientelization is the tendency . . . for repetitive purchasers of particular goods and services to establish continuing relationships with particular purveyors of them, rather than search widely through the market at each occasion of need" (p. 30). The kind of information provided is more detailed than that available in impersonal markets. "Search is primarily intensive because the sort of information needed most cannot be acquired by asking a large number of diagnostic questions of a handful of people"—it is "exploring nuances rather than canvassing populations" (p. 32).

Affiliate-shareholders have learned about each other through ongoing trading relationships and through various collaborative projects and other forms of interaction that provide information not available in financial statements. If, for example, product quality begins to decline, the group trading firm and other affiliated trading partners are likely to be among the first to know this through their purchasing connections. The kind of in-depth information that the firm's main bank acquires in order to extend loans is utilized as well in its decisions as shareholder.

These banks know their customers well and are able, in the words of one observer, to distinguish between "inspired entrepreneurs and blind reck-lessness" (Suzuki, 1980).

How information is understood also differs. Affiliate-shareholders are managers with concrete knowledge about and experience in running companies. To the extent that management is best thought of not as a set of recipes that can be transferred cookbook-style from one individual to another, but as a focal point of implicit routines, tacit knowledge, and hands-on experience (Nelson and Winter, 1982), these professional managers may be better able to evaluate the performance of other managers across a range of criteria than are professional investors whose skills come in other forms.

Alliance partners are also linked through various forms of personnel connections that improve information and serve as a source of discipline. Employee transfers are common among business partners, particularly among banks and their client firms and among large manufacturers and their subcontractors. Interfirm executive councils bring together man-agers from various levels in firms within the bank-centered and vertical keiretsu groupings. The Sumitomo group, as noted earlier, has monthly councils not only for the presidents and chairmen of group companies, but for vice presidents of corporate planning, research and development, and other fields. In addition, group projects bring together personnel from the middle and technical levels of several firms. As a reflection of the increasing need for interfirm information flows, group projects pro-liferated in the 1980s, and an average of ten to twenty new projects were started within each group every year.

Incentives

The informational and governance advantages to alliance structures outlined above may have the result of lowering de facto capital costs for Japanese firms even if direct costs, when measured by adjusted interest rates, are not significantly lower. Affiliate-shareholders may also be willing to accept lower returns from their investments for an entirely different reason: promotion of their long-term strategic interests (see also Aoki, 1984b).

The argument in brief is that intercorporate alliances have brought together investment and managerial decisions within an ongoing cooper-ative relationship between firms. Capital has been moved closer to the point of investment decision, resulting in a general pattern of rapid entry into new industries by existing firms with the early and continued support of allied companies. Group firms, as equity shareholders, receive first-order returns on their investment when other group firms are profitable. More important in many cases, however, are their second-order returns as business partners. Product improvement and volume expansion redound to the benefit of group financial institutions that extend loans for new investments, trading concerns that manage the goods that result, and manufacturers that use the products. In cases where social benefits for investment outweigh private benefits, therefore, it makes sense for affiliate-shareholders to permit "over-investment" in certain projects if they are able to capture a sufficient portion of the benefits themselves.[12]

With the merging of shareholding positions into ongoing trading relationships, the long-term viability of the firm as a reliable supplier and customer becomes important. The continual improvement in the quality and features of firms' product lines takes on significance in and of itself— even where these improvements are not captured in improved equity returns—because investors receive benefits in other forms. Financial institutions, for example, are among the top shareholders in large Japanese firms, yet their equity positions are typically only a fraction of the loans and other business they carry on with the same firms.[13] Not surprisingly, these institutions are interested in ensuring that their corporate borrowers are around over the long term to service their financial obligations.

Even where direct equity returns are low, continued expansion by the firm leads to new business for the group banks and insurance companies (in the form of loans, deposits from employees of group companies, and other business), for the group trading firm (as the commercial representative of the firm's products), as well as for other affiliated manufacturing concerns (which supply parts for and use the products). As a result of the importance of these kinds of strategic linkages, new market entry in Japan has been dominated by larger and older firms with substantial backing from their affiliates. There is really nothing equivalent in Japan to California's Silicon Valley, though pockets of regional high-tech entrepreneurism exist. Rather, as Chapter 6 pointed out, advanced industries such as biotechnology, electronics, and new materials have been entered by well-established firms seeking expansion into new but related growth areas with the support of their larger group. While this may discourage some entrepreneurs, it also means that new entrants have a ready market to tap in the form of other affiliated firms. In addition, when industries reach a point at which plant and equipment with greater capacity become necessary, these firms have an accessible pool of motivated capital through their banking connections.

STRUCTURAL BARRIERS TO MARKET ENTRY

What is one to make of the persistent trade imbalances that have plagued the U.S.-Japan economic relationship since the 1960s? The explanation of Japan's inroads into U.S. markets seems relatively straightforward. The high value of the dollar combined with the poor performance of American products in certain sectors in comparison with their Japanese counterparts led to a surge in Japan's exports in the early 1980s. These markets were aggressively maintained even as this exchange rate advantage disappeared in the mid-1980s, as Japanese companies sacrificed profits rather than pass the full brunt of price increases on to overseas customers and investors absorbed earnings losses rather than pressure corporate managements into holding margins.

More vexing, however, has been the difficulty firms from the United States and elsewhere have had in making inroads into Japan's own markets, including many industries where U.S. products are fully competitive. Recent trade statistics show some improvements, but the bilateral imbalance remains enormous even in the early 1990s despite the doubling in the value of the yen against the dollar since 1985, as well as market-liberalization efforts initiated by the Japanese government much earlier.[14]

Both macroeconomic changes, embodied in currency realignments, and changes in government trade policies, in the form of formal tariff and nontariff barriers, have proved less powerful in explaining U.S. corporate performance in Japanese markets than many scholars of trade have suggested.[15] A significant reason for this is a simple but often overlooked point: international trade is based not only on exchange rates set by capital markets and legal barriers set by governments but also on the concrete relationships among the firms that actually make the buying and selling decisions, both in financial and in industrial (intermediate product) markets.

Preferential trading patterns characterize a wide variety of product and service markets in Japan. Firms are aware of the identity of their lenders and trading partners and of the history and nature of their relationships with them. This does not necessarily mean that there is an especially strong "buy Japanese" bias among Japanese buyers. Consumer nationalism probably exists in all economies, although it is not clear that it is more pervasive in Japan than elsewhere. (Consider the "Made in America" logos imprinted on red-white-and-blue insignias and patriotic music used to promote American products on TV and radio.) Nor is this an argument for barriers resulting from the "complexity" of the Japanese distribution system or the number of levels between producer and consumer. There is already well under way a movement to reduce the complexity by consolidating retail and wholesale outlets in Japan. It is not the absolute number of outlets or levels that is important so much as the relationships of these outlets with upstream producers and downstream users. The argument here is that there are preferential biases built into the structure of Japanese product markets—biases that have certain economic benefits for their participants but that also raise de facto barriers to entry for market newcomers.

The source of these preferential biases lies in part in the rationality involved when affiliate-shareholders consider strategic interests in their investments—that is, when they accept lower rates of financial return because their business interests benefit. Equally important is the fact that the reverse is also true: Japanese companies rationally take into consideration the identity of their shareholders and board members when choosing with whom to trade or bank. A supplier firm in which 30 or 40 percent of equity and half a dozen board seats are controlled by its parent company must factor in this set of external constraints in making product-pricing and downstream-sales decisions. Similarly, when a share of the parent's equity and several board seats are held by its lead bank, this too weighs into the parent company's decisions about where to open a new line of credit or place newly issued securities.

The reality of business reciprocity of this sort was expressed to me in the course of several interviews. A top executive in NEC told me that his company planned to use the long-distance lines of NTT's new competitors in direct proportion to the amount of equipment those carriers purchased from his company. A director in one of these common carriers, Teleway Japan, confirmed that this was likely to be the common pattern and added that his company used engineers from their shareholding companies. He expected to get banks and life insurance companies on board as both equity investors and large-scale users of his company's services. Especially clear evidence of the consequences of these forms of business reciprocity for market newcomers comes in the following matter-of-fact quotation from the financial vice president of Japan Air Lines: "We have 16 banks in our syndicate, each of which is a shareholder. . . . Therefore, we have to borrow from all 16 banks, and we could not think of borrowing from foreign banks" (quoted in *The Economist,* August 22, 1987).

Even observers who are otherwise unsympathetic to a structural approach to Japan's trading relations acknowledge that institutional differences do exist. Gary Saxonhouse (1988, p. 247), for example, notes the role of industrial groups and other "distinctive Japanese institutions" and recognizes that these institutions may have repercussions for international trade:

> Many of Japan's distinctive institutions may involve the creation of market power or the alteration of the terms under which pre-existing market power is exercised. The theory of international trade would conventionally suggest that where such market power results in nontrivial distortions, intervention of some kind by trading partners is justified. (A nontrivial distortion is one that significantly changes the terms under which goods and services are offered for sale either in Japan or abroad.)

Saxonhouse nevertheless remains unconvinced that nontrivial distortions actually exist in Japan. He concludes his analysis with sufficient confidence to end in an exclamation point: "The case remains to be made . . . that Japanese institutions do, in fact, create the kinds of distortions that invite Japan's trading partners to demand changes!" (p. 248).

The structuralist perspective faces the difficult challenge of moving beyond quotes and anecdotes to a systematic demonstration of deviations from orthodox market rationality. One approach has been to focus on overall patterns of trade in order to infer more microlevel institutional differences. The problem with this approach, however, is that overall patterns reflect a large number of factors, only some of which are related to institutional differences in market structure. Thus, the high ratio of exports to imports in Japan's overall trade can be attributed theoretically not only to preferential trading patterns but also to straightforward macroeconomic forces. Along these lines, Bergston and Cline (1985) and others argue that a large part of the U.S.-Japan trade imbalance can be understood as a natural outgrowth of financial imbalances between aggregate investment and aggregate savings by Japanese and American households, resulting in Japan's producing more than it spends and the United States's spending more than it produces.

An alternative is the microanalytic study of concrete patterns of relationships among economic decision makers. One way of getting at these relationships is to study the extent to which the identity of trading partners is an important characteristic of actual trading patterns. In arm's-length markets, identity should be unimportant and traders will freely trade with those who offer the best combination of price, quality, and features. Where identity is important, on the other hand, one will find various patterns of long-term trading among relatively exclusive groupings. The importance of identity in different markets can be set along a continuum of preferential trade, ranging from zero (the identity of traders is irrelevant to trading patterns) to one (all trades are among exclusive buyer-seller combinations).

Using an extensive network database and new methods of analysis, I have identified clear, systematic evidence of preferential trading across a range of markets. The importance of identity turns out to vary by type of transaction as well. In product markets, intermarket keiretsu members are on average about three times more likely to trade with their affiliates than with companies in other groups. In the case of bank and equity capital—seemingly homogeneous media of exchange—figures rise to over ten times. The result of these analyses moves beyond the standard debate over whether Japanese markets are "open" or "closed" to a more subtle view of markets as ranging in degrees of preferential trading in ways that will affect cross-border trades.

Preferential trading patterns pose special problems for public policy. Far from being a mere "market imperfection" that leads to inefficiencies in Japanese markets, identity-based trade represents a form of system-level rationality that emphasizes development of reliable trading systems with reduced governance costs. As Ben-Porath (1980, p. 1) puts it, "Some transactions can take place only between mutually or unilaterally identified parties. Investment in resources specific to a relationship between identified parties can save transaction costs and stimulate trade. Such investment gives rise to what I call specialization by identity— concentration of exchange between the same parties—analogous to specialization by impersonal dimensions of transactions." And herein lies the public policy dilemma: although identity-based trading systems can lead to certain efficiencies, they also result in differential access to the fruits of that efficiency. In other words, the benefits of the system can only be enjoyed if one is a part of it.

JAPAN'S INTEGRATION
INTO THE INTERNATIONAL ECONOMY

The challenge facing Japan, as with any country, is to build on its economy's inherent strengths while overcoming its distinctive weaknesses. No doubt the Japanese economy has proved remarkably resilient in the past and has responded effectively to external shocks that would have devastated many other economies. And it has done so while maintaining features that have been keys to its effectiveness, including those patterns of firm and interfirm organization that are at the center of this study.

As Japan now takes its place as a leader in the global trading system, it faces what is perhaps its biggest challenge. There remains widespread perception among its trading partners that in "playing by different rules" Japan has gained a disproportionate share of the benefits of international trade. The resulting pressures have been highlighted in recent years with the onset of the Structural Impediments Initiative (SII) talks between the Japanese and American governments in the late 1980s. One consequence of these negotiations has been a new focus in Japan on intervention in the private sector with the goal of increasing the "transparency" of business relations and facilitating access to Japanese markets by foreign companies. Specific policy reforms now being considered touch on issues discussed at length in earlier chapters, among them reducing cross shareholdings, increasing the number of outside directors sitting on Japanese boards, and strengthening the rights of individual shareholders.

Nevertheless, there is substantial ambivalence in Japan concerning the SII process and its outcomes, especially where reforms might affect fundamental business practices. In a recent survey, for example, one hundred top executives in Japan were asked for their opinions on America's SII-related demands. More than four-fifths found merit in reforms that would directly affect Japanese consumers, including policies affecting land prices and the distribution system. In contrast, only one-fifth found any merit in the U.S. position regarding keiretsu-based trade and stock crossholdings (Gerlach, 1992a). There does not appear to be any significant domestic coalition to push for serious keiretsu reform—at least not yet and not among the leading companies within the Japanese business community.

It is possible, of course, that Japan's increasing presence in the world economy will bring fundamental changes to its own system through an ongoing process of internationalization. To date, however, this has largely involved the expansion of production and other business activities of Japanese companies overseas without a commensurate increase in the penetration by foreign firms directly in Japan. This has provoked two sets of concerns among Japan's trading partners, the first related to the openness of the Japanese market itself, the second to the possibility that keiretsu patterns are being exported to their own markets.

The issue of market openness, as I have suggested, is strongly affected by patterns of preferential trading that exist in Japan. Those large firms that are most likely to act as major importers of foreign products—especially the general trading companies that serve as a central import window to Japanese markets—also sit at the middle of a complex nexus of vertical and intermarket groupings. For these firms, importing substantial numbers of products that compete with those of key affiliated companies runs the risk of harming this nexus. It is of more than passing interest, in this light, that the lowest import penetration ratios in Japan tend to be in industrial product markets, where the role of intercorporate trade is greatest (Lawrence, 1991).

It is also of interest that some of the most successful foreign firms in Japan have been those that have acknowledged and worked within the keiretsu structure. Kodak, for example, is reported to have become sufficiently "Japanese" that it has developed its own family of companies, with some of its largest business customers asking it to take a small equity stake in them (*The Economist*, November 10, 1990). Also noted in Chapter 4 was the evolving set of relationships among IBM-Japan and several companies of the Mitsubishi group. The effectiveness of these relationships depends to a large degree on the distinctive capabilities that foreign firms bring in and on the extent of competitive overlap that exists with domestic competitors. Although the number of cross-border alliances has increased in recent years (Imai, 1990), there remains widespread feeling among many outside Japan that not enough is being done to encourage penetration of trading networks in Japan by foreign firms.

Given the close relationships that characterize the Japanese market, it is not surprising that overseas patterns tend to recreate domestic patterns. The dramatic increase in Japanese direct investment in foreign markets has introduced a new worry among Japan's trading partners that keiretsu patterns are being introduced into their own economies. There is certainly anecdotal evidence of preferential trading with affiliated firms overseas. An article on preferential trading among "compatriot" firms in the *Wall Street Journal* (April 12, 1984), for example, reported that Canon USA relies on Fuji Bank and Bank of Tokyo to provide import financing when it buys products from its Japanese parent, has the products insured in transit by Yasuda Fire and Marine, and stores them in the United States in east-coast warehouses owned by Nippon Express. It is worth noting here that Canon participates in the presidents' council of the Fuyo group, as do Fuji Bank and Yasuda Fire and Marine.

More systematic data are provided in a recent survey of Japanese transplant automobile assembly plants and suppliers in the United States. Florida and Kenney (1991) found that over three-quarters of the suppliers they surveyed had set up U.S. operations to maintain close relationships with a major Japanese customer and nine-tenths chose their specific locations to be close to that customer. In contrast, traditional economic considerations, such as local labor costs, had little impact on locational choices. Most of these suppliers were located within a short driving distance of their primary customer and maintained a variety of forms of close interaction, including on-site visits by their customers' engineers.

Further evidence that trading patterns overseas follow those at home was provided in Chapter 4, utilizing detailed information on Japanese trading companies' business transactions with steel companies. These data show that trading companies represent primarily their own affiliated steel producers in overseas markets and are much less likely to be involved in transactions with producers in other groups. Elsewhere (Gerlach, 1992a), I have extended this analysis to overseas plant contracts managed by these trading firms. Despite encompassing a far broader range of trading partners than just steel producers, the similarities in preferential trading in overseas markets are striking. Overall, trading companies are about ten times more likely to handle contracts to build overseas plants that involved firms in their own group than they are with firms in another group.

In short, it is clear that the increasing activity of Japanese companies in international markets has not led to the kind of dramatic changes in its business structure that some observers have predicted. This is not to say that important changes in Japanese industrial organization cannot or will not occur. Undoubtedly, liberalization of Japanese financial markets and Japan's inexorable push into high technology industries and overseas markets will continue to provide the impetus for an ongoing evolution in Japan's own firm and market organization. But there is nothing inevitable about the direction of these changes, and the move toward more impersonal or "Western" forms of market transaction is only one possibility. Just as Japan's corporations have proved themselves adaptive to changes in their environment, so too have its intercorporate networks. The decline of alliance structures will become apparent when long-term relationships, business reciprocity, and the role of extended families of companies decrease in importance in the Japanese industrial landscape. The evidence to date indicates that this has yet to happen.

The problem in the policy arena this creates, as Yamamura (1990) points out, results from an asymmetry between the need for rapid adjustments in business behavior in order for Japan to appease its trading partners and the slow pace of structural changes that are likely actually to emerge. In the scenario that he outlines, "Neither market forces nor foreign and domestic political and economic pressure to change Japan's economic structure will be exerted in sufficient amounts or in ways necessary to fundamentally alter it" (p. 17). As rates of change lag behind external demands, Japan will face continued and perhaps even exacerbated problems in managing its international relationships. It is essential, therefore, that Japan and its trading partners work toward establishing some kind of modus vivendi for integrating their distinctive economic systems.

CONCLUSION

Perhaps the strongest argument for the Japanese business system has been its remarkable ability and willingness to experiment—to try new things and to look outside and learn. This has been carried out enthusiastically on all fronts in the development of Japanese technical, organizational, managerial, and production skills. Japanese industry has been marked by rapid entry into new fields by firms that have the early and continuing support of affiliated companies. Competition within markets has been balanced by cooperation across markets among financial, commercial, and manufacturing concerns.

This argues for an extremely relativistic view of organizations and markets. Considering each in isolation impoverishes our understanding of the other, and hard-and-fast boundaries between the two are inadequate for comparative organizational and economic analysis. Acknowledging this close relationship, however, requires overcoming traditional distinctions in the social sciences. In economic thought, the firm has long led a strange and precarious existence in the background of the subject of main interest, the market. In organizational theory, it is the market itself (defined, if at all, as part of the organization's "environment") that has been neglected.

Over the past decade, this artificial bifurcation has been attacked from both directions and has eroded considerably. Economists have entered the firm and found it not to be a relatively straightforward production function of neoclassical market theory but, rather, a complex institution in which organizational form matters. They have had to develop new tools to understand internal organization, the most influential of which is the idea of transaction-costs minimizing contracting (Williamson, 1975, 1985). Firms and markets are, in this new view, not fundamentally different, but alternatives in the terms of the contracts linking parties.[16]

In contemporary organizational theory as well, firm and market distinctions have blurred. Within resource-based theories of organization, boundaries are drawn "as a matter of analytical convenience, much as analytical boundaries are drawn in the analysis of heat-transfer systems. For some purposes, then, customers might be considered part of the organization, and for others they might not" (Pfeffer and Salancik, 1978, p. 30). Sociological theories of institutions have focused on the ways in which firms and their environments lead mirror lives, with each embedded in the other as a result of the interpenetration of the structures and symbolic forms of society. In the words of Meyer and Rowan (1977, p. 346), "Quite beyond the environmental interrelations suggested in open systems theories, institutional theories in their extreme forms define organizations as dramatic enactments of the rationalized myths pervading modern societies, rather than as units involved in exchange—no matter how complex—with their environments."

As we have seen in this study, firms and markets in Japan are merged in a common process of the contracting of terms of trade as well as in a social framework organized by broader sets of rules and rituals. Alliance forms organize business networks both by symbolically identifying group members and by structuring concrete exchange relationships. They represent a significant middle ground between, on the one hand, tightly organized internal operations and, on the other, loosely organized and impersonal markets. As such, they have altered the nature of each in important ways. Organizations are nested in markets, while markets are organized. Studies of the social organization of Japanese business must recognize this dual embedding.

Appendix A: Data Sources and Coding Methods

The quantitative analyses in Chapters 3 through 5 of this study rely heavily on an extensive network database that is described in more detail in this appendix. Funding from the University of California's Pacific Rim research program covered a team of data coders and Japanese language translators for the period 1987–88 when the bulk of the database was assembled (see Gerlach, Harris, and Teece, 1987). Additional funding from the Pacific Rim program and from the National Science Foundation since 1989 has allowed for completion of documentation and analysis (Gerlach and Lincoln, 1989; Gerlach, Lincoln, and Teece, 1989).

The focus on concrete networks of relationships among corporations that is the hallmark of this database required that choices be made as to which network actors and network variables to include. Both the Japanese and American economies are made up of millions of firms of varying sizes and industries linked through a wide variety of formal and informal relationships. It is obviously unrealistic to attempt to cover empirically anything more than a fraction of these.

The choice to focus on large firms was both practically and theoretically motivated. Detailed information on ownership, control, and business relationships is most widely available for public corporations, and these tend to be larger enterprises. This is especially true in Japan, where only a small fraction of firms are publicly traded (see Chapter 2). In addition, by focusing primarily on major business concerns, it was possible to reduce substantially the number of firms covered while nevertheless incorporating a significant portion of each economy, as measured both by total market share and by range of industries.

The largest 200 industrial firms in Japan were identified from a list provided in *Nihon kigyō shūdan bunseki* (1980, pp. 25–31), based on company sales. Commercial, utility, and service industries were excluded from the sample, in keeping with the criteria utilized by the *Fortune 500*. The 50 major financial institutions in Japan included in the sample were drawn from listings in the final section of the 1982 volume of *Industrial Groupings in Japan*, based on total assets. For the American sample, the top 200 industrial corporations were identified from the 1980 *Fortune 500* listings, based on company sales. The top 50 financial institutions in the United States came from the *Fortune* financial institutions list from the same year. This American sample provided the basis for the comparative ownership analyses in Chapter 3.

Brief company histories, including important name changes and major restructurings, were written for each company in the sample. *Kaisha nenkan* provided this information for the 250 Japanese firms, while *Moody's* provided the same information for the 250 American firms. For the Japanese sample, formal affiliations with industrial groupings were coded based on listings in two publications, *Industrial Groupings in Japan* and *Kigyō keiretsu sōran*. A listing of the Japanese and American firms in the sample is provided in Appendix B.

A second decision concerned the type of network information to include in the database. Ideally, a network database should cover the complete panoply of linkages that connect any actors within the sample. Since this is obviously impractical, choices must be made about what relationships to include. Most interfirm network studies in the United States, when faced with this dilemma, have relied on interlocking directorships as their focal measure (e.g., Mizruchi, 1982, Burt, 1983). These interlocks are used as "traces" of other ongoing business relationships among firms. Just how closely interlocks actually follow capital or trading patterns among firms remains uncertain, however, and it is important to supplement these ties with detailed information on other intercorporate linkages.

The wide availability of network data in Japan presents an opportunity to expand the range of important business relationships considered and to develop a rigorous, empirically based approach to the mapping of a much broader range of key industrial organization relationships. The database used here systematically maps intercorporate structure in Japan across four different, but fundamentally important, network variables: equity shareholdings, borrowed capital, interlocking directorships, and major trading relationships. To facilitate comparisons, data on intercor-

TABLE A.I.   DATA VARIABLES, YEARS,
AND SOURCES USED IN THE STUDY

Japanese Network Data

Top-ten shareholders
  Companies: largest 250 Japanese industrials and financials
  Sources: *Keiretsu no kenkyū* (for industrials);
            Kaisha nenkan (for financial institutions)
  Volumes: 1970, 1972, 1974, 1978, 1980, 1982, 1984, 1986, 1988
Outside directors
  Companies: same 250 firms
  Source: *Kaisha nenkan*
  Volume: 1980
Top-ten debtholders
  Companies: top-200 industrials only
  Source: *Keiretsu no kenkyū*
  Volumes: 1970, 1972, 1974, 1978, 1980, 1982, 1984, 1986, 1988
Trading partners
  Companies: top-200 industrials only
  Source: *Kaisha nenkan*
  Volume: 1980

U.S. Network Data

Top-ten shareholders
  Companies: largest 250 U.S. industrials and financial institutions
  Source: *Spectrum*
  Volumes: 1980, 1984
Outside directors
  Companies: same 250 firms
  Source: *Dun & Bradstreet's Guide to Corporate Managements*
  Volume: 1980

porate relationships among American firms have been collected for the two types of relationships in which similar data were available—equity shareholdings and interlocking directorships. The data included in this study, their years, and their sources are summarized in Table A-1.

The identity of industrial companies' top-ten shareholders and the amount of their holdings were translated and coded from a Japanese annual, *Keiretsu no kenkyū*. Since the lists of leading shareholders compiled by this source excludes financial institutions, ownership information on banks and other financial corporations were coded from another annual, *Kaisha nenkan*. The volumes of each source utilized began in 1970 and continued biannually until 1988. (The exception was 1976, a year in which *Keiretsu no kenkyū* did not publish a volume.) Each volume covers ownership data from between one and two years earlier.

Also translated and coded from *Keiretsu no kenkyū* from the same years were industrial companies' leading lenders and the amount of their loans. In this part of the database, industrial firms appear only as "receivers" of ties and banks and other financial institutions appear only as "senders."

Until recently, no comparable information on capital investors was available for American firms. While this is still true for debt capital, systematic data on corporate ownership have been available for the past decade through the *Spectrum* series. *Spectrum* relies on information resulting from 13f reporting requirements filed by institutional investors with the U.S. Securities and Exchange Commission. This source has provided on a quarterly basis since 1980 detailed breakdowns of institutional investors and the amount of their holdings for over five thousand listed and unlisted companies, including all of those traded on the New York and American stock exchanges. Volumes from *Spectrum* for the second quarter in 1980 and the second quarter in 1984 were used for coding ownership data for all American industrial and financial firms in the sample.

Data on all Japanese companies' outside directors were located through *Kaisha nenkan*. This publication provides information on firms' officers, including the current or former affiliations of outside directors. This feature is important in studying directorship flows in Japan since many "inside" directors have actually moved in midcareer from another company, such as the receiving company's bank. Unlike in the United States, these dispatched directors (*haken yakuin*) typically take on full-time managerial positions in their new firm while retaining ongoing contacts with their former employer (see Chapter 4). These data were translated and coded from the 1980 volume. For the American sample, outside directors and their affiliations were identified through *Dun and Bradstreet's Guide to Corporate Managements,* also the 1980 volume.

The final set of network measures, trading relationships, was identified for the industrial firms in the Japanese sample from the 1980 volume of *Kaisha nenkan,* which provides the names of companies' leading suppliers and customers for industrial firms. It does not, however, include information on the amounts of purchases or sales. These data were supplemented by specific figures on purchases and sales among trading companies and steel producers provided in *Sōgō shōsha nenkan,* which are used in analyses in Chapter 4.

Appendix B: Companies in the Network Database

JAPANESE FINANCIAL INSTITUTIONS

Number	*Name*
1	Dai-Ichi Kangyo Bank
2	Fuji Bank
3	Sumitomo Bank
4	Mitsubishi Bank
5	Sanwa Bank
6	Industrial Bank of Japan
7	Long-Term Credit Bank of Japan
8	Tokai Bank
9	Taiyo Kobe Bank
10	Mitsui Bank
11	Nippon Credit Bank
12	Kyowa Bank
13	Saitama Bank
14	Bank of Tokyo
15	Hokkaido Takushoku Bank
16	Bank of Yokohama
17	Hokuriku Bank
18	Shizuoka Bank
19	Joyo Bank
20	Chiba Bank
21	Ashikaga Bank

JAPANESE FINANCIAL INSTITUTIONS—*(continued)*

Number	Name
22	Bank of Hiroshima
23	Bank of Fukuoka
24	Daiwa Bank
25	Gunma Bank
26	Mitsubishi Trust and Banking
27	Sumitomo Trust and Banking
28	Mitsui Trust and Banking
29	Yasuda Trust and Banking
30	Toyo Trust and Banking
31	Chuo Trust and Banking
32	Tokio Marine and Fire Insurance
33	Yasuda Fire and Marine Insurance
34	Taisho Marine and Fire Insurance
35	Sumitomo Marine and Fire Insurance
36	Nichido Fire and Marine Insurance
37	Dai-Tokyo Fire and Marine Insurance
38	Nippon Fire and Marine Insurance
39	Chiyoda Fire and Marine Insurance
40	Fuji Fire and Marine Insurance
41	Nissan Fire and Marine Insurance
42	Nishi-Nippon Sogo Bank
43	Kinki Sogo Bank
44	Tokyo Sogo Bank
45	Hyogo Sogo Bank
46	Nagoya Sogo Bank
47	Nomura Securities
48	Nikko Securities
49	Daiwa Securities
50	Yamaichi Securities

JAPANESE MANUFACTURING FIRMS

Number	Name
1	Toyota
2	Nippon Steel
3	Nissan
4	Nippon Oil
5	Matsushita Electric

JAPANESE MANUFACTURING FIRMS—(continued)

Number	Name
6	Hitachi
7	Mitsubishi Heavy Industries
8	Toshiba
9	NKK
10	Sumitomo Metal Industries
11	Kawasaki Steel
12	Mitsubishi Electric
13	Honda
14	Kobe Steel
15	Maruzen Oil
16	Kirin
17	Ihi
18	Toyo Kogyo
19	Mitsubishi Petrochemical
20	NEC
21	Daikyo Oil
22	Isuzu
23	Toa Nenryo
24	Sanyo Electric
25	Showa Oil
26	Mitsubishi Chemical
27	Taiyo Fisheries
28	Kawasaki Heavy Industries
29	Nihon Kogyo
30	Kubota
31	Fujitsu
32	Sumitomo Chemical
33	Asahi Chemical
34	Snow Brand
35	Sony
36	Toray
37	Komatsu
38	Nippondenso
39	Matsushita Denko
40	Nippon Suisan
41	Takeda Pharmaceuticals
42	Bridgestone Tires

JAPANESE MANUFACTURING FIRMS—*(continued)*

Number	Name
43	Kanebo
44	Nissan Shatai
45	Ajinomoto
46	Sharp
47	Dai Nippon Printing
48	Teijin
49	Hino
50	Fuji Heavy Industries
51	Asahi Glass
52	Sumitomo Electric
53	Furukawa Electric
54	Mitsui Toatsu
55	Ube Industries
56	Nisshin Steel
57	Arabian Oil
58	Yamaha Motors
59	Meiji Milk Products
60	Showa Denko
61	Fuji Film
62	Toppan Printing
63	Mitsui Mining
64	Nippon Gakki
65	Suzuki Motors
66	Shiseido
67	Dai Nippon Ink
68	Hitachi Zosen
69	Daihatsu
70	Koa Oil
71	Mitsui Shipbuilding
72	Toyo Aluminum
73	Mitsubishi Oil
74	Morinaga Milk
75	Sapporo Breweries
76	Fuji Electric
77	Sekisui Chemical
78	Jujo Paper
79	Nippon Light Metals

JAPANESE MANUFACTURING FIRMS—*(continued)*

Number	Name
80	Nisshin Flour
81	Sanyo Kokusaku Pulp
82	Oji Paper
83	Kao Corp.
84	Toyobo
85	Daido Steel
86	Ito Ham
87	Nippon Reizo
88	Nissan Diesel
89	Mitsubishi Metals
90	Onoda Cement
91	Ricoh
92	Tokyo Sanyo Electric
93	Sumitomo Heavy Industries
94	Mitsui Petrochemicals
95	Hitachi Metals
96	Nippon Meat Packers
97	Nippon Victor
98	Asahi Breweries
99	Unitika
100	Mitsubishi Mining and Cement
101	Honshu Paper
102	Mitsui Mining and Smelting
103	Meiji Seika
104	Aisin Seiki
105	Toyota Automatic Loom Works
106	Kanto Auto
107	Sumitomo Metal Mining
108	Toyota Autobody
109	Pioneer
110	Kuraray
111	Kyokuyo
112	Nichiro Gyogyo
113	Nihon Agriculture
114	Hitachi Cable
115	Fuji Kosan
116	Toyo Soda

JAPANESE MANUFACTURING FIRMS—*(continued)*

Number	Name
117	Yokohama Tire
118	Daishowa Paper
119	Prima Meat Packers
120	Mitsubishi Rayon
121	Kyowa Hakko
122	Denki Kagaku
123	Niigata Engineering
124	Japan Steel Works
125	Yamazaki Baking
126	Sumitomo Light Metals
127	Canon
128	Oki Electric
129	Rengo
130	Sumitomo Forestry
131	Konishiroku
132	Showa Sangyo
133	Sankyo Co.
134	Nihon Cement
135	Gunze
136	Kanegafuchi Chemical
137	Matsushita Reiki
138	Mitsubishi Gas Chemical
139	Fujisawa Pharmaceutical
140	Hitachi Chemicals
141	Nippon Seiko
142	Kurashiki Boseki
143	Sumitomo Cement
144	Shionogi
145	Topy Kogyo
146	Tokuyama Soda
147	NTN Toyo Bearing
148	Kikkoman
149	TDK
150	Central Glass
151	Morinaga Seika
152	Nisshin Spinning
153	Nisshin Oil Mills

JAPANESE MANUFACTURING FIRMS—*(continued)*

Number	Name
154	Q.P.
155	Matsushita Communications
156	Fujikura Densen
157	Japan Synthetic Rubber
158	Aichi Steel Works
159	Aichi Machine Industry
160	Fujiya
161	Toto
162	Mitsubishi Paper
163	Marudai Food
164	Iseki and Co.
165	Nippon Flour Milling
166	Diesel Kiki
167	Brother Industries
168	Daikin Kogyo
169	Ebara
170	Lion Corp.
171	Ezaki Glico
172	Omron Tateishi
173	Nakayama Steel Works
174	Toshin
175	Daicel Chemical
176	Nissan Chemical
177	Toyo Ink
178	Toyo Kohan
179	Toyo Rubber
180	Shin-Etsu Chemical
181	Nippon Sheet Glass
182	Koyo Seiko
183	NGK Insulators
184	Yodogawa Steel Works
185	Nippon Zeon
186	Sankyo Aluminum
187	Dowa Mining
188	Tanabe Seiyaku
189	Matsushita Kotobuki Electric
190	Daiwa Spinning

JAPANESE MANUFACTURING FIRMS—*(continued)*

Number	Name
191	Showa Aluminum
192	Nitto Boseki
193	Daiken Trade and Industry
194	Nissin Food Products
195	Tokyu Car Corp.
196	Kayaba Industries
197	House Food Industries
198	Kokuyo
199	Alps Electric
200	Tokyo Steel Manufacturing

AMERICAN FINANCIAL INSTITUTIONS

Number	Name
1	Citicorp
2	Bankamerica Corp.
3	Chase Manhattan Corp.
4	Manufacturers Hanover Corp.
5	J. P. Morgan and Co.
6	Chemical New York Corp.
7	Continental Illinois Corp.
8	First Interstate Bancorp
9	Banker's Trust New York Corp.
10	Security Pacific Corp.
11	First Chicago Corp.
12	Crocker National Corp.
13	Wells Fargo and Co.
14	Interfirst Corp.
15	Mellon National Corp.
16	Marine Midland Banks
17	Irving Bank Corp.
18	First National Boston Corp.
19	Texas Commercial Bancshares
20	Northwest Bancorp
21	Republicbank Corp.
22	First Bank System
23	First City Bancorp of Texas

AMERICAN FINANCIAL INSTITUTIONS—*(continued)*

Number	Name
24	Bank of New York Co.
25	NBD Bancorp
26	NCNB Corp.
27	Mercantile Texas Corp.
28	Seafirst Corp.
29	Republic New York Corp.
30	European American Bancorp
31	Federal National Mortgage Assoc.
32	Aetna Life and Casualty
33	Cigna
34	American Express
35	Travelers
36	Merrill Lynch and Co.
37	First Boston
38	H. F. Ahmanson
39	American General
40	Great Western Financial
41	Transamerica
42	Loews
43	Lincoln National
44	First Financial Charter
45	Baldwin-United
46	American International Group
47	Continental
48	E. F. Hutton Group
49	Golden West Financial
50	FN Financial

AMERICAN MANUFACTURING FIRMS

Number	Name
1	Exxon
2	General Motors
3	Mobil
4	Ford Motor Corp.
5	Texaco
6	Standard Oil of California

AMERICAN MANUFACTURING FIRMS—*(continued)*

Number	Name
7	Gulf Oil
8	IBM
9	General Electric
10	Standard Oil (Indiana)
11	ITT
12	Atlantic Richfield
13	Shell Oil
14	US Steel
15	Conoco
16	EI Dupont De Nemours
17	Chrysler
18	Tenneco
19	Western Electric
20	Sun
21	Occidental Petroleum
22	Phillips Petroleum
23	Proctor and Gamble
24	Dow Chemical
25	Union Carbide
26	United Technologies
27	International Harvester
28	Goodyear Tire and Rubber
29	Boeing
30	Eastman Kodak
31	LTV
32	Standard Oil (Ohio)
33	Caterpillar Tractor
34	Union Oil of California
35	Beatrice Foods
36	RCA
37	Westinghouse Electric
38	Bethlehem Steel
39	RJ Reynolds Industries
40	Xerox
41	Amerada Hess
42	Esmark
43	Marathon Oil

AMERICAN MANUFACTURING FIRMS—*(continued)*

Number	*Name*
44	Ashland Oil
45	Rockwell International
46	Kraft
47	Cities Service
48	Monsanto
49	Philip Morris
50	General Foods
51	Minnesota Mining and Manufacturing
52	Gulf and Western Industries Inc.
53	Firestone Tire and Rubber
54	McDonnell Douglas
55	WR Grace
56	Georgia Pacific
57	Pepsico
58	Armco
59	Coca Cola
60	Deere
61	Colgate Palmolive
62	Getty Oil
63	Aluminum Co. of America
64	Consolidated Foods
65	Greyhound
66	International Paper
67	Ralston Purina
68	TRW
69	Allied Chemical
70	American Can
71	Weyerhauser
72	Continental Group
73	Borden
74	Charter
75	Signal Companies
76	National Steel
77	Iowa Beef Processors
78	Johnson and Johnson
79	Honeywell
80	Sperry

AMERICAN MANUFACTURING FIRMS—*(continued)*

Number	Name
81	Litton Industries
82	Lockheed
83	General Dynamics
84	Union Pacific
85	Republic Steel
86	Champion International
87	Farmland Industries
88	Bendix
89	American Brands
90	General Mills
91	IC Industries
92	Raytheon
93	CPC International
94	CBS
95	Inland Steel
96	Owens-Illinois
97	United Brands
98	Dresser Industries
99	American Home Products
100	Textron
101	Eaton Corp.
102	FMC Corporation
103	Reynolds Metals
104	Texas Instruments
105	Warner-Lambert
106	American Cyanamid
107	Celanese
108	J Ray McDermott
109	American Motors
110	PPG Industries
111	NCR
112	BF Goodrich
113	Kaiser Aluminum and Chemical
114	Boise Cascade
115	Amax
116	Carnation
117	Crown Zellerbach

AMERICAN MANUFACTURING FIRMS—*(continued)*

Number	Name
118	Burroughs
119	Anheuser Busch
120	Dana Corp.
121	Combustion Engineering
122	Bristol Myers
123	Pfizer
124	Borg-Warner
125	Motorola
126	Teledyne
127	Norton Simon Inc.
128	Kerr McGee
129	Burlington Industries
130	Emerson Electric
131	Standard Brands
132	Singer
133	Northwest Industries
134	Uniroyal
135	Mead
136	Ingersoll Rand
137	Time Inc.
138	St. Regis Paper
139	HJ Heinz
140	Fruehauf
141	Central Soya
142	Land O' Lakes
143	Kennecott Copper
144	American Standard
145	North American Philips
146	Dart Industries
147	Merck
148	Avon Products
149	Nabisco
150	Hewlett Packard
151	Diamond Shamrock
152	Hercules
153	Archer-Daniels Midland
154	General Tire and Rubber

AMERICAN MANUFACTURING FIRMS—*(continued)*

Number	Name
155	Walter Kidde Inc.
156	Johns-Manville
157	Whirlpool
158	Campbell Soup
159	Control Data
160	Owens-Corning Fiberglass
161	Ogden
162	Kimberly-Clark
163	Eli Lilly
164	Pillsbury
165	Colt Industries
166	NL Industries
167	Levi Strauss
168	Martin Marietta
169	American Broadcasting
170	Pennzoil
171	Agway
172	Gould
173	White Consolidated Industries
174	Gillette
175	Allis Chalmers
176	Quaker Oats
177	Jim Walter
178	Tosco
179	Scott Paper
180	Paccar
181	Interco
182	Williams Companies
183	Kellog
184	JP Stevens
185	Marmon Group
186	Koppers
187	Digital Equipment
188	Squibb
189	Olin
190	McGraw Edison
191	National Distillers and Chemical

AMERICAN MANUFACTURING FIRMS—*(continued)*

Number	Name
192	Cummins Engine
193	SCM
194	Clark Equipment
195	Asarco
196	Revlon
197	Abbott Labs
198	Ethyl
199	Warner Communications
200	Gold Kist

Notes

1. OVERVIEW

1. It is doubly ironic, therefore, to see how far attitudes have reversed: a recent survey of Japanese attitudes began with a picture of a feeble Statue of Liberty, limping slowly with cane in hand under a rising sun (*Business Week*, December 18, 1989). The survey reported that nearly half of a sample of one thousand adult Japanese believed that the United States was being eclipsed by Japan as the world's leading economic and political power, a surprisingly large proportion in a country not known for overly optimistic opinions about themselves; only a third expressed admiration for American people or for the U.S. economy.

2. Hoshi and his colleagues measure access to capital in terms of the degree of corporate "liquidity," defined as sensitivity of corporate investment to cash flow. In one study, they show that the marginal effect of liquidity investment is nearly ten times higher for firms without strong affiliations than for those with these affiliations (Hoshi et al., 1990b). In an extension of this analysis in another study, they demonstrate that firms that reduced dependence on debt capital from group banks increase the effects of liquidity on their investment rates (Hoshi, et al., 1990a).

3. The indicators tested were Tobin's q (the ratio of the market value of debt and equity to the replacement cost) and realized investment rates.

4. Two useful compendia of the network approach are Wellman and Berkowitz, *Social Structures: A Network Approach* (1988), and Mizruchi and Schwartz, *Intercorporate Relations: The Structural Analysis of Business* (1987). The first provides an overview of the structural or network perspective, and the second a series of specific applications to intercorporate relationships.

5. Among the influential studies reflecting this movement away from vague conceptualizations of "organizational environments" to the detailed study of

specific patterns of interorganizational relationships are Pfeffer and Salancik (1978), Aldrich (1979), and Burt (1983).

6. As we see in Chapter 2, individual shareholding continued to decline in Japan even during the stock price boom of the 1980s, while shareholding by Japanese banks increased at a sufficient rate to offset this.

7. For a useful discussion of the logistics of share-voting coalitions, see Leech (1987).

8. An exception to this is Nakatani (1984). Note, however, that Nakatani's results, while showing differences between "keiretsu" and "non-keiretsu" firms that are consistently in the same direction and statistically significant, also find these differences to be quite small, averaging less than 2 percent across all variables.

9. That alliances help to stabilize critical uncertainties, however, does not mean that they are stagnating or anti-change. Rather, actors pursue alliances in some arenas in order to free them up to focus on the elements of change in other arenas. Nation-states create military alliances for geopolitical stability while continuing to pursue their own independent economic interests. Kinship groups use marriage and other personal alliances in order to further the social interests of the clan. And companies seek intercorporate alliances in some markets (e.g., capital) in order to further their business interests in other markets (e.g., development of new technologies).

10. As chapters 4 and 5 demonstrate, these forms of reciprocal trading exist whether the companies are linked through formal keiretsu ties or not. This becomes readily apparent when intercorporate relationships are studied as complex networks rather than as unitary groups.

11. The importance of establishing credible commitments in market exchange (Williamson, 1985) is taken up in the following chapter.

12. Institutional approaches to organization have received considerable attention within both economics and sociology in recent years. The contributions of institutional economics to this issue are considered in the following chapter. Here I focus primarily on sociological interpretations of organizational forms, which provide a more skeptical account of rationality and efficiency than their economic counterparts. See, for example, Zucker (1977), Meyer and Rowan (1977), DiMaggio and Powell (1983), and Meyer and Scott (1983).

13. As DiMaggio and Powell (1983, p. 148) put it in their well-known formulation of the institutionalist perspective, "We ask, instead, why there is such startling homogeneity of organizational forms and practices; and we seek to explain homogeneity, not variation."

14. Insofar as alliance forms in Japan predate the widespread adoption of permanent employment, the historical accuracy of the argument that internal labor markets were the primary impetus for the emergence of the keiretsu (as suggested in recent risk-sharing explanations) is unclear.

15. It is interesting in this light that, although the multidivisional form has also made inroads in Japan, it is not nearly as widespread as in the United States or the United Kingdom (Yoshihara et al., 1981). One reason may be, as Cable and Yasuki (1985) suggest, that enterprise groups create the same kind of separation of strategic and operating decisions as the M-form, the first taking place at the group level and the second at the firm level.

16. One former business executive now working as a consultant explained this as follows: "People contacts are more important than money. That's why I always go to cocktail parties and other functions—to renew these contacts. Altogether, I have more than 20,000 *meishi* [calling cards] in my file. Of course, I don't remember them all, but I do remember the important ones."

17. Notably lacking are incentives based on the financing of wholly new enterprises in which entrepreneurs stand to receive significant capital gains by taking the company public or merging it with another company.

18. Aoki (1987) provides a particularly effective discussion and critique of the managerialist viewpoint. He asks, if the Japanese company were really "owned" by its employees, as some have argued, "why does the body of employees not have the power to regain more explicit control over the firm in the event of bankruptcy? Why are employees susceptible to discharges at their own cost? Why are senior employees the ones most vulnerable to layoff? Are they not in the strongest position with respect to the property ownership of the firm, by virtue of their seniority?" (p. 101).

19. It should be noted that shareholders will be interested in both capital gains and in dividend income, which was not included as a separate item. However, given the low rates of dividend payouts (see Chapter 8), it seems unlikely that higher dividends are being substituted for capital gains as a corporate goal.

20. As Chapter 3 shows, an average of one-half of the top-ten shareholders of large Japanese companies also hold major, identifiable banking or trading relationships with those same firms. The true figures, including those investors that hold business relationships that have not been identified, are probably much higher than this.

21. Among the non-profit-maximizing criteria that have received attention are Baumol's (1959) maximization of sales revenues, subject to a profit constraint; Marris's (1964) constrained maximization of the firm's growth rate; and Williamson's (1964) tripartite model comprising staff, discretionary spending for investments, and managerial slack absorbed as a cost. Various theories of subgoal pursuit have also been developed within organizational theory, probably the best-known of which is Cyert and March's (1963) model of the firm as a shifting set of coalitions.

22. Advocates of perfect competition models recognize that their assumptions may be unrealistic. But the standard response, following from Friedman's (1953) well-known article on the methodology of economics, has been that it is not necessary that the assumptions be true, only that they lead to useful predictions. An unanswered question in this interpretation is how far these assumptions must deviate before they become counterproductive. As Loasby (1976, p. 15) points out, if Galileo had followed Friedman's prediction rule, he would never have gotten in trouble with the Roman Church, for the church was quite willing to acknowledge and make use of Copernican theory. But Galileo was interested as well in the "structure" of a theory, and the result has opened up new avenues of research.

23. In this context, Loasby (1976, p. 163) points to the inherent contradiction in the textbook emphasis on the virtues of equilibrium models in advocating the free movement of prices in response to changing circumstances—by no

means a logical outcome of a theory that is concerned with stable prices in a stable situation.

24. This literature dates from at least Akerlof (1970). For influential analyses applied to capital investment, see Myers (1984) and Williamson (1988).

25. Even successful "mixed" economies, like those of Scandinavia, are largely market capitalist by the above standards.

26. As Williamson points out, economic organization reflects a "syndrome of characteristics" in which "distinctive strengths and distinctive weaknesses, in a comparative institutional sense, appear nonseparably—albeit in various proportions—as a package" (1975, p. 130, emphasis deleted).

2. RETHINKING MARKET CAPITALISM

1. Although the conditions of change are more readily apparent in modern economies, where technological and organizational innovations have led to an ongoing process of economic evolution, even traditional economies face changing conditions in the form of poor weather, wars, and so on.

2. A fourth pattern, householding (the pattern of peasant agriculture), was introduced in *The Great Transformation* (1944) but was ignored in his classic piece, "The Economy as Instituted Process" (Polanyi, 1957). He returned to it in his last work, *Dahomey and the Slave Trade* (1966).

3. Although Polanyi wrote in several places that the twentieth century had seen the return of some important nonmarket elements, notably the role of the state in regulating markets and in redistributing income, this argument was not well developed in his work and his primary empirical contributions came in the analysis of ancient economies.

4. E.g., premodern Africa (Braudel, 1984, pp. 430–41), Turkey (pp. 467–84), and India (pp. 484–523).

5. These statistics are reported in Cable and Dirrheimer (1983, p. 43), based on Prais (1976).

6. Even here, however, the anonymity of trading has been brought into doubt. See especially Baker's (1984) work on the emergence of trading cliques in securities markets.

7. Evidence for the ongoing "keiretsu-ization" of the Japanese economy and its implications for firm organization is discussed in Chapters 5 and 6.

8. Williamson writes, "Contrary to earlier conceptions—where the economic institutions of capitalism are explained by reference to class interests, technology, and/or monopoly power—the transaction cost approach maintains that these institutions have the main purpose and effect of economizing on transaction costs" (1985, p. 1).

9. A foreign manager of a joint venture company in Japan described his own impressions as follows: "One has to build confidence between partners. Can they trust you? 'Sincerity' is a word that comes up often. . . . It takes time and a lot of interaction to build this sort of trust between partners. The Japanese do not like to rush headlong into relationships. . . . Their bonds of friendship are slowly won but deep."

10. For a somewhat different treatment of Japan's low litigation rates, but

equally skeptical about their cultural bases and compatible with Haley's institutional barriers argument, see Ramseyer (1988). Ramseyer attributes lower rates to the fact that court cases are tried by judges rather than juries in Japan. This increases the predictability of outcomes insofar as judges tend to follow common judicial procedures and to standardize their results far more than juries.

11. Braudel (1984) himself is clear on this distinction, arguing that the market economy represents the flow of social life: transactions with one's local merchants, bartering at the village bazaar, and so forth. Capitalism, in contrast, represents a higher level control structure: decisions made by key actors in the "central cities" of the world economy.

12. These figures come from *Venture Japan* (vol. 1, no. 3), *Forbes* (November 11, 1988), and Komatsu (1990). The pattern of very low public listings in Japan seems to be changing, however, with a relaxation in listing standards. The number of annual initial public offerings in Japan has increased from less than fifty in the early 1980s to more than 100 in 1988 and 1989, half of these in over-the-counter markets.

13. The subject of just how the Japanese and U.S. systems of managerial discipline actually operate is taken up in several later chapters. Not surprisingly, given the stakes involved, reality is more complex than the skeletal differences outlined here. This is perhaps demonstrated most clearly in the in-depth case studies.

14. This process also reflects the inevitable workings of organizational life cycles, as companies' original owner-founders are often not the right people to manage their enterprises when they grow beyond a certain size.

15. Note that the company-centered focus of the owner-founder can remain even if the owners choose to hire professional managers to manage their businesses. The professionalization of management is a different issue from the professionalization of the investment function.

16. The importance of individual and institutional investment can be measured as a share of either overall ownership or of trading volume. I focus on the share of overall ownership, because trading volume can be strongly affected by the goals of the investor. Institutional investors trade far less on average than individual investors in Japan but far more in the United States.

17. Precise figures on this are difficult to come by. The numbers reported here are reported in *Business Week* (February 4, 1985).

18. West Germany represents a mixture of Japanese and Anglo-Saxon patterns of ownership. On the one hand, large banks are prominent shareholders in important companies with which they do business. A leading example of this is Deutschebank, which owns over 20 percent of its most important client, Daimler-Benz. Investment trusts are also prevalent, however, constituting a greater share of stock market investment, about 50 percent of total, than in other countries, excluding Britain (Futatsugi, 1982, p. 110).

3. THE ORGANIZATION OF JAPANESE
BUSINESS NETWORKS

1. As a result, the volume of wholesale trade is proportionately far larger in Japan than in other advanced industrial countries. Whereas the ratio of whole-

sale to retail transactions is 1.6 in the United States, 1.9 in the United Kingdom, 1.2 in France, and 1.7 in Germany, the figure in Japan is 4.0 (Okumura, 1990). These wholesalers represent intercorporate mediaries in a chain of relationships between producer and final consumer.

2. For example, into the early 1980s, about 60 percent of the external capital of large Japanese semiconductor firms came from bank loans, in contrast to only about 30 percent in the United States (Flaherty and Itami, 1984, p. 141).

3. For a critique of the dual structure perspective applied to the U.S. economy, see Baron and Bielby (1984) and Hodson and Kaufman (1982). Regarding Japan, Clark (1979) has argued compellingly that a "graded hierarchy" more accurately captures contemporary reality than the discrete partitions implied by the dual structure terminology.

4. Useem's view need not be incompatible with a firm-stratification view. Indeed, the "inner circle" terminology itself suggests that the centrality of actors in an economy differs. This might be interpreted as reflecting different positions in a business hierarchy.

5. In network theory terms, these can be understood as relatively stable and coherent cliques or clusters of relationships. The cliques are marked by high levels of intensity of transactions within and low intensity across groupings.

6. A number of studies have attempted to test the extent of dispersal in the United States, as well as the associated prediction that diffusely held ("management-controlled") corporations will perform more poorly than companies with concentrated ownership ("owner-controlled") because of the lack of managerial discipline. Although these studies have consistently found that even the largest shareholders of most major corporations rarely control more than a few percent of shareholdings, the evidence for systematic relationships between ownership structure and company performance has proved generally weak (see Demsetz and Lehn [1985]). The ownership-performance relationship would appear to be more complicated than any simple, monotonic function would predict.

7. Aoki (1984a) estimates that banks account for only 2.9 percent of shares traded on the Tokyo Stock Exchange, life insurance companies only 0.8 percent, and nonfinancial corporations 6.9 percent. In other words, institutional investors account for only 10 percent of total transactions, despite holding two-thirds of total shares on the exchange.

8. Using a somewhat different classification, Futatsugi (1976) finds much higher percentages of reciprocity. For most firms in his overall sample, reciprocity exceeds 20 percent and in some cases exceeds 50 percent. The reasons for these higher figures seem to be (1) the use of top-twenty versus top-ten shareholders; and (2) limiting shareholders to those listed on the first section of the Tokyo Stock Exchange, which effectively excludes mutual life insurance companies and other investors that cannot have their shares reciprocated.

9. Many of the remaining 51.5 percent of the equity ties probably also involve simultaneous relationships of other kinds that were not coded. Employee stockholding plans and family foundations, for example, were common investors in the firms with which they are associated.

10. Calculated from *Nihon kigyō shūdan bunseki* (1980), pp. 25–31, table 10.

11. In most cases where two or more companies are listed under the same category, they represent different areas or product lines. For example, within the Mitsui group, Mitsui and Co. and Mitsukoshi are, respectively, a multinational trading company and a department store chain; Mitsui Construction is a large building firm, while Sanki Engineering specializes in equipment installation; and Mitsui Toatsu covers a broad spectrum of chemicals, but leaves petroleum-related products like polyethylene to Mitsui Petrochemicals.

12. *Shūkan Bunshun* (March 15, 1990) reported that this decision was a collective one made by the entire Mitsui group at its presidents' council, the Nimoku-kai.

13. In general, keiretsu members are over twenty times as likely to have outside directors from affiliated companies and over ten times as likely to borrow from affiliated financial institutions and have affiliated companies as equity holders. The picture in intermediate product market trade is complicated by the fact that preferential trading patterns vary substantially by industry; steel and chemical firms rely heavily on intermarket keiretsu affiliates (especially the group trading companies), whereas assembly industries rely more on vertical keiretsu affiliates. Methods and findings are discussed in Chapter 4.

14. An article in the *New York Times* (October 28, 1989) on the takeover of Sansui Electric by Polly Peck notes that Sansui had been losing money for years, had paid no dividend for four years, had lost $50 million on $190 million in sales, and had been able to find no buyer in Japan.

15. Detailed histories of the Sumitomo group may be found in Miyamoto et al. (1979) and Noguchi et al. (1968).

4. THE BASIC FORM AND STRUCTURE OF THE KEIRETSU

1. As a reflection of the increasing need for interfirm information flows, these projects have been proliferating in the 1980s, and an average of ten to twenty new products are being started within each group every year.

2. Unlike the United States, where the chairman of the board is usually CEO, in Japan it is the company president that tends to wield most power.

3. As noted in Chapter 3 and discussed in more detail in Chapter 5, by the late 1980s, the councils had grown to a membership of twenty companies for the smallest, Sumitomo, twenty-four for Mitsui, twenty-nine for Mitsubishi, twenty-nine for Fuji, forty-four for Sanwa, and forty-seven for Dai-Ichi Kangyo.

4. The Mitsui zaibatsu apparently did not have a formal *kyōryoku-kai*. Instead it included in its *rijikai* (directors' meeting) the presidents of the Mitsui subsidiaries, so it did not require a separate association for intragroup interaction.

5. This name has an interesting etymology. It was created by taking the ideograph for the name of the original Sumitomo copper shop, *Izumi*, and breaking it into two parts. The top part alone, in its Chinese reading, is *haku*, or white, while the bottom part is *sui*, or water.

6. The *Oriental Economist* has published periodic articles on the groups since the 1950s, which discuss the shachō-kai in varying degrees of detail and plausibility. See also Okumura (1983, pp. 90–105).

7. This relationship is structured into the Japanese language, as the forms and vocabulary of discourse change dramatically depending on the respective social positions of the speaker and listener and the length of time they have known each other.

8. The chairmen have their own meeting, the Izumi-kai, whose purpose apparently is largely centered on playing golf.

9. For example, following the crash of a Japan Air Lines 747 in 1985, in which over five hundred passengers died, JAL made a series of very public apologies through the mass media and sent its executives out on personal visits to the families of the deceased. Its president, Yasumoto Takagi, shortly thereafter acknowledged his responsibility by stepping down.

10. This role is discussed again in the following chapter. For a detailed case study of Sumitomo Bank's assistance in the turnaround of Mazda in the 1970s, see Pascale and Rohlen (1983).

11. On the other hand, while Japanese banks are able to hold shares themselves in companies, most are not permitted to act as a representative of trust or pension funds. For U.S. banks, in contrast, this is an important source of business. A study by the office of the late Senator Metcalfe (reported in Aoki, 1984a, pp. 10–11) found that U.S. banks manage trusts and pensions that represent about one-quarter of total voting shares. These banks, however, are required by laws on fiduciary responsibility to vote their shares in the interests of the actual holder, and this law is maintained by a "China Wall" separating a bank's trust business from its lending business.

12. This is determined by taking the number of nondirectional linkages possible in a network of eleven actors (55) and dividing it into the number of ties actually observed (in this case, 39). Considering the direction of the ownership tie in calculations of density would double the number of possible linkages and alter the density figures. It would be biased, however, by the fact that one important shareholder, Sumitomo Mutual Life, cannot have its own shares held by other companies, since it is a mutual company. Nondirectional measures in this case seem more appropriate.

13. That is, 22 out of 55 possible nondirectional ties are completed.

14. These are the group bank, trading company, life insurance company, and eight largest industrial firms.

15. Figures for share purchases are based on book value, and come from *Nikkei bijinessu* (January 15, 1990). Figures for total ownership come from *Securities Market in Japan, 1990*, p. 10.

16. Data derived from *Kabushiki ashidori 20 nenkan* and *Japan Company Handbook*. The one company that switched affiliations is Sumitomo Marine and Fire, which had used Yamaichi as its lead underwriter in the late 1960s but later changed to Daiwa Securities.

17. These regulations limit banks in all major industrialized countries to holding total assets no more than 12½ times their equity capital base by March 1993. Prior banking regulations in Japan allowed much higher capital ratios, and as a result, Japanese banks have had either to limit their loan portfolio or else to increase their equity base in order to meet these new requirements. The BIS-imposed regulations also allow banks to apply a portion of the unrealized

gains on their own equity holdings in companies and other hidden assets toward their equity base. While most major Japanese banks had met these restrictions by 1989, the rapid decline in the Tokyo stock market in 1990 wiped out much of the value of their stock-based hidden assets, forcing them once again to consider other means of raising equity. Nevertheless, this arrangement has allowed these financial institutions to continue to invest in new securities of nonfinancial firms at a rate that would have otherwise been impossible, in the expectation that appreciation on these shares would help their own capital positions.

18. It is not surprising, therefore, to hear an official in one long-term credit bank report that, among the various means of meeting BIS rules, "the most efficient, most influential way is equity finance" (*Wall Street Journal,* May 13, 1991).

19. Statistics on Japanese bank growth come from *The Economist* (November 11, 1989). Of course, a substantial portion of this growth comes from *endaka*-induced asset inflation. Nevertheless, more informal indices also suggest the continuing strength of financial institutions in the Japanese economy. For example, annual surveys of college graduates' preferred employers—a widely cited and closely watched measure in Japan—continue to place major banks and insurance companies among the most desired employment destinations.

20. Hirschmeier and Yui (1975, p. 350) report that in only 22 percent of the firms do important matters like changes in company structure or new product development come before the full board in Japan.

21. Mitō (1983) calculates that outside directors constitute 33 percent for the two hundred largest corporations listed on the Tokyo Stock Exchange in 1976, up slightly from 31 percent in 1966. *The Oriental Economist* (December 1975) gives a figure of 31 percent for all 1,667 listed firms. The U.S. figures cited here are from Mintzberg (1983, p. 93).

22. Another possible interpretation of the sparsity of intragroup director interlocks is the existence of presidents' councils. These may serve as a substitute for boards of directors among large firms in a way that reinforces not just bilateral linkages but the interests of the group as a whole. See Chapter 7.

23. The predominance of full-time transfers rather than part-time appointments was also confirmed. Of the 160 total outside directorships, two-thirds (66.3 percent) were full-time transfers, while only one-third (33.7 percent) maintained full-time positions in their old firm.

24. In reality, the distinction between these two often blurs—major construction projects, for example, typically involve elements of both direct sourcing of project supplies from one partner to another and joint investment.

25. This has historically constituted nearly half of the sōgō shōsha's business, though this share has been decreasing in recent years. The proportion of third-country trade (off-shore transactions not directly involving Japan), on the other hand, has been increasing.

26. Goto (1982, p. 57) cites a figure for overall trade moving between group companies and group sōgō shōsha of 30 percent. Somewhat lower figures are given in a study in 1977 by the Long-Term Credit Bank of Japan (cited in Okumura, 1983, p. 138). This study finds that 28 percent of all sales and 27 percent of all purchases in the Mitsubishi group go to the group's trading firm,

while the figures for Mitsui are 18 percent for sales to and 9 percent for purchases from the group trading firm in the Mitsui group. According to the same study, the sōgō shōsha appear less dependent on their groups than vice versa, as sōgō shōsha purchases from group companies constitute a little less than 20 percent of their total purchases, while sales to group companies account for only about 5–6 percent of their total sales.

27. This theme was reflected in each pavilion's title. Sumitomo's was "Man's Love of Nature—Our Hope for the Future"; Mitsui's was "Man and Science, Man and Nature—A Wonderful Relationship"; and Fuyō's Robot Theater was entitled "Tomorrow's Science for the Enrichment of Mankind." The most astonishing title, however, would have to have been that of the Mitsubishi group, which was simply "Wonderful World, Beautiful People."

28. A group-wide marriage system would appear to have the advantage of pooling a larger population of eligible personnel, thereby improving the chances of finding compatible partners.

5. PATTERNS OF ALLIANCE FORMATION

1. The literature on the goals of the firm is enormous. In addition to an obvious interest in profits, other purposes ascribed to corporate managers are discussed in March and Simon (1958), Marris (1964), Williamson (1964), Thompson (1967), and Pfeffer and Salancik (1978).

2. Many international joint ventures are rather unwieldy in management but serve a broader set of strategic interests held by the partner firms. The Toyota-General Motors joint venture (NUMMI), for example, ensured Toyota a manufacturing presence in the United States as a hedge against trade restrictions while General Motors was introduced to modern Japanese manufacturing and management techniques.

3. A pattern very much like Marsden's restricted-access networks was demonstrated in Chapter 4 in the structures of interfirm exchange networks constituting the keiretsu—patterns that we saw involved a partial internalization into the group of debt, equity, directorship, and trade linkages.

4. The literature on the institutionalization of broader patterns of economic and social organization has expanded rapidly since the late 1970s. See, for example, Zucker (1977), Hannan and Freeman (1977, 1989), DiMaggio and Powell (1983), and Meyer and Scott (1983).

5. Bonds accounted for an additional 22 percent of funds, with much of the remainder coming from internally generated funds.

6. These relationships were established using information provided in *Keiretsu no kenkyū* (1967, pp. 53–68, 138–91), and the *Japan Company Directory* (1968).

7. The number-two ranked institutions for these same companies provided an average of 14 percent of capital.

8. Kubota had borrowed a total of ¥3.20 billion from both Sumitomo Bank and Fuji Bank in 1982, while Kobe Steel had borrowed a total of ¥40.38 billion from the Dai-Ichi Kangyo Bank and Sanwa Bank. That loan amounts should be precisely equal in both of these cases is an indication of the symbolic importance of these figures for Japanese executives.

9. Significantly, this source does not use the Japanese word for independent (*dokuritsu*) to describe firms without apparent affiliation, but a term meaning "affiliation unclear" (*fumei*). The implication seems to be that affiliations probably exist, but cannot be determined with certainty.

10. For example, *Keiretsu no kenkyū* classifies Matsushita Electric as an affiliate of Sumitomo, with which it has long-standing historical ties, while *Industrial Groupings in Japan* classifies it as an independent firm at the head of its own vertical grouping. Intermarket and vertical alliances, however, are not mutually exclusive categories, and many firms maintain positions as members or quasi-affiliates of an intermarket keiretsu while heading their own vertical grouping of subcontractors and distributors.

11. This source uses as the basis for its categorization of group affiliations both "hard" criteria, such as the extent of group equity holdings and borrowings, and "soft" factors, primarily historical associations between firms.

12. Another difference in this example is the dispersion of ownership. The ten leading holders of Nippon Steel control only 19.5 percent of shares, while the ten leading holders of Sumitomo Metal Industries control 30.3 percent. However, the dispersion of ownership does not appear to be a widespread difference between independent and group firms, and examples of closely and widely held firms can be found in both categories. What is significant, it is argued here, is shareholder identity.

13. That these small differences nevertheless demonstrate statistical significance in some cases is probably the result of the very large number of observations available in the pooled cross-sectional approach employed.

14. Market-orientation classifications were as follows. Producer-oriented industries included industrial transport equipment, iron and steel products, oil and coal products, industrial electronics, chemicals, nonferrous metals, industrial machinery, textiles, printing, glass/ceramics/cement, ore mining, metal products, paper and wood products, and miscellaneous industrial manufacturing. Consumer-oriented firms included beverages, food and agricultural products, pharmaceuticals and cosmetics, tires, automobiles, photographic film and equipment, consumer electronics, and household products.

15. Several managers in firms with a dominant position mentioned that while they might welcome the stability that comes from group membership, their own firms would find it too constraining to become a group affiliate. By remaining independent, they believed, they improved the chances that they would be able to capture a significant share of the market.

16. For example, Nippon Steel, the world's largest steel company, sold in 1981 more than double the amount of steel of its next leading competitor, Nippon Kokan. Matsushita Electric has long been the dominant electric appliance manufacturer in Japan, more than triple the size of the next leading firm, Sanyo. While Sony was the first to introduce a VCR system, the Betamax, it was Matsushita, using its marketing clout and its strong chain of distributors and retailers, that set what has become the industry standard, its own VHS system. Similar positions of industry dominance are found for Komatsu (four times the sales of Hitachi Construction Equipment), Takeda Chemicals (twice the sales of Kyowa Hakko in pharmaceuticals), Bridgestone Tire (two-and-one-half times the sales of Yokohama Tire), Fuji Photo Film (twice the film sales of Konishiroku), and so on.

17. The 10 percent criterion is widely considered in research on corporate governance to be sufficient to constitute "effective" control over a firm.

18. These variables are the rate of GNP growth (1976–85), average compensation to employees, and total assets of the company.

19. Nakatani's study uses the classification of *Keiretsu no kenkyū,* the main determinant of which is the stability of banking ties over time. Because banking relationships tend to be stable over time for most large Japanese firms, only 69 firms in Nakatani's total sample of 317 firms are classified as "non-keiretsu," or 22 percent of the total. In contrast, over half of our sample (111 of 200 firms) are classified as non-shachō-kai firms.

20. Export ratios, also discussed in Table 5.8, were excluded from this model since these did not differ significantly between the two sets of firms.

21. One of the distinguishing characteristics of the six main keiretsu as compared to several smaller groups (e.g., those centered on the Tokai, Daiwa, and Saitama banks) is the extent of inclusion. The large keiretsu are represented in a far wider variety of industrial sectors.

6. NEW VENTURE DEVELOPMENT AND TECHNOLOGICAL INNOVATION IN JAPAN

1. A somewhat different argument is that the lack of consistent results is a product of the difficulty in measuring appropriate inputs (e.g., degree of market competition) and outputs (e.g., rates of inventive activity), which has resulted in the employment of a variety of imperfect substitutes (concentration ratios, levels of R & D spending). Better measures, this argument goes, would yield more consistent results.

2. A few exceptions to this general pattern existed—e.g., Oji Paper, which controlled over 75 percent of Japan's Western-style paper industry before the war—but these were infrequent.

3. In practice, of course, it is often difficult to separate these twin considerations. For example, ensuring continuing transactions through long-term equity positions also ensures continuing processes of interfirm learning.

4. Bakalar (1988) finds that 75 percent of venture capital funds in the United States are managed by independent partnerships measured primarily by return-on-investment criteria.

7. THE JAPANESE FIRM IN CONTEXT

1. In addition to Aoki, notable exceptions are Yoshino (1968) and Clark (1979).

2. Indeed, agency theorists argue that the separation of ownership and control is actually *efficient,* for it allows for an economic division of labor. Owners bear the risks of investment and managers specialize in running the companies. The original concerns of Berle and Means have, in this new formulation, been turned into virtues.

3. The problem at the CEO level is typically resolved by making the older of the two presidents *kaichō* (chairman), and the younger *shachō* (president).

4. According to Heftel (1983), over two-thirds of the companies ended their meetings in less than twenty minutes, and over 95 percent in less than half an hour.

5. These new laws have five main features:

(1) Attendees at the sōkai must now hold a minimum number of shares. This is usually 1000 shares on a ¥50 face-value stock. These new requirements eliminate almost one-quarter of Japan's shareholders—including, especially, marginal sōkai-ya—from meetings (Heftel, 1983, p. 163).

(2) Leading shareholders—defined as those who hold more than 1 percent of the company's shares or a minimum of 300,000 shares—must be informed not later than six weeks prior to the meeting about its agenda.

(3) The rights of shareholders to question management are now strengthened. The former practice of management's refusing to answer difficult questions is now forbidden.

(4) A new written voting system is now required. Even those who do not attend meetings receive the right to vote by written ballot and can now vote directly on directors.

(5) Shareholders' reports must now include detailed explanations of the company's expenses, future budgeting, and other important matters.

6. Various other claims and counterclaims were made during this period, perhaps the most important of which was that Pickens did not really own the shares he purported owning and was simply serving as a front for Watanabe Kitarō, president of Azabu Jidosha and a well-known greenmailer.

7. A somewhat softer version of the same concern, which emphasized the strategic disadvantage at which Mitsubishi Oil might be placed, is related in another contemporaneous account (*Zaikai*, February 7, 1984).

8. ALLIANCE CAPITALISM AND THE JAPANESE ECONOMY

1. These deviations imply market imperfections in the technical sense that equilibrium conditions are indeterminate. One cannot assume that a given market will "clear" when factors exogenous to the equilibrium model, such as preferential trading, are introduced. Since much of the apparatus of orthodox economic analysis relies on a general equilibrium model, the theoretical deviations implied by these deviations are not trivial.

2. Ronald Dore (1986) captures the paradox of simultaneous adaptability and stability in the title of his book, *Flexible Rigidities*. He points out how labor, product, and capital markets are all "sticky" in Japan and asks, "Why on earth, then, should Japan, an economy which almost flaunts its rigidities as a matter of principle, be the most successful among the OECD countries at dynamically adjusting to the three challenges—absorbing the oil-price rises, controlling inflation at a low figure, and shifting the weight of its industrial structure decisively away from declining to competitive industries?" (p. 6). One can add to this a fourth challenge, the more recent doubling in the value of the yen against the dollar and other currencies.

3. Basis trading does not consider any of the traditional reasons for buying or selling stocks—overall economic health, companies' long-term performance

outlook, etc. It depends instead on two financial measures: a stock market index, usually the Standard & Poor's 500-stock index, and the price of a futures or options contract that gives the investor the right to buy that index at some future date. The difference between these two, the "basis," determines trading.

4. Junk bonds are low-grade, high-yield bonds that take secondary position to other bond issues in claims against the company. These serve as a relatively cheap, albeit risky, way of financing takeovers.

5. Typically, banks cover about half of the takeover cost, junk bonds about 30–40 percent, and the remainder comes from the raiders themselves.

6. Other tactics include working with the company's charter by staggering the elections on the board of directors or requiring super-majorities on major corporate policies, and leveraging firms through debt to become as unattractive to potential suitors as possible.

7. *Business Week* (November 24, 1986). There had been, as of November 1986, 2,500 mergers and buyouts, worth $118 billion, and in 1985, 2,463 deals, worth $96 billion. These numbers have declined in recent years.

8. For a critical view of the hostile takeover movement, see Drucker (1986).

9. A detailed case study of how this process worked in the rejuvenation of Mazda is provided in Pascale and Rohlen (1983). See also Chapter 5.

10. According to figures reported in *The Economist* (September 3, 1988), for the period 1980–87, Japan had a higher rate of gross fixed capital formation than any country except South Korea. Japanese investment averaged nearly 29 percent of the GNP, as compared with about 22 percent in France and West Germany and under 20 percent in the United States and Britain.

11. In addition, leveraging through banks keeps a company's equity base small so profits can be concentrated. As a result, when measured by return on equity rather than return on sales or assets, Japanese firms appear to perform quite well relative to their American counterparts (Abegglen and Stalk, 1985, p. 149), at least until the recent market crash.

12. These indirect (strategic) benefits are common in the area of technological innovation. Kline and Rosenberg (1986) have calculated that the social returns to innovation far exceed the portion that can be captured by the inventor.

13. To take one case, the top shareholder of NEC in 1982 was its affiliated life insurance company, Sumitomo Mutual Life. Whereas Sumitomo Mutual Life held 8.1 percent of NEC's shares, valued at $15.8 million, its outstanding loans to NEC were over eight times higher, $126.0 million. NEC's second-leading shareholder was also a Sumitomo affiliate, Sumitomo Bank, which held 5.8 percent of NEC's shares. This accounted for $11.3 million in external capital but was only a small fraction of the bank's total commitment to NEC, for Sumitomo Bank extended $184.0 million in loans during the same year (calculated from data provided in *Industrial Groupings in Japan*, 1982).

14. The advances into Japanese markets now being made by companies from the newly industrializing economies of East Asia and by some European firms in Japanese markets, though impressive, must be placed in perspective. Products from the first have increased substantially the share of Japanese imports comprising manufactured goods, but this has come largely in areas where added value is lowest (e.g., commodity steel and low-end textiles). European manufac-

turers, in contrast, have been most successful in sophisticated and name-brand luxury goods where domestic Japanese competition is minimal. The competitive advantage of U.S. firms, in contrast, is often in high-value-added services and technology-based products in which several domestic competitors exist.

15. It was commonly asserted in macroeconomic arguments in the early 1980s that the yen had to rise to somewhere just under 200 to the dollar in order to bring bilateral merchandise trade between the United States and Japan into balance. Beginning in 1985 the yen rose much further than that. Not only did the current account not balance, but the deficits look at present as though they will continue well into the future.

16. The commissioned salesperson, for example, might be viewed as either an employee or a market representative, depending on one's purposes. The firm is no longer a problem because, in a sense, it no longer exists: "According to one's view a 'firm' may be as small as a contractual relationship between input owners or, if the chain of contracts is allowed to spread, as big as the whole economy" (Cheung, 1983, p. 17).

References

Abegglen, James C., and George Stalk, Jr. (1985) Kaisha: The Japanese Corporation. New York: Basic Books.

Akerlof, George A. (1970) "The market for 'lemons': Qualitative uncertainty and the market mechanism." Quarterly Journal of Economics. 84:488–500.

Akerlof, George A. (1983) "Labor contracts as partial gift exchange." Quarterly Journal of Economics. 97:543–69.

Aldrich, Howard (1979) Organizations and Environments. Englewood Cliffs, N.J.: Prentice-Hall.

Allen, G. C. (1940) "Japanese industry: Its organization and development to 1937." In E. B. Schumpeter (ed.) The Industrialization of Japan and Manchukuo, 1930–1940: Population, Raw Materials, and Industry. New York: Macmillan.

Allen, G. C. (1981) The Japanese Economy. New York: St. Martin's Press.

Amihud, Yakov, Peter Dodd, and Mark Weinstein (1986) "Conglomerate mergers, managerial motives, and stockholder wealth." Journal of Banking and Finance. 10:401–10.

Ando, Albert, and Alan J. Auerbach (1988) "The cost of capital in the United States and Japan: A comparison." Journal of the Japanese and International Economies. 2:134–58.

Ando, Albert, and Alan J. Auerbach (1990) "The cost of capital in Japan: Recent evidence and further results." Journal of the Japanese and International Economies. 4:323–50.

Aoki, Masahiko (1983) "Managerialism revisited in the light of bargaining-game theory." International Journal of Industrial Organization. 1:1–21.

Aoki, Masahiko (1984a) "Aspects of the Japanese firm." In Masahiko Aoki (ed.) The Economic Analysis of the Japanese Firm. Amsterdam: North-Holland.

Aoki, Masahiko (1984b) "Shareholders' non-unanimity on investment financing." In Masahiko Aoki (ed.) The Economic Analysis of the Japanese Firm. Amsterdam: North-Holland.

Aoki, Masahiko (1984c) The Co-operative Game Theory of the Firm. Oxford: Oxford University Press.

Aoki, Masahiko (1987) "The Japanese firm in transition." In Kozo Yamamura and Yasukichi Yasuba (eds.) The Political Economy of Japan, vol. 1. Stanford, Calif.: Stanford University Press.

Aoki, Masahiko (1988) Information, Incentives, and Bargaining in the Japanese Economy. Cambridge: Cambridge University Press.

Aoki, Masahiko (1990) "Toward an economic model of the Japanese firm." Journal of Economic Literature. 28:1–27.

Arrow, Kenneth (1974) The Limits of Organization. New York: W. W. Norton.

Asajima, Shoichi (1984) "Financing of the Japanese zaibatsu: Sumitomo as case study." In Akio Okochi and Shigeaki Yasuoka (eds.) Family Business in the Era of Industrial Growth. Tokyo: University of Tokyo Press.

Asano Junji (1978) Sumitomo gurūpu [Sumitomo Group]. Tokyo: Kyōikusha.

Asanuma, Banri (1985) "The organization of parts purchases." Japanese Economic Studies. Summer:32–53.

Asanuma, Banri (1989) "Manufacturer-supplier relationships in Japan and the concept of relation-specific skill." Journal of the Japanese and International Economies. 3:1–30.

Atsuta Masanori (1979) Sumitomo no Senryaku [Sumitomo's Strategy]. Tokyo: Tokubun Shoten.

Auerbach, Alan J. (1983) "Taxation, corporate financial policy and the cost of capital." Journal of Economic Literature. 21:905–40.

Averitt, Robert T. (1968) The Dual Economy. New York: Norton.

Bacon, Jeremy, and James K. Brown (1978) The Board of Directors: Perspectives and Practices in Nine Countries. New York: Conference Board.

Bakalar, Steven D. (1988) "Japanese venture capital and entrepreneurship." Stanford, Calif.: Stanford University. Mimeo.

Baker, Wayne E. (1984) "Social structure of a securities market." American Journal of Sociology. 89:775–811.

Baldwin, C. Y. (1986) "The capital factor: Competing for capital in a global environment." In Michael E. Porter (ed.) Competition in Global Industries. Boston: Harvard Business School Press.

Ballon, Robert J., Iwao Tomita, and Hajime Usami (1976) Financial Reporting in Japan. Tokyo: Kodansha International.

Barnes, J. A. (1972) Social Networks. Reading, Mass.: Addison Wesley.

Baron, James N., and William T. Bielby (1984) "The organization of work in a segmented economy." American Sociological Review. 49:454–73.

Baumol, W. J. (1959) Business Behavior, Value, and Growth. New York: Macmillan.

Belshaw, Cyril S. (1965) Traditional Exchange and Modern Markets. Englewood Cliffs, N.J.: Prentice-Hall.

Ben-Porath, Yoram (1980) "The F-connection: Families, friends, and firms and the organization of exchange." Population and Development Review. 6:1–30.

Berglof, Erik, and Enrico Perotti (1989) "The Japanese keiretsu as a collective enforcement mechanism." Cambridge, Mass.: Harvard Law School. Mimeo.

Bergston, C. Fred, and William R. Cline (1985) The United States–Japan Economic Problem. Washington, D.C.: Institute for International Economics.

Berle, A. A., and G. C. Means (1932) The Modern Corporation and Private Property. New York: Commerce Clearing House.

Bieda, K. (1970) The Structure and Operation of the Japanese Economy. Sydney: John Wiley.

Braudel, Fernand (trans. Sian Reynolds) (1979) The Wheels of Commerce. New York: Harper and Row.

Braudel, Fernand (trans. Sian Reynolds) (1984) The Perspective of the World. New York: Harper and Row.

Burt, Ronald S. (1983) Corporate Profits and Cooptation. New York: Academic Press.

Burt, Ronald S., and Debbie S. Carlson (1989) "Another look at the network boundaries of American markets." American Journal of Sociology. 95:723–53.

Cable, John, and Manfred J. Dirrheimer (1983) "Hierarchies and markets: An empirical test of the multidivisional hypothesis in West Germany." International Journal of Industrial Organization. 1:43–62.

Cable, John, and Yasuki Hirohiko (1985) "Internal organisation, business groups, and corporate performance: An empirical test of the multidivisional hypothesis in Japan." International Journal of Industrial Organization. 3: 401–20.

Carlton, Dennis W. (1986) "The rigidity of prices." American Economic Review. 76(4):637–58.

Carrington, John C., and George T. Edwards (1981) Reversing Economic Decline. London: Macmillan.

Carroll, Glenn (1984) "Organizational ecology." In R. Turner and J. Short (eds.) Annual Review of Sociology, vol. 10. Palo Alto, Calif.: Annual Review Press.

Caves, Richard, and Masu Uekusa (1976) Industrial Organization in Japan. Washington, D.C.: Brookings Institution.

Chandler, Alfred D. (1962) Strategy and Structure. Cambridge, Mass.: MIT Press.

Chandler, Alfred D. (1977) The Visible Hand: The Managerial Revolution in American Business. Cambridge, Mass.: Harvard University Press.

Chandler, Alfred D. (1984) "The emergence of managerial capitalism." Business History Review. 58:473–503.

Cheung, Stephan (1983) "The contractual nature of the firm." Journal of Law and Economics. 26:1–21.

Clark, Rodney (1979) The Japanese Company. New Haven: Yale University Press.

Coase, Ronald H. (1937) "The nature of the firm." Economica. 4:386–405.

Coffee, John C., Jr., Louis Lowenstein, and Susan Rose-Ackerman (1988) Knights, Raiders, and Targets: The Impact of the Hostile Takeover. New York: Oxford University Press.

Collins, Randall (1986) Weberian Sociological Theory. New York: Cambridge University Press.

Cyert, Richard, and James G. March (1963) A Behavioral Theory of the Firm. Englewood Cliffs, N.J.: Prentice-Hall.

Demsetz, Harold, and Kenneth Lehn (1985) "The structure of corporate ownership: Causes and consequences." Journal of Political Economy. 93:1155–77.

DiMaggio, Paul (1988) "Interest and agency in institutional theory." In Lynne G. Zucker (ed.) Institutional Patterns and Organizations: Culture and Environment. Cambridge, Mass.: Ballinger.

DiMaggio, Paul, and Walter W. Powell (1983) "The iron cage revisited: Institutional isomorphism and collective rationality in organizational fields." American Sociological Review. 48:147–60.

Dodd, E. Merrick (1932) "For whom are corporate managers trustees?" Harvard Law Review. 45:1145–63.

Dore, Ronald (1983) "Goodwill and the spirit of market capitalism." British Journal of Sociology. 34:459–82.

Dore, Ronald (1986) Flexible Rigidities. Stanford, Calif.: Stanford University Press.

Dore, Ronald (1987) Taking Japan Seriously. Stanford, Calif.: Stanford University Press.

Dosi, Giovanni (1990) "Finance, innovation, and industrial change." Journal of Economic Behavior and Organization. 13:299–319.

Dosi, Giovanni, and L. Orsenigo (1988) "Coordination and transformation: An overview of structures, behaviours, and change in evolutionary environments." In G. Dosi, C. Freeman, R. Nelson, G. Silverberg and L. Soete (eds.) Technical Change and Economic Theory. New York: Columbia University Press.

Drucker, Peter F. (1986) "Corporate takeovers—what is to be done?" The Public Interest. 82:3–24.

Dumont, Louis (1957) "Hierarchy and marriage alliance in South Indian kinship." Occasional Papers of the Royal Anthropological Institute, no. 12. London.

Durkheim, Emile (trans. George Simpson) (1933) Division of Labor in Society. New York: Free Press.

Eccles, Robert G. (1981) "The quasifirm in the construction industry." Journal of Economic Behavior and Organization. 2:335–57.

Eccles, Robert G., and Dwight Crane (1987) "Managing through networks in investment banking." California Management Review. 30:176–95.

Eccles, Robert G., and Dwight B. Crane (1988) Doing Deals: Investment Banks at Work. Boston: Harvard Business School Press.

Eliasson, Gunnar (1990) "The firm as a competent team." Journal of Economic Behavior and Organization. 13:275–98.

Encaoua, David, and Alexis Jacquemin (1982) "Organizational efficiency and monopoly power: The case of French industrial groups." European Economic Review. 19:25–51.

Fama, Eugene (1985) "What's different about banks?" Journal of Monetary Economics. 15:29–39.

Fama, Eugene F., and Michael Jensen (1983) "Separation of ownership and control." Journal of Law and Economics. 26:302–26.

Federal Trade Commission (1976) Statistical Report on Mergers and Acquisitions. Washington, D.C.: Bureau of Economics.

Feld, Scott L. (1981) "The focused organization of social ties." American Journal of Sociology. 86:1014–35.

Ferguson, Charles H. (1988) "From the people who brought you voodoo economics." Harvard Business Review. May–June:55–62.

Ferguson, Charles H. (1990) "Computers and the coming of the U.S. keiretsu." Harvard Business Review. July–August:55–70.

Flaherty, M. Therese, and Hiroyuki Itami (1984) "Finance." In Daniel I. Okimoto, Takuo Sugano, and Franklin B. Weinstein (eds.) Competitive Edge: The Semiconductor Industry in the U.S. and Japan." Stanford: Stanford University Press.

Fligstein, Neil (1985) "The spread of the multidivisional form among large firms, 1919–1979." American Sociological Review. 50:377–91.

Florida, Richard, and Martin Kenney (1991) "Transplanted organizations: The transfer of Japanese industrial organization to the U.S." American Sociological Review. 56:381–98.

Fox, Robin (1967) Kinship and Marriage: An Anthropological Perspective. Cambridge: Cambridge University Press.

Frame, J. Davidson, and Francis Narin (1990) "The United States, Japan, and the changing technological balance." Research Policy. 19:447–55.

Friedman, David (1988) The Misunderstood Miracle: Industrial Development and Political Change in Japan. Ithaca, N.Y.: Cornell University Press.

Friedman, Milton (1953) "The methodology of positive economics." In Essays in Positive Economics. Chicago: University of Chicago Press.

Friend, Irwin (1972) "The economic consequences of the stock market." American Economic Review. 62(2):212–19.

Fruin, Mark (1992) The Japanese Enterprise System: Competitive Strategies and Cooperative Structures. Oxford: Oxford University Press.

Futatsugi Yusaku (1976) Gendai nihon no kigyō shūdan—Dai-kigyō bunseki o Mezashite [Enterprise Groups in Contemporary Japan: Focusing on an Analysis of Large Firms]. Tokyo: Tōyō Shinpōsha.

Futatsugi Yusaku (1982) Nihon no kabushiki shoyū kōzō [Japan's Stockholding Structure]. Tokyo: Dōbunkan Shuppan.

Futatsugi, Yusaku (1986) Japanese Enterprise Groups. Kobe: School of Business, Kobe University.

Geertz, Clifford (1973) The Interpretation of Cultures. New York: Basic Books.

Geertz, Clifford (1978) "The bazaar economy: Information and search in peasant marketing." American Economic Review. 68(2):28–32.

Gerlach, Michael L. (1987) "Business alliances and the strategy of the Japanese firm." California Management Review. 30:126–42.

Gerlach, Michael L. (1989) "Keiretsu organization in the Japanese economy: Analysis and trade implications." In Chalmers Johnson, Laura D'Andrea Tyson, and John Zysman (eds.) Politics and Productivity: The Real Story of Why Japan Works. Cambridge, Mass.: Ballinger.

Gerlach, Michael L. (1990) "Trust is not enough: Cooperation and conflict in Kikkoman's American development." Journal of Japanese Studies. 16(2): 389–425.

Gerlach, Michael L. (1992a) "Twilight of the keiretsu? A critical assessment." Journal of Japanese Studies. 18(1):79–118.

Gerlach, Michael L. (1992b) "Alliance strategies and technological innovation in Japan." Berkeley: University of California. Mimeo.

Gerlach, Michael, Robert Harris, and David Teece (1987) "The Effect of Public Policies, Organizational Structures, and Corporate Strategies on Technological Innovation, Adoption, and Diffusion in Japan and the U.S." Berkeley: Proposal to the Pacific Rim Research Program, University of California. Mimeo.

Gerlach, Michael, and James Lincoln (1989) "The Organization of Business Networks in the U.S. and Japan." Berkeley: Research proposal funded by the National Science Foundation and the University of California Pacific Rim Research Program.

Gerlach, Michael, James Lincoln, and David Teece (1989) "The Organization of Business Networks in the U.S. and Japan." Berkeley: Proposal to the Pacific Rim Research Program, University of California. Mimeo.

Gerschenkron, Alexander (1962) Economic Backwardness in Historical Perspective. Cambridge, Mass.: Harvard University Press.

Gertler, Mark (1988) "Financial structure and aggregate economic activity." Journal of Money, Credit, and Banking. 20(3):559–96.

Giddens, Anthony (1984) The Constitution of Society. Berkeley and Los Angeles: University of California Press.

Gilder, George (1988) "The revitalization of everything: The law of the microcosm." Harvard Business Review. March–April:49–61.

Goldberg, Victor (1980) "Relational exchange: Economics and complex contracts." American Behavioral Scientist. 23:337–52.

Goldsmith, Raymond A. (1983) The Financial Development of Japan, 1868–1977. New Haven: Yale University Press.

Gordon, Andrew (1985) The Evolution of Labor Relations in Japan: Heavy Industry, 1853–1955. Cambridge, Mass.: Council on East Asian Studies, Harvard University.

Gordon, Robert J. (1982) "Why U.S. wage and employment behavior differs from that in Britain and Japan." Economic Journal. 92:13–44.

Gordon, Robert J. (1990) "What is new-Keynesian economics?" Journal of Economic Literature. 28:1115–71.

Goto, Akira (1981) "Statistical evidence on the diversification of Japanese large firms." Journal of Industrial Economics. 29(3):271–78.

Goto, Akira (1982) "Business groups in a market economy." European Economic Review. 19:53–70.

Goto, Akira, and Kazuyuki Suzuki (1989) "R & D capital, rate of return on R & D investment, and spillover of R & D in Japanese manufacturing industries." Review of Economics and Statistics. 71(4):555–64.

Granovetter, Mark (1973) "The strength of weak ties." American Journal of Sociology. 78:1360–81.

Granovetter, Mark (1985) "Economic action and social structure: A theory of embeddedness." American Journal of Sociology. 91:481–510.

Graves, Samuel B. (1988) "Institutional ownership and corporate R & D in the computer industry." Academy of Management Journal. 31(2):417–28.

Grossman, Sanford, and Oliver Hart (1986) "The costs and benefits of ownership: A theory of vertical and lateral integration." Journal of Political Economy. 94:691–719.

Hadley, Eleanor (1970) Antitrust in Japan. Princeton: Princeton University Press.

Hadley, Eleanor (1984) "Counterpoint on business groupings and government-industry relations in automobiles." In Masahiko Aoki (ed.) The Economic Analysis of the Japanese Firm. Amsterdam: North-Holland.

Haitani, Kanji (1976) The Japanese Economic System. Lexington, Mass.: Lexington Books.

Hai-teku jidai kigyō henshin [Changes in Enterprises in the High Technology Era], vols. 1 and 2 (1984). Tokyo: Nihon Keizai Shinbunsha.

Haley, John O. (1978) "The myth of the reluctant litigant." Journal of Japanese Studies. 4:359–90.

Haley, John O. (1982) "Sheathing the sword of justice in Japan: An essay on law without sanctions." Journal of Japanese Studies. 8(2):265–81.

Haley, John O. (1990) "Weak law, strong competition, and trade barriers: Competitiveness as a disincentive to foreign entry into Japanese markets." In Kozo Yamamura (ed.) Japan's Economic Structure: Should It Change? Seattle: Society for Japanese Studies.

Hamada, Koichi, and Akiyoshi Horiuchi (1987) "The political economy of the financial market." In Kozo Yamamura and Yasukichi Yasuba (eds.) The Political Economy of Japan. Stanford, Calif.: Stanford University Press.

Hamilton, Gary, and Nicole Woolsey Biggart (1988) "Market, culture, and authority: A comparative analysis of management and organization in the far east." American Journal of Sociology. 94 (supplement):s52–s94.

Hamilton, Gary G., Marco Orru, and Nicole Woolsey Biggart (1987) "Enterprise groups in east Asia." Shōken Keizai. 161:78–106.

Hannan, Michael T., and John H. Freeman (1977) "The population ecology of organizations." American Journal of Sociology. 82:929–64.

Hannan, Michael T., and John H. Freeman (1989) Organizational Ecology. Cambridge, Mass.: Harvard University Press.

Hansmann, Henry (1988) "Ownership of the firm." Journal of Law, Economics, and Organization. 4(2):267–304.

Hattori, Ichiro (1985) "Product diversification." In Lester C. Thurow (ed.) The Management Challenge: Japanese Views. Cambridge, Mass.: MIT Press.

Hattori, Tamio (1984) "The relationship between zaibatsu and family structure: The Korean case." In Akio Okochi and Shigeaki Yasuoka (eds.) Family Business in the Era of Industrial Growth. Tokyo: University of Tokyo Press.

Heftel, Christopher Lee (1983) "Corporate governance in Japan: The position of shareholders in publicly held corporations." University of Hawaii Law Review. 5:135–206.

Helfat, Constance E., and David J. Teece (1987) "Vertical integration and risk reduction." Journal of Law, Economics, and Organization. 3(1):47–67.

Herman, Edward S. (1981) Corporate Control, Corporate Power. Cambridge: Cambridge University Press.

Higashi, Chikara, and G. Peter Lauter (1987) The Internationalization of the Japanese Economy. Boston: Kluwer Academic Publishers.

Hirsch, Paul M. (1986) "From ambushes to golden parachutes: corporate takeovers as an instance of cultural framing and institutional integration." American Journal of Sociology. 91:800–837.

Hirschman, A. O. (1970) Exit, Voice, and Loyalty. Cambridge, Mass.: Harvard University Press.

Hirschmeier, Johannes, and Tsunehiko Yui (1975) The Development of Japanese Business, 1600–1973. Cambridge, Mass.: Harvard University Press.

Hodder, James (1988) "Capital structure and the cost of capital in the U.S. and Japan." Stanford, Calif.: Stanford University. Mimeo.

Hodder, James (1991) "Is the cost of capital lower in Japan?" Journal of the Japanese and International Economies. 5:86–100.

Hodgson, Geoffrey M. (1988) Economics and Institutions: A Manifesto for a Modern Institutional Economics. Cambridge: Polity Press.

Hodson, Randy, and Robert L. Kaufman (1982) "Economic dualism: A critical review." American Sociological Review. 47:727–39.

Horiuchi, Akiyoshi, Frank Packer, and Shin'ichi Fukuda (1988) "What role has the 'main bank' played in Japan?" Journal of the Japanese and International Economies. 2:159–80.

Hoshi, Takeo, Anil Kashyap, and David Scharfstein (1990a) "Bank monitoring and investment: Evidence from the changing structure of Japanese corporate banking relationships." In R. Glenn Hubbard (ed.) Asymmetric Information, Corporate Finance, and Investment. Chicago: University of Chicago Press.

Hoshi, Takeo, Anil Kashyap, and David Scharfstein (1990b) "Corporate structure, liquidity, and investment: Evidence from Japanese industrial groups." Quarterly Journal of Economics. 106:33–60.

Hoshi, Takeo, Anil Kashyap, and David Scharfstein (1990c) "The role of banks in reducing the costs of financial distress in Japan." San Diego: University of California. Mimeo.

Imai, Ken-ichi (1982) "Japan's industrial structure and United States-Japan industrial relations." In Kozo Yamamura (ed.) Policy and Trade Issues of the Japanese Economy. Tokyo: University of Tokyo Press.

Imai, Ken-ichi (1984) Jōhō nettowāku shakai [Information Network Society]. Tokyo: Iwanami Shinsho.

Imai, Ken-ichi (1989a) "Kigyō grūpu" [Enterprise groups]. In Imai Ken-ichi and Komiya Ryūtarō (eds.) Nihon no Kigyō [Japan's Enterprises]. Tokyo: Tōkyō Daigaku Shuppankai.

Imai, Ken-ichi (1989b) "Latecomer strategies in advanced electronics: Lessons from the Japanese experience." Tokyo: Hitotsubashi University. Mimeo.

Imai, Ken-ichi (1990) "Japanese business groups and the structural impediments initiative." In Kozo Yamamura (ed.) Japan's Economic Structure: Should It Change? Seattle: Society for Japanese Studies.

Imai, Ken-ichi (forthcoming) "Japan's corporate networks." In Henry Rosovsky and Shumpei Kumon (eds.) The Political Economy of Japan, vol. 3. Stanford, Calif.: Stanford University Press.

Imai, Ken-ichi, and Itami Hiroyuki (1984) "Interpenetration of organization and market: Japan's firm and market in comparison with the U.S." International Journal of Industrial Organization. 2:285–310.

Imai, Ken-ichi, Itami Hiroyuki, and Koike Kazuo (1982) Naibu-soshiki no keizai-gaku [The Economics of Internal Organization]. Tokyo: Tōyō Shinpōsha.

Imai, Ken-ichi, Ikujiro Nonaka, and Hirotaka Takeuchi (1985) "Managing new product development: How Japanese companies learn and unlearn." In Kim B. Clark, Robert H. Hayes, and Christopher Lorenz (eds.) The Uneasy Alliance. Cambridge, Mass.: Harvard Business School.

Inbesutomento [Investment] (1984) "Wa ga kuni kabushiki shoyū kōzō no tokuchō" [Special characteristics of Japanese ownership structure]. December:4–26.

Industrial Bank of Japan (1983) "Gijutsu no jidai ni ikiru [Living in the age of technology]." Tokyo: Medium- and Small-Firm Center, Industrial Bank of Japan.

Industrial Groupings in Japan (various years). Tokyo: Dodwell Marketing Consultants.

Inohara, Hideo (1972) "Shukkō: Loan Personnel in Japanese Industry." Sophia University Socio-Economic Institute Bulletin, no. 42.

Ishida, Hideto (1983) "Anticompetitive practices in the distribution of goods and services in Japan." Journal of Japanese Studies. 9:319–34.

Itc, Shoji (1984) "Ownership and management of Indian zaibatsu." In Akio Okochi and Shigeaki Yasuoka (eds.) Family Business in the Era of Industrial Growth. Tokyo: University of Tokyo Press.

Itozono Tatsuo (1978) Nihon no shagai-kō seidō (Japan's Outside Subcontracting System). Kyoto: Minerva Shobō.

James, Christopher (1987) "Some evidence on the uniqueness of bank loans." Journal of Financial Economics. 19:217–35.

Japan Company Directory (various years). Tokyo: Oriental Economist.

Japan Company Handbook (various years). Tokyo: Oriental Economist.

Jenkinson, T. J. (1990) "Initial public offerings in the United Kingdom, the United States, and Japan." Journal of the Japanese and International Economies. 4:428–49.

Jensen, Michael C. (1986) "Agency costs of free cash flow, corporate finance, and takeovers." American Economic Review. 76(2):323–29.

Jensen, Michael C. (1989) "Eclipse of the public corporation." Harvard Business Review. September–October:61–74.

Jensen, Michael C., and William H. Meckling (1976) "Theory of the firm: Managerial behavior, agency costs, and ownership structure." Journal of Financial Economics. 3:305–60.

Johanson, Jan, and Lars-Gunnar Mattsson (1987) "Interorganizational relations in industrial systems: A network approach compared with the transaction-cost approach." International Studies of Management and Organization. 17:34–48.

Johnson, Chalmers (1982) MITI and the Japanese Miracle. Stanford, Calif.: Stanford University Press.

Johnson, Chalmers (1987) "How to think about economic competition from Japan." Journal of Japanese Studies. 13:415–27.

Johnson, Chalmers (1990) "Trade, revisionism, and the future of Japanese-American relations." In Kozo Yamamura (ed.) Japan's Economic Structure: Should It Change? Seattle: Society for Japanese Studies.

Jorde, Thomas M., and David J. Teece (1987) "Using antitrust's 'state action doctrine' to promote beneficial collaboration and cooperation among California firms: An exploration." Berkeley: University of California Business School Working Paper Series.

Jorde, Thomas M., and David J. Teece (1990) "Innovation and cooperation: Implications for competition and antitrust." Journal of Economic Perspectives. 4:75–96.

Kabushiki ashidori 20 nenkan [Twenty Years of Corporate Trends] (1969). Tokyo: Nissho Shuppansha.

Kagono, Tadao, Ikujiro Nonaka, Kiyonori Sakakibara, and Akihiro Okumura (1985) Strategic vs. Evolutionary Management: A U.S.-Japan Comparison. Amsterdam: Elsevier North-Holland.

Kaisha nenkan [Company Annual] (various years). Tokyo: Nihon Keizai Shinbun-sha.

Kameoka Kataro (1969) Mitsubishi tai Sumitomo [Mitsubishi vs. Sumitomo]. Tokyo: Bunkei Shunshu.

Kamien, M., and N. Schwartz (1982) Market Structure and Innovation. Cambridge: Cambridge University Press.

Kawamoto, Ichiro, and Ittoku Monma (1976) "Sōkai-ya in Japan." Hong Kong Law Journal. 6:179–88.

Kawasaki, Seiichi, and John McMillan (1987) "The design of contracts: Evidence from Japanese subcontracting." Journal of the Japanese and International Economies. 1:327–49.

Keiretsu no kenkyū [Research on Industrial Groups] (various years). Tokyo: Keizai Chosa Kyōkai.

Kester, W. Carl (1991) Japanese Takeovers: The Global Contest for Corporate Control. Boston: Harvard Business School Press.

Keynes, John Maynard (1936) The General Theory of Employment, Interest and Money. New York: Harcourt, Brace.

Kinoshita Masatoshi (1989) "Atarashii kin'yū no nagare" [New trends in finance]. In Yoshio Suzuki (ed.) Nihon no kin'yū to ginkō [Japanese Finance and Banks]. Tokyo: Tōyō Keizai Shinpōsha.

Kline, Stephen J., and Nathaniel Rosenberg (1986) "An overview of innovation." In Ralph Landau and Nathaniel Rosenberg (eds.) The Positive Sum Strategy: Harnessing Technology for Economic Growth. Washington, D.C.: National Academy Press.

Knight, Frank H. (1957) Risk, Uncertainty and Profit. New York: Kelley and Millman.

Kobayashi Yukio (1979) Shin kigyō shūdan monogatari [Stories about Enterprise Groups]. Tokyo: Tōyō Keizai Shinpōsha.

Kodama, Fumio (1986) "Technological diversification of Japanese industry." Science. 233(July):291–96.

Koike, Kazuo (1983) "Internal labor markets." In Taishiro Shirai (ed.) Contemporary Industrial Relations in Japan. Madison: University of Wisconsin Press.

Komatsu Akira (1983) Kigyō no ronri: Shakai kagaku toshite no keiei-gaku [Logic of Enterprise: Management as Social Science]. Tokyo: Mitsumine Shobō.

Komatsu Akira (1990) Kigyō keitai-ron [Theory of Enterprise Form]. Tokyo: Shinseisha.

Komiya, Ryutaro, and Motoshige Itoh (1988) "Japan's international trade and trade policy, 1955–1984." In Takeshi Inoguchi and Daniel Okimoto (eds.) The Political Economy of Japan, vol. 2: The Changing International Context. Stanford, Calif.: Stanford University Press.

Kōsei Torihiki Iinkai [Japanese Federal Trade Commission] (1983a) "Juyō dai-kigyō no kabushiki shoyū no jōkyō ni tsuite" [On the state of stock owner-ship of important large companies]. Tokyo: Kōsei Torihiki Iinkai.

Kōsei Torihiki Iinkai [Japanese Federal Trade Commission] (1983b) "Kigyō shūdan no jittai ni tsuite" [On the state of affairs of enterprise groups]. Tokyo: Kōsei Torihiki Iinkai.

Kotabe, Masaaki (1989) "How cooperative are member companies in the Japa-nese industrial group?" Paper presented to the Association of Japanese Busi-ness Studies, San Francisco.

Kotz, David M. (1978) Bank Control of Large Corporations in the United States. Berkeley and Los Angeles: University of California Press.

Kreinin, Mordechai E. (1988) "How closed is Japan's market?" World Economy. 7:529–41.

Krugman, Paul (1987) "Is free trade passé?" Journal of Economic Perspectives. 1:131–44.

Larner, Robert J. (1966) "Ownership and control in the 200 largest nonfinancial corporations, 1929 and 1963." American Economic Review. 56:777–87.

Lawrence, Robert Z. (1987) "Imports in Japan: Closed markets or minds?" Brookings Papers on Economic Activity. 2:517–54.

Lawrence, Robert Z. (1991) "Efficient or exclusionist? The import behavior of Japanese corporate groups." In William C. Brainard and George L. Perry (eds.) Brookings Papers on Economic Activity. Washington, D.C.: Brookings Institution.

Leblebici, Huseyin, and Gerald R. Salancik (1982) "Stability in interorganiza-tional exchanges: Rulemaking processes of the Chicago Board of Trade." Administrative Science Quarterly. 27:227–42.

Leech, Dennis (1987) "Corporate ownership and control: A new look at the evidence of Berle and Means." Oxford Economic Papers. 39:534–51.

Leff, Nathaniel H. (1978) "Industrial organization and entrepreneurship in the developing countries." Economic Development and Cultural Change. 26: 661–75.

Leifer, Eric, and Harrison White (1987) "A structural approach to markets." In Mark S. Mizruchi and Michael Schwartz (eds.) Intercorporate Relations: The Structural Analysis of Business. Cambridge: Cambridge University Press.

Leland, Hayne, and David Pyle (1977) "Informational asymmetries, financial structure, and financial intermediation." Journal of Finance. 32(2):371–87.

Levi-Strauss, Claude (1969) The Elementary Structures of Kinship. London: Eyre and Spottiswoode.

Lincoln, Edward J. (1990) Japan's Unequal Trade. Washington, D.C.: Brookings Institution.

Lincoln, James R. (1982) "Intra- (and inter-) organizational networks." In Samuel B. Bacharach (ed.) Research in the Sociology of Organizations. Green-wich, Conn.: JAI Press.

Lincoln, James R. (1989) "Japanese organization and organization theory." In Barry M. Staw and L. L. Cummings (eds.) Research in Organizational Behavior, vol. 12. Greenwich, Conn.: JAI Press.

Loasby, Brian J. (1976) Choice, Complexity, and Ignorance. Cambridge: Cambridge University Press.

Lockwood, William W. (1968) The Economic Development of Japan: Growth and Structural Change. Princeton: Princeton University Press.

Macaulay, Stewart (1963) "Non-contractual relations in business." American Sociological Review. 28:55–70.

Mace, Myles L. (1971) Directors: Myth and Reality. Boston: Harvard Business School Press.

MacKie-Mason, Jeffrey K. (1990) "Do firms care who provides their financing?" In R. Glenn Hubbard (ed.) Asymmetric Information, Corporate Finance, and Investment. Chicago: University of Chicago Press.

Macneil, Ian R. (1974) "The many futures of contracts." Southern California Law Review. 47:691–816.

Macneil, Ian R. (1978) "Contracts: Adjustments of long-term economic relations under classical, neoclassical, and relational contract law." Northwestern University Law Review. 47:854–906.

Malkiel, Burton (1973) A Random Walk down Wall Street. New York: Norton.

Manne, Henry G. (1965) "Mergers and the market for corporate control." Journal of Political Economy. 73:110–20.

March, James G., and Johan P. Olsen (1984) "The new institutionalism: Organizational factors in political life." American Political Science Review. 78:734–49.

March, James G., and Herbert A. Simon (1958) Organizations. New York: Wiley.

Marris, Robin L. (1964) The Economics of "Managerial" Capitalism. New York: Macmillan.

Marsden, Peter V. (1983) "Restricted access in networks and models of power." American Journal of Sociology. 88:686–717.

Masaki, Hisashi (1978) "The financial characteristics of the zaibatsu in Japan: The old zaibatsu and their closed finance." In Keiichiro Nakagawa (ed.) Strategy and Structure of Big Business. Tokyo: University of Tokyo Press.

Matsui, Kazuo (1977) "Institutional investors and stock prices." Tokyo Money. 2(3):14–19.

Matsui Kazuo (1988) "Beikoku ni okeru tāmu rōn to kyōchō yūshi seido no hatten" [Development of term loans and syndicated loan system in the U.S.]. Shōken Keizai.

Mauss, Marcel (1954) The Gift: Forms and Functions of Exchange in Archaic Society. New York: Free Press.

Mayer, Colin (1990) "Financial systems, corporate finance, and economic development." In R. Glenn Hubbard (ed.) Asymmetric Information, Corporate Finance, and Investment. Chicago: University of Chicago Press.

Mayer, Colin, and Ian Alexander (1990) "Banks and securities markets: Corporate financing in Germany and the United Kingdom." Journal of the Japanese and International Economies. 4:450–75.

Meltzer, Allan H. (1988) Keynes' Monetary Theory: A Different Interpretation. New York: Cambridge University Press.

Meyer, John W., and Brian Rowan (1977) "Institutionalized organizations: Formal structure as myth and ceremony." American Journal of Sociology. 83:340–63.

Meyer, John W., and W. Richard Scott (1983) Organizational Environments: Ritual and Rationality. Beverly Hills: Sage Publications.

Miles, Raymond E., and Charles C. Snow (1987) "Organizations: New concepts for new forms." California Management Review. 28:62–73.

Mintz, Beth, and Michael Schwartz (1985) The Power Structure of American Business. Chicago: University of Chicago Press.

Mintzberg, Henry (1983) Power in and Around Organizations. Englewood Cliffs, N.J.: Prentice-Hall.

Mitchell, J. Clyde (1969) "The concept and use of social networks." In J. Clyde Mitchell (ed.) Social Networks in Urban Situations. Manchester, Engl.: Manchester University Press.

Mitchell, J. Clyde (1974) "Social networks." Annual Review of Sociology. Palo Alto, Calif.: Annual Reviews Press.

Mitō Hiroshi (1983) Nihon dai-kigyō no shoyū kōzō [The Structure of Ownership of Large Japanese Firms]. Tokyo: Bunshindō.

Mitsubishi Research Institute (1987) "The relationship between Japanese auto and auto parts makers." Tokyo: Japanese Automobile Manufacturers Association.

Miwa Yoshirō (1990) Nihon no kigyō to sangyō soshiki [Japan's Enterprise and Industrial Organization]. Tokyo: Tōkyō Daigaku Shuppankai.

Miyamoto M. et al. (1979) Sumitomo no keiei shi-teki kenkyū [Research on Sumitomo's Management's History]. Tokyo: Jikkyō Shuppansha.

Miyazaki Yoshikazu (1976) Sengo nihon no kigyō shūdan [Enterprise Groups in Postwar Japan]. Tokyo: Nihon Keizai Shinbunsha.

Mizruchi, Mark (1982) The American Corporate Network: 1904–1974. Beverly Hills, Calif.: Sage.

Mizruchi, Mark S., and Michael Schwartz (1987) "The structural analysis of business: An emerging field." In Mark S. Mizruchi and Michael Schwartz (eds.) Intercorporate Relations: The Structural Analysis of Business. Cambridge: Cambridge University Press.

Morikawa, Hidemasa (1975) "Management structure and control devices for diversified zaibatsu business." In Keiichiro Nakagawa (ed.) Strategy and Structure of Big Business. Tokyo: University of Tokyo Press.

Morishima, Michio, and George Catephores (1988) "Anti-Say's law versus Say's law: A change in paradigm." In Horst Hanusch (ed.) Evolutionary Economics: Applications of Schumpeter's Ideas. Cambridge: Cambridge University Press.

Mowery, David C. (1986) "Market structure and innovation: A critical survey." In G. D. Libecap (ed.) Advances in the Study of Entrepreneurship and Innovation. Greenwich, Conn.: JAI Press.

Murakami, Yasusuke (1987) "The Japanese model of political economy." In Kozo Yamamura and Yasukichi Yasuba (eds.) The Political Economy of Japan, vol. 1. Stanford, Calif.: Stanford University Press.

Murakami, Yasusuke, and Hugh T. Patrick (1987) "Preface by the general editors." In Kozo Yamamura and Yasukichi Yasuba (eds.) The Political Economy of Japan, vol. 1. Stanford, Calif.: Stanford University Press.

Myers, Steward C. (1984) "The capital structure puzzle." The Journal of Finance. 39(3):575–92.

Myers, Steward C., and N. J. Majluf (1984) "Corporate financing and investment decisions when firms have information that investors do not have." Journal of Financial Economics. 13:187–221.

Nakamura, Takafusa (1983) Economic Growth in Prewar Japan. New Haven: Yale University Press.

Nakamura Tsutomu (1983) Chūshō-kigyō to dai-kigyō [Medium-Small-Sized Companies and Big Companies]. Tokyo: Tōyō Keizai Shinpōsha.

Nakane, Chie (1972) Japanese Society. Berkeley and Los Angeles: University of California Press.

Nakatani, Iwao (1984) "The economic role of financial corporate groupings." In M. Aoki (ed.) The Economic Analysis of the Japanese Firm. Amsterdam: North-Holland.

Nasu Masahiko (1987) Gendai Nihon no Kin'yū Kōzō [The Financial Structure of Contemporary Japan]. Tokyo: Tōyō Keizai Shinpōsha.

Nelson, Richard R. (1981) "Research on productivity growth and productivity differences: Dead ends and new departures." Journal of Economic Literature. 19(3):1029–64.

Nelson, Richard R., and Sidney G. Winter (1982) An Evolutionary Theory of Economic Change. Cambridge, Mass.: Harvard University Press.

Nihon Keizai Shinbun (1987) Kabushiki tōshi no tebiki [Introduction to Stock Investment]. Tokyo: Nihon Keizai Shinbun.

Nihon kigyō shūdan bunseki [Analysis of Japanese Enterprise Groups] (various years) Tokyo: Sangyō Dōkō Chōsa-kai.

Nishiyama, Tadanori (1982) "The structure of managerial control: Who owns and controls Japanese business." Japanese Economic Studies. Fall:37–77.

Noguchi Tasaku et al. (1968) Sumitomo konzern: Keiei to zaimu no sōgō bunseki [The Sumitomo Group: A General Analysis of Management and Finances]. Tokyo: Shin-Hyō-Ron.

North, Douglass C. (1977) "Markets and other allocation systems in history: The challenge of Karl Polanyi." Journal of European Economic History. 6:703–16.

North, Douglass C. (1981) Structure and Change in Economic History. New York: W. W. Norton.

Odagiri, Hiroyuki, and Hideki Yamawaki (1986) "A study of company profit-rate time series: Japan and the United States." International Journal of Industrial Organization. 4:1–23.

Odaka, Konosuke, Keinosuke Ono, and Fumihiko Adachi (1988) The Automobile Industry in Japan: A Study of Ancillary Firm Development. Tokyo: Kinokuniya.

Ohkawa, Kazushi, and Henry Rosovsky (1973) Japanese Economic Growth:

Trend Acceleration in the Twentieth Century. Stanford, Calif.: Stanford University Press.

Okimoto, Daniel I., and Gary R. Saxonhouse (1987) "Technology and the future of the economy." In Kozo Yamamura and Yasukichi Yasuba (eds.) The Political Economy of Japan, vol. 1. Stanford, Calif.: Stanford University Press.

Okumura Hiroshi (1975) Hōjin shihonshugi no kōzō: Nihon no kabushiki shoyū [The Structure of Corporate Capitalism: Share Ownership in Japan]. Tokyo: Nihon Hyōronsha.

Okumura Hiroshi (1978) Kigyō shūdan jidai no keieisha [The Managers of the Enterprise Group Era]. Nihon Keizai Shinbun.

Okumura Hiroshi (1983) Shin nihon no roku dai-kigyō shūdan [Japan's Six Major Enterprise Groups]. Tokyo: Daiyamondosha.

Okumura Hiroshi (1988) Nihon no kabushiki shijō: Tōki jidai no kabuka wa kō kimaru [Japan's stock markets: How stock prices are determined in a speculative era]. Tokyo: Daiyamondosha.

Okumura Hiroshi (1990) Kigyō baishū [Corporate Mergers and Acquisitions]. Tokyo: Iwanami Shoten.

Okun, Arthur M. (1981) Prices and quantities: A macroeconomic analysis. Washington, D.C.: Brookings Institution.

Orru, Marco, Gary G. Hamilton, and Mariko Suzuki (1989) "Patterns of inter-firm control in Japanese business." Organization Studies. 10(4):549–74.

Ornstein, Michael D. (1984) "Interlocking directorates in Canada: Intercorporate or class alliance?" Administrative Science Quarterly. 29:210–31.

Osano, Hiroshi, and Yoshiro Tsutsui (1986) "Credit rationing and implicit contract theory." International Journal of Industrial Organization. 4:419–38.

Ouchi, William G. (1980) "Markets, bureaucracies, and clans." Administrative Science Quarterly. 25:125–41.

Palmer, Donald (1983) "Broken ties: Interlocking directorates and intercorporate coordination." Administrative Science Quarterly. 28:40–55.

Pascale, Richard, and Thomas P. Rohlen (1983) "The Mazda turnaround." Journal of Japanese Studies. 9:219–63.

Patrick, Hugh T., and Thomas P. Rohlen (1987) "Small-scale family enterprises." In Kozo Yamamura and Yasukichi Yasuba (eds.) The Political Economy of Japan, vol. 1. Stanford, Calif.: Stanford University Press.

Patrick, Hugh, and Henry Rosovsky (1976) "Japan's economic performance: An overview." In Hugh Patrick and Henry Rosovsky (eds.) Asia's New Giant. Washington, D.C.: Brookings Institution.

Perlo, V. (1957) The Empire of High Finance. New York: International.

Perrow, Charles (1984) Normal Accidents: Living with High-Risk Technologies. New York: Basic Books.

Perrow, Charles (1986) "Economic theories of organization." In Complex Organizations. 3d ed. New York: Random House.

Pfeffer, J., and G. R. Salancik (1978) The External Control of Organizations: A Resource Dependence Perspective. New York: Harper and Row.

Piore, Michael J., and Charles F. Sabel (1984) The Second Industrial Divide: Possibilities for Prosperity. New York: Basic Books.

Polanyi, Karl (1944) The Great Transformation. Boston: Beacon Press.

Polanyi, Karl (1957) "The economy as instituted process." In Karl Polanyi,

Conrad M. Arensberg, and Harry W. Pearson (eds.) Trade and Market in the Early Empires. Chicago: Free Press.

Polanyi, Karl (1966) Dahomey and the Slave Trade: An Analysis of an Archaic Economy. Seattle: University of Washington Press.

Polanyi, Karl, Conrad M. Arensberg, and Harry W. Pearson (1957) "The place of economies in societies." In Karl Polanyi, Conrad M. Arensberg, and Harry W. Pearson (eds.) Trade and Market in the Early Empires. Chicago: Free Press.

Porter, Michael E. (1980) Competitive Strategy: Techniques for Analyzing Industries and Competitors. New York: Free Press.

Posner, Richard A. (1980) "A theory of primitive society, with special reference to law." Journal of Law and Economics. 23:1–53.

Powell, Walter W. (1987) "Hybrid organizational arrangements." California Management Review. 30:67–87.

Powell, Walter (1990) "Neither market nor hierarchy: Network forms of organization." In B. Staw and L. Cummings (eds.) Research in Organizational Behavior. Greenwich, Conn.: JAI Press.

Prais, S. (1976) The Evolution of Giant Firms in Britain. Cambridge: Cambridge University Press.

Prindl, Andreas R. (1981) Japanese Finance: A Guide to Banking in Japan. New York: John Wiley.

Ramseyer, Mark (1987) "Takeovers in Japan: Opportunism, ideology and corporate control." UCLA Law Review. 35(1):1–64.

Ramseyer, Mark (1988). "Reluctant litigant revisited: Rationality and disputes in Japan." Journal of Japanese Studies. 14(1):111–23.

Ramseyer, Mark (1991). "Legal rules in repeated deals: Banking in the shadow of defection in Japan." Journal of Legal Studies. 20:91–117.

Rapp, William V. (1986) "Japan's invisible barriers to trade." In Thomas A. Pugel (ed.) Fragile Interdependence: Economic Issues in U.S.-Japanese Trade and Investment. Lexington, Mass.: Lexington Books.

Rappa, Michael A. (1985) "The capital financing strategies of the Japanese semiconductor industry." California Management Review. 26(2):85–99.

Ravenscraft, David J., and F. M. Scherer (1987) Mergers, Selloffs, and Efficiency. Washington, D.C.: Brookings Institution.

Richardson, G. B. (1960) Information and Investment. Oxford: Oxford University Press.

Richardson, G. B. (1972) "The organization of industry." The Economic Journal. 82:883–96.

Roe, Mark J. (1989) "The political origins of American corporate finance." New York: Columbia University. Mimeo.

Roe, Mark J. (1990) "Political and legal restraints on ownership and control of public companies." Journal of Financial Economics. 27:7–41.

Roe, Mark J. (1991) "A political theory of American corporate finance." Columbia Law Review. 91:10–67.

Roehl, Thomas (1983) "A transactions cost approach to international trading structures: The case of the Japanese general trading companies." Hitotsubashi Journal of Economics. 24(2):119–35.

Roehl, Thomas (1989) "Japanese industrial groupings: A strategic response to rapid industrial growth." Paper presented to the Association of Japanese Business Studies, San Francisco.

Rosenbluth, Frances (1989) Financial Politics in Contemporary Japan. Ithaca, N.Y.: Cornell University Press.

Rotwein, Eugene (1964) "Economic concentration and monopoly in Japan." Journal of Political Economy. 72:262–77.

Rumelt, Richard P. (1974) Strategy, Structure, and Economic Performance. Boston: Harvard Business School Press.

Rumelt, Richard P. (1989) "How much does industry matter?" Los Angeles: University of California. Mimeo.

Sahlins, Marshall (1972) Stone Age Economics. Chicago: Aldine-Atherton.

Sakamoto T. (1983) "Kigyō shūdan zaimu ni okeru naibu torihiki to gaibu torihiki" [Internal and external trade in the financial affairs of the enterprise groups]. Keiei Ronshu. 31:151–63.

Samuels, Richard J. (1987) The Business of the Japanese State. Ithaca, N.Y.: Cornell University Press.

Saxonhouse, Gary (1988) "Comparative advantage, structural adaptation, and Japanese performance." In Takashi Inoguchi and Daniel I. Okimoto (eds.) The Political Economy of Japan, vol. 2. Stanford, Calif.: Stanford University Press.

Scherer, Frederic M. (1980) Industrial Market Structure and Economic Performance. 2d ed. Chicago: Rand McNally.

Schotter, Andrew (1981) The Economic Theory of Social Institutions. New York: Cambridge University Press.

Schumpeter, Joseph (1934) The Theory of Economic Development. Cambridge, Mass.: Harvard University Press.

Schumpeter, Joseph (1939) Business Cycles, vol. 1. New York: McGraw-Hill.

Schumpeter, Joseph A. (1950) Capitalism, Socialism, and Democracy. New York: Harper and Row.

Schwert, G. William (1983) "Size and stock returns, and other empirical regularities." Journal of Financial Economics. 12:3–12.

Scott, John (1979) Corporations, Classes, and Capitalism. London: Hutchinson University Library.

Scott, John (1986) Capitalist Property and Financial Power. Brighton, Engl.: Wheatsheaf Books.

Scott, W. Richard (1987) "The adolescence of institutional theory." Administrative Science Quarterly. 32:493–511.

Securities Market in Japan, 1990 (1990). Tokyo: Japan Securities Research Institute.

Sheard, Paul (1985) "Main banks and structural adjustment in Japan." Research Paper, no. 129. Australia-Japan Research Centre. Australian National University.

Sheard, Paul (1986) "Main banks and internal capital markets in Japan." Shōken Keizai. 157:255–85.

Sheard, Paul (1989) "The Japanese general trading company as an aspect of interfirm risk-sharing." Journal of the Japanese and International Economies. 3:308–22.

Sheard, Paul (1991) "The role of firm organization in the adjustment of a declining industry in Japan: The case of aluminum." Journal of the Japanese and International Economies. 5:14–40.

Shiller, Robert J. (1981) "Do stock prices move too much to be justified by subsequent changes in dividends?" The American Economic Review. 71: 421–36.

Shimokawa, Koichi (1985) "Japan's keiretsu system." Japanese Economic Studies. 12:3–31.

Shinkai, Yoichi (1988) "The internationalization of finance in Japan." In Takashi Inoguchi and Daniel I. Okimoto (eds.) The Political Economy of Japan, vol. 2. Stanford, Calif.: Stanford University Press.

Shleifer, Andrei, and Lawrence H. Summers (1988) "Breach of trust in hostile takeovers." In Alan J. Auerbach (ed.) Corporate Takeovers: Causes and Consequences. Chicago: University of Chicago Press.

Shubik, Martin (1982) Game Theory in the Social Sciences. Cambridge, Mass.: MIT Press.

Simmel, Georg (ed. K. Wolff) (1950) The Sociology of Georg Simmel. New York: Free Press.

Simon, Herbert A. (1957) Models of Man. New York: John Wiley.

Simon, Herbert A. (1961) Administrative Behavior. 2d ed. New York: Macmillan.

Sōgō shōsha nenkan (1985) Tokyo: Seikei Tsūshinsha.

Staff Report for the Subcommittee on Domestic Finance, Committee on Banking and Currency, House of Representatives (1968) Commercial Banks and Their Trust Activities: Emerging Influence on the American Economy. Washington, D.C.: U.S. Government Printing Office, July 8.

Stein, Jeremy C. (1988) "Takeover threats and managerial myopia." Journal of Political Economy. 96(1):61–80.

Stern, Louis W., and Adel I. El-Ansary (1977) Marketing Channels. Englewood Cliffs, N.J.: Prentice-Hall.

Stokman, Frans N., Rolf Ziegler, and John Scott (1985) Networks of Corporate Power. Cambridge: Polity Press.

Suzuki Sadahiko (1980) "Kyūsai yūshi ni okeru 'meinu banku' chikara" [The strength of relief-capital from main banks]. Keiō Keiei Ronshū. December:18–39.

Suzuki Sadahiko (1982) "Nihon ni okeru hi-baishū jōjō-kigyō no tokuchō" [Special characteristics of acquired listed firms in Japan]. Keiō Keiei Ronshū. July:23–44.

Suzuki, Yoshio (1980) Money and Banking in Contemporary Japan. New Haven: Yale University Press.

Swiddler, Ann (1986) "Culture in action: Symbols and strategies." American Sociological Review. 51:273–86.

Taira, Koji (1970) Economic Development and the Labor Market in Japan. New York: Columbia University Press.

Teece, David J. (1980) "Economics of scope and the scope of the enterprise." Journal of Economic Behavior and Organization. 1:223–47.

Teece, David J. (1982) "Toward an economic theory of the multiproduct firm." Journal of Economic Behavior and Organization. 3:39–63.

Teece, David J. (1986) "Profiting from technological innovation: Implications for integration, collaboration, licensing, and public policy." Research Policy. 15(16):285–305.

Teece, David J., and Sidney G. Winter (1984) "The limits of neoclassical theory in management education." American Economic Review. 74(2):116–21.

Telser, Lester G. (1980) "Why there are organized futures markets." Journal of Law and Economics. 23:1–22.

Thakor, Anjan (1990) "Investment myopia and the internal organization of capital allocation decisions." Journal of Law, Economics, and Organization. 6(1):129–54.

Thompson, James D. (1967) Organizations in Action. New York: McGraw-Hill.

Titman, Sheridan, and Roberto Wessels (1988) "The determinants of capital structure." Journal of Finance. 43(1):1–19.

Ueda, Yoshiaki (1986) "Intercorporate networks in Japan." Shōken Keizai. 157: 236–54.

Ueda, Yoshiaki (1989) "Similarities of the corporate network structure in Japan and the U.S." Ryūtsū Kagaku Daigaku Ronshū. 2:49–61.

Uekusa, Masu (1987) "Industrial organization: The 1970s to the present." In Kozo Yamamura and Yasukichi Yasuba (eds.) The Political Economy of Japan, vol. 1. Stanford, Calif.: Stanford University Press.

Useem, Michael (1984) The Inner Circle. New York: Oxford University Press.

USITC (1990) "Phase I: Japan's distribution system and options for improving U.S. access." Washington, D.C.: United States International Trade Commission.

Vogel, David (1983) "Trends in shareholder activism: 1970–1982." California Management Review. 25(3):68–87.

Vogel, Ezra F. (1979) Japan as Number One. Cambridge, Mass.: Harvard University Press.

von Hippel, Eric (1988) Sources of Innovation. New York: Oxford University Press.

Wakasugi Ryūhei (1984) "Sangyō no R & D katsudō to seisaku kainyū [Industrial R & D activities and policy intervention]." Nihon keizai seisaku gakkai nenpō. 32:40–47. Tokyo: Keiso Shobō.

Wallich, Henry C., and Mable I. Wallich (1976) "Banking and finance." In Hugh Patrick and Henry Rosovsky (eds.) Asia's New Giant. Washington, D.C.: Brookings.

Weick, Karl E. (1986) "Organizational culture and high reliability." California Management Review. 29(2):112–27.

Wellman, Barry, and S. D. Berkowitz (1987) "Introduction: Studying social structures." In Barry Wellman and S. D. Berkowitz (ed.): Social Structures: A Network Approach. Cambridge: Cambridge University Press.

Westney, D. Eleanor (1987) Imitation and Innovation: The Transfer of Western Organizational Patterns to Meiji Japan. Cambridge, Mass.: Harvard University Press.

White, Harrison C., Scott A. Boorman, and Ronald L. Breiger (1976) "Social structure from multiple networks: I. Blockmodels of roles and positions." American Journal of Sociology. 81:730–80.

White, Harrison (1981) "Where do markets come from?" American Journal of Sociology. 87:517–47.

Williamson, Oliver E. (1964) Economics of Discretionary Behavior: Managerial Objectives in a Theory of the Firm. Englewood Cliffs, N.J.: Prentice-Hall.

Williamson, Oliver E. (1975) Markets and Hierarchies: Analysis and Antitrust Implications. New York: Free Press.

Williamson, Oliver E. (1979) "Transaction-cost economics: The governance of contractual relations." Journal of Law and Economics. 22:233–61.

Williamson, Oliver E. (1985) The Economic Institutions of Capitalism. New York: Free Press.

Williamson, Oliver (1988) "Corporate finance and corporate governance." Journal of Finance. 43(3):567–89.

Williamson, Oliver (1991) "Comparative economic organization: The analysis of discrete structural alternatives." Administrative Science Quarterly. 36: 269–96.

Winter, Sidney G. (1988) "On Coase, competence, and the corporation." Journal of Law, Economics, and Organization. 4(1):163–80.

Wolff, Alan Wm. (1990) "U.S.-Japan relations and the rule of law: The nature of the trade conflict and the American Response." In Kozo Yamamura (ed.) Japan's Economic Structure: Should It Change? Seattle: Society for Japanese Studies.

Wray, William D. (1984) Mitsubishi and the N.Y.K., 1870–1914: Business Strategy in the Japanese Shipping Industry. Cambridge, Mass.: Council on East Asian Studies, Harvard University.

Yamada Ichirō (1971) Kigyō shūdan keiei-ron [A Theory of Enterprise Group Management]. Tokyo: Maruzen.

Yamamura, Kozo (1974) A Study of Samurai Income and Entrepreneurship. Cambridge, Mass.: Harvard University Press.

Yamamura, Kozo (1976) "General trading companies in Japan: Their origins and growth." In Hugh Patrick (ed.) Japanese Industrialization and Its Social Consequences. Berkeley and Los Angeles: University of California Press.

Yamamura, Kozo (1978) "Entrepreneurship, ownership, and management in Japan." In Peter Mathias and M. M. Postan (eds.) The Cambridge Economic History of Europe, vol. 7. Cambridge: Cambridge University Press.

Yamamura, Kozo (1982) "The role of the zaibatsu in the adoption of new technology and creation of internal capital and labor markets in Meiji Japan." Eighth International Economic History Congress, the University of Lund, Budapest.

Yamamura, Kozo (1990) "Will Japan's economic structure change? Confessions of a former optimist." In Kozo Yamamura (ed.) Japan's Economic Structure: Should It Change? Seattle: Society for Japanese Studies.

Yasuoka, Shigeaki (1975) "The tradition of family business in the strategic decision process and management structure of zaibatsu business: Mitsui, Sumitomo, and Mitsubishi." In Keiichiro Nakagawa (ed.) Strategy and Structure of Big Business. Tokyo: University of Tokyo Press.

Yasuoka, Shigeaki (1984) "Capital ownership in family companies: Japanese firms compared with those in other countries." In Akio Okochi and Shigeaki

Yasuoka (eds.) Family Business in the Era of Industrial Growth. Tokyo: University of Tokyo Press.

Yonekura, Seiichiro (1985) "The emergence of the prototype of enterprise group capitalism: The case of Mitsui." Hitotsubashi Journal of Commerce and Management. 20:63–104.

Yoshihara Hideki, Sakuma Akimitsu, Itami Hiroyuki, and Kagono Tadao (1981) Nihon kigyō no tayō-ka senryaku: Keiei shigen apurōchi [The Diversification Strategy of Japanese Firms: A Managerial Resource Approach]. Tokyo: Nihon Keizai Shinbunsha.

Yoshihara, Hideki (1987) "Some questions on Japan's sōgō shōsha." In Shin'ichi Yonekawa and Hideki Yoshihara (eds.) Business History of General Trading Companies. Tokyo: University of Tokyo Press.

Yoshihara, Kunio (1982) Sōgō Shōsha: The Vanguard of the Japanese Economy. Oxford: Oxford University Press.

Yoshino, M. Y. (1968) Japan's Managerial System: Tradition and Innovation. Cambridge, Mass.: MIT Press.

Yoshino, M. Y., and Thomas B. Lifson (1986) The Invisible Link. Cambridge, Mass.: MIT Press.

Zeckhauser, Richard J., and John Pound (1990) "Are large shareholders effective monitors? An investigation of share ownership and corporate performance." In R. Glenn Hubbard (ed.) Asymmetric Information, Corporate Finance, and Investment. Chicago: University of Chicago Press.

Zeitlin, Maurice (1974) "Corporate ownership and control: The large corporation and the capitalist class." American Journal of Sociology. 79:1073–119.

Zielinski, Robert, and Nigel Holloway (1991) Unequal Equities. Tokyo: Kodansha.

Zucker, Lynne G. (1977) "The role of institutionalization in cultural persistence." American Sociological Review. 42:726–43.

Zucker, Lynne G. (1983) "Organizations as institutions." In Samuel B. Bacharach (ed.) Advances in Organizational Theory and Research, vol. 2. Greenwich, Conn.: JAI Press.

Zucker, Lynne G. (1988) "Where do institutional patterns come from? Organizations as actors in social systems." In Lynne G. Zucker (ed.) Institutional Patterns and Organizations: Culture and Environment. Cambridge, Mass.: Ballinger.

Index to References

Subject Index